Whaikōrero

Whaikōrero
The World of Māori Oratory

POIA REWI

AUCKLAND
UNIVERSITY
PRESS

First published 2010
Reprinted 2011, 2013, 2016, 2019, 2022, 2024

Auckland University Press
University of Auckland
Private Bag 92019
Auckland 1142, New Zealand
www.auckland.ac.nz/aup

© Poia Rewi, 2010

ISBN 978 1 86940 463 5

Publication is kindly assisted by

National Library of New Zealand Cataloguing-in-Publication Data
Rewi, Poia.
Whaikōrero : the world of Māori oratory / Poia Rewi.
Includes bibliographical references and index.
ISBN 978-1-86940-463-5
1. Speeches, addresses, etc., Maori. 2. Maori language—
Rhetoric. 3. Maori language—Spoken Maori. [1. Whaikōrero. reo]
I. Title.
808.5108999442—dc 22

This book is copyright. Apart from fair dealing for the purpose of private study, research, criticism or review, as permitted under the Copyright Act, no part may be reproduced by any process without prior permission of the publisher.

Front cover: Hieke Tupe, of Ngāti Haka, holds a *tokotoko* on his maiden *whaikōrero* at Waiohau (n.d.). Photograph by Te Whānau Tupe.

Back cover: Renowned orator Pou Temara, of Ngāi Tūhoe, December 2005. Photograph by Poia Rewi.

Cover design: Jacinda Torrance

Printed in China by Everbest Printing Investment Ltd

Contents

Acknowledgements vi

Explanatory Comments vii

Map of Tribal Lands viii

One Introduction 1

Two What is *Whaikōrero*? 10

Three How to Learn *Whaikōrero* 21

Four *Whaikōrero* as Rituals of Encounter 37

Five Who can Perform *Whaikōrero*? 56

Six What Skills are Required for Oratory? 77

Seven The Mana of *Whaikōrero* 103

Eight Protocols of Place 114

Nine The Structure of *Whaikōrero* 135

Ten The Future of *Whaikōrero* 163

Appendix Sample *Whaikōrero* 183

Notes 210

Bibliography 221

Index 228

Acknowledgements

He mihi

I tīmata ēnei mahi rangahau āku i ngā tini hāereere i ngā huihui a Ngāi Tūhoe, kātahi ka pīkautia e Te Whare Wānanga o Waikato, nā reira, aku mihi ki Te Tari Māori, ki Te Pua Wānanga o te Ao, mō ngā mahi tautoko i aku mahi rangahau i tērā wā, i tērā o ngā kura wānanga: ko Ahorangi Tamati Reedy, ko Ahorangi Winifred Crombie, ko Tākuta Ray Harlow, ko ngā toi huarewa, arā, ko Te Wharehuia Milroy rāua ko Hirini Melbourne. Ko te pāpā tautōhito whāngai reo, ko Tīmoti Kāretu, tae atu ki ngā pūkenga whakawairua i ngā kōrero tikanga. Tēnā koutou i tuarā mai i te tuhinga nei.

Nō te tau rua mano mā whā i whakawhitihia ai taku mahi ki Te Whare Wānanga o Otāgo: ko Te Ihorei, ko Tania Ka'ai, tēnā, ko te Tūāhoanga Matarehu o Te Mātauranga, ko Murumāra Moorfield, tēnā, ko Ahorangi Michael Reilly tēnā. Tēnā koutou, Te Tumu, i kawe ai i tēnei tuhinga kia pae ki uta. Tēnā hoki koutou Te Kura Aronui o Otāgo, tēnā koutou Auckland University Press i te whakapukapukatanga mai: Anna Petersen, Sam Elworthy, Vani Sripathy, Ginny Sullivan, Jane McRae, Katrina Duncan.

Murumāra, me kore ake koe i eke ai ngā waituhi ki te kōmata o te rangi, ināhoki ko te putanga tuatahi kei te reo Māori tonu me ōna āhuatanga kāore noa i māu rawa i tēnei whakapākehātanga mā Ngāi Kiritea. Nā tō whakapono kei te reo Māori te panekiretanga o te whakaaro Māori, ā, mā te reo Māori anō e taea katoatia ai te ao Māori te whakaataata, te whakawairua, te whakaihi, te whakawehi, te whakawana, i hūtia ai e koe ngā paiaka o te whare wānanga mai kore e tāhurihuri mahurangihia ai te ture me reo Pākehā te tuhi' He aroha nōu ki te reo, he ūpoko mārō rānei, i pakaru rawa ai te ūpoko, nāwai i tika, nāwai i whakaaehia taku tuhi ki te reo Māori, nāwai i ea ai tētahi manako o te whakapuakanga o Mātaatua e kī ana: 'Insist that the first beneficiaries of indigenous knowledge (cultural and intellectual property rights) must be the direct indigenous descendants of such knowledge,'* nāwai i whakaaehia kia whakawāhia te tuhinga reo Māori, nāwai i whakaaehia tō Aotearoa nei hunga pūkenga ki te kaupapa hei hunga aro matawai. Anei tō hoa e mihi nei ki a koe; e kurupākara ana a roto, engari e mū ana a waho.

Ki a koe Tākuta Reilly, hei mātua kaiārahi i te tuhinga reo Māori, kei te poho te ngārahu hei kāinga mō te hana o te kupu paremata ki a koe. Ahakoa te kupu whakamihi kei te ngaro i a au, tēnei te kirihou nei i te aroha ki a koe i tō whakarangatira mai nei i te kaupapa. Kia mao te marangaipāroa, kia whiti te rangipaihuarere ka hōngongoi te kaupapa.

Ki ngā maunga kōhā, ki ngā roma wai terenga kōrero mai i ngā puna mātinitini.
E Koro mā, e Kui mā, i te pō.
Ko koutou te iwi tuaroa i roto i ngā tau whakapūrehurehu
Kia papakura mai koutou i te kākarauritanga o te rā
E kore rawa koutou e ngaro i te mahara.

---

* The Mātaatua Declaration on Cultural and Intellectual Property Rights of Indigenous Peoples, online.

E ngā pāpara, e ngā whaea, e ngā karawa, e ngā hoa piripono i te ao.

Kai te whānau tē kōrerotia, tē utaina ki ngā momo urupare, noho ake koutou hei ihi kōrangaranga, hei ā tē kitea, hei ā tē rangona, hei hiringa taketake i hua mai nei i a koutou, ahakoa piki, ahakoa heke.

Ki aku kamo, ki a miromiro: Tīmoti Kāretu, Te Wharehuia Milroy, Koro Tihema.

Tēnā koutou katoa i rite tonu ai te whakakipakipa mai i ahau kia whakaoti i te tuhinga nei hei ekenga mā tātou katoa, inā tā koutou kōrero, tō koutou whakaaro 'ko koe, ko tātou katoa tēnā. Kia toa koe hei iti kotahi harakoa mō te iwi.'

Explanatory comments

Direct quotations are presented in the text in accordance with the informants' dialects. In doing so, my intention is to acknowledge their individual styles of speaking as well as their dialectal distinctiveness, and to retain and represent their particular language use. I implore any linguists or anyone else who reads these quotations not to assess or evaluate what were oral comments as if they were written statements, and additionally, not to assume that this is the correct written form of the Māori language.

I believe that the initial consent given by informants to share their knowledge with me was based on Māori principles. It was the consent of an elder handing on knowledge to a younger person. It was consent purely in support of the request and the merit of the request. The only restrictions were those employed because my research was being conducted under the auspices of a Western tertiary institution. I sincerely appreciate the spirit in which the information was shared with me.

All informants who consented to the inclusion of their names alongside their comments have been referenced accordingly. Those who did not want to be named have been assigned a nom de plume. The option to remain anonymous is not an evasive move on their behalf to eliminate the possibility of people contesting their comments; they chose to do so as a show of humility. Half of the informants died before this text was printed, and consent to include their names was given by their descendants, wives or children.

The appendix is a compilation of sample *whaikōrero* that I acquired from the Radio New Zealand Archives in Auckland. Extracts from them are included in the text to illustrate the different models that people use to structure their *whaikōrero*. It is important to note that *not all* of these samples are top quality examples of *whaikōrero*.

The Māori words in this book, with the exception of those appearing in direct quotations, have been italicised to signal that they retain their full contemporary and traditional meanings and belong to a different language to that of the commentary text. It does not assert that the Māori language is a 'foreign language'. The italicisation and macronisation of Māori words in direct quotes follow the orthographic conventions applied by the original authors.

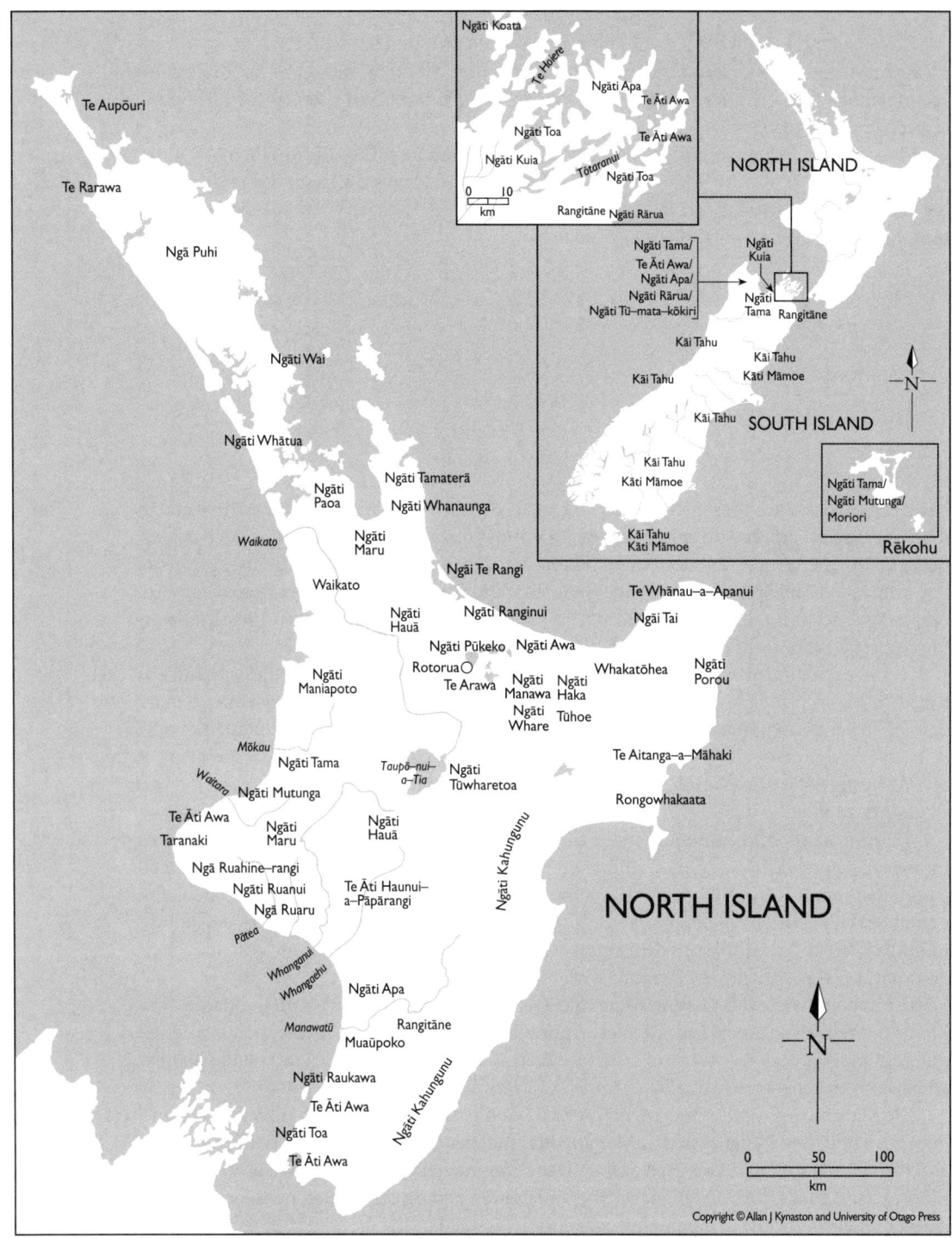

MAP OF TRIBAL LANDS

Chapter One

Introduction

This book, *Whaikōrero: The World of Māori Oratory*, explores the complexity of Māori oratory, both past and present. While *whaikōrero* continues to be a central element in Māori gatherings and culture, there is a notable absence in the literature of an analysis of its depth, its delivery, and its cultural and social context. What makes *whaikōrero* more than merely a theatrical speech is the origin and function of the various components, the rites associated with the selection and qualification of its exponents, and the way it is delivered. This book is an investigation into not only the art of oratory itself, but also related cultural aspects. It delves into the underlying philosophies inherent in *whaikōrero* that impact on, and are influenced by, the culture, etiquette and belief system of the Māori world.

It was my interest in learning about the Māori people in general as well as the tribes with which I have affiliations that provided me with the motivation and passion to find out more about Māori culture and lore. I believe that this passion, this interest, was imbued in me as I traversed the Bay of Plenty, Gisborne and bordering areas as a small boy with the grandfather I knew and loved, Sonny White. We would attend Ringatū days in the Mātaatua area where I recall sleeping at the feet of elders. The last thing I would hear at night were Ringatū prayers, and the first thing to enter my ears in the morning were Ringatū prayers again. Although what was going on at the time was not always apparent to me, I think the teaching began there. Perhaps the spiritual elders, with all their knowledge, humility and compassion, thought that their *mokopuna*, me, might be worth cultivating. I believe they consciously, or subconsciously, opened the corridors of learning to me, and from there I was drip-fed knowledge selectively chosen that was appropriate to the various stages of my maturity. I think that they saw this knowledge as invaluable for my future survival, and perhaps more importantly, for the preservation of tribal information for future generations beyond me.

'One of the fundamental notions of Māori society is the respect for elders whose wisdom embodies the past', says Reilly,[1] and it is with this thought in mind that I will be forever grateful to all of my *kuia* and *koroua* who have added to the *tukutuku* of Māori knowledge that has fashioned me. I sincerely hope that the knowledge they have passed on as the living breath of their words will continue to enhance the sovereignty, independence and honour that will become part of each and every Māori generation hereafter, '*hei pūtiki kōrero whakawhiti ki tēnā reanga, ki tēnā whakapaparanga*'.

The Search for Knowledge

In order for research on Māori to be conducted in an appropriate manner, it needs first to be unbiased. Durie expressed his view that researchers –

> . . . must come to a better understanding of Māori society if they are to measure past conflict and conduct in cultural context. To understand that society they must look inside its thought concepts, philosophy and underlying values and avoid interpretations from an outward appearance. They must consider the social structure not just in terms of how it looks but with regard for the likely reasons for it. It will be important to consider the poetry, songs, legends, proverbs, idiom and forms of speech-making.[2]

If we align Durie's expectations with the study of *whaikōrero*, we become aware of the diverse factors that are associated with speech-making, including cultural context, values and meaning. *Whaikōrero* is more than mere discourse. One of the purposes of this book is to examine the multifaceted nature of *whaikōrero* – as ritual, as history, as *tikanga* – which is often overlooked by the very people to whom it belongs.

Where does one search for knowledge about the world of Māori oratory? Much of the literature on *whaikōrero* gives a similar account, almost as if one author has regurgitated the writings of another: there is little newly introduced information and the approaches bear a close resemblance to each other. What also astounds me is the lack of data on *whaikōrero* recorded by ethnographers such as Elsdon Best and John White. Why was this the case when people such as Best and Grey wrote volumes of material on Māori history, Māori lore, Māori belief systems, Māori genealogy? I am inclined to presume that it is because in the nineteenth century *whaikōrero* was a thriving practice with a relatively large number of practitioners. Because it did not face the possibility of extinction, ethnographers felt less compulsion to write about it.

Sir Peter Buck mentions Western scholars' scepticism about the ability of uncivilised peoples to transmit information orally.[3] Despite this scepticism, I view oral information as an integral component of this research, especially in light of the fact that the majority of written literature on *whaikōrero* is repetitive. I would like to believe that the intricacies and subtle differences that give colour to this account of *whaikōrero* come from the oral informants themselves. Conducting interviews, for me, was also a way of reinstating the validity of oral transmission and recognising the power of its mnemonic capacity, especially in the face of sceptics who are reliant on the written word and do not or cannot accept the dynamism of orality. Cox, amongst others, points to the functions and centrality of oral traditions within Māori culture:[4]

> It is important to remember that oral tradition has not ceased just because a more 'acceptable' alternative is available. Māori continue to store, maintain, and transmit historical details orally. For Māori, this information is vital to the social, economic, and political well-being of groups, and is consequently a dynamic resource. The same events in which many ancestral figures have played a part are retold through waiata (songs), whakatauaki (proverbial expressions), whakapapa (genealogical tables), and whaikorero (formal speeches).[5]

Facing the paucity of material in the written record, I decided that oral interviews were the most effective means of eliciting quality information. I conducted 31 interviews over the period 1995–2003. The majority of interviews were formally structured. Five respondents chose to divulge the knowledge they had on the subject of *whaikōrero* less formally by way of 'loose chats', rather than following the more standard 'question and response' format. Two elders died just before I was about to interview them, and this prompted me to prioritise the interviewing process. The venue where the interviews were conducted was determined by the informants: they decided on the location where they felt most comfortable, whether it was in the privacy of their own homes, the *marae,* my home, a hospital, a workplace or at a university.

I would like to express deep gratitude to all of them for making themselves available to my research. The majority of these elders were familiar with me or my family, but there were some who were unknown to me, and I to them. They agreed to share their knowledge, their memories, and even their *kai,* with me. I must confess that there were times when I felt like a secret forager for information, becoming privy to knowledge that I thought may have been rightfully destined for their own children or grandchildren, or people from their immediate tribe or subtribe. It was indeed a privilege to have these people talk with me, and I will probably spend the rest of my life finding a way to reciprocate. Where words fail to acknowledge such people fully, I must be content, at this point in time, with the moral gratitude that will forever sit close to my heart for all that they have shared.

Most of the people interviewed were chosen because they were renowned as quality practitioners of *whaikōrero*, well known throughout their tribal boundaries, or recognised as great orators because of the memorable *whaikōrero* they had delivered. As a consequence, their fame had spread throughout the country. Some of the respondents were referred to me as people with knowledge about *whaikōrero*. All of these *kuia* and *koroua* of the 1990s embodied a link with highly skilled orators they would have witnessed who would, in turn, have been educated by elders schooled in *wānanga*, the special schools of learning of the early twentieth century.

I made initial contact with informants via telephone, and once I had arrived for the interviews they were asked whether they agreed to have the interview tape-recorded. Two male respondents declined to be recorded. Bearing in mind the fact that *whaikōrero* is a male-dominated area of responsibility on most *marae*, most of the people interviewed were male. However, I also interviewed *kuia*, and the approach with them was slightly different. They tended to be more informal, and talked about any area of *whaikōrero* they wished to discuss. I sensed some reluctance by two of the *kuia* to talk about *whaikōrero*, probably because it is generally accepted that *whaikōrero* is a male role in most tribes. There were others who were not approached who, upon hearing that I was researching *whaikōrero*, volunteered information or views they had in regard to the practice. Most informants agreed to divulge their knowledge with the understanding that I safeguard it. It is from this understanding that I recorded the discussions and completed transcription of the dialogue. I still have the records in my possession. Transcribed segments from the interviews have been incorporated in this work. The year that the discussion took place has been provided, and brief biographies of the informants can be viewed in the bibliography section.

Perhaps this is an opportune time to express my one regret in regard to the interview process. Eleven of the informants died before their contribution to this work went to print, and I sincerely apologise for my tardiness in completing the writing. Perhaps if I had been more conscientious and less procrastinating, they would have seen the fruits of their information. Their comments, nonetheless, are central to the text, and

I am grateful to them, along with all of the informants, for their contributions, their trust and their openness.

Hohepa Kereopa, an expert on Māori medicine, once provided a hint on procuring leaves for the preparation of medicine. It is preferable, he said, to refrain from gathering the leaves off one single tree or plant. The inadvertent effect of gathering leaves from one tree, he went on, means that the person who has gathered the leaves has empowered that one tree to be the sole healer. Because Māori believe that trees have a living form, similar to that of people, this gives that one tree, or plant, exceptional *mana*, that is, it raises the status and authority of that tree which may then become the target of jealousy and envy. This then gives root to animosity. What Hohepa proposes is that the leaves from different trees are gathered so that many trees, as opposed to one, will then have the power to heal, thereby minimising the likelihood of one tree becoming superior to others. This ensures that the *mana* is shared. In forming this text, information has been acquired from a range of sources including people now dead or alive, published and unpublished literature, public and private documents, and the internet. Like the trees with their remedial properties, the collective of elders who were interviewed gives authority to the knowledge I have brought together, and the means by which this knowledge of Māori cultural practices and *whaikōrero* can be transmitted over generations. .

Royal is critical of people who research and publish work on Māori culture and history and consequently 'have attempted to create a common version of tribal traditions, thereby undermining tribal diversity and ultimately tribal authority'.[6] It is my hope that the main focus of this text falls sharply on *whaikōrero* in the areas of its core values and principles, its intricacies and nuances, its diversity and variability. By allowing difference, complexity and context, and by examining both oral and written literature, it is my hope that I will be able to paint a worthwhile insight into tribal and individual uniqueness and specificity, as well as to reveal comparative differences and similarities. Perhaps this will encourage a shift from 'standardising' the way *whaikōrero* is delivered.

The tribal affiliations of the informants include Tūhoe (Ngāi Tūhoe), Kahungunu (Ngāti Kahungunu), Te Arawa, Ngāti Porou, Ngāti Awa, Waikato–Maniapoto, Te Whakatōhea, Ngā Puhi and Ngāti Whare; the majority being from the Tūhoe tribe. The general belief, when I began, was that Tūhoe have managed to evade the assimilation process, in comparison with other tribes, and therefore orators from Tūhoe were referred to me as knowledgeable in the arena of *whaikōrero*. I am not totally sure why the other tribes were represented, but I am compelled to believe that the participation of informants from outside of my immediate tribal affiliations is the work of my *taha Māori*, my Māori side, and that it is likely that I have genealogical ties to those tribes. Two of the *kuia* who were interviewed are from Ngāti Porou. Another *kuia* lived in Te Tairāwhiti and has connections to Ngāti Kahungunu. Yet another is from Tūhoe. It must be stated here that although I intended to gather information representative of all tribes, informants from Ngāti Whātua, Taranaki, Whanganui, Rangitāne, Muaupoko, Te Whanganui-a-Tara, Te Waipounamu, Wharekauri and Rakiura were not included in this research.

Who Does Knowledge of the Past Actually Belong To?

Regardless of the venue or the speaker, I have always wondered who the knowledge of the past actually belongs to. I have heard the accolades of people seated around me being generously accorded to various speakers as they delivered *whaikōrero*, lectures and seminars, or *wānanga*, extended discussion forums. Some of this awareness has arisen because I know I have listened to similar utterances being expressed by other speakers, and what is being said on this occasion is, in part, merely the regurgitation of eloquent and profound material that is part of the cultural canon of *whaikōrero*. It has always seemed a little unjust that there is no acknowledgement of the predecessors from whom these intelligent views and philosophies originated. But it is not my intention to censure the repetitions and similarities, since without them, the treasured history of former times may have perished along with the memories of those esteemed repositories.

My aim here is to share the credit between both the source of the information and the speaker, should they not be the same person. How can we not give due recognition to the current repository of that knowledge and its role in transmitting that knowledge to future generations so that they will be proud in their heritage as Māori? And likewise, it would be a disservice not to acknowledge those ancestors with their wealth of experience and knowledge who coined beautiful phrases, who received knowledge from numerous people before them, and who opened the portal to esoteric knowledge of the Māori people which was secured and passed on from generation to generation.

When knowledge is passed on, it is not only its content that is important, but also the manner in which it is transmitted, that is, the ethos, integrity and spirituality that make those teachings so special. It is as a result of this passing on of knowledge that Māori are distinctly Māori and that individual tribes are unique and distinguishable from one another. These distinct tribes and subtribes also define us as special individuals. Such characteristics are also the cornerstones of identity for future generations of Māori that they will be able to use as treasures and as signposts that will enable them to know forever who they are and where they come from. This is held together by a genealogical thread that ties Māori to the primal gods Rangi-nui and Papa-tū-ā-nuku, to their offspring, and then down to the human form fashioned from mother earth, Hine-ahu-one, from whom Māori people believe their very existence came to be. This text follows the same path in that this is a collection of knowledge and heritage passed down.

We know that the transmission and dissemination of knowledge is a vast topic and this focus on *whaikōrero* is merely a ripple in that great sea of knowledge. We might extrapolate from the comment by King that education 'is a direction, not a destination',[7] that not all knowledge can be acquired in its entirety. The journey is, in itself, satisfying, and its progress is just as important as the knowledge which may or may not be acquired along the way. A learned man, Te Wharehuia Milroy, once said to me, '*ki te kore he whakakitenga, ka mate te iwi*', interpreted as, 'a people without a vision will perish'. One of the teachings of the prophet Te Kooti Arikirangi Te Tūruki is embodied in the words, '*Kei roto i te pōuri te māramatanga e whiti ana, engari, kīhai i mau i roto i te pōuri*', meaning 'Although enlightenment resides in darkness, it cannot be acquired within this darkness'. The *pōuri* or 'darkness' he mentions suggests naivety and ignorance. But when uninformed individuals such as these begin to learn, they must also gain understanding, by which the 'darkness' lifts and ignorance is replaced by knowledge. Keeping the statements by Michael King and Te Kooti in mind, it would be over-ambitious and arrogant for me to assume that all knowledge on the topic of *whaikōrero* is contained in this single text. There are numerous outcrops of information on this topic that still remain to be explored.

This book is subtitled 'the world of Māori oratory' because *whaikōrero* is such a diverse topic and involves much more than mere 'speech'. It begins with the origin of *whaikōrero*, after which modes of learning and the acquisition of *whaikōrero* are described. Understanding the origins of *whaikōrero* provides the background for a discussion of the locations where *whaikōrero* takes place and who is permitted to deliver *whaikōrero*. Having designated the space for delivery and the orators, the book then examines the attributes that qualify a particular individual to speak and the type of delivery that is acceptable. The issue of quality, or lack of it, is of paramount importance in terms of the *mana* – the integrity, status, pride, honour and social standing – of the individual performer and the people (s)he represents.

'Geomentality', the type of behaviour that a person adopts for different occasions, is central to understanding *whaikōrero*. When we talk about behaviour in regard to *whaikōrero*, this covers the stance the speaker uses, their attire, the style of their delivery, the content of their delivery, the way they structure their delivery, the way they present *koha*, the song they use to round off their speech and the way they are selected to speak. There is clearly a lot involved, and each of these facets has a bearing on and is connected to *mana*. When a speaker delivers *whaikōrero* with conviction and gains a high level of respect, then they make the occasion an important one that is imbued with greater *mana*, that in turn is accorded to all the people present. This is why I value geomentality as an important condition that underpins *whaikōrero*.

Genealogy is another important theme, introducing Māori gods and their association with *whaikōrero*, as well as the effect of genealogy on speaking rights and sibling status. In chapter 6, which outlines the skills and qualities of an orator, we talk about the style – verbal and paralingual – and the theatrics of *whaikōrero*. We draw some comparisons between how *whaikōrero* were delivered in former times and how they are delivered now. We compare individuals and modes of teaching that Māori used in former days. One issue that is unclear is what types of speech-making fall under the term *whaikōrero*. Deference during the delivery and content, as opposed to an informal, low-key delivery style, may be the main criterion that distinguishes *whaikōrero* from other forms of discourse. The process of selecting speakers requires wide consideration when culture and etiquette are applied, and on this note, we discuss challenging views in regard to who may speak. We then enter briefly into the issue of women and *whaikōrero*.

The range of information discussed up to this point is historical and tracks the evolution of *whaikōrero* to the present. We then proceed to discuss the location of *whaikōrero* and the physical seating arrangements. This includes the *marae* complex and buildings where *whaikōrero* take place. We also talk about the order of speakers and the differences between tribes and their tribal rules. We note the role of each designated speaker and the order of speakers, which ensures they successfully fulfill their function as the speaking body during the welcoming ceremony. Visitors are cognisant of honouring the host people and this is commonly done via the presentation of a *koha* to the hosts. We discuss the type of *koha*, how it is presented and how it is received. Chapter 6 discusses what qualities make up *whaikōrero* and in chapter 9 we examine the structure of *whaikōrero* and its various components.

The conclusion addresses some of current issues that are potentially challenging adherence to traditional custom and etiquette. This opens the window into the future of *whaikōrero*, and what adaptations may lie ahead.

It is my hope that, by providing an in-depth account of the context of *whaikōrero*, and in particular an explanation of its diversity, this book will provide a means by which the spirit of older *whaikōrero* can be reinstated in the modern context and upheld by current and potential orators. A more informed appreciation of *whaikōrero* will, I hope, lead to an invigorated approach to practice among all those learning the art of Māori oratory.

Chapter Two

What is *Whaikōrero*?

Ko te whaikōrero, ko ia nei ngā mihi nui a ngā kaumātua i runga i ngā marae i roto i ngā huihuinga a te iwi.[1]

Whaikōrero, or formal speech-making, according to Barlow is performed by male elders on the *marae* and at social gatherings.[2] A definition of this type is a useful starting point for a person unaccustomed to Māori culture and etiquette, or to a tourist in New Zealand. However, it is not a definition that will satisfy the Māori mind or belief system. The boundaries of this belief system span from one horizon to the next, and its philosophies originate from the beginning of time with links to the present, and encompass the Māori and non-Māori worlds and the evolution that continues to take place within, between and around them.

The Origin of *Whaikōrero*: Cosmogony

Understanding the origin of *whaikōrero* poses some difficulty. Who delivered the first *whaikōrero*? Where was the first *whaikōrero* delivered? Where did the template for *whaikōrero* come from? When did *whaikōrero* begin? If these questions were raised with exponents of oratory, it would not surprise me if their replies differed from each other and revealed some uncertainty. When I asked a number of scholars and practitioners the same questions, the overwhelming feeling was that '*whaikōrero* just is'. They were hard pressed to find answers, but they generally agreed that *whaikōrero* is not a recent development. So let us begin these discussions by casting back into the cosmogonical past, before moving through to the colonisation era and the twenty-first century.

We start with Barlow's comments about the Māori creation story and the separation of Rangi-nui and Papa-tū-ā-nuku:[3]

> The wheiao is that state between the world of darkness and the world of light, but it is much closer to the unfolding of the world of light. The first wheiao occurred during the time that Ranginui (the Sky Father) and Papatūānuku (the Earth Mother) lived together with their children locked within their embrace. After a considerable time, the children became restless and were intent upon escaping from the confines of their parents into the world of light beyond. They convened a council to discuss a plan for making their escape.[4]

Following on from Barlow's explanation, Te Kei Merito says that, according to the accounts of his elders, speech began when three of Rangi-nui and Papa-tū-ā-nuku's children – Tāne, Paia and Tū-mata-uenga – brought about the separation of their parents and the liberation of their offspring onto the earth:

> *E ai ki ngā kōrero a aku koroua, i tīmata mai te kōrero, te whakatakoto i ngā kupu i reira. I te wā i whakaarotia ai e Tāne me Paia, me Tūmatauenga kia whakawehetia ō rātou pākeke, engari, i roto i ngā whakaaro o ētahi atu, perā i a Whiro, me Tāwhiri-mātea, me ētahi atu o ngā tuākana o te hunga nei, kāore rātou i manako, kāre rātou i whakaae, anā, i tērā tonu ka tautohetohe, ana, i roto i te tautohetohe koirā te tīmatatanga o te whaikōrero e mōhiotia nei e tāua.*[5]

Te Wharehuia Milroy elaborates on these comments by Te Kei Merito, and introduces the element of discourse, of discussion of opposing ideas, when some of the children, such as Whiro and Tāwhiri-mātea, did not support the separation. This discussion resulted in 'the great debate', which was the beginning of *whaikōrero* as we know it.

Hirini Melbourne, Tāmati Kruger, Hue Rangi, Te Wharehuia Milroy and Te Kei Merito share another view. In that account, *whaikōrero* eventuated in the darkness when Papa-tū-ā-nuku and Rangi-nui were still bound to each other in close embrace. Their offspring were disenchanted with their existence in a world without light, which resulted in a discussion between the siblings about whether or not to separate their parents. Hirini Melbourne states that this family quarrelling constitutes the origin of *whaikōrero*, as well as the origin of particular styles of *whaikōrero* that will be discussed later.

While Te Ariki Morehu also places the origin of *whaikōrero* with Rangi-nui and Papa-tū-ā-nuku, in his account the debate was over the issue of who should have care of their children when they passed from the land of the living. Papa-tū-ā-nuku declared, 'They were born of me and should return to my ward', which is interpreted as meaning that *whaikōrero* came to exist purely as a result of the deities communicating with one another. Māori believe this was one of the earliest forms of *whaikōrero*.

Te Hiko Hohepa goes as far as to state that, for Te Arawa, *whaikōrero* was handed down from the *atua*[6] of war, Tū-mata-uenga, who was associated with the sacred teachings from the school of combat in the uppermost heaven, with *whaikōrero* being a safe and stylised means of airing differences and resolving conflict.

We now take leave of the separation of Rangi-nui and Papa-tū-ā-nuku, and skip to the period of the demigod Māui-tikitiki-a-Taranga and Hine-nui-te-pō, the goddess of death, some generations later. In Kimoro Pukepuke's reflections on mythology and the origin of *whaikōrero*, he refers particularly to an episode between Māui-tikitiki and Hine-nui-te-pō, when they argue about the permanence of death for humanity.[7] They discuss whether a person should die only for a month and then come back to life again, or die for all eternity. My interpretation of Kimoro Pukepuke's comments is that this argument between deities is a model of *whaikōrero*, and was in fact one of the first examples of it.

Another theory is that *whaikōrero* resulted from the Māori creation of humanity whereby Tāne fashioned the first woman, breathing life into her and naming her Hine-ahu-one.[8] They cohabited and begat Hine-tītama, whose incestuous relationship with her father resulted in the birth of the first humans, and with humanity came speech, from which, says Pou Temara, *whaikōrero* eventuated.

The Origins of *Whaikōrero*: Geography and History

Hapi Winiata and Patu Hohepa are of the view that *whaikōrero* began in the Pacific Islands, in Rangiātea, prior to the migration to New Zealand. There are divergent references to this place called Rangiātea.[9] Rangiātea has been mentioned as an altar in Hawaiki. Theogonical Māori tradition affords this name to the house from which all Māori knowledge hails or the structure in which this knowledge was housed.[10] Despite Tīmoti Kāretu stating that he did not know where *whaikōrero* originated, he expressed his own view that it may have begun with Io-matua-te-kore's comments to Tāne while on his quest to procure the baskets of knowledge.[11]

Raiatea is an island in the Society Islands (sometimes spelt 'Ra'iatea') that is 'widely regarded as the center of Polynesia and it is likely that the organised migrations to Hawaii, Aotearoa (New Zealand) and other parts of East Polynesia started at Ra'iatea'.[12] In this account of history, the Māori language and *whaikōrero* were brought to New Zealand by these ancestors when they migrated.[13]

Te Poroa Malcolm says that *whaikōrero* is inherent in the procedures of Te Arawa, and those procedures were received directly from the *atua*, from the supreme God and the cosmogonical beginnings of the people.[14] Around the time of the great migration, when each tribe discussed and appointed their representative leader, Mauriora Kingi says, *whaikōrero* came to be.[15]

Another explanation is given by Hieke Tupe, who admits that he does not really know where *whaikōrero* came from, but extrapolates that it was a form employed by Māori in the 1800s. He bases his surmise on a discourse set up by the Māori prophet, Te Kooti, who after prophesising the eruption of Tarawera in 1886, requested land from the Ngāti Whare,[16] Ngāti Manawa,[17] Ngāti Haka[18] and Patuheuheu[19] people who were residing together at the time. According to Hieke, his request was presented in the form of *whaikōrero*:

> *Kāore au i te tino mōhio i puta mai tēnei mea te whaikōrero i hea, engari i te wā i ngā koroua tonu, me kī, kua tāti kē te whaikōrero i mua noa atu . . . te whaikōrero i te 1800, ināhoki, ngā kōrero i kōrerotia i te wā e noho tōpū ana a Ngāti Whare, a Ngāti Manawa, a Ngāti Haka, Patuheuheu. Kua tāti kē ngā whaikōrero i reira. I reira hoki te haerenga mai o te koroua nei, o Te Kooti, kātahi ka kōrero . . . tono kia hoatu e ngā koroua he takoha ki a ia, ko mōhio kē ia ka hū a Tarawera, koirā te kaupapa.*[20]

The Functional Essence of *Whaikōrero*

Our account of the theories relating to the origin of *whaikōrero* has taken us from the world of *atua*, to the Pacific Islands and to the present.

Comments by informants and in the literature indicate a functional diversity as well as a diverse range of opinion about what *whaikōrero* is.

Whaikōrero, according to Ward, allowed a speaker, or a leader, to present issues to the people in an open address.[21] As he explains:

> The Maories are fond of public speaking, and opportunities for such an exercise often occurred. To consider an affront given by another tribe, to determine on war, to make arrangements of peace, and to discuss any other affair of general interest, a numerous meeting was convened, and their oratorical powers were freely displayed.

Smith says that 'set speeches were made by the principal men' when the tribe gathered to discuss affairs pertaining to the tribe or other matters.[22] McGuire emphasises the value of *whaikōrero* to ancient Māori who 'expected problems to be thrashed over on the marae'.[23] He further stresses that *whaikōrero* was not lost through the years of colonisation, war, land loss, disease and depopulation. It is clear that Māori continued to value this art form as a manifestation of all they still valued.

In support of Ward, Mataira makes the following comment:

> *I mua i te taenga mai o te pākehā ko te whaikōrero anake te āhua whakaputa whakaaro, whakatakoto kaupapa, whitiwhiti kōrero, e pai ai te whakatau a te iwi i ngā take katoa e whai pānga ana ki tō rātou noho, ki ā rātou mahi, ki ngā whakahaere o ia rā, o ia marama, o ia tau, e ora pai ai rātou . . . mehemea he take nui kei mua i te minenga, arā, ka tūtū mai ia kaikōrero me ōna whakaaro mō taua take, me te whitiwhiti whakaaro kia tau rā anō ngā whakaaro o te katoa.*[24]

Mataira describes *whaikōrero* as an important Māori custom which, prior to European colonisation, was the primary medium for expressing opinion and presenting topics for discussion. It helped people make decisions with regard to all matters affecting their living arrangements, their work, and their daily, monthly and yearly activities that would keep them safe. If there were any major issues put before the people, each speaker would stand and air their opinion until all concerned had expressed what they wanted to say.

Mahuta also describes *whaikōrero* as an integral part of any social gathering amongst Māori, particularly in more formal surroundings.[25] Its absence from such occasions could be seen as a lack of fulfilment of Māori etiquette. Indeed, even the omission of a particular component, such as declining to reply, could indicate cultural conflict between visitor and host,[26] and be interpreted by the host or visitor as evidence that they are not being afforded due respect in such an important cultural exchange. We will address the effects of *whaikōrero* on peer esteem in a later chapter (see chapter 10).

Ranginui Walker expresses the view that *whaikōrero* originated from the period of inter-tribal feuding amongst Māori and that *whaikōrero* was put in place to assess the intent of visitors. This confirms Te Kotahitanga Tait's comment that *whaikōrero* originated as a ritual of encounter. The following descriptions published by John White in the nineteenth century are illustrative of this interpretation:

> They went on over the hard scoria flat on the east of the pa, and ascended the hill by a path that led from the Tiko-puke (Mount St. John) Pa, and sat down on the marae (courtyard) of the pa, where speeches of welcome were uttered by the chiefs and answered by some of the young men of the guests.[27]

He also described how:

> The visitors had not been there long when an Awhitu chief rose and made a speech of welcome, and was followed by a Mount Eden chief.[28]

According to Te Wharehuia Milroy:

> *Ko te tangata e tū ake ki te whakatakoto i ētahi kōrero i roto i te reo Māori i ngā wā e whakatauria ai te manuhiri i ngā wā o te tangihanga, i ngā wā rānei e huihui ai ngā tāngata ka mihimihi ki a rātou anō . . . hāunga ia ngā mihimihi he kōrero ērā, he whakatau ērā, engari kia tae mai ki te āhua o te whaiwhai kaupapa haere i konā kua kī ake au hei reira kē koe āta kite ai i tēnei mea te whaikōrero e whakatakotoria ana, e whakapuakina ana, e whakamahia ana.*[29]

Te Wharehuia explains that *whaikōrero* can be defined as a particular kind of language use, for example, during rituals of encounter, when welcoming visitors, at times of bereavement, or on other occasions when two or more autonomous entities gather together. Apart from the acknowledgements exchanged, the real essence of *whaikōrero* is the fact that a theme is expressed and maintained by follow-up and discussion, becoming a common topic for various speakers.

Although *whaikōrero* is a dominant feature in rituals of encounter by Māori, it is by no means limited to this.[30]

The Innate Meaning of the Term *Whaikōrero*

It is often assumed that the word '*whaikōrero*' is derived from a combination of '*whai*', meaning 'to follow' and '*kōrero*' 'to speak'. According to Te Wharehuia Milroy, the word *whaikōrero* may also simply mean having something to say, that is, *whai* (meaning 'to be in possession of something'), and *kōrero* (meaning 'to speak'). But even if the word has this derivation, it is mandatory that topic continuity is involved.

We now shift our focus to definitions of *whaikōrero*, or the other forms of this term, such as *whaiwhaikōrero* or *whaikī*:

> The term whaikoorero when used as a noun means formal speech. When used verbally it means to make a formal speech. It may also be used to refer to the ceremony of formal speech-making on the marae (courtyard) or in the tribal meeting-house.[31]

Ryan explains that *whaikī* means making a 'solemn declaration', or speaking formally.[32] Williams defines *whaikī* as 'formal speech', *whaikōrero* as to 'make an oration, speak in a formal way', *whaikupu* as to 'make a formal speech' and *whaiwhaikōrero* to 'hold a formal discussion involving speeches by several persons'.[33]

Clearly, *whaikōrero* is unassailably a particular expression of the Māori language. 'For a man to speak one language rather than another is a ritual act.'[34] Is this a fair representation with regard to *whaikōrero*? The following statements provide a diversity of views.

Whaikōrero, says Salmond, 'is a true example of "in-group" language, clear only to initiates, and this at least in part is the reason it is so highly valued'.[35] This endorses the status of *whaikōrero*, the language of *whaikōrero* and the esteem inherited by speakers of *whaikōrero*.

Salmond, again, writes:

Maori is spoken on the marae because it is an art-form, and because the marae is tapu, like the old chants and songs '. . . . there is safety and sanctity in the old ways of speaking and people defend them strongly, so that although Maori may fade altogether as an everyday language, one might expect it to remain the ceremonial language of the *marae* for a long time to come'.[36]

Kernot makes the comment that Māori is the language of formal occasions if the context is Māori.[37] This point is reiterated by Te Wharehuia Milroy who says that *whaikōrero* is a Māori word, and therefore the language of *whaikōrero* must also be Māori. In other words, part of the definition of a *whaikōrero* is that it is delivered in Māori: there is no such thing as a *whaikōrero* that is delivered in a language other than Māori. A translation of a *whaikōrero* is not in itself a *whaikōrero*. Nor is a speech composed and delivered in English, or any other language, a *whaikōrero*:

> When Pakeha groups visit the marae, the tangata whenua may ask visitors not to use English during the whai kōrero exchange on the marae-atea. Māori speakers among the manuhiri should respond to this request to honour the marae-atea by standing and replying in Māori, though it might have been their intention to allow their Pakeha friends to speak . . . . [speaking in English in this forum] is sometimes interpreted as the height of rudeness.[38]

In relation to this, Te Wharehuia Milroy suggests, '*taihoa kia oti katoa mai ngā whakaritenga tapu o te whakatau manuhiri, mō muri kē nei tukuna ai rātou kia kōrero Pākehā*', simply stating the case that should an individual intend to deliver in English, then this can be accommodated after the formal components of the welcome have been fulfilled.

Mataira further recognises the importance of *whaikōrero* as being the major custom of Māori whereby a speaker can truly demonstrate their eloquence in their mother tongue, that is, in the Māori language. In her own words, '*tētahi o ngā tino tikanga a te Māori e kitea ai te tohungatanga o te tangata ki te whakaputa whakaaro i roto i tōna reo tūturu*'.[39]

The Content and Thematic Integrity of *Whaikōrero*

A *whaikōrero* that is part of a ceremonial does not exist in isolation: it exists as part of a discourse. Thus, *whaikōrero* not only relates to the purpose of a meeting, but also picks up on and develops earlier topics and discussions. It emerges out of listening and involves thematic development: expounding on a particular point that was made, analysing and developing that point, and either supporting it or critiquing it, or both.[40] One important aspect of *whaikōrero* appears to be reiteration. Hohepa Kereopa makes this point:

> *Ko te pūtake o te whaikōrero ko tana uru atu ki te tapu o te huna wairua koi riro ai ko te tangata e kawe ana i te kaupapa, koirā te anga o te huna wairua e kōrero ana i ngā kaupapa kia rongo mai ngā taringa o ētahi atu. Mehemea te rongo na taringa o ētahi i tētahi kōrero kua whāia e tētahi te wairua, te kaupapa, kua rangahau haere i taua kōrero.... te mutunga o tērā kua whakatinana haere taua kōrero, nā reira kua kōrerohia te kōrero, kua whāia te kōrero, kua whakatinana haerehia te kōrero. Kia tinana rānō, kātahi anō kua mau, ka mau te moko o te kōrero. Koirā te āhua o te whaikōrero.*[41]

An integral component of *whaikōrero* that Hohepa Kereopa refers to here is the connection between the speaker and the sacredness of the spiritual world, so that the orator in effect becomes the means of communication for all those who are present on that occasion. Once a comment is made, the essence of the comment is pursued and discussed: this essence exists in the spiritual domain and is given expression in the earthly domain. If one speaker were to mention land confiscation in their area, for example, another speaker might mention land of their own that was acquired by way of confiscation.

Kāretu has noted that topic development is now often neglected and speakers do not tend to focus on the views and opinions of others. They are more inclined to develop and impart their own knowledge.[42] For example, the first speaker may present a topic, but successive speakers may raise unrelated topics of their own.

However, in comparing past and present practices, Te Wharehuia maintains that this dual process of thematic development and discursiveness is by no means a departure from the traditional approach:

> *I ngā wā o mua, ko ngā mihimihi ko ngā whakatau kua mutu ērā kua tahuri te hunga nei ki te kōrero i ā rātou kaupapa, he aha rā te kaupapa, he kōrero whenua, he kōrero muru, he*

kōrero whakaea mate, e hia ngā āhuatanga, he mahi kai, he aha rānei, whakatakotoria ana e rātou ō rātou nā whakaaro i aua wā, ka rārangihia atu, ka horaina atu te kaupapa e tētahi tangata nāna pea i kawe ake te kōrero. Kua whaiwhaihia taua kaupapa e ētahi kē e tū ake ana ki te whakatakoto i ō rātou nā whakaaro . . . kei te whaiwhai haere koe i ngā whakaaro o tētahi i whakatakotoria ai e ia.[43]

Certainly, a typical gathering would have begun with salutations and cordial greetings, followed by a speech in which the significant issues for the gathering (whether pertaining to land confiscation, exacting revenge, procuring food or other issues) were set out. Later speakers would then develop the topics and follow up on any issues raised. Such a system allowed a certain amount of flexibility and robustness into the proceedings.

Te Poroa Malcolm of Te Arawa and Katerina Mataira of Ngāti Porou suggest that *whaikōrero* always involves thematic development, and point out that the person who expresses a particular 'issue' is irrelevant, the main focus being the 'issue' itself.[44] This view reiterates the spiritual dimension of the theme and the emphasis on meaning and discourse rather than personality and performance.

The effect of two distinctive procedures pertaining to the order of speakers adopted by different tribes is important here, these being *pāeke* and *tauutuutu*, which we will describe in more detail later on (see chapter 8). Briefly, *tauutuutu* is an alternating speaking pattern between host and visitor, whereas *pāeke* requires all host speakers to orate before their visitors do so, and consequently the length of time between the speech of the first host speaker and the visiting speakers may be more than half an hour. As a result, the visiting speaker's memory may be unable to maintain the theme(s) of discussion raised by the opening host speaker, let alone issues mentioned or alluded to by subsequent speakers. Some funeral occasions that I have attended have seen deliveries of more than two hours' duration.

Rhetorically, I would argue that the sense of continuity that is fundamental to *whaikōrero*, as explained above, may still be present through reference to topics raised at earlier meetings. Māori do not always anchor themselves into specificities of time. Generations may even pass and a topic of discussion of bygone years, perhaps with some relevance to the present, may be revisited.

Thematic development may also occur through the use of idiomatic expressions, through *tauparapara* (opening chants), and through the use of formulaic expressions voiced by earlier speakers and repeated by a speaker at a later stage or on another occasion.

We may, therefore, be prompted to ask why a speaker may opt not to discuss issues raised by others. In the Bay of Plenty area, each speaker has a designated role to perform. The opening speaker for the host group has the task of linking local people and visitors through genealogy. The speakers who follow must focus on the event that has brought everyone together. And finally, the last host speaker has the duty of summarising what has been said and introducing anything that has been omitted. Because specific roles have been designated, it may therefore be illogical to duplicate what another speaker has said, unless it is wittily cast to avoid sounding repetitive. Duplication, or repetition, is often viewed by listeners as below par, illustrating a lack of ability by the speaker to offer new opinion. Thus, it is an over-simplification to say that speakers should, under all circumstances, develop previously introduced topics. The development must be approached freshly. There are also occasions when it is appropriate for speakers to deviate from previous comments and to introduce new themes at their discretion.

Tamati Reedy does not define *whaikōrero* by language alone. As indicated in the following comment, *whaikōrero* involves the whole physical delivery, the psychological revere afforded to it and the spirit in which it is expressed:

> . . . ko te whaikōrero he tū-ā-tinana, he tū-ā-tangata, he tū-ā-hinengaro, he whakatū-ā-wairua o te tangata i a ia ki runga i te kaupapa e kōrero ana ia.[45]

Conclusion

By giving a brief explanation of what *whaikōrero* is and tracing its possible origins, we have now built a platform upon which it can be discussed in more detail. From here we begin a critical review of existing works dealing with *whaikōrero*, and incorporate information provided by *kaumātua* to illustrate the intricacies inherent in this supposedly 'simple' tradition. In this way we may further our understanding of the development and expression of *whaikōrero* over time and as it is in today's world.

Chapter Three

How to Learn *Whaikōrero*

The Transfer of Knowledge

How have Māori acquired the appropriate skills to deliver *whaikōrero*? In addressing this question, the first thing we might consider is how Māori transmitted knowledge through the generations and the issues surrounding transmission now:

> The handing down of knowledge by old people is a very difficult thing now. They have a look at their own children, perhaps the eldest son. If he is mature enough or interested enough in his Maori, he might become the repository. But a lot of people say no. They would sooner take a knowledge of their own traditions with them than pass them on to the present generation. They believe that if it goes out to another person outside the family, in a short time it will have dissolved, absorbed by all the other people who have access to it. There is also a fear that by giving things out they could be commercialised. If this happens, they lose their sacredness, their fertility. They just become common. And knowledge that is profane has lost its life, lost its tapu.[1]

Te Uira Manihera raises three key issues: the appropriate transmission from father to son; a preference for taking information to the grave rather than handing it on to a generation not embedded in the traditions; and a perception by Māori that when knowledge is transferred beyond the family it becomes *noa* or common, and no longer holds its sacredness.

But in the face of loss of cultural knowledge, others espouse the critical importance of transmission. A former statesman of the Tūhoe people, the late John Rangihau, in direct reference to his own people, once said that in order to pass knowledge on, 'the main thing we have to overcome is the conservative nature of Maori elders, particularly elders who have withdrawn as a result of pressure from the outside'.[2] Royal argues that the greater good of continuance is served by transmission of knowledge, and explains that –

> . . . this knowledge is never divorced from its cultural reality . . . . tribes should come to an understanding of what is contained in their oral traditions and keep them alive. We must not allow the oral tradition to erode even further. Therefore, we need to create systems to ensure that it is never lost. This means convening regular wānanga and ensuring that the younger generations attend.[3]

This awareness of the importance of transmission and knowledge transfer is not new. Orbell writes:

> In an extraordinary literary outpouring, Maori tribal authorities of the second half of the nineteenth century recorded in great detail their mythology, history, poetry and folklore. Some of their writings appeared in print, in Maori-language periodicals and in early books and articles published by interested Pakeha; many more manuscripts remained unpublished, but are now preserved in public collections. These men knew that the knowledge they possessed was in danger of being lost, and they wished to record it for future generations. They left a rich heritage; and they were followed by many more Maori and Pakeha students of Maori tradition.[4]

Over the mid-to-late twentieth century, perhaps as a reaction to the erosion of culture and language that resulted from colonisation, elders tended to be reluctant to share their pearls of knowledge, until sufficient Māori became aware that they were receiving only droplets of knowledge and would not be able to educate the next generation when their time finally came. Fortunately, as Rangihau says, a mindshift occurred in the 1970s amongst Tūhoe elders mainly due, first, to their own awareness that not a single person amongst them had complete knowledge of all aspects of Māori culture and that they therefore needed to 'pool their information' in order to establish an extensive knowledge base; and, second, to a realisation that the reluctance to share did not bode well for future generations who would face the same dilemma. From the 1970s, John Rangihau was principal in encouraging the revitalisation of tribal knowledge forums amongst Tūhoe, known as 'Kura Wānanga a Tūhoe', and since the 1980s there have been further developments and adoption of similar institutions amongst other tribes. These forums have been a personal motivating factor: they encouraged me to record information lest it be lost forever and to overcome concerns about my own shortcomings in the face of the importance and urgency of the task.

Pre-contact Māori Knowledge Forums: Knowledge, Memory and Transmission

Traditional Māori knowledge institutions were in operation prior to European arrival and were known as *whare wānanga*, with different names for more specific purposes. The forum known as *whare maire* taught ritual prayers associated with witchcraft, as well as legends and historic narratives, and the *whare takiura* imparted esoteric knowledge.[5] Both were held at night.[6] The *whare pōrukuruku* specialised in teaching similar topics to that of the *whare maire,* but on an individual basis;[7] and the *whare kura* taught livelihood. The *whare kau pō* ran from midday to sunset and focused on cultural practices and customs. Māori with affiliations to tribes that descend from the Tākitimu canoe were known to conduct their learning forums during the winter months between April and September from sunrise to midday.[8]

After being selected for the *wānanga,* successful candidates would be taken to a waterway of special sacred significance and would undergo a baptismal ceremony of knowledge. Standing in the river, the *tohunga* (an expert) would cut the hair of the student while uttering a prayer. This would take place at night and the candidates would return to their own homes the next morning.[9]

Having a good memory was one of the criteria by which students were accepted to attend traditional *whare wānanga*. Limiting external stimuli and keeping students isolated were thought to be conducive to developing mnemonic abilities. But if it was deemed to be correct for someone to be invested with particular knowledge, 'then that person would be blessed with the appropriate talent'.[10]

John White, in *The Ancient History of the Maori*, and Best's *The Maori School of Learning*, differ somewhat on the issue of whether these schools existed as permanent physical buildings dedicated to teaching specific disciplines, or whether they were conceptual and behavioural. Best says that the 'house' of learning is figurative, denoting a course of teaching practised at a certain place, and a curriculum.[11] He further explains that 'Whare wananga taught: the inner teachings, the superior versions, of Io (the Supreme Being), and the higher phases of religious belief and practices, and cosmogonic myths.' The objective of *whare wānanga* was the preservation of 'all desirable knowledge' pertaining to religious belief of the upper echelon, cosmogony and other traditional lore, and to hand this down to succeeding generations as accurately as possible. In opposition to the Western view of Māori as a culture devoid of literacy and literary artefacts, Māori scholars in the past were trained in oral history and had a 'highly developed mnemonic capacity' that 'astounded counterparts from other traditions'.[12] The historical *whare wānanga* was clearly an important institution for the oral perpetuation and transmission of knowledge.

Māori Modern Schools of Learning: Memory and Regeneration

The phrase '*whakairohia ki tōu rae, ki ōu toto*' was hammered home by one of my former Māori language lecturers[13] at the University of Waikato in his attempts to emphasise mnemonic retention. The expression literally means 'to carve it into your forehead with your blood'. Without dictaphones, pens, paper and other such recording devices, the ability of the individual to memorise material was considered an asset, and this has not changed much, even in the modern environment.

Best talks about the powers of memory that Māori possessed: memory was central to the success of the student who attended the *wānanga* of old whose tutors viewed these institutions as sanctuaries in which Māori could aspire to conserve knowledge in its purest form.[14] Ignorant of any form of script and cut off from knowledge of other cultures, Māori depended entirely on memory and mnemonic devices and oral tradition to preserve and communicate all prized lore (and the passing of this to their descendants). Instant recall was an asset for both the scholar and orator, and the mnemonic capacity of students was acknowledged and respected.

Pita Sharples, Māori cultural performance ambassador, academic and politician, in an informal discussion with me, compared the capacity of Māori of former times to memorise with the ability of their Polynesian relatives in the late 1900s. To exemplify this, Pita recalled an occasion when he visited one of the Pacific Islands. Being a renowned tutor and practitioner of performing arts, and in particular, *kapa haka*, he was invited to teach a *haka* to the adult men of one particular island community. Pita assumed that their ability to learn the *haka* would be similar to his own cultural performance group in New Zealand. With this in mind, he prepared the first half of the *haka* to teach, expecting it to take a day. To his amazement, the words and actions were acquired in half the time. Rather than have his lack of preparation revealed, Pita astutely explained that it 'wasn't Māori custom to learn a whole *haka* in one day', and he released the men so that he could finish preparing the remainder of the *haka*. Upon his return the following morning, a row of boys was lined up, none of whom he had instructed before. They appeared to be the children of the men he had taught the previous day, and they performed the first part of the *haka* with uniform accuracy of both words and actions. This was an example of the memory capacity Pita thought Māori possessed in the past, but unfortunately had failed to maintain through to the present.

McGuire surmises that it became less necessary to preserve knowledge by way of memorisation when written Māori language developed and the ability to commit information to memory merely served as a show of pride for Māori elders.[15] 'Dependence on retrievable records', says Cox, 'diminishes the need and therefore the faculty to memorise.'[16]

The *wānanga* model has been modified over the years, and successful candidates no longer go through an initiation process or are expected to show an extraordinary ability to memorise. Nowadays, learning forums continue to take place within Western tertiary educational institutions, such as universities, polytechnics and private training enterprises. Candidates generally require some formal qualification in order to gain entry, so the baptismal ceremony associated with the old *wānanga* has essentially been replaced with the enrolment process of modern-day education providers.

Some education bodies today are Māori and tribe-specific, the entry criteria being blood affiliation, invitation or sheer determination. These current Māori educational forums cover a vast range of discussion topics, for example, tribal genealogies and histories, pedagogy and educational practices, politics, land settlements and tribal development.

Alternatively, Māori youth often ask to attend *marae* where they can be educated by their elders about Māori custom.[17] The Ngāi Tūhoe people, from Eastern Bay of Plenty, held their own *wānanga* throughout the 1960s and 1970s primarily for Tūhoe descendants to learn about their specific practices with regard to *whaikōrero*, *karanga* and *waiata*. During one of these forums, attendees were required to present a body of discussion with substance on a particular topic. The peripheral elements of *whaikōrero* such as introductory chants, formulaic acknowledgements and farewells were to be left until the speakers were proficient in speaking about the main topic. Knowledgeable elders were present to critique components that were effective, appropriate, valuable or otherwise. Koro Dewes and Te Poroa Malcolm corroborate that tribal *wānanga* such as these also took place in their respective tribes of Ngāti Porou and Te Arawa. While not devoted purely to the teaching of *whaikōrero*, these *wānanga* passed on information about genealogy and tribal migratory histories that could be included in *whaikōrero*.

I know of tribal *wānanga* that have been held between 1970 and 2004 amongst Te Arawa, Te Tairāwhiti, Taranaki and Ngāi Tahu. The *wānanga* hosted by Tūhoe that I attended did not focus solely on *whaikōrero*, but discussed many tribal issues and practices.

In 2001, Tūhoe hosted a *wānanga* on one of its own *marae* specifically to teach the rudiments of *whaikōrero* and *karanga* to its own people. As the late Hohepa Kereopa explains:

> I remember Wharehuia Milroy and Pou Temara, they started classes, or wananga, about the whaikorero of Tuhoe. The simple reason was that some of our young people were not up to the sort of standards when it came to speaking on the marae. It was not up to the standard that we as Tuhoe expected. They can do whaikorero, but then we are sometimes ashamed because it is not as good as it needs to be. So that is why we had to go around saying that this is our tikanga and this is how to do the whaikorero, and this is why we are like this. And we did this for the simple reason that we do not want to go out there and be seen as people who can't whaikorero, and we don't want other people to comment on that.[18]

The majority of those who attend these Tūhoe *wānanga* are Tūhoe themselves, but they are not stipulated as 'Tūhoe only' *wānanga*. There is usually an understanding that when tribes are hosting *wānanga*, attendance is reserved for those with affiliation, residence or invitation because the knowledge shared is specific to that tribe. An advantage of hosting Tūhoe *wānanga*, for example, on Tūhoe *marae* is that emphasis is clearly placed on the particularities of tribal practice. Many Tūhoe descendants have relocated outside of the Tūhoe area to live amongst other tribes, and it can be easy for them subconsciously to adopt practices adhered to by the tribe in which they now reside, and in turn to bring these practices back to Tūhoe where they may not align with Tūhoe teachings and philosophies. Now, in the Te Arawa area, subtribes, such as Tūhourangi and Ngāti Whakaue, also organise their own *wānanga* to address cultural practices specific to them as a subtribe. Elders have requested that younger tribal members be permitted to attend.

These are just some examples of tribal self-determination focusing on the regeneration of *whaikōrero*.

Western Academies

From the pre-contact period through to the post-contact epoch, traditional forms of learning have included *wānanga* and observation of *whaikōrero* exponents, but there has been some debate about the effectiveness of these forms in today's world. New Zealand universities and schools have also offered *whaikōrero* instruction as part of their curricula:

> City-born children can learn oratory skills in universities, training-colleges, Maori studies courses at high school, and culture clubs; via newspaper articles and Maori language broadcasts, and by studying chants and genealogies in published collections.[19]

Secondary school is one avenue for learning how to *whaikōrero*. In 1965, a school speech competition in English, known as the 'Korimako Contest', was initiated 'to encourage a greater command and fluency of spoken English amongst secondary Māori students'.[20] In 1977, a new section, the Pei Te Hurinui Jones competition, was introduced focusing on the students' command of the Māori language. Teachers, and sometimes mentors, of students provide guidance for these speakers and the normal format of speeches adopted by the male contestants is that of *whaikōrero*.

Another competition held as part of Te Hui Ahurei a Tūhoe, the Tūhoe Festival,[21] a tribal sports and cultural festival hosted for and by the Tūhoe people, has a *whaikōrero* component in which males 25 years of age or under compete. There is the assumption that these speakers will have been tutored by advisers from the regional group to which they belong and that they represent.

The entrance criterion for university *whaikōrero* courses is always a specified level of Māori language proficiency, which provides an instant filtering device. Once the candidates have been accepted, they are usually taught various language forms that may be included to enhance *whaikōrero*, as well as customs associated with the art form. *Whaikōrero* courses, at postgraduate level, have been taught out of Victoria University of Wellington since 1978. I attended one such programme hosted there by Te Kawa A Māui, in 2002. Attendance was by invitation only, and the convenors selected candidates on the basis of their ability to acquire the depth of knowledge surrounding *whaikōrero*, their language ability, their familiarity with tribal knowledge and custom, and their maturity. Tuition was '*wānanga* style', that is, interactive immersion over two nights interspersed with lecture-type delivery. Massey University, Palmerston North, offered a course to assist teaching assistants of limited Māori language proficiency with their pronunciation, grammar use, vocabulary and actual oratory itself.[22]

However, it is possible for the teaching of *whaikōrero* in such settings to result in cultural degradation, since what is being imparted becomes a commodity and is cut loose from its cultural context. Elam School of Fine Arts in Auckland allows students to pursue numerous Māori subjects, including *whaikōrero*, if students so desire.[23] This suggests the acquisition of information about rather than immersion in *whaikōrero*.

Another factor involved in the universalising of *whaikōrero* teaching within universities is that cultural particularities and diversities are unlikely to be maintained, as both students and teachers come from all over the country and their cultural practices may differ. This sometimes results in students attempting to apply the protocols they learn at the university back in their home areas, inadvertently riding roughshod over local practices and needing to be 'gently reminded' of this.

There are some Māori educational providers that have resulted from the aspiration that Māori should educate Māori, some of which include Te Wānanga o Aotearoa, Anamata, Te Whare Wānanga o Awanuiārangi and Te Wānanga o Raukawa. One advantage of Māori providers such as these is that education is offered locally so students are not required physically to relocate themselves, and sometimes their whole families, to main centres where Western tertiary providers are situated in order to learn Māori language and culture about their own areas. Subjects such as *whaikōrero* are now taught by these institutions. Universities, such as Waikato, were prime movers in bridging the physical divide between Māori and tertiary education by moving tutors from Māori Studies to hubs where their students lived and conducting the introduction of a *wānanga*-style delivery of courses. This distance education has been further enhanced by technological tools such as digital platforms.

Apprenticeship and Learning through Birth, Aptitude or Ability

Maori Marsden, according to Shirres,[24] spoke of being 'bonded to particular powers through a ritual dedication and consecration'. This is a rite known as *tohi* that some children undergo whereby they are 'dedicated and consecrated at birth' to Māori deities representative of particular disciplines: for example, Tū-mata-uenga, to receive his special powers as a warrior, or Rongo, for peace.

So what is the connection with *whaikōrero*? Many, if not all, parents have ambitions and ideals for their children. Traditionally, Māori ideally wished for a son who would ultimately have the skills of a warrior, a chief or an educated person. In terms of the latter, the parents would hope to see the child fittingly baptised and dedicated to a supernatural being synonymous with knowledge, like Tāne-i-te-wānanga or Rua-i-te-pūkenga. This begins while the unborn is hosted in the womb of the mother. The mother, the father, or both, begin to recite lullabies so that the child will hear genealogies and tribal histories. Among other things, they will hear cultural explanations.[25] The belief is that by dedicating their son to such entities, the child will be imbued with knowledge. Perhaps this is the beginning of oratorical potential, because knowledge and oratory of high quality go hand in hand.

Orbell provides the following example describing the use of sympathetic magic amongst aristocratic people, which shows how much skills such as oratory were desired and wished for in the young:

> An early missionary, Richard Taylor, says that at Taupo it was the custom, at the ceremony marking the birth of a boy of high rank, to cook a bellbird in a tapu oven 'that the child might have a sweet voice, and become an admired orator'.[26]

However, some individuals are born with the 'gift' of oratory.[27] The late Eruera Stirling of Te Whānau-a-Apanui, Ngāti Porou and Ngāi Tahu, was an elder nationally renowned as an exponent of quality *whaikōrero*. He was deemed to be blessed with the necessary skills to orate from birth. When he was born, there were two moles, one on his upper lip and another on his jaw or chin. These were interpreted as signs that knowledge would bestow itself upon him and therefore he should be sent to the traditional Māori schools of learning.[28]

We need to be aware of the fact that in former times not all people were privileged to receive traditional teachings. Most elders as well as other experts 'will probably not agree to teach higher or deeper knowledge (mātauranga tapu) of the Māori world in the forum of general iwi hui wānanga'.[29] They preferred to identify talent, or potential, and then to mentor such individuals on a one-to-one basis.

It was not a given that, just because someone was Māori, they could ask that teachings about Māori history and practices be taught to them. To some extent, this is still the case. In fact, if an individual were to ask outright, it is more likely that an elder would decline without reservation or hesitation, or at the most respond by giving a smattering or diluted version of information.[30] Māori educators tended to divulge the knowledge appropriate for the maturity of the individual. This poses difficulty nowadays when someone pays for education and is entitled to receive it, regardless of the personal wishes or otherwise of the teacher. In terms of teaching, Ngoi Pewhairangi provides the following account:

> When you learn anything Maori, it has to be taken seriously. It involves the laws of tapu: genealogies, history, traditional knowledge, carving, preparing flax, in fact, nature itself. Tapu is something that teaches you how to respect the whole of nature, because Maori things involve the whole of nature.
>
> Awareness of tapu associated with learning is something we grew up with. If you are born on a marae, there are certain qualities about you that are recognised by elders. They don't actually teach you. They select you and place you in a situation where you absorb knowledge. When you're asleep on your own, they're singing waiatas or reciting genealogies in the next room. As you're lying in the dark, you absorb everything that's going on. And before you realise what you're doing, you've learned how to recite too, or you've learned the words of a certain song. And this can go on for three or four years. But you don't realise that they're putting you into the situation to learn.
>
> Suddenly, later, they take you to a meeting house and they recite these genealogies or sing these waiata and deliberately forget a line. And you find yourself singing by yourself because you've recited and learned these things by heart. And you sing this line they've left out. And after a while they say to you 'why don't you learn other songs or other genealogies?'
>
> Then again you hesitate. You know the restrictions placed on these sorts of things. But they take you in hand. The tapu is so great they wouldn't take you in hand and teach you unless you yourself had done work in your own time and shown yourself able and suitable.[31]

'In time, elders and other knowledgeable people will pass over more knowledge as they become more confident in you and your abilities.'[32] Another determining factor is proficiency in the Māori language, because Māori knowledge is believed to be transferred most effectively if the medium of transfer is also the Māori language.

One of my *kaumātua*, Koro Hieke Tupe, showed potential as a learner while he was attending church and was taken by his elders and sent to work alongside one of them. That elder then began to teach him how to deliver orations as well as types of expressions that can be introduced into *whaikōrero*. Another of my informants, Joe Malcolm, of Te Arawa, was himself taught by his elders. Te Ariki Morehu, with reference to pupils taken under the wing of an elder to be taught, explained that the mentor also stipulated when a pupil was ready to stand and deliver *whaikōrero*. Witnesses of such occasions would then comment that 'he is a student of so and so', or, 'that's so and so's style'. In these circumstances, the pupil carries the status of their mentor/tutor, and the behaviour and performance of the pupil therefore reflects directly upon the mentor. This inadvertently shifts the responsibility on to the pupil to 'do their mentor proud', so to speak, because failings of the pupil are equally viewed as a failing of that mentor. Perhaps prior to the death of an elder, that elder would seek to invest his knowledge in one of his close kin if he could identify someone with the willingness to learn.[33]

Hirini Melbourne recalled one of his elders being sent to the back of the house to practise *whaikōrero*, and when the elder mentor saw the cows running off this indicated that the budding young man had acquired the optimum level of vocal projection to qualify him as an orator.

Hohepa Kereopa suggests that *whaikōrero* itself was not actually taught. Instead, formulaic expressions, proverbial sayings, geographical identity markers, metaphor and simile, genealogies, cosmogonical and cosmological information, past tribal encounters and memorable events, any of which could be included in *whaikōrero*, were taught. Other pupils were systematically instructed in how to stand, how to turn, how to walk, and how to hold and manipulate things such as *tokotoko*. Some were encouraged to emulate other practitioners and others to express their own individuality.

Salmond describes how there were times when aspiring orators would congregate at someone's house or at the milking shed and practise *whaikōrero*.[34] She mentions one expert orator who, along with his friend, would practise speaking to a beer crate draped with a blanket as the target audience. Beaglehole makes mention of similar cases whereby developing speakers would have mock *whaikōrero* sessions in order to refine their skills. This method was not sanctioned by all people, however, because it was viewed as improper practice to make mock farewell speeches to the deceased without actually having the dead lying in state. Neither was it deemed appropriate to make speeches without actually having visitors present.[35]

The Experiential Acquisition of *Whaikōrero*

We have discussed *whaikōrero* being systematically taught, as well as some of the more esoteric ways Māori have endeavoured to encourage the skills of oratory in their children and young people. Another method of learning *whaikōrero* is through absorption as a natural facet of human development:

> The individual compares what they think to what the greater population models in order to ascertain what is right and wrong, what is important and what is insignificant. This learning is by no means limited to young children and rather extends throughout adulthood whereby the individual defines the world in terms of how they experience it.[36]

One mode of educating a person in the area of *whaikōrero* is during the developmental stage of young adulthood when they are cast into the *marae* environment to learn basic principles:

> In country areas, oratory is learned by a natural process. Children hang around the fringes of the marae at local gatherings to watch the elders perform. Proverbs, genealogy and local history soon become familiar, and the formal constraints of speech-making are unconsciously acquired.[37]

Kohere in Heuer concurs that –

> The art of public speaking, the allusions contained in the numerous proverbs often used, and the rhetoric which was deeply admired by all, was learned by listening to such stories and by attending tribal gatherings. He tangata i akona ki te whare, tunga ki te marae tau ana (a man performs well on the marae because he learned at home).[38]

Tauroa also says that Māori are 'expected to learn by seeing, by hearing, and by doing'.[39] And as Siers explains:

> First the child's vocabulary was developed, a most necessary attribute because of the importance placed on oratory by the Maori. A child's entry into adolescence opened for it a new life with emphasis on rounding out and deepening its education. This phase was particularly important for a boy as it introduced him to oratory. It was used on all occasions, and children learned not only conversational speech but also the higher forms which contained references to mythology, traditions and genealogies and which were

enriched with chants and songs. Oratory was frequent and what was more important, was open to all. The orators carried a club and moved to and fro in making a speech. They punctuated their speech with gestures and inflections.[40]

These references reflect the zonal or spatial relationship that is conducive to learning *whaikōrero,* a paradigm strongly embedded in Māori methods of knowledge transfer. As Royal describes it:

> Sitting with kaumātua, and other knowledgeable people, allows you to grasp a sense of wider family and tribal life that is unobtainable from books, films, and other media.[41]

Two of my own elders told me that in their youth they attended Māori gatherings and amidst their minor roles of splitting wood, lighting fires and running errands they would move behind the bench of speakers on the *marae* whenever they were free.[42] A common phrase that one might hear being uttered with reference to this is '*he noho, he mātakitaki*', meaning, to 'sit and observe'.[43] Salmond also talks about elders 'doing the rounds' and constantly being exposed to phrases, proverbs and chants preceding orations and genealogy.[44] Some of these elders carried books so they could note down new or varying examples that they might be able to employ in their own orations. These serve as stock phrases or, as Lord describes them, as a 'stock of formulae'. The compositions, he says, 'are not delivered by rote memory, but, rather, are rebuilt anew with each performance, within the same broad outline, by weaving together ready-made elements at a number of levels'.[45]

This notion of oral formulaic theory refers to rote-learned phrases that orators use in their deliveries, a practice I often saw being employed by many different speakers on many different occasions.[46] It also refers to a familiar construction of conjunctives, or adjectives and nouns, that provides a template that allows some variation and creativity, but a structure that keeps the narrative moving forward.

Some people hold the opinion that any individual who is keen and/or sharp can learn *whaikōrero* if they attend tribal gatherings, because it is there that they hear expressions and become adept at selectively picking up specific utterances, at summarising, or at formatting and presenting their own orations.[47] When the time was right, says Salmond, then a person simply involved themselves.[48] Tamati Reedy comments that while he was a university student he would go and listen at *wānanga*, such as the *wānanga* on *whaikōrero* held at Waahi Marae in Huntly in 1960, and there he would listen to the likes of Paraire and Whati Tāmati, Piri Poutapu, Arapeta

Awatere and Koro Dewes.[49] He would also move around the East Coast of the North Island and observe orators. Te Hiko Hohepa, on the other hand, accompanied his grandfather and grand-aunt who raised him because his own father had died young (aged in his forties).[50] Later on, he was initiated into formal speech-making within the confines of the meeting house by delivering eulogies on the night immediately prior to the interment of the deceased, the *pō poroporoaki*. After this, Te Hiko graduated to sit alongside his grandfather and other elders, where he did not orate but observed orations while receiving counsel from those around him. Similarly, another of my elders, John Tahuri, would go and listen to the old people because he enjoyed doing so. Consequently, upon the premature death of his own father, he was required to assume his father's role as speaker with the guidance and support of his elders in attendance. Mauriora Kingi was also young when he was taken to Māori forums such as *tangi* by his *kaumātua* where he would watch and listen.[51] The late Sir Robert Mahuta learnt in a similar way by listening to elders such as King Korokī, the fifth Māori King, and others as they simply talked amongst themselves.[52]

Whitu Waiariki once remarked '*māu anō koe e whakaako*', alluding to the fact that 'one may merely take it upon himself to acquire the skills to orate'.[53] Salmond talks about 'aspiring young orators' who, instead of becoming fluent speakers of the Māori language, 'memorise special set speeches, rather like a priest memorising the Order of Service in Latin'.[54] She explains that, surprisingly, there are a number of people who, 'in adulthood, set about learning Maori from scratch'. I also know of such cases.[55] Mahuta alerts us to the fact that certain individuals aspire to become orators 'because of the prestige associated with oratory', so that young Māori 'entering the ministry are actively encouraged to learn how to whaikoorero'.[56]

Salmond explains that the reason that some make a late run to learn is that they want to 'recapture the knowledge they ignored as children'.[57] My own parents disregarded the opportunities readily available to them when they were young to access forums where Māori cultural practices were deliberated at length. Now, having been promoted to roles as *marae* elders, they feel the pressure and a sense of regret for not being better equipped with a vaster knowledge base from which to draw.

Te Poroa Malcolm of Te Arawa emphasises that there was a period when some Te Arawa elders were precious about their knowledge and reluctant to part with it.[58] People were, therefore, sometimes left to their own devices to learn, sometimes by trial and error.

Kimoro Pukepuke adds that many people today learn their speeches from texts.[59] His comment is particularly directed at people who have attended New Zealand universities in order to learn the Māori language, and Māori cultural practices and histories, and so are labelled as having 'learnt from the book'. Morehu is also critical of people who aspire to become speakers and learn oral forms such as introductory chants for *whaikōrero* as well as traditional incantations but are not proficient in speaking Māori.[60] Younger people these days tend not to prepare themselves for the ensuing roles they will take on as orators and, before they realise it, the responsibility is upon them.[61]

Radio broadcasts are another medium from which people can learn about *whaikōrero*. Sometimes there are speakers from different tribes talking about Māori tribal customs, including *tauparapara* (introductory chants for *whaikōrero*) and their explanations, and *whaikōrero* itself. Some *whaikōrero* from important events, such as the formal Māori welcome for the Duke of Edinburgh, have been recorded and broadcast, serving as examples of *whaikōrero* that encapsulate many personal and tribal variations.

Some individuals are pushed to the fore as orators purely because of their linguistic competence in the Māori language and the lack of other speakers. Pita Iraia was encouraged to *whaikōrero* by his own elders but refused when he was first urged to speak because he was a junior in the family.[62] Over time, though, he eventually agreed because there was no one else to do it. Salmond mentions one speaker from Te Whakatōhea who attended a *hui* with a number of his elders and received the cue from the host speakers to be the opening speaker.[63] In such a situation, the novice can be fairly certain that the more experienced elders who follow after him will be able to make amends for any of his comments if necessary.

There are, therefore, many avenues by which a person aspiring to *whaikōrero* can learn, and we have only mentioned some of them. Perhaps the phrases 'if there is a will, then there is a way' and 'to each his/her own' are apt in this context. The likes of Kei Merito explains that he used every available approach in order to learn to *whaikōrero*: he learnt through the teaching of his grandfather; he absorbed even more by taking his *kuia* to Ringatū church services; and, after serving in the military, he began to school himself in the art of *whaikōrero*.[64]

Conclusion

This chapter has sought to show the many ways in which *whaikōrero* has been learnt over the last 50 years, as well as touching on traditional, pre-contact and contact modes of knowledge transmission amongst Māori. This began with traditional *wānanga* when the Māori language was flourishing and constituted the primary medium of teaching. Then in the 1900s, there was a rapid decline in the number of Māori speakers and the Māori language itself faced extinction. *Whaikōrero* was indirectly impacted upon by the suppression of the Māori language.[65]

This language loss was compounded by the death of numerous Māori males fluent in the Māori language who perished in World War II. With their demise, the next generation who should have naturally inherited their knowledge and oratorical eloquence was left bereft and untutored. During the 1940s, Māori were part of the urban drift looking for employment. The Māori language again suffered because of this as Māori took a liking to the English vernacular at the expense of their own language.

After that, the Māori renaissance took effect on a national scale, with many programmes deployed to revitalise the Māori language. And now, in the twenty-first century, Māori is spoken by more than 135,000 people. The primary aim, therefore, for orators aspiring to deliver fine *whaikōrero* is to attain a high level of proficiency. This has seen numerous people attend tertiary institutions with the primary goal of learning the Māori language and gaining the additional cultural knowledge that accompanies it. The more *whaikōrero* can be experienced, the greater the chance to progress on to actual delivery of *whaikōrero*. The adoption of formulaic, rote-learned expressions is the major tool by which this can achieved. We address this topic further in chapter 9.

Chapter Four

Whaikōrero as Rituals of Encounter

We have looked at the origins of *whaikōrero*, what *whaikōrero* actually is and how *whaikōrero* has been transmitted. We now examine *whaikōrero* in terms of rituals of encounter because they are integral to the form (discourse, space and formality) and function (conduct, identity and connectedness) of *whaikōrero*.

Discourse, Space and Formality

Māori customs of encounter are central to cultural practice, etiquette and realisation, and in fact the interrelatedness between *whaikōrero* and encounters between host and visitor is seminal within Māori culture:

> When a group of visitors arrived at the village of their hosts, for instance, they would come on in battle formation and be met outside the palisade by the warriors of the settlement. There the two groups would defiantly challenge each other and perform the terrifying war dance, the *haka*, with all its threatening gestures, brandishing of weapons, and ferocious grimaces. While a foreign observer might fear that their frenzy would culminate in a bloody fray, the sequel would actually be speeches of greeting and welcome, followed by both parties entering the fortified village for a feast.[1]

The three main characteristics of the delivery of *whaikōrero* are, first, that a discourse is exchanged between visitor and host; second, that this meeting takes place in an assigned space, usually a *marae*; and third, that the occasion is formal.

What follows is a discussion of the encounter between two entities, *tangata whenua*, the hosts, and *manuhiri*, the visitors; followed by a description of the *marae* as space; and an account of the levels of formality and informality that may inform, and be informed by, the verbal expressions of encounter within that space.

Discourse: The Encounter Between Hosts and Visitors

Although Māori are perhaps most familiar with the term *tūrangawaewae* to describe the host people, other terms such as *hunga marae*, *hau kāinga* and *iwi kāinga* are also used. From a Māori perspective, each continent, country, region and *marae* has its own 'people of the land' or 'original inhabitants'. This, however, does not presuppose that the original inhabitants of a country are afforded ultimate authority over a particular *marae* or region. When we reflect on New Zealand on a world scale, Māori are viewed as original inhabitants with sovereignty because of first occupation. When we reduce the scale to the nation itself, there are tribal identities assigned to specific regions. To downsize further to each region, there are subregions and subtribes with designated *marae* and autonomous sovereignties. Urban drift by Māori, especially over the last 60 years, has brought with it a new understanding of *tangata whenua*, which does not see it limited merely to *marae* as it was perhaps in the past. The constant, however, is that there is an affinity between the people and the land.

Salmond defines *tangata whenua* as having long-term occupation and as having acquired the land through Māori means.[2] To Takino, 'tangata whenua refers to the "home people". The people of the placenta, the lands and environs.'[3]

When asserting whether people are *tangata whenua* or otherwise, the following criteria are important:

- they have sovereign occupation in the area;
- they have long-term residency, whether by means of first discovery, occupation, force, purchase, cession or by gift;[4]
- they have tribal affiliation to the land;
- they have governance over the land, regardless of the duration of their occupation.

While residency is important, true local affiliates, *tangata whenua,* are quick to remind individuals of the 'limitation' of their residency, and to suggest that their true right and sovereignty may actually lie within the area of their birth. However, when *tangata whenua* are affiliated to an area by birth, their affiliation is assured only through the practice of *ahi kā*, which was used to validate occupancy prior to the advent of European colonisation. Thus, *tangata whenua* status is attained and maintained through occupancy, residency or frequent visits, and when someone does not physically maintain his or her ties they may be subject to criticism and even social eviction:

> Perhaps in the more contemporary situation, the ahi kā concept can be sustained by one's meeting one's tribal obligations, that is, being seen at the more important rites of passage of the tribe. In this way one is seen to care because one's 'face is seen', an extremely important aspect of being Māori. It is all that is necessary, one need not say anything. Not to be seen over a long period of time would be tantamount to ahi mātao, to the extinguished fire, and could be interpreted as an attitude of not caring.[5]

Melbourne explains *tūrangawaewae* as follows:

> Tūrangawaewae literally means *a standing place for the feet*, but it means a lot more than its present use to describe one's association with the quarter acre suburban paradise. Tūrangawaewae means a great deal more as it applies to a shared or collective hapū or tribal identity and of belonging within a recognised geographic region.[6]

Tauroa refers to *tūrangawaewae* when explaining *tangata whenua* in the following account:

> Tangata whenua are the local people who, by genealogy and by association, claim the marae as their turangawaewae – their standing place or identity base. This turangawaewae gives them the right to belong, to determine *kawa* (protocols), to define roles on the marae and to be responsible for its *mana* (status). It also implies that they have responsibilities and obligations in extending hospitality to manuhiri. They will prepare the marae for visitors and generally do all they can to make hui a success and ensure that visitors are well looked after. Tangata whenua contribute to the food supplies, provide the ringa wera – the work force for the kitchen, dining room, meeting house and upkeep of the ground and marae facilities – and the paepae for welcoming visitors.[7]

Barlow, in explaining *manuhiri* or visitors from a Māori perspective, refers to a person or persons who attend a *marae* other than their own for an engagement with Māori.[8] The easiest way to define a visitor is as anyone who is not host.

The term *manuhiri* refers to all ethnicities and is used irrespective of the distance travelled. Even Māori with affiliations to a particular *marae*, and who may also have been raised there, may fall into the *manuhiri* category because they have been away for a long period of time.[9] In this case, even someone with strong ties is required to go onto the *marae* like a visitor.

Because I have lived much of my life away from my town and *marae* of origin, I have often felt in a quandary, not quite sure whether I am host or visitor at my own *marae*. I have, on occasion, been sent out to the front after trying to take a shortcut and enter by the 'back door', so to speak. I suppose this is the way my host *whānau* remind me of how I am viewed after I have been absent for so long (or too long). The following comment by Tauroa, therefore, rings true for me:

> Manuhiri need not be only people of other tribes or marae. Tangata whenua can be welcomed as manuhiri to their own marae, particularly when they have been absent from the marae for a long period, or they are attending a tangi.[10]

The Marae: *Place or State of Mind?*

While *tūrangawaewae* is used to refer to the people who belong to a place, or to the host people, it is also used to refer to the *marae*, a 'locale with deeply imbedded identity'.[11] This locale symbolises Māori chieftainship, Māori integrity, Māori geomentality, Māori hospitality and the succession of things Māori from generation to generation. *Marae*, says Awatere, encompasses all that Māori promote as fundamental to their beliefs, and the social systems that emerge from and mark their very existence.[12]

Tauroa endorses the importance of *marae*, claiming that 'Only in such a special case can the high levels of wairua (spirituality), mana (prestige), and tikanga (customs) be practised in their true setting':[13]

> A marae is a place where Māori culture can be celebrated to the fullest extent, where the language can be spoken, where Māori can meet Māori, where intertribal obligations can be met, where the customs can be explored, practised, debated, continued, or amended, and where necessary ceremonies – such as welcoming visitors or farewelling the dead – can be carried out. It is the place where the generations before the present ones held the mana of the iwi or the hapū, maintained the tikanga to the best of their ability and kept

the culture alive. It is a named piece of ground, registered as a Māori reservation where tikanga Māori has pride of place. It is a wāhi tapu, a place of great cultural significance . . . . It is a place to be kept 'warm' by the owning group, and as one generation passes on another takes their place in looking after the marae. People of other cultures often see the marae as the institution that saved Māori culture from being assimilated by western civilisation. It was a place of cultural resistance that helped Māori enjoy what others have called de-facto sovereignty.[14]

Each *marae*, according to Salmond, has –

. . . a meeting-house, a dining-hall and other small buildings set in about an acre of land and fenced off from surrounding properties. Sometimes though, the total *marae* reserve can be thirty acres or more. Directly in front of the meeting-house lies an empty expanse of lawn, and this, although physically inconspicuous, is the focus of the complex – the *marae ātea* or ceremonial courtyard.[15]

Let us look at a few other definitions and descriptions of *marae*.

The word [marae] literally means an expanse of anything. Thus *marae roa* or the long expanse was the ocean. Normally however the word was applied to the large open space or village green where social observances were conducted in a Maori community. Nowadays it refers to any place where Maoris gather but specifically to the large open space in front of a carved Maori meeting house. In ancient Maoridom, (and also in this present day) guests were welcomed and farewelled on the *marae*. Here the tribal chiefs and speechmakers addressed the people and all free men had the chance to agree or disagree with the opinions of their leaders. It was the setting of the councils of war and peace, indeed the heart of the community.[16]

The *marae* of a village was bound up with all the most vital happenings, with warm and kindly hospitality, stately and dignified ceremonials, and groupings of hosts and visitors in positions determined by etiquette and traditional procedure. This helps to account for the fact that to the native it was more than a simple open space in the village or a convenient assembly ground, and bore a distinct social importance.[17]

The *marae* symbolises the close relationship between land and people and is the focal point of Maori community life . . . .

All important gatherings will be held on the marae and here one most often hears Maori spoken and Maori social forms followed.[18]

While the term *marae* usually has specific spatial meanings, sometimes it is used to refer to the larger communal dwelling complexes of Māori known as *pā*.[19] Salmond concurs: 'The term "*marae*" is ambiguous, since it denotes both the total complex and the ceremonial courtyard, so in some areas the complex is referred to as a "*Pā*" instead.'[20]

In dissecting the term *marae*, it is possible to see it as the conjunction of two words: *mā* and *rae*. If *mā* means to be clear of restriction, and *rae* anatomically refers to the forehead, possibly extended to refer to the cerebellum, then *marae* could be interpreted as the 'space clear of obstruction'.[21]

Thus, Walker in King describes *marae* as –

> . . . an institution that has persisted from pre-European Maori society. While a whole living complex may be referred to as a marae, the marae proper consists of an open space of ground in front of an ancestral meeting house. In traditional times the marae and the meeting house together made up the focal point of every permanently inhabited village.[22]

So why are *marae* so important for Māori, and how does an examination of *marae* help us understand *whaikōrero*? Robb writes:

> Marae are places of refuge for our people and provide facilities to enable us to continue with our own way of life within the total structure of our own terms and values. We need our marae for a list of reasons –
>
> > that we may rise tall in oratory
> > that we may weep for our dead
> > that we may pray to God
> > that we may have our feasts
> > that we may house our guests
> > that we may have our meetings
> > that we may have our weddings
> > that we may have our reunions
> > that we may sing
> > that we may dance
> > And then know the richness of life and the proud heritage which is truly ours.[23]

Marae continue to act as the focal point where 'public speech still represents the major tool of Maori political exchange'.[24] But whereas Mataira states that *whaikōrero* is the ultimate form of discourse that takes place on *marae*,[25] Patu Hohepa says that it need not necessarily be limited to the *marae* and may be in a building, apart from a house. It may take place wherever Māori meet and speeches are exchanged in acknowledgement of one another.[26] In other words, it is possible for *marae* to be more a state of mind than a specific and traditional 'place', for the purpose, function and complexion of an event to determine what it is, rather than simply the physical space in which it occurs. Many places and spaces are thus capable of being or becoming what we have called 'pseudo *marae*' because of temporal, spatial or social circumstance.

For example, as Ranginui Walker states:

> One of the bastions of cultural conservatism in the alien environment of the city is the tangi, the mortuary customs for farewelling the dead. The most appropriate place to conduct the rituals of the tangi is the marae, the other bastion and focal point of the culture. Although there were tribal marae engulfed by urban sprawl in Auckland and Wellington, the first wave of pre-war migrants felt they needed a hall or marae of their own. In any case as the number of urban Maori increased exponentially, tangata whenua marae were unable to cope with the need. In the meantime, the normal life-crisis of birth, death and marriage had to be met with what was at hand, the family dwelling. The head of a whanau responded to death by turning the suburban state house into a 'mini-marae'.[27]

Regardless of where someone is, says Temara, the *marae* can be psychologically translocated to wherever it is that the occasion is being hosted. In such cases, formality and reverence are imparted to the occasion through the manner in which the event unfolds.[28] Walker describes this application of geomentality in relation to the Māhurehure Community Centre, which differs from what we might normally understand to be a *marae*:

> The land on which the centre stands has not been declared a Maori reserve, nor is there a traditional meeting house and marae where generations of ancestors have stood to deliver their orations. Yet despite the absence of these traditional criteria, ideologically the centre is spoken of as a marae because it serves as a focal point for the community sentiment of the urban Maori. Above all, the centre meets the social and cultural needs of the Maori in a way that cannot be met by equivalent Pakeha institutions.[29]

Mauriora Kingi makes a more political point that a discourse can still be *whaikōrero* even if it is not performed on the *marae* because the ground upon which the structure, such as a municipal hall or a school, is erected is the determining factor, and in New Zealand, the land belongs to Māori.[30]

Whether or not *whaikōrero* occurs indoors or outdoors was traditionally determined by local, or subtribal, culture. Some tribes in Northland, Auckland, Waikato, Te Arawa, Ngāi Tahu, Taranaki, Rongowhakaata and Kahunganu conduct welcome ceremonies indoors, and the speeches are still regarded as *whaikōrero*.

Nowadays such differences in protocol and behaviour are complicated by the existence of non-traditional and Western-style buildings, as well as buildings that are part of Western rather than Māori culture. Formerly, in accordance with Māori protocol, the deceased would be laid in state outside in front of a meeting house, or in a non-permanent structure especially erected to the side of the meeting house as a shelter for the deceased and the family in mourning for the duration of the funeral. Western buildings, says Merito, are different from Māori ones because they are not constructed within the philosophies and spirituality of the Māori meeting house.[31] For tribes that accommodate the deceased inside, orations are still understood to be *whaikōrero*. To orate indoors, says Temara, prompts a particular approach to *whaikōrero*, which requires the speech to maintain a high level of importance, reverence and spirituality but without invective or vilification. *Whaikōrero* indoors restricts the use of oratorical gestures and hand movements involving *tokotoko*, *patu* and the like, which are used outside.[32]

Tahuri, Iraia and Milroy all put forward the idea that *whaikōrero* may take place either outside on the open courtyard (for those tribes that afford *pōhiri* outside) or inside (for those tribes that conduct *pōhiri* inside).[33] Milroy explains that there are times when issues discussed outside on the open courtyard are not finished. If these topics are later taken inside the meeting house, then they still constitute *whaikōrero* under the process of *whaikōrero* and thematic development.[34]

For the Tūhoe people, according to Kruger, *whaikōrero* is synonymous with *marae ātea* (the open courtyard of the *marae* complex), where they conduct *pōhiri* and *whaikōrero*. Tūhoe *whaikōrero* exponent Pou Temara views the *marae* as the primary location for *whaikōrero*. If he orates outside, says Pou, on the *marae*, then his orations are more serious and carry more weight.[35] Colloquialisms, informal expressions and items of little consequence are abandoned. Issues of significance can be raised during *whaikōrero* – the Tūhoe people have an expression, '*te umu pokapoka*', meaning 'the dust can be stirred' and 'the throat of a person slit'. There is an understanding that verbal or physical attacks may take place – '*Me marae puehu e kīia ai te marae, he marae*'. A *marae* is not fully certified as a *marae* until it has had the dust upon it stirred: that is, until some form of confrontation has taken place there:

> In the past it was not uncommon to 'raise the dust' on the marae with vigorous body language. When feelings ran high, arguments were occasionally settled by bruising physical contact, hence the courtyard in front of the ancestral house was also known as 'the marae of Tūmatauenga', the god of war. When there is tension and conflict between groups, the marae is as much a bear-pit as Parliament. . . . So when government ministers go to marae, as they did at Waitangi, they can expect a rough time, to be called to account by the people. Theatrical gestures, the prancing haka, baring buttocks, spitting on the ground, stomping on a flag, are ritual gestures of defiance against the power of government.[36]

The *marae*, Pou Temara stresses, is where this diatribe ends. Like Milroy, he makes the point that once people gather inside the meeting house, the verbal exchanges are more tempered and physical attacks are not, in the main, acceptable.[37]

Tūhoe also refrain from offering visitors a formal welcome at night. If visitors turn up after dark then they forfeit the formal call of welcome and full orations – *whaikōrero*. Instead, such visitors congregate inside the meeting house and receive the less formal exchange of speeches – *mihimihi, mihi whakatau* – inside the *wharenui* (*marae* meeting house). Kereopa, Tupe and Merito take the position that speeches made inside a dining room, for example, are not *whaikōrero*.[38]

There are other types of discourse, similar to *whaikōrero*, that take place inside the meeting house, such as *mihimihi* or *whakatau*. *Whakatau* are words of acknowledgement, including sentiments of welcome to visitors, and include information sharing, especially with reference to the purpose of the meeting. *Whakatau* also constitute an exchange of discourse that reduces or removes the feelings of unfamiliarity that a new visitor may experience in unfamiliar surroundings. *Whakatau*, to me, means 'to settle': that is, to make a person feel more comfortable in their surroundings. Therefore one would expect that following the *whakatau* visitors would feel relaxed, less inhibited and psychologically reassured. This would encourage a total stranger to befriend and talk with the newly met hosts.

To a large extent the host people control the level of formality during a welcoming ceremony. If they wish to be formal then it usually follows that the visitors will reply accordingly. Morehu believes that whenever a person stands to greet you, that is *whaikōrero*, regardless of where you are – home, school or hospital. The visitor is being acknowledged on the host's land.[39] Likewise, if there is formality in the proceedings, says Mataira, then it is *whaikōrero*.[40]

Formality

We have already alluded to possible circumstances that bring visitor and host together and consequently dictate whether the practices and tenor surrounding the meeting of these two entities should be formal, semi-formal or informal. This raises the larger issue of what practices or exchanges Māori view as formal, which would then require *whaikōrero*. Firstly, let us take a look at the requirements on the individual under 'formalisation', which Bloch explains to be the process by which the speaker 'removes the authority and the event from . . . himself so that he speaks when using formalisation less and less for himself and more and more for his role'.[41] Because the speaker is the representative for his group, he is afforded a great deal of responsibility and status within that role. The position is synonymous with expertise in oration and, therefore, what he says and how he says it tend to be formal rather than colloquial.

The level of formality is influenced by a phenomenon that Yoon refers to as 'geomentality', or a particular behavioural pattern that occurs in response to a specific environment.[42] In this context, my interpretation of geomentality is that it is a set of responses governed by the psychological and spiritual perception of an individual about a particular scenario. I remember the advice given to me by one of my elders, a *tohunga* in his own right, when I asked whether the information he was imparting should have an aura of stricture, of sacred inhibition, to be accessed only carefully and respectfully. He replied that it was not he who placed a sense of stricture on his words, but rather the recipients, if they chose to do so. In this case, the prominence of the informant and the privilege associated with receiving his knowledge carried their own sense of reverence that in turn added to the formality with which the knowledge, as words, was treated. It is the entire complex that carries meaning and mood in a particular social and ritual context.

So what discourse is deemed formal and what is informal? Is it dependent on grammatical constructions employed? Is it the size of words used? Is it the philosophical profundity of the discourse? Is it the frequency with which stock phrases are used? Is it the intonation employed by the speaker? Is it the inclusion of pre-contact expressions, chants, prayers, incantations? Is it a combination of all of these?

Sinclair defines formal speech, actions and occasions as having the following characteristics:

1. Formal speech or behaviour is very correct and serious rather than relaxed and friendly, and is used for example in official situations or when you are talking to someone important.
2. A formal statement, decision, action etc. is one that is officially declared, done, or accepted so that it becomes publicly known or recognized.
3. Formal occasions are ones at which people wear smart clothes and behave correctly in accordance with particular conventions.[43]

Kruger says that a person must adopt the correct posture and delivery during *whaikōrero*.[44] They must be well-informed and adept at critiquing the topic for discussion from a position of knowledge. The delivery must be in Māori and it must be language commonly heard on the *marae*. The level of proficiency in the Māori language must be of a high standard in order to uphold the pride and esteem of the *marae* and the affiliates of the speaker. *Whaikōrero*, says Kruger, stand in contrast to *mihimihi* that are comparatively short speeches of superficial content.[45]

The following is a comparison provided by Bloch between formal and informal speech.[46]

TABLE 4.1 **CHARACTERISTICS OF FORMAL AND INFORMAL SPEECH**

FORMALISED SPEECH ACTS	EVERYDAY SPEECH ACTS
Fixed loudness pattern	Choice of loudness
Extremely limited choice of intonation	Choice of intonation
Some syntactic forms excluded	All syntactic forms available
Partial vocabulary	Complete vocabulary
Fixity of sequencing of speech acts	Flexibility of sequencing
Illustrations only from limited sources	Few illustrations from a fixed body
Stylistic rules applied at all levels	No stylistic rules consciously held to operate

In former times, when inter-tribal feuding was common amongst Māori, the intention or purpose of a visit was often in question and formal welcomes were implemented to ascertain whether the visit was one of just cause. In this context, all visitors had by necessity to be viewed as significant, in order to determine whether they were friend or foe, allies or threats.

Today, the purpose of the encounter is unlikely to be a matter of survival or annihilation, but the rituals remain important as ways to establish relationship, find common ground, discuss differences, accord honour, or acknowledge status or difference. Speakers might take more liberty to tweak their words and the manner of their delivery to a particularly high standard in accordance with the perceived importance of the visitor. Western views generally afford formalities to people of status – Ministers of Parliament, chief executive officers, royalty, elite athletes, television celebrities, the wealthy, religious ministers and famous scientists. During official gatherings, which usually include the sorts of individuals mentioned above, the welcome speeches often begin with a high level of formality.

Although 'Formal speech or behaviour is very correct and serious rather than relaxed and friendly', this may not be the case all the time.[47] For Māori, sometimes less conventional expressions may be included in the speech. Funeral ceremonies remain occasions that are synonymous with high formality, and while the overall spirit of the discourse is formal, less formal exchanges may take place. I recall attending a funeral at which the welcome and the speeches began very formally, but subsequent speakers added some lighthearted humour into the mix. I did not view this as detracting in any way from the sacredness of the funeral, and I think it was the honest intention of the speakers to comfort the bereaved family and friends with humour and warmth. Humorous comments sometimes carry a double edge whose purpose is to confront the listener with a more serious issue.

Funerals are not the only occasions that Māori revere. The solemn acknowledgements that Māori afford to those in the spirit world are resurrected with every *marae* visit because part of the protocol requires Māori to refer to the deceased and bring them into the present. This forces the people on the *marae* into a state of mourning by default. Following this, the speaker delivers as the spirit of the occasion dictates – speaking in a serious manner or tending to be humorous and entertaining. The second part of Sinclair's definition of formality, referring to public recognition, is appropriate when we consider the *marae* complex as a public domain. By bearing in mind the form of the congregation and the level of formality required for that event, perhaps we can further ascertain when the discourse of exchange is *whaikōrero* and the extent to which this is formal or informal.

On any occasion of tribal importance, it is most likely that the welcome will be formal and accompanied by full speeches. The level of formality, in my opinion, is to some extent dependent on who the visitors are. If they are people from outside the family and subtribal affiliation, it is likely that the welcome will be pre-arranged. There is no chance appearance. The visitors are well aware of the time that they must arrive for the formal rituals to take place. I remember visiting one *marae*, at Maungapōhatu, after an absence of ten years or so. An aunty of mine residing there promptly sent me to the *marae* where I was issued the formal call of welcome even though I was the only visitor. There was no exchange of speeches, however, perhaps because I was not important enough – I was not a 'real' visitor – and there were no other practitioners of speech-making available at the time.

Pōhiri are more formal oratorical exchanges as opposed to the low-key, more casual, exchange of pleasantries known as *whakatau*. *Whaikōrero* and *whakatau* appear to share similar content, for example, the exchange of words of welcome between host and visitor, acknowledgements and words of farewell to the deceased, proverbs and mottos of identity, and the expression of genealogical ties. There are, however, some verbal entities that are considered part of *whaikōrero* that are not used in *whakatau*, for example, *tauparapara* (chant-like recitations).

The most salient difference between *whaikōrero* and *whakatau*, to me, is the style of vocal delivery employed by the speakers, especially in terms of volume and tone. During *whakatau*, the volume and intonation are a little more restrained, less forced and more relaxed. There is no requirement to project the voice so loudly, as with *whaikōrero*, so that people across town can hear. With *whaikōrero*, the tone or pitch is higher than that of *whakatau*. Thus, *whaikōrero* carries further. The kinesics applied during *whaikōrero* also tend to be more animated. In simple terms, the difference can be described as one of degrees of formality.

Visiting relatives, or unannounced friends, may receive the informal welcome (*mihimihi* or *mihi whakatau*). They may also be gestured to make their way to another part of the *marae* where host relatives are working, and informally greeted with a Western-style peck on the cheek or the ritual *hongi* (pressing of noses). Acknowledgements, such as *kia ora*, may be the only verbal exchange, followed by a cup of tea and perhaps something to eat. The casual, uceremonious exchange of greetings in the kitchen remain the only recognition they receive.

I was told by my own elders that before 1980 it was normal practice for visitors to sleep at the *marae* for at least the first night of their stay so that they could be afforded proper greetings. Now, visitors are often accommodated by relatives and friends, which means that there is less chance for cordial greetings of the type mentioned above to occur in the meeting house.

The degree of formality governing encounters between hosts and visitors is to some extent fluid and flexible. When I was an employee of the Department of Māori Studies at the University of Waikato in 1998, the staff were informed that a visitor was arriving. One of my colleagues raised the question of what form the welcome should take – formal (*pōhiri*) or informal (*whakatau*). Because this visitor was not *waewae tapu* (a total stranger to the place), an informal welcome was considered an option.

Another colleague suggested, however, that because it had been over a year since the person's last visit, a formal welcome should take place, and that is what happened. A large teaching room was booked to accommodate the welcome.

Whaikōrero is revered because of its inherent seriousness and the rules surrounding its delivery. But as this account indicates, it is not hard and fast. While at its very core, it encapsulates and upholds a formal type of discourse between host and visitor, it exists along a formal–informal continuum that is more heavily weighted at the formal end, but has some flexibility as to role, place, style and content.

Conduct, Identity and Connectedness

Māori with an in-depth working knowledge of Māori custom and *whaikōrero* are generally able to identify what is *whaikōrero* and what is not. Perhaps it is safe to say that if the encounter requires a formal welcome, a *pōhiri*, then oratorical exchanges will take the form of *whaikōrero*. There are certain determinants to be taken into account when deciding on a suitable form of speech-making:

- whether the visitors are newcomers;
- whether they have visited before and how long ago;
- the arrangements already agreed to by the hosts and visitors;
- the composition of the visiting group;
- the venue;
- the purpose of the gathering;
- the host's tribal and other protocols;
- the attitude of the hosts and whether or not this makes formality mandatory to the ceremony.

It would appear to be difficult to link *whaikōrero* solely and unassailably with *marae*. As the final point above indicates, the primary governing power rests with the host people, after which some degree of negotiation might occur between host and visitor prior to the gathering.

Conduct

We have established *whaikōrero* as part of a ritual of encounter, but beyond this, it has several cultural functions. The first of these is fundamental and timeless, and places human encounter in a cosmogonical context. As described in chapter 2, it is the very nature of the relationship between Māori and the Māori gods that provides a model of human discourse and argument, and a vehicle for its conduct. As well-known historian and ethnographer Elsdon Best notes, 'the maintenance of law and order within the commune was based upon belief in the gods'.[48]

The majority of Māori tribes accept that Rangi-nui, the Sky-father, and Papa-tū-ā-nuku, the Earth-mother, are the primal beings of Māori genealogy and origin. The genealogical representation in figure 4.1 is generic, with some tribes having subtle variations, mainly with names. There are four main departmental gods who play roles within *whaikōrero*: Tū-mata-uenga, Rongo (sometimes referred to as Rongo-mā-tāne or Rongo-marae-roa),[49] Tahu and Tāne-mahuta.

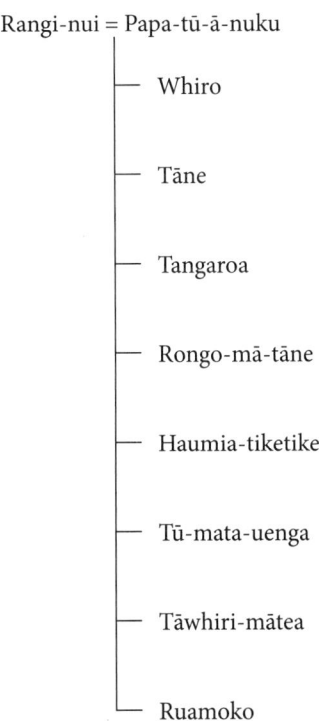

Figure 4.1 The Generic Genealogical Representation of Rangi-nui and Papa-tū-ā-nuku

Creation narratives of the Māori have it that the primal Māori gods lived –

> ... in perpetual darkness, and the nakedness of Papa was covered with vegetation that thrived in dark moisture. The many sons of Rangi and Papa constantly lamented the miserable conditions that they had to endure between their parents. Eventually they resolved to do something about them.[50]

While Tū-mata-uenga[51] preferred to slay his parents, the majority of the offspring opposed this and eventually Tāne-mahuta,[52] with the power of growth, separated them.

Tū-mata-uenga is one of the most frequently referred to of the Māori gods when the *marae* or *whaikōrero* are the focus of discussion:

> The full name for the sacred courtyard in front of the meeting house is Te Maraenui-Atea-o-Tumatauenga (the larger marae of Tumatauenga, the Guardian of War). Going on to the marae means entering into an encounter situation, where challenges are met and issues are debated.[53]

According to Tregear, Tāne is 'one of the greatest divinities of Polynesia'.[54] Buck describes him as –

> ... the most important of the departmental gods in New Zealand. He had been the leader among the sons of the primary parents [Ranginui and Papatūānuku] during the creation period.[55]

Tāne has been attributed to a number of representations, for example,

> ... the greatest son of the Sky-father, he was Tanenuiarangi; as proper-up-of-the-sky, Tanetokorangi; as the parent of man and other progeny, Tanematua; as the producer of life, Tanetewaiora; and because of his association with knowledge, Tanetewananga and Tanetepukenga.[56]

'One Punaweko is said to have been the origin of forest-birds, and he [Tāne] is certainly viewed as the personified form thereof.'[57] He is the progenitor of humankind, the primal ancestor.

Another prominent Māori deity is Rongo, said by Tautahi to be the eldest sibling.[58] Prytz-Johansen views Rongo-marae-roa as synonymous with 'kumara (root)' and responsible for 'providing food, sending people on travels, dancing, and building houses', with 'additional duties as a peacemaker' which 'were probably of more recent date'.[59]

The relevance of Rongo, or Tahu, for promoting peaceful endeavours is therefore antithetical to Tū-mata-uenga and his capacity for conflict. The common perception amongst Māori is that the Māori god Tū-mata-uenga takes precedence out on the open *marae*, whereas Rongomaraeroa takes governance inside:[60]

> When stranger groups are meeting on the marae, they are in the territory of the traditional war god, and oratory is a tenuous bridge between them . . . . In the meeting-house, Rongo the god of peace holds dominion, yet paradoxically, the most heated speeches are delivered in this context.[61]

Tāmati Kruger thinks that when the orators of today speak, they actually have the choice of speaking under the mantle and in the spirit of Tū-mata-uenga or Tāne-i-te-wananga.[62]

Timutimu explains that, being an old practice, *whaikōrero* also serves to stimulate thinking about current and past practices, maintaining a link between ancestors and modern Māori. Through geomentality, *whaikōrero* promotes interaction between the speaker and the spiritual domain whereby the speaker becomes the medium of that spiritual past, a presence by proxy who embodies the direct ancestors.[63] I always remember one of my elders advising me that when I stand, regardless of the forum, I should call my ancestors to support me. Carrying the spirit of the ancestors automatically sanctifies the speaker and their *whaikōrero*. This aura of sanctity is increased when speakers begin their *whaikōrero* with traditional (pre-contact) Māori chants, incantations, prayers, proverb and *haka*.

Identity

A description of early speech-making suggests that *whaikōrero* served as a means of enhancing identity and thus of underlining who is *tangata whenua* and who is *manuhiri*. In this context, it would be used principally to incite protectiveness and aggression:

> There was no need to call a meeting of Parliament to declare war and mobilise troops. The Maori tribe was quickly assembled in the tribal house or on the marae and the insult

or other cause was made known. Inflammatory speeches were made, and if the meeting was held on the marae, the leading warriors punctuated their speeches with a display of their agility and skill in handling their favourite weapons. Speeches were also enriched with songs and chants appropriate to war . . . . The orators thus worked the people up into a state of excitement and military fervour, making them impatient to set out to raid the enemy.[64]

However, the paramount functions of *whaikōrero* appear to be in the realm of the actual encounter or meeting between host and visitor. The protocol governing *whaikōrero* reflects the identity and history of the host tribes. All visitors are expected to adhere to these protocols, above all, as a show of respect to the host.[65]

Connectedness

Whaikōrero express aspects of social concern to the people present[66] and serve to introduce the main topic that has brought the two entities together for discussion on a particular day. Through *whaikōrero*, says Milroy, the individual ensures that a particular issue is recognised and promoted with the view that perhaps the vision and insight expressed will be critiqued, endorsed and/or validated by those in attendance.[67]

Whaikōrero also reflect the complexity of human emotion and experience. I attended a funeral in Te Whakatōhea on one occasion, arriving on the actual day of the burial. While *whaikōrero* were taking place, the hearse arrived. The speaker referred to the arrival of the hearse in his speech, advising that the rest of the speeches should be short. After he had sat down, one of the speakers from the visiting group stood up to speak. He referred to Alamein Koopu, a parliamentary member, sitting on the verandah of the meeting house. In jest he said, 'Don't be concerned about the cost of the hire for the hearse, the minister can pay for it.' Well, the congregation burst into laughter. But after this, he returned to the more serious mood of his *whaikōrero* that was more appropriate to the occasion. Later on, I asked why he had added humour to his *whaikōrero*, and he said that it was not intended to be humorous. It contained a hidden challenge, drawing attention to his belief that 'cost or time restraints should not take priority over Māori protocol'. Another government minister, Tuariki Delamere, came onto the *marae* a bit later and the speaker again alluded to the cost, inferring that he, Tuariki, would probably place a million dollars on the *marae* as his *koha*. This again brought smiles to those gathered together. The grief of the funeral and the sanctity associated with death had been suspended, albeit briefly, and I think that this also served to lift the burden of death that nestled upon the bereaved family and friends.

Whaikōrero give voice to the exchange of genealogical links and the reaffirmation of relatives, creating a vehicle of oral exchange across the *marae ātea* (real or pseudo) that divides the speakers. *Whaikōrero* remove the psychological division that separates visitor and host when they first meet, and ascertains the intentions of the visitors. After this, the 'visitor is no longer a visitor' because the ritual exchanges 'decontaminate them from their alien tapu', says Walker.[68] Of course, this does not go so far as to mean that the visitor is now the host, but it does show how the visitor has been accorded more freedom to relax within the space dominated and occupied by the host. Dewes suggests that the main function of *whaikōrero* to this day is in discharging hospitality to visitors.[69]

Interestingly, Salmond explains that 'Oratory among the Maori of New Zealand has always been a main avenue for the achievement and exercise of power.'[70] Mahuta concurs, saying that *whaikōrero* has been used by some individuals of recent times to advance themselves and their social standing.[71] A difference between past and present practice is that, in former times, those selected to speak were assigned to this elevated role because of the status they already had and it was not through *whaikōrero* that they were promoted to a position of importance.

Chapter Five

Who Can Perform *Whaikōrero*?

Now let us look at who, exactly, has the right to deliver *whaikōrero*, and how this relates to knowledge, status, genealogy and aristocracy. We also consider the forum as a factor that determines who may speak, the issues involved in assigning the role of speaker and the importance of ensuring that the integrity of the speaking bench is upheld. Gender responsibilities and, in particular, the issue of women and *whaikōrero* are also examined.

Let us start with the overview given by Te Kotahi Mahuta that 'the three main qualifications for ceremonial speech-making are maleness, maturity and status', in other words, that those who can speak are men who, 'by virtue of their qualifications and position in the community, have assumed leadership'.[1] It is an honour, say Pat and Hiwi Tauroa, 'to be given the right to speak on a marae. This is because a person speaks on behalf of others, not only for himself. He is the spokesman, and his performance enhances, or otherwise, the mana of the group he represents. Some will positively refuse to speak, rather than risk bringing dishonour to themselves or their people.'[2]

The Knowledge and Lineage of Speakers of *Whaikōrero*

Winiata says that performers of *whaikōrero* are born with the skills that will set them apart as orators: natural ability, high intellectual capacity and/or aristocratic lineage.[3]

We must be mindful of the comment made by the late Ngoi Pewhairangi that 'anyone can speak on a marae once they've been shown the proper procedure. This is just scratching the surface',[4] that is, where it may appear to be straightforward, there are more issues that need to be considered.

Kāretu makes the point that:

> If one considers the marae, one will appreciate that by its very ethic and philosophy, competition is an integral part of the rituals of welcome . . . . only the most articulate, the most eloquent and the most learned rise to speak . . . . The response from the guests is in similar vein because the reputation of both host and guest depend to such a high degree on the quality of performance of all the participants.[5]

In general, it is the elders who decide who may speak on the *marae*.[6] Pita Iraia, of Ngāti Whare, was encouraged to *whaikōrero* by the elder women of the tribe. If you belong to the *marae*, says Pita, then this affiliation serves as the first prerequisite for speaking on that *marae*. This does not mean, however, that any old fool can speak purely because of tribal affiliation.[7]

Having high status is of huge significance, according to Te Ariki Morehu; and Timutimu says that if a boy is from an agnatic line, his father usually assumes that his status will pass to this son in due course.[8] But neither Te Ariki nor Timutimu believe that this criterion is as important now as it used to be.

Rangi says that a person of low status, a commoner, should not front the *marae* as a speaker, a view supported by Te Mātorohanga:[9]

> *Kaua e waiho mā te ware e tū te marae kōrero, te papa tauā, te aroaro ope tūārangi, koi uia ka ngaro i a ia, ka hē. Mō te tū, koi tae ki roto i te mura o te ahi, ka kōmutu tangata ware i a ia ka mutua koe ki runga i te mura o te ahi, koi tū ki te kōrero, he tohungatanga ware, ka hapa ngā kupu, ka tau te whakahāwea ki runga i te iwi, i te hapū rānei. Waiho tonu i ngā uri tuku o te matapihi he tangata kawe i te iwi ki te marae tangata, kia whai manawa ai te kupu Mana Whakaora.*[10]

Tauroa makes the point that 'people's mana could be belittled by a poor speaker', and that, therefore, specific qualities in oratory need to be present.[11]

In the past, having the correct genealogy went some way towards deciding who could speak. In the 1960s, it counted for a great deal 'if a person is a rangatira in the old genealogical sense. Certainly this entitles him to be the speaker and representative when prominent visitors come to the marae'.[12] I think that this prerequisite has been compromised to some degree because the *rangatira* in its 'old genealogical sense' probably does not apply to all speakers today. Speakers often refer to each other rhetorically as *rangatira* during exchanges of speeches. The main point here is that when visitors of high social standing arrive, they should be commensurately afforded *whaikōrero* by high-ranking host speakers, not speakers of drastically lower status. If the visiting group was comprised of young people, then having equally young host speakers would not be a problem, but having an uninitiated youth address senior tribal members would not be viewed as being respectful.

Sometimes it is said that a particular stage of maturity or age qualifies a person to speak on *marae*. Generally, I would say that when someone has been present for many years, they acquire an in-depth working knowledge of *marae* protocol, history and genealogy. Before the twenty-first century, it would have been acceptable to say 'The kaumatua front the marae to welcome visitors, take care that the kawa is followed and set an example to the young'.[13] For example, in the 1970s elders were described as follows:

> Qualified elders are men over 50 who have proved themselves competent in speech-making, although younger men with responsible positions in the European world (Maori welfare officers, Maori M.P.s, lawyers, doctors, university and training college teachers, ministers) may also be admitted as honorary elders, providing they too can speak.
>
> They are usually elderly with a command of the language; its formal rhetoric, idioms, myths, *pepeha, whakataukī,* and *mōteatea* as well as a thorough knowledge of tribal history, genealogies and protocols.[14]

For these *kaumātua*, knowledge and status were acquired through immersion, by a process of osmosis and sometimes by a form of apprenticeship: 'in the Maori situation, one has graduated to the paepae after a number of years of listening, observing and being involved in other marae activities such as the preparation of food'.[15] However, some people who were regarded as elders in the 50–60 year age bracket, and even some in their seventies, never graduated to speak on *marae*. These men were fluent native speakers and well-grounded in Māori custom and history, but this did not automatically mean that they became orators. In fact, the mantle of oratory was very much an honour and not a given.

At the same time, there were certain circumstances, as Kernot relates, in which the role of *kaumātua* was actually eclipsed, perhaps where *marae* ceased to be functional and an aging population was not able to maintain and pass on the traditions without a viable and dynamic community to form the nucleus of cultural knowledge and practice.[16]

A decline in the number of speakers on *marae*, especially rural *marae*, has highlighted the need to address the issue of succession of speakers and to make sure there are those who can 'fill the boots of those who have died and vacated the role of speaker'. Tamati Reedy explains that, through necessity, elders who may be clearly lacking in cultural knowledge are pushed into these positions solely because of their age.[17]

Amongst Māori, it is considered desirable to have a healthy stock of speakers on the host side, maybe because it highlights the capacity of the host speakers to maintain their speaking functionality during encounter rituals as well as offering a show of their knowledge base. Some men are assigned seats amongst the designated speakers although it is understood that they are not put there in a speaking capacity, at least on this occasion.[18]

To have a number of seats filled with potential speakers, or even non-speakers, can only enhance the *mana* of the hosts. This is also seen as a mark of high respect for the visitors. The orations may be given by those in the first and last seats with the three or four people seated in between merely 'warming' those seats.

Opinion is somewhat divided over the significance of status – whether it is agnatic and genealogical, or whether it is the result of cultural immersion, knowledge and competency. Armstrong, for one, does not seem to support the supremacy of status, explaining that *whaikōrero* 'was an art not confined to the noble or high born, as in many cultures, but one which was encouraged in all free men'.[19] It could be assumed that, when Armstrong refers to a 'free' man, he means any person who is not enslaved.

The Passing of the Cloak

It is generally accepted that speakers 'must qualify by age, seniority of birth (i.e., a younger brother or sons of a living father should not speak), and competence in the conventions of whaikoorero, before they may venture to stand upon the marae'.[20] Put another way, 'Men with tangata whenua status in the district, either by long residence, or by ownership of Maori land, who can also claim good descent, qualify as potential speakers.'[21]

Primary authority to orate rests with the father. With the failing health, mental incapacitation or death of the father, a son may assume the role of orator and spokesperson for the family. For a son to assume the speaking rights without the previous conditions occurring removes the authority of the father and diminishes the authority and respect accorded to the son. Such actions are seen as indicative that the son is ready, perhaps over zealously, to replace the senior position of the father.[22] It may also be interpreted, says Hue Rangi, as demonstrating a desire (by the child) that the father should die:[23]

> I heard a young man say recently he was trying to equip himself so that when the time came for him to take his place on the marae he would have learned all the things required of him. Most people would support him in this. But he and others like him have to wait.
> . . . We believe that everytime you give of yourself you are starting to lose some of the aura, some of the life force, which you have for yourself. In the case of my son, if he starts to get up [and whaikōrero] then he's drawing something from me and eventually I will be left an empty hulk. This is the real reason behind not allowing the young man to speak before the father dies. Because it is possible that he will take some of the mauri which rightly belongs to the father.[24]

Te Rangihau actually saw this happen. Contrary to advice, a son spoke and delivered *whaikōrero*, after which the father faded out of recognition because the son had taken over, so to speak. Another circumstance, says Malcolm, is where the father's mental stability is under question. In a case like this, the family or the subtribe may absolve the father of responsibility to orate and sanction the son to speak.[25]

Hohepa of Te Arawa explains that there are some tribes and subtribes that allow the son to orate if the father is absent from that occasion and has given his prior consent, not only to the son, but also to the people.[26] 'Elders can delegate their right to speak.'[27] Mataira of Ngāti Porou concurs that in these circumstances it is acceptable for the son to deliver *whaikōrero*. This has the added bonus of allowing the son to hone his skills of oratory in preparation for the role he will inherit, and will eventually make for a more rounded orator.[28]

Failure to allow this practice, Mataira warns, potentially opens up *marae* in the twenty-first century to degradation and loss of the formal language of *whaikōrero* and the speaking of English: potentially a generation of orators may be lost because they were not afforded an initiation period. '*Ngarongaro manu kōrero; he puehu te kai a te manuhiri*' – bereft of proficient orators on the host side, the visitors are afforded rhetoric with little substance. Some elders I interviewed were pessimistic about allowing a son to *whaikōrero*, and were concerned that once a father relinquishes his right to *whaikōrero*, it cannot be restored to him. Once this responsibility is ceded, the esteem that accompanies it passes to the son.

Taua Pouwhare recollected an instance where a father handed over the right to *whaikōrero* to his son and subsequently sought to take back the role. His two sons died after he had resumed the role of orator which, Taua infers, was a direct result of their *mana* being eroded in competition with their father and with each other.[29] Examples such as this serve as cautionary tales that illustrate the possible repercussions of unsanctioned actions. It must be a right to speak unto eternity, and not a 'short-term', 'relief speaker'-type appointment.

This restriction to *whaikōrero* in the presence of the father also applies to uncles, says Melbourne.[30] Pita Iraia, in honouring this arrangement, chose not to speak on some occasions so his 'nephews' could *whaikōrero* without transgressing any cultural protocols.[31] I am aware of similar practices taking place throughout Tūhoe where able speakers have consciously chosen not to speak in order to make way for others. Metge describes an instance when Epa Awanui had arranged to take a group of visitors onto his own *marae*. On arrival, his father did not speak so that Epa Awanui could do so.[32]

A disadvantage of this system is the time that might elapse before the position of speaker is vacated by the father:

> The practice of the father speaking 'on behalf of' gives very limited opportunities for the youngest [son] to speak.... In other areas, where the number of elders is greater, the older leaders may be very old, so the younger ones have to wait 'in the wings' until given the opportunity to participate in the formal arena.[33]

As Salmond mentions: 'One Northland elder was 75 when he gave his first speech, because his father died at 95.'[34]

When the father finally relinquishes the right to speak, this must be viewed as a permanent handover of responsibility to the eldest sibling. There has been little doubt in the past that the right has principally rested with the eldest son. The voice of the eldest born is respected.[35] This person has seniority and is therefore recognised as the speaker on the *marae*.[36] Even today the situation is seldom contested by the younger sibling. There is usually an implicit agreement that sees siblings mutually supporting each other.

In Māoridom this extends beyond immediate sibling relationships and includes cousins. Tihema says that this means that speakers tend to be as far away as possible from each other genealogically, which is a good thing.[37] Salmond explains that 'Only if they [younger men] show exceptional ability can they hope to outshine their senior relatives and supersede them as speakers.'[38]

The following anecdotal accounts illustrate the kind of resistance levelled by the older generation against changes to this tradition. Tahuri told me about seeing younger relatives deliver *whaikōrero* while more senior relatives were present. On this occasion they were verbally reprimanded, but on another day the younger speaker was actually struck with a *toki*[39] by one of the elders.[40] Hohepa recalled a similar instance when a speaker of *koroua* status was part of a visiting group to Te Puke[41] who spoke while his older brother was seated amongst the host speakers. The speaker was verbally chastised for breaching Te Arawa protocol and told two or three times to sit down. When these attempts to make him sit down failed, an elder from the host side removed his shoe and threw it at the speaker, hitting him in the chest.[42]

I myself have attended a *marae* ceremony when a local elder was being conferred with an Honorary Doctorate. An attendee stood to acknowledge this great occasion and to say how fitting the honorary conferment was. He was interrupted by the host people and told to sit down, with remarks by the local people that his father was still alive. This speaker had not actually spoken during the formal exchange of speeches, but waited until after the formal conferment. He did not stop speaking immediately, nor did he make a lengthy delivery. This raises the question of whether his speech qualified as *whaikōrero* or whether it was merely an acknowledgement made after the formalities. In any case, it was regarded as breaching protocol.

Challenges to protocol occur, nevertheless. Salmond recounts a time when a visiting elder arrived on a *marae* and, during the exchange of speeches, expressed his disapproval to the speakers of that particular *marae* for allowing a younger sibling to *whaikōrero*. The response from the host tribe was 'Put your kawa (etiquette) in your bag and take it home with you.'[43]

Sometimes when accusations of breach of protocol are made, they are based on misconceptions. I remember an uncle of mine returning to our *marae* and being told off by one of the elders for not speaking as part of the visiting group. The elder did not realise that my uncle actually had an older brother who was still alive, and that he was therefore not allowed under tribal protocols to orate. No one qualified this 'public scolding' of my uncle, but the erring elder was duly reminded of the fact after the *whaikōrero* exchange. This incident serves to illustrate that 'speakers need good genealogical knowledge to avoid an embarrassing *faux pas*'.[44]

As we have seen, protecting and/or maintaining the senior status of the father is vital and this consideration is also important in terms of the younger sibling deferring to the older. '*He nui muringa hei kī mai i tōna angaanga*' ('No matter how important the younger may become, he must defer to his elder brother'). [45] The Te Arawa and Tūhoe tribes are particularly stoic in maintaining this practice. Cleave says, 'the teina or younger brother may not speak on the marae while the tuakana or elder brother is alive unless a special arrangement has been made whereby the older brother forfeits his rights to speak'.[46]

If consent has been given by both the father and the eldest son to a younger son or brother, the rule ceases to have salience and there is no transgression.

There are cases where the oldest brother has absolutely no intention of assuming the orator's role, when the father can confer it on the younger sibling instead. In other instances, a younger family member may have higher Māori language and cultural proficiency, or the elder may be incapacitated by illness. An aunt of mine told me about her brother, of Tamakaimoana, who wanted to *whaikōrero*, but when the opportunity finally came, he stood up to speak and nothing came out. He never attempted again after that and left the speaking to his younger brother.

Such circumstances come about because of personal or inter-family choices. At other times, a more pragmatic decision may be made, for example, when the confirmed speaker is absent. There are varying opinions about whether the younger brother can orate in such a case. Some tribes have established the rule that regardless of whether the older brother is present or not, the younger does not speak. There appears to be a general consensus that if both siblings are present, then only one of them may speak. But there are exceptions to every rule and sometimes room for compromise. A senior member of the family with good intention and in good spirit may unselfishly defer to a younger man to allow him to speak. Rangi has actually seen a senior and junior from the same family orate at the same time on the same occasion.[47] There are tribal members who humour each other under the etiquette that the *teina* defers to the *tuakana*. It is also true that by pulling this '*tuakana-teina* card' and applying this principle, an individual can avoid having to *whaikōrero*.

In the case where more than one sibling is eloquent, it seems a shame to see such qualities unutilised. Pouwhare and Tait both view it as acceptable for two brothers whose father has died or relinquished the role as speaker to orate at different places.[48] To ensure a healthy succession of orators, Tauroa explains that 'In some districts where there are few older folk, the younger group of men and women assume the role of the elders.'[49] I envisage more allowances taking place with regard to this in the upcoming generations.

Reedy makes a simple case that a person can *whaikōrero* because they have suitable qualities, for example, an extensive knowledge of genealogy. They are then able to do justice to the job of acknowledging visitors by relating their genealogical ties which may extend back some generations.[50]

When a host speaker struggles with the language or makes errors in front of visitors, it is embarrassing. This serves as a caution that –

> . . . *tuakana* cannot 'rest on their laurels' – so a *tuakana* who constantly permits the *teina* to run the show may be 'usurped' and, in effect, become the *teina*. There is a fine line . . . between maintaining *tuakana* status and delegating roles without [the] latter leading to usurpation of the former. The *tuakana* needs to define who's boss.[51]

The elder sibling, therefore, needs to stay ahead of the younger in terms of oratorical skills and cultural knowledge.

In discussing the regulatory conditions imposed on male siblings, Kruger suggests that in the case where an elder brother is not fulfilling the role as orator, the family may decide that the younger brother will be given this responsibility.[52] '*Ki te kore e taea e te tuakana, mā te teina e hiki.*' The elder brother, the *tuakana*, may take exception and contest this redistribution of power. As Douglas stresses, the older brother with his ascribed status defends his position, his *mana*, and the younger brother disadvantaged by birth is more 'ambitious, achievement-oriented . . . aggressive, shrewd'[53] and barely manages to succeed in life because he is the younger.

The desire of a younger sibling to contest the seniority of an elder brother is nothing new: there are instances in Māori cosmogonical narratives of family feuding between the primal gods in which the younger sibling prevails. One merely needs to recollect past escapades between Tūhoe–pōtiki and Puhi-kai-ariki, Whatihua and Tūrongo, and Māui-tikitiki-a-Taranga as classic illustrations of a younger sibling emerging with significant autonomy.

In the past, a rebellious younger brother could always go and establish himself in some distant part of the country beyond the boundaries of local restrictions and there assert his knowledge and authority, his *mana whakatipu*. Māori histories maintain that this is one of the very reasons that motivated the relocation of siblings and the emergence of new autonomous tribes.

While leadership can be ceded to a younger sibling, the status that is inherent 'as of right' in seniority cannot be transferred. Seniority is passed through descent lines, and there is no contesting this, although there are many accounts where a younger son has been prominent and –

> ... feels himself free to act as he pleases, and does so more promptly than his elder brother, whose behaviour is determined by ritual considerations ... and by etiquette and kinship obligations.... the elder brother fails because he lacks decision. His indecision can be correlated with his overgrown social and ritual conscience, and the decision of the younger brother with his freedom from this restriction.[54]

So there does actually appear to be some leeway for a younger brother to *whaikōrero*, with the appropriate blessing. Failing to get clearance from the people or the tribe, however, will only result in the admonishment of the 'uncertified younger brother' by his peers, a most shaming experience if done within the public domain of the *marae*.

While the restrictions between father, son and siblings are generally upheld, Merito of Ngāti Pūkeko says that if an individual shows a strong desire and aptitude, and establishes his identity and ties to a particular *marae*, then the *marae* may afford him the right to *whaikōrero*.[55] This may restore cultural vitality and continuation. Generally, it is thought that such changes need to be tempered, however. Sometimes people are motivated to *whaikōrero* because it is through this that they receive recognition,[56] and *whaikōrero* becomes a means of self-elevation and self-promotion. But this motivation is neither valid nor traditional, and is not supported by Māori protocol. I have observed cases where youth who have appeared somewhat overzealous have been made to wait longer by their elders. If the individual does not appear to possess the mental maturity, he may be denied. Impatience, in other words, may delay any elevation to this role of high importance.

Such cosmogonical and historical instances are examples of the sorts of mutations and changes that can occur within a culture, perhaps opening up new areas for settlement, or allowing a new form of succession to be established. If leadership is weak, failing or lacks potency, and the stock of knowledge-holders and orators is dwindling, for instance, then there may be times when regeneration is allowed at the expense of *kawa* and *tikanga*. In some of these cases, younger siblings may become orators, fathers may relinquish their role or members of the same family may speak on the same occasion.

The Special Case of Bereavement and the Ties of Genealogy

Assigning speakers in the case of a funeral brings with it additional considerations. Once again genealogies come into play, as it is necessary to know the relationship between a potential speaker and the deceased. If this person is a brother, sister, parent, uncle or aunt of the deceased, then the convention is that they will refrain from speaking. Outside of these relationships, there is more flexibility, and sometimes *taokete* (brothers-in-law) provide a good substitute in such cases.

Dewes says that if one of the close family members were to speak on behalf of the host-tribe, it would be like the actual deceased speaking,[57] in effect acknowledging himself. Similarly, should a close family member speak as a visitor, this would be perceived as self-indulgent and egotistical. Kereopa states that with the death of a child, the father does not speak, but a grandfather or great-grandfather may speak at such a *tangi*.[58] Both Morehu and Kāretu disclose occasions at which they were present when close relatives gave *whaikōrero* on the *marae* at the funeral of the relative lying in repose. Disapproval was openly expressed at their doing so, with Kāretu observing the people who disapproved launching into a chant to make the speaker stop.[59]

There are some anomalies amongst tribes, as Pukepuke points out. In the case of the Tūhoe people, if the relationship of the deceased is twice removed from the speaker, then the individual is free to *whaikōrero* if they so choose. Pukepuke adds that this is not an issue if the relationship is four times removed.[60] Pouwhare, Herewini and Pukepuke are all affiliated to the Tūhoe tribe whose orators generally do not speak if they are closely related to the deceased. The result is that Tūhoe attending the death of a relative may be left in a position in which there is no one to speak on behalf of the visitors.

In describing this inability to speak because of close genealogical ties, Kāretu applies the following description – 'all the guns have been silenced' – which was, in fact, the literal case, 'as all the better waiata, whaikōrero and karanga men and women were all within degrees of prohibition and unable to perform their roles'.[61] Some tribes do not apply this strict rule.

Women and *Whaikōrero*

When host or visiting groups seat themselves on *marae*, men occupy the front benches and women sit at the back. This gender division relates to the principle that men are *tapu* and are therefore qualified to perform *tapu* activities such as oratory, and women are *noa*.[62]

The general restriction on women throughout New Zealand to *whaikōrero* has been a hotly debated topic. Twenty-four of my 39 informants explained that women are not permitted to *whaikōrero*. It was no surprise to me that the majority of the 24 were Tūhoe, one was Ngāti Awa, one Te Whakatōhea, five were Te Arawa, two were Ngāti Porou and one Kahungunu (but speaking about Ngāti Porou where she was raised). Interestingly, three *kuia* residing in Ngāti Porou were of the opinion that women did not traditionally deliver *whaikōrero*. Unfortunately, I did not pursue this topic further, but it certainly provides more 'food for thought'.

Anne Salmond makes mention of Mihi Kotukutuku, of Te Whānau-a-Apanui, who proceeded to orate within the Te Arawa area. This was not viewed favourably by Te Arawa,[63] and it is an occasion well etched in the memories of Te Arawa and Te Whānau-a-Apanui descendants.[64] In Te Tairāwhiti, Ngāti Porou, Kahungunu and some northern areas of the North Island, *whaikōrero* is not limited to men, but the female speakers in question were recognised as descending from chiefly lines and the event seems now to occur only rarely. Does this suggest that there are no women of high enough status left, that the genealogical lines of aristocracy have been watered down, obliterated or consciously hidden so that women no longer view themselves as having the pure bloodline that would warrant their speaking? Is this an indication that they feel the men are servicing this role adequately? Or is it an admission that women do not regard *whaikōrero* as a woman's role?

On the one occasion in the mid-1990s when I witnessed a woman of high status speak, the event occurred at a recently built complex with a specific area designated for formal ritual encounters. It was regarded as a pseudo- rather than a true *marae*, and the *iwi* in question did not allow women to *whaikōrero*. After the *tauutuutu* speaking pattern had ended, the highly ranked woman opened her 'address' by saying '*ehara tenei i te whaikōrero*', 'this isn't a *whaikōrero*'. Being respected in her own right throughout the country, I doubt that she said this to placate the male speakers or the *iwi*. I viewed it as a show of respect by this woman, this person of high standing, and perhaps it was said to allay any unease the men may have felt in the face of this potentially embarrassing situation.

It is possible that the question of whether prominent women may speak has been given new weight by the theory that women from particular tribes actually delivered *whaikōrero* in pre-colonial times:

> Ngati Porou women as of traditional right may speak on the marae; they assume this right if the men do not measure up or at the request of their male kinsmen, e.g. Materoa Reedy, mother of a noted East Coast leader, Arnold Reedy, was the Ngati Porou spokesman at the Waitangi hui in 1934.[65]

In this particular case, according to one of my informants, Materoa did not volunteer her services as spokesperson. The Waitangi occasion required a speaker and, out of respect for each other, none of the tribal leaders felt comfortable about being leader or spokesperson for another tribe. This then prompted one of the senior members present to offer Materoa as speaker.

Even the question of Ngāti Porou women delivering *whaikōrero*, which is frequently cited as 'proof' that women can and even should deliver *whaikōrero*, is not at all straightforward. Archer writes that it is degrading for women to *whaikōrero* on *marae* outside of Ngāti Porou, and even while on home territory, visitors may not be receptive to women speaking, although it is the way of the host people. There is a solution: if visitors are uncomfortable with this, they can always 'take the highway'.[66]

I have been present on one occasion when no one considered it appropriate even for the women to seat themselves on the front seats designated for male speakers, regardless of their status. Tauroa says –

> ... women may speak on the marae-atea on special occasions, under exactly the same conditions as men. But they, too, must be accepted by their people as having the necessary mana to speak on behalf of others. This expectation applies also to Ngati Porou, a tribal area that accepts the right of women to stand and whai korero.[67]

In contrast, 'When women, who would not normally claim that right [to speak], are accorded that honour by a marae, they will, most often, go to the porch of the whare and speak from there – from the shelter of the ancestor.'[68]

The historical argument is fraught with disagreement. The Tūhoe and Te Arawa tribes maintain that women have never been permitted to *whaikōrero* on their *marae*. On the other hand, Katerina Mataira says that colonisation and the introduction and adoption of Christianity from the reign of Queen Victoria brought about these restrictions, because women did not tend to speak publicly in Europe.[69] This is debatable, however, considering that Her Majesty, Queen Victoria herself, frequently orated to her subjects. And closer to home, there is evidence in Polynesia that high-ranking women addressed the people on occasion after the advent of colonisation.[70] In considering Mataira's inference about the oppression and exclusion of women, it is interesting to examine Tauroa's explanation of the place of women on the *marae* that asserts the holism and functionality of the *marae* system in which everyone has a role of equal significance:

> Many of those who argue that women should have the right to speak on the marae-atea claim that the situation is one of female suppression. . . . Māori people, both men and women, see their involvement on the marae not only as a role but as a personal contribution to the identity of their people. By contributing to the whole tikanga, their own mana, and the mana of their marae, is uplifted . . . . [Māori women] do not consider themselves oppressed.[71]

Ani Mikaere cautions against adopting the European viewpoint that there is a gender inequality issue. It is more an issue of complementarity:

> The roles of men and women in traditional Maori society can be understood only in the context of the Maori world view, which acknowledged the natural order of the universe, the interrelationship or whanaungatanga of all living things to one another and to the environment, and the over-arching principle of balance. Both men and women were essential parts in the collective whole, both formed part of the whakapapa that linked Maori people back to the beginning of the world, and women in particular played a key role in linking the past with the present and the future. The very survival of the whole was absolutely dependent upon everyone who made it up, and therefore each and every person within the group had his or her own intrinsic value. They were all a part of the collective; it was therefore a collective responsibility to see that their respective roles were valued and protected.[72]

Tait says that the specific roles of men and women are essential for the survival of the people.[73] Kereopa elaborates:

> Now I agree that women should not whaikorero, but they should be respected for the special knowledge that they have . . . . There has to be a role that women play, and a role

that men play. The women should not try to take over a man's role, because otherwise they are going to lose the role they were put on this earth for.[74]

The perception that women are prohibited from speaking because of an inherent inequality in Māori society must therefore be challenged, since arguably it reflects the ethnocentricity of a Western view and the application of this view prescriptively to a society with a completely different – but cohesive – *kaupapa*.

There are many instances when women have affirmed their roles as valuable within Māori society.[75] In addition to *karanga* and *waiata*, say Kingi and Walker, women have played important roles in advising men. If the men say something wrong, women may correct them. If their concluding song is not in check, women may set this straight as well. Women may even go so far as to advise the men on how they might improve their speeches.[76]

When the issue of equality was raised, Melbourne posed the question as to why, then, men are not allowed to *karanga*? And if, indeed, all things were meant to be equal, men would have been blessed with the facility to give birth. He further asserts that it is only of late, since the mid-to-late 1990s, that role division has been viewed as gender inequity, and suggests that this may be a result of Māori practices being evaluated by Māori who have been raised outside of the traditional Māori forum.[77]

Reedy further espouses the importance of women as being the foundation of *marae* practices. Ancestral houses are named after prominent Māori women in the tribe. They have been the backbone of the tribe and visible in battle as well.[78]

Women, according to Māori views expressed in the nineteenth century, were seen to possess *mana tapu,* or spiritually ordained potency that was different from but complemented that of men. This capacity for *tapu*, or an intimate connection with the divine, meant that women were the key actors in certain ritual ceremonies.[79] One only needs to consider the opening, or blessing, of a new house (building or complex), the *kawanga whare*, whereby a *puhi* or a *ruahine* are critical in lifting the *tapu* off a new building:

> *Ko te wahine hoki he tapu,* in her own right. Lives of our *tūpuna* have been spared by the *mana*, or the tapuness of a woman. *Ētehi o ō tātou iwi i patua ai, ka peke te whanaunga wahine i roto i te taua, ka peke ki runga i te whare, ka nōhia e ngā hūhā, e te tara o te wahine, ka oma ōna whanaunga ki roto i te whare, ka ora, ka kore e patua e te taua.*[80]

Hohua Tutengāehe gives the example of a woman who, through her divine sacredness, was able to save her kinsmen from being killed during conflicts simply by straddling the gable of the meeting house and having those men enter the house by passing beneath her, underneath her vagina. This act prevented the aggressors from pursuing her kinsmen, so great was the protection she offered by virtue of the sanctity of her femaleness.

I was always told that the practice of having men positioned at the front, on the sides and at the back on the *marae* and elsewhere was specifically to protect the womenfolk who were located in the middle. In other words, the men acted as the first line of defence. Mātaatua and Te Arawa peoples assert this philosophy as justification for their prohibition of women delivering *whaikōrero*: on the *marae* women do not sit at the front, and this inherently means they are not at the forefront and are not therefore able to speak; in addition, their position symbolically places them at one and the same time in a space where they are protected by the men and where their sanctity is upheld.

There is a common proverb that reads '*He rākau e taea te karo, he tao kī e kore e taea*',[81] which basically means 'physical attacks can be parried whereas verbalised curses are not easily deflected'. Tauroa says that 'The tapu of all women requires that they be protected from the possibility of abuse'.[82] They must sit behind the men so they cannot be spiritually attacked, through *mākutu, whaiwhaiā* and *kangakanga* that could affect not only the woman, but also her progeny for all time to come.[83] This way the men 'take the hit', so to speak:[84]

> Women were revered in Māori society for their ability to give life and to take it away as the following *whakataukī* notes, '*He wahine, he whenua, i ngaro ai te tangata*' (It is because of women and land that men perish). Therefore, Māori were conscious not to expose women to curses or threats that might be made on the *marae ātea*, lest these affect subsequent generations.[85]

Because of the potential for curses that could result in the loss of capacity to bear children, there have been times when, even when I was just acting as a seat warmer, I have not allowed my daughters to sit beside me during the *whaikōrero* so that they are not subjected to the potential 'spoken spear'. It is this 'spoken spear' that Māori are cautious of invoking lest it result in the female who is still capable of childbearing becoming *wharepā*, or *wharengaro*, unable to conceive. Katerina Mataira raises an exception to this. If a woman is in a post-menstrual state, she is exempt from this vulnerability.[86] This is the understanding amongst Ngāti Porou, Te Whānau-a-

Apanui and Kahungunu people. Regardless of the way we view it, men have tended to maintain that the potential for womenfolk to be cursed is the primary reason for prohibiting women from *whaikōrero*:

> Maori women are primarily defined in our society as whare tangata even if we are women without children, either wharepa or lesbian or whatever. The responsibility and the role of whare tangata means that through our collective and individual wisdom, through the decisions we make, and through the vision we have – through all those different elements – we shape a world for our children and succeeding generations. Women in Maori society will always carry that particular responsibility, which without doubt is a task we have endured or enjoyed for countless generations.[87]

It is widely acknowledged that one of the perceived purposes of the *marae* is to provide a space where potential physical conflict may be expressed, which is another reason that is sometimes given for the banning of women from taking a 'front row' role on the *marae*:

> Maori people believe the marae atea is the domain of Tu, the god of war, where bad feelings, arguments or nasty comments can be aired. Some tribes believe women must be protected from this behaviour, and don't allow women to whaikorero or make speeches on the marae.[88]

If this is one of the main functions of the *marae*, then it can be asked whether women are able to enter into physical confrontation, should a challenge be issued against them. But such a question could equally be asked about aged men well beyond their years of combat, in pre-contact as well as contemporary Māori society, and whether there is an age, or point of maturation, when even they cease to front the *marae*. It is clear that some of today's speakers have been appointed because of their age and wisdom, as opposed to their physical potential to defend their 'ground'. Generally, this is to do with *mana* rather than actual physical ability, but it is clear that physical confrontation is regarded as the realm of men. Nevertheless, Best documented the ability of some women to defeat men in battle.[89] And there are some very physical women who I believe would put up a good fight if called to task by some of these aging orators as well as some younger ones.

Where many tribes assert that Tū-mata-uenga reigns outside on the open courtyard, it is generally accepted that a non-confrontational deity, such as Rongo or Tahu, resides within the meeting houses. Although Tūhoe and Te Arawa do not allow women to speak outside on the *marae*, they do allow them to speak inside the *wharenui* after the formalities on the *marae* have ended. Personally, I have never viewed these deliveries as *whaikōrero* because they have taken the form of discussion rather than true orations. For example, they are not prefaced with sacred chants but may begin with brief introductory comments about who the speaker is.

There is an additional understanding that when women speak inside the *wharenui*, they adopt a different posture to that of the men. For example, they can speak while they are sitting, or even kneel and speak. This particular posture is sometimes perceived as a show of deference, or humility, on the part of the woman. But regardless of the stance they adopt while speaking, their comments have weight and are equally considered during the discussions.

Many people argue that one of the assigned roles of women on the *marae* – delivering the *karanga* – can be regarded as the first *whaikōrero*, on both the host and visiting sides. In this case, an important rite of passage is guided and actuated by women, further endorsing and expressing their status and significance in Māori society:

> That is why the woman is the person who takes the first step onto the marae, whose voice is heard first in karanga – to clear the pathway with her words and to introduce her people – where they come from, who they are tribally. She clears the way for her speakers as they move forward and eases the hearts and minds of the tangata whenua as she calls in answer to their call. Their whaikorero will go smoothly because of her.[90]

One could assert that the *karanga* is very similar to *whaikōrero*, only shorter. Like *whaikōrero*, *karanga* often provide genealogical links, acknowledgements of the dead and reference to the occasion that has brought the people together on that day. The function of this delivery is just as crucial in terms of establishing the identity and sanctity of those present, and taking them across the liminal threshold, as is the ensuing delivery of *whaikōrero*. This would seem to preclude the argument that women are being discriminated against or treated unequally in not being assigned to the role of delivering *whaikōrero*. Shirres explains:

> Understanding noa both as a positive reality and noa as a negative reality, are important in seeing what is meant by the noa of women and by their power to make noa. When women are called noa, the noa referred to is a positive noa, a positive freedom from restriction.

When women are called noa, it does not mean that they have no intrinsic tapu of their own, but that they are free from restriction, especially when it comes to dealing with other tapu. They have a special tapu[,] a special mana, to whakanoa, to make situations noa, especially when the clash of tapu is between the tapu of the local people and the tapu of a people outside their own area. Perhaps this is the underlying reason why the women are asked to give the karanga, to call visitors onto the marae, and why, in some tribal areas, the women in a visiting party are asked to take the lead as the visitors move onto the marae. The same tapu and mana to whakanoa, to make situations noa, is called upon when particular women, sometimes ariki, sometimes first-born, sometimes virgins, are asked to be the first to step into a new meeting house. They are asked to do this in order to make noa, by the power of their tapu, any destructive powers.[91]

It has already been stated that observing the protocol established by the host *marae* is paramount. Acknowledging that some *marae* allow women to stand and speak must also be accepted by visitors to those *marae*, although some may show a reluctance to be received by women. In considering women and *whaikōrero*, Mataira says that although it may be appropriate for women to *whaikōrero* on their own *marae* where it is accepted, it would be arrogant to stand and speak on *marae* of other tribes that do not condone this practice.[92]

Metge writes about one formal welcoming ceremony held on a particular *marae* where women were allowed to speak. The problem was that the male speakers given the responsibility to orate on behalf of the hosts were from tribes that do not allow women to speak. Following after the host speaker, when one of the women (a visiting speaker, I presume) began her farewell comments, one of the male speakers openly disapproved. The people of the host *marae* were embarrassed because this woman was prevented from speaking even though she was on a *marae* where women were allowed to speak.[93]

Let us refocus our discussion on women within Ngāti Porou, Ngā Puhi and Kahungunu, since these have been identified as tribes that allow women to *whaikōrero*. Can all women from these tribes *whaikōrero*? Can they only *whaikōrero* on their own tribal *marae*? Are there separate arrangements and protocols for women who *whaikōrero*? We have heard mention that they must be of noble lineage. Dewes explains that they must be proficient in speaking, knowledgeable, well-grounded and have good voices. They should also be learned in genealogy and leaders of the people.[94] Kuia Te Wai says that they must be strong women.[95] I am not sure, however, whether she was referring to strength of character or to physical strength.[96]

There appears to be little doubt about the ability of women to fulfil the role as orator, as a repository of knowledge or as an educator. Whaia McClutchie, of Ngāti Porou, was an authoritative speaker, confident and with good voice projection who structured and presented her words well and was better to listen to than many men, according to Reedy.[97] She is but one example of many women who possessed these attributes.

Ngahuia Te Awekotuku refers to the fact that it is not inherent inequality between men and women and their roles in Māori society that is the problem. It is more that the effects of colonisation and Christianity have eroded some of the old spiritual power of women. Whereas in traditional Māori society, women had roles of knowledge and power, the changes brought about by the dominant European social model upset the complexity of the *noa* and *tapu* system described by Shirres, and replaced it with a dualistic system that was also hierarchically ranked. Te Awekotuku therefore argues that it is more important for Māori women to reclaim and extend their traditional roles so that they are experts in both the realisation and the rich complexity of those roles. *Karanga*, in this setting, would therefore take on its critical significance in juxtaposition with *whaikōrero*:

> There is another part to our natures, however, which I believe Christianity and colonisation effectively undermined and certainly damaged, and that is the warrior, the shaman, the initiator, the visionary, the groundbreaker – the women at the front. Although some of that knowledge is retained by the karanga, I even think that within our role as kai karanga, as the first voice, as the sole voice, much of our dignity and our significance has been downplayed, so that today we witness the truly heartbreaking arguments that occur in certain tribal regions – and most notably my own of Arawa – regarding the rights of women to speak on the marae, and the mana and authority and status invested in the male voice.
>
> What I believe has happened in the last 200 years, is the reduction of the female voice. Personally I have no wish to whaikorero, but I believe it is our responsibility as Māori women to revive and to really celebrate and strengthen the beauty and the knowledge of karanga. Karanga in its richest form – the apakura, the whakatangitangi, the maioha. Again, the root issue is language. We hear those voices mainly in places like Tūhoe and Waikato, just occasionally in other parts of the land. We should hear them everywhere – wherever our people gather.[98]

The latter section of this chapter has raised the issue of points one must consider when applying and/or maintaining protocols during *whaikōrero*. Kruger raises concerns about particular cultural practices and the physical boundaries within which they apply. When we consider the *marae ātea*, he says, one must recognise the fact that the elders' authority does not extend beyond that particular domain.[99] If someone is not comfortable with a particular person present on the *marae*, there is nothing to stop him from going to the gate, or to the entrance of the *marae*, and voicing his disapproval from there. Because this is not actually on the *marae ātea,* technically they are not transgressing any speaking protocols regulated by the *marae* proper. Host elders have been empowered by the host people to officiate on the *marae*, but that is where their authority ends.

Chapter Six

What Skills are Required for Oratory?

In the mid-1970s, Mahuta explained that it was a generally accepted belief throughout New Zealand that Māori 'are gifted speakers (in their own language), and that the Maori language is particularly well-suited to elegant, formal and ceremonial speech-making'.[1] By the mid-1980s, he was starting to make different observations, describing orations during which 'poor or boring speakers may hear comments such as <u>kaatahi</u> how unnecessary, <u>paanguu</u> how tiring, <u>hoohaa</u> boring, or <u>puku kau</u> empty stomach'.[2]

In the mid-1990s, Tīmoti Kāretu was of the view that there were many people who could speak Māori, but few who were proficient in oratory – '*He nui ngā tāngata kōrero, engari ngā tāngata whaikōrero*'.[3] Milroy makes the observation that speakers from the 1970s to 1980s were better than speakers in the mid-1990s,[4] the difference being the body of knowledge and vocabulary that more recent speakers no longer seemed to possess. Good speakers, says Milroy, tended to have at their disposal a language bank specific to each of them, and an ability to articulate clearly what they wanted to say and to utilise it to full effect. Tahuri views the language of former speakers as classical language, a diglossic language, a prestigious language.[5]

It is clear, then, that there are identifiable characteristics that mark good oratory from bad oratory, that include aesthetic, stylistic, linguistic and cultural factors. The best way to ascertain what these are is to identify individuals of high repute who serve as exemplars of oratorical prowess. The oration, says Mahuta, must be fitting for the occasion,[6] and the orator must have the skills to meet the requirements of the occasion and give expression to the *mana* of all those involved.

In this chapter we look at stylistic approaches in terms of language constructions and forms, and the paralanguage of the orator that all contribute towards this. Let us take a look at what makes a great orator, a great *whaikōrero* person, in the Māori environment. Mataira, in talking about the importance of oratory, recognises the skill involved in a speaker being able to express their thoughts and to enhance their delivery by including various song forms and proverbs.[7] Add a bit of eye contact and paralanguage, and the ingredients are all there to move the audience. As Schrempp reiterates, '"Rhetoric" may be defined generally as the skill of, or the study of the skill of, verbal persuasion, and the concern of rhetoric as an intellectual discipline, is to discover the means and strategies by which a speaker renders his speech persuasive.'[8]

Colenso made the observation in the middle of the nineteenth century that –

> To the ancient New Zealanders . . . the great value of their proverbs and proverbial sayings appeared in their oratory, of which they were passionately fond, and in which they excelled. At such times (as I myself have heard them with delight some 40–45 years ago!) their orators, by some well-chosen, some fitting proverb, carried everything before them, winning over their attentive auditory as if they were but one man! In which, no doubt, they were ever largely aided by the very genius and structure of their noble Maori language, it being so highly terse, pregnant with meaning, and abounding in paronomasia and antithesis.[9]

Oratorical skill, then, starts to emerge as a marrying of personal qualities, *mana* and charisma, with linguistic skills and cultural knowledge. Kāretu and Winiata define quality as the ability of a speaker to structure and present their words, of being knowledgeable and skilled at thematic development – that is, skilled in expanding on an idea expressed by a previous speaker and potentially turning the idea, or part of it, into an expression that will provoke thinking in the listener.[10] Clear articulation of thought, says Milroy, is one quality. Tupe adds that the speaker's selection of language is another.[11] Rangi explains that the great orators know how to structure their addresses and add myriad linguistic accoutrements to beautify their speech.[12] Winiata identifies three particular skills: high proficiency in the Māori language; cultural competency, genealogy, a knowledge of proverb and tribal motto-maxims; and awareness of tribal, governmental and national events.[13] In other words, there are inherent and personal skills involved in fine oratory, as well as an ability to communicate and to persuade through language use, as well as a powerful awareness of the social, tribal and even national context in which these words emerge. Mahuta refers to chiefs in their conversations with Governor Grey who 'frequently quoted in explanation of their views and intentions, fragments of ancient poems or proverbs, or made allusions which rested on an ancient system of mythology'.[14]

The two quotations below idealise oration. The first was given by Tīmoti Kāretu, a stickler for Māori language quality:

> What was once a noble and lofty art is fast degenerating into a perfunctory, platitudinous, recited litany of rote-learned words and phrases. The occasions are becoming fewer when one could be moved and stirred by the command of rhetoric, of metaphor, of mythical allusion, of pithy and apposite aphorism, of wit and candour, of subtlety and nuance interspersed with chant where appropriate and concluded with haka.[15]

The author of the following description is unknown, but there is a similar focus on content and vocal expression:

> The Maori language contains a rich treasury of proverbs, wise and/or witty sayings which sum up the experience of generations in small compass. These proverbs display most of the main features of oral literary art . . . have marked rhythmic patterns . . . are economical of words – terse, condensed, and elliptical . . . use concrete images to convey rich abstract and symbolic meanings . . . can legitimately be interpreted in more than one way.[16]

Having the ability to 'prick the conscience' of the audience and arouse their minds is a quality that Kereopa views as a major attribute in an orator.[17] Kereopa, himself, tested those of his own generation by adopting this facility. I know he sometimes annoyed people, but nonetheless, he succeeded in provoking thought amongst those gathered on the *marae*. He was a 'shit stirrer'. Speakers with the facility to stimulate discussion, he said more than once, were beneficial for prompting the lazy brain into action. The audience simply had to be attentive, with the capacity to interpret hidden linguistic nuances, the messages, taunts, digs and revelations; and to recognise the cultural and historic significance of what was being said. (The description of the funeral in Te Whakatōhea mentioned in chapter 4 is a classic example of this.)

The quality of *whaikōrero* has never been dependent on length. As Salmond points out, if it 'has been brief (say ten to fifteen minutes), dramatic and well-delivered, he [the speaker] has won more *mana* for his group'.[18] Judging from discussions with individuals, and through personal observation, some notable *whaikōrero* have been short. Te Pairi Tuterangi, of Tūhoe, was mentioned by some elders as being particularly memorable in this respect. One *whaikōrero* he delivered was very brief, when he used gesture more than words to make his point and to captivate his audience.[19]

Amongst others, Kāretu makes mention of the late Hamuera Mitchell, a very adept Te Arawa speaker who was economical with words and not one to draw out his *whaikōrero*.[20] Te Wharehuia Milroy of Tūhoe, Huirangi Waikerepuru of Taranaki, Hohua Tutengaehe of Taurangamoana were some exemplars, says Kāretu, because they were skilled in presenting and structuring their speeches, and extrapolating from comments made by other speakers.[21] Other admirable speakers included Haupeke Piripi of Ngā Puhi, Hieke Tupe of Ngāti Haka, Ru (John) Tahuri of Tamakaimoana, Kimoro Pukepuke, Apirana Mahuika of Ngāti Porou, Pihopa Kingi of Te Arawa, Hoani Rangihau of Tūhoe, Waea Mauriohooho of Waikato and Pumi Taituha of Waikato-Maniapoto.

Mahuta describes *whaikōrero* as a 'mixture of poetry, prose and song . . . [that] tend to be abstract, dwell on the symbolic and supernatural, and possess an esoteric quality absent in other forms of discourse'.[22]

The Content of *Whaikōrero*

Old Expressions, New Ideas

Expressing fresh ideas, complemented with original and clever approaches, are characteristics that always have their own appeal, to me anyway. Having a body of significant content to share with an audience is normally much appreciated. Having the facility, says Tahuri, to vary one's oration from that of another is an indication of a learned speaker.[23] This might be effected through possessing an 'older form' of Māori language; by having in-depth cultural knowledge; or because of personal skill, creativity and dynamism.

Schrempp analyses the use of formulae as a way not only of ascertaining an orator's facility with traditional language forms but also as a way of determining the nature and quality of a speaker's own repertoire and linguistic skills:

> There is one sense in which the possibility of formulaic analysis of *whaikoorero* may to some extent reflect a regrettable contemporary tendency. For it has been suggested that in recent times, decreasing fluency among Maori speakers has lead to a greater domination of the specifically formulaic aspects of *whaikoorero*, over the

more fluid *ad hoc* exposition that can take place within the *kaupapa* section of the speech.

Detailed formulaic analysis can often be carried out most effectively through careful study of transcribed texts. Compounding the demands posed by this type of analysis, is the probability that the greatest number of formula are distinctive, or at least, partially distinctive to a particular speaker. They therefore stand to be revealed most fully through considering a number of speeches given by the same orator on different occasions, rather than through study of a number of speeches by different orators. A given speaker might use a particular phrase or pattern only once within a given speech and the student would not realize its formulaic character until confronting it in other speeches by the same orator.[24]

For some fifteen or so years, I accompanied Wharehuia Milroy at funerals and meetings, predominantly in the Mātaatua and Waikato areas. I would listen to his orations and found he was able to vary each *whaikōrero* in language and content. It took about ten occasions, maybe more, before I heard him recycle a portion of a previous *whaikōrero*. In contrast, I would hear other speakers using parts of other people's *whaikōrero*, and sometimes repeating much of what they had said on a prior occasion.

Having a Supporting Song Form

The combination of complementary songs and speeches with good voice projection and intonation, and valuable and carefully placed content helps create *whaikōrero* of high quality.

Ruka Broughton describes the importance of possessing a large enough suite of *waiata* for the intentions or words of *whaikōrero* always to be matched to the song[25] – the song could act as important reinforcement for a message. Although speakers at the time – in the 1970s and 1980s – did not have a large enough repertoire to achieve that effect, there are now speakers who possess a vast knowledge of Māori songs or chants, and even include English songs in part, or whole, to strengthen their orations. This is nothing new. In the mid-1800s, Shortland observed Māori drawn to Christian teachings and including passages from the scripture in their *whaikōrero*. They also used Christian hymns to finish off their *whaikōrero*, as opposed to traditional Māori *waiata*.[26]

Strong Christian teachings influenced Māori oratory in the speaker's conscious selection of words, constructions, paradigms, genealogical inclusions and structures.

These affected thought patterns of orators through the 1900s. By the late twentieth and turn of the twenty-first century, the renaissance saw Māori invigorated with a resurgence in Māori identity, Māori language revitalisation, Treaty of Waitangi claims and settlements. The language shifted amongst younger speakers, who were less influenced by Christianity.

Humour and Entertainment

On occasion, there are adept speakers who cleverly intermingle humour with their *whaikōrero*. The following is an extract from a *whaikōrero* by Haupeke Piripi at a venue I cannot identify. I have provided an English translation.

> *Nā reira, ka hari hei hakarongotanga mai mā Ngāti* Blow *e tāhae ana [a] Ngāti Awa nei i wā rātou haka, pēnei i a Ngāti Awa i mea nei, 'E Ngā Puhi, nā koutou i tāhae tō mātou waka'. Nā tū ake ana a mātou whaikōrero, 'Taku rākau e . . .'. Ka pai ana hoki tāku nei tāhae mea kē. Homai taku tāhae, māku e kī ake ngā korokē nei, korokē koretake. Tukuna e rātou tō rātou tuahine, tō rātou whaea tupuna kia kauria te waka nei a Mātaatua 'Kia whakatāne hoki au i a au.' Koretake ana werā korokē. Ka pai ki te hakapai a te korikori kai o te tinana, engari, mangere riro atu i a Puhi-kai-ariki te waka, ka nuihia atu ki Tākou, huri ana, hei kōhatu, hei kōhatu, hei kōhatu. Nō reira, i roto i te rā nei ka mahia e rātou he waka hou mō rātou, Mātaatua, ka piri mai ai ki tēnei o ngā waka. E toru kē ō tātou nei waka. Nā, koretake ngā korokē nei te tiaki i tō rātou waka, mā tātou anō e tāhae, kei te pai, kei te pai, kei te pai.*[27]

It is entertaining to hear that Ngāti Awa are pinching the *haka* of Ngāti Blow [Ngāti Porou], like Ngāti Awa asserting, 'Ngā Puhi, you stole our canoe'. So when we deliver *whaikōrero*, we sing '*Taku rākau e . . .*'. It is very good indeed to pinch things that belong to others. Give it to me to pinch. And I say to them, they are useless elders. They allowed/sent their ancestress to retrieve the Mātaatua canoe, whence she uttered the words, 'Let me assume the status of a man.' How useless they were. Good at physical endeavours, but lazy, a dispute over food, and thus the vessel was commandeered by Puhi-kai-ariki [and taken north to its final resting place] where it was petrified in the Takou Bay [Bay of Islands]. Now the Mātaatua people are building a new vessel for them, to add to this one. That will make three. The old people were useless at protecting their vessel, but that's okay, we'll pinch this [new] one.

This section of Haupeke Piripi's *whaikōrero* has humorous components, as well as a challenge, and perhaps a criticism, depending on the audience's viewpoint. I have no record of the responses of the speakers who followed, but candid expressions such as these sometimes prompt a 'tit for tat' exchange between speakers.

Haupeke's delivery also indirectly alludes to the genealogical affiliations between the Ngā Puhi people (as descendents of Puhi-kai-ariki through the cohabitation of his daughter Te Hauangiangi with Rāhiri) and the Mātaatua people of the Bay of Plenty (descendants of Toroa, Tāneatua and Muriwai), this giving the *whaikōrero* some traditional authority and gravitas that are counterbalances to the humour and invective.

Using Proverbs

The occasion itself plays a part in the quality of *whaikōrero* being delivered, says Reedy.[28] It not only focuses on a place and an encounter between at least two peoples; it also brings out the expertise of an orator to pull together their mastery of the Māori world and to incorporate markers and signifiers such as proverbs in their oration. These expressions are informative and clever, and orators are skilled at recalling and expressing them at the appropriate time. Proverbs, referred to as *whakataukī*, or *whakatauākī*, capture an audience by evoking a myriad of images. The saying goes, 'a picture paints a thousand words', so does a proverb capture a thousand more?

Pei Te Hurinui Jones, in *Ngā Mōteatea,* wrote that, 'In former times a wealth of meaning was clothed within a word or two as delectable as a proverb in its poetical form and in its musical sound'.[29] *Whakataukī*, says Grove, are generational and many refer to 'localities or personalities; others allude to events in traditional accounts or mythology'.[30] Proverbs take history and compress it into brief, short phrases, and their inclusion in *whaikōrero* involves the listeners in acts of recognition and identity.

Reciting Genealogies

Genealogical affiliations have always been an important part of the Māori worldview. They inform and reaffirm familial relationships, from the cosmogonical gods to Māori pre-existence in the Pacific, to migration to New Zealand. They draw relationships with the environment, the social spheres in which different entities interact, and the cultural practices and belief systems. On occasion I have witnessed *whaikōrero* where the content has been largely *whakapapa*, genealogy. In one case, the speaker recited genealogical links between the hosts and the visitors and then sat down immediately afterwards. This illustrates how integral genealogical ties are to Māori in terms of their identity and their customary practices, and in this case, rituals of encounter.

As Reilly explains:

> Māori creation narratives... stressed the important place of genealogies and kinship relations in Māori society. Kinship has been described as one of 'the fundamental categories of knowledge' for Māori. Not surprisingly, Māori take care to establish their kinship ties with both the natural world, and with other human beings.[31]

The following example of a genealogically-based *whaikōrero* was delivered by Pei Te Hurinui Jones in 1966 at his farewell to King Korokī, the fifth Māori King:

> *Kua rewa atu too waka, e te Ariki, maa roto i too awa i Waikato*
> *he wai pounga hoe mai naa oo maatua.*
> *E huri too kanohi ki te Hauaauru*
> *ki Whaaingaroa, ki Aotea, ki Kaawhia.*
> *Ka ahu mai ai, e Tama, too tira ki te ara mauii ki runga o*
> *Maungatautari, ki te hikonga uira i runga o Wharepuuhunga i Rangitoto.*
> *Ngaa tohu eenaa aa oo tuupuna.*
> *Takahia e koe, e Tama, te ara ki Rotorua-nui-aa-Kahu.*
> *Ka tae atu ai koe ki Te Rotoiti, kei konaa, e Tama,*
> *ngaa wai kaukau aa oo tuupuna oo Ngaati Pikiao oo runga i a Te Arawa,*
> *i too ara taane, mai i a Tamatekapua.*
> *Taiaawhio te haere i runga i oo waka i a Maataatua, Horouta,*
> *Taakitimu, kia mihia mai koe e ngaa uri a oo tuupuna, a Toroa, a*
> *Porourangi, a Kahungunu.*
> *Whakamau mai maa te uupoko o te Ika*
> *ki oo kaawai maha, ki a Raukawa....*[32]

The *whaikōrero* tracks affiliations, first referring to the ties of Korokī close by – that is, to the Waikato people who are the current guardians of the Kīngitanga, the Kingite movement. The words then extend the links to the west coast – Whāingaroa (Raglan), Aotea (a harbour approximately 100 kilometres south of Whāingaroa), and Kāwhia (the next bay immediately south of Aotea). The links then come back inland to Mounts Maungatautatari and Wharepūhunga, on to Rotorua (Rotorua-nui-a-Kahu-mata-momoe) and Rotoiti where the Ngāti Pikiao people reside – their ancestor being the origin of the King line in Waikato, from which Korokī is descended – and continue across the North Island to the Bay of Plenty and around the East Coast, to incorporate the descendants of the Mātaatua, Horouta and Tākitimu canoes. Pei then tracks down to the Wellington region, and Raukawa.[33] These simple genealogical recitations therefore serve to inform the audience of intermarriages and alliances. They are historic references as extensive, or limited, as the knowledge of the audience who interprets them.

A major reason for including genealogies, especially when recounted by the host speakers, is that the host speaker may make the familial connections of all parties gathered known to all, thereby helping to remove the feeling of separateness that an individual can experience as a newcomer.

Archaic Utterances, Metaphor and Simile

When oratory flourishes, richer forms of expression in metaphor, simile and poetic phrases are composed to please the ears of listening audiences and add to the orator's reputation as a scholar.[34]

Archaisms are viewed as valuable ammunition for a speaker to have at their disposal. Metaphor and simile are viewed as language representative of an older society, a society that depended largely on the natural environment, when people were highly cognisant of their relationship with the environment in which they lived. Such archaisms include old knowledge, esoteric knowledge about cosmogony, references to the primal deities and information about social behaviour amongst Māori.[35]

Shortland described the language as arcane, and went on to say that if Polynesian peoples are to uphold their language with veneration and respect, and weave it with multiple contextual messages, orators run the risk of making their speeches accessible only to a 'privileged' audience, to the exclusion of, for example, younger generations.[36] Mahuta refers to Piri Poutapu, an esteemed carver of the Waikato, as a speaker who included these dual-meaning expressions into his *whaikōrero*, leaving the audience to pursue the spirit of his words in any way they could – literally or figuratively.[37]

I have extracted a portion of the speech by Haupeke Piripi, of Ngāti Wai, orating at Waitangi in the north of the North Island:

E Ngā Puhi. Hīpokina Te Tiriti o Waitangi ki tōna ake kākahu, kāhore ki te kākahu, ki te kara o Ingarangi.

[Literal translation by author]
To you, Ngā Puhi. Cover the Treaty of Waitangi with its own garment, rather than clothe it with the colours of England.

[Interpretation and translation by author]
To you, Ngā Puhi. Recognise the Treaty of Waitangi in its distinct form, rather than accept it as a subjugate of English rule.

Reedy views these types of utterances with their secret meanings as hidden treasures, and it is because of their subtlety that they are such wonderful pieces. They are not recycled by the average Joe Bloggs and that makes them a gem to hear. This, says Reedy, defines the speakers themselves as learned on another level:[38]

> The language of the Maoris was limited in its range of sounds but not in its expression of ideas. The Maoris were imaginative people, fond of speech-making. Upon all public occasions, such as greeting guests, or speaking farewells to the dead, words flowed from the lips of elders. These orators created colourful word pictures rich in imagery.[39]

Another extract from Haupeke Piripi, in one of his orations regarding the Treaty of Waitangi, reads:

> *Ko koutou, e te iwi Māori, he para whenua, he para whenua, he para whenua. Ahakoa pēhea tō koutou haere atu ki roto i te moana, te mātauranga o te iwi tauiwi, ka tuhaina mai koutou ki uta, nā te mea, he para whenua koutou . . . .*[40]

Meaning: You, the Māori people, are refuse on the land. No matter where you venture on the ocean, in the academic arena of the Pākehā, you will only be cast ashore. A number of strong metaphors are used whereby Haupeke has likened the Māori he was addressing and their pursuit of Western knowledge to debris washed ashore after being put through the ringer by the Western academic environment. The vastness of academia has been likened to a great sea of knowledge and the verb '*tuha*', 'to spit', is used to describe how Māori would be unceremoniously disposed of by the education system.

In his farewell to Frederick Augustus Bennett[41] in 1950, Kepa Hamuera Anaha Ehau, of Te Arawa, employs several examples of metaphor and simile.

> *Heoi raa, e Paa maa haere i te ringa kaha o te mate!*
> *Ngaa tootara haemata, ngaa tootara whakahiihii o te wao tapu nui a Taane Mahuta.*

Ngaa taangata hautuu, ngaa haumi, ngaa whakatakere o ngaa waka.
Ngaa toka tuu moana aakinga aa tai, aakinga aa hau, aakinga aa ngaru tuuaatea. Aku parepare, aku whakaruruhau.
Te muurau a te tini, te wenerau a te mano.
Aku manu tiioriori, aku manu hoonenga, ngaa kaakaa waha nui o te pae, ngaa kaakaa haetara ki te iwi i ana raa.

This translation is provided by Brooke-White.

Whichever of these, e Paa maa
Go under the strong arm of death.
(You were all like) the strong totara, the lofty totara from the great sacred forest of Taane Mahuta, the *tangata hautuu*, the *haumi*, the *whakatakere* of the canoes [the leaders, the bow, the stern].
(You were all like) the sentinel rocks defying the tides, defying the winds, defying the ocean waves.
(You were all like) my *parepare*, my windbreak [my protection, my shelter]
the guiding star of the multitudes [the expression of many], the envy of thousands
My *manu tiioriori* [eloquent speaker], my *manu honenga*, my strong voiced *kaakaa*
Of the threshold, you were the greatly admired *kaakaa* of your time.[42]

If we look back to the mid-nineteenth century, Angas documented how Pōtatau Te Wherowhero, the first Māori King, used imagery and figurative language, as did many Māori orators of that time.[43] Figurative language was not limited to oratory, of course, and was used in the composition of other oral art forms such as song (*waiata*), chant and recitations (*haka, karakia, tauparapara* etc.). One merely has to turn to any page of the edited series by Ngata, *Nga moteatea: he maramara rere no nga waka maha*, and the frequency of usage is clear. It was a natural feature of Māori composition.

References to Landmarks

Landmarks are cited by almost every Māori who stands to introduce himself, but they are often mentioned with little thought and in relative ignorance. In other words, they often become clichés. When they are incorporated into *whaikōrero*, however, they are consciously and purposefully applied by the orator. The landmarks are usually in the form of *pepeha*, which are apposite phrases that function as a geographical reference of tribal identity for Māori:

> Pēpeha are not just proverbs; the term includes charms, witticisms, figures of speech and boasts. Neither are they historical relics; they feature in the formal speeches heard everyday on the marae, and in the oral literature handed down from past generations.[44]

During his experiences in the field, Yoon was inclined to believe that 'all Maori of any distinction, that is those who are eligible to speak at the marae, were able to recite their own pepeha (popular or tribal sayings) of tribal identity'.[45] These *pepeha*, or motto maxims, are used to 'introduce the speaker (announce where they are from), and acknowledge and compliment the host people in terms of their territory and ancestral heritage'.[46]

> In te kawa o te whaikorero, orators lace their performances with literary and historical allusions (e.g. proverbs, battle names and stock ancestors) which assume some understanding on the part of the audience . . . . Another essential element is the audience, which is often directly involved in the creation or performance of a piece of oral literature. The oral artist can exploit this face-to-face situation or be influenced by it, or the type of audience can affect the presentation of an oral piece . . . . The significance of the occasion can affect the content and form of a piece being performed.[47]

'Their speeches also employed imaginative language enriched by references to old Polynesian myths and legends and to ancestral deeds'.[48] Some examples of landmarks can be viewed in the appendix in Sample whaikōrero 17, Sample whaikōrero 18, Sample whaikōrero 19 and Sample whaikōrero 20.

Allusion – to location, past events and people – is another key feature employed in *whaikōrero*. Some of these utterances are not full accounts or references and are elliptic in their use, for example:

> . . . the omission of one or more words in a sentence which would be needed to complete the grammatical construction or fully to express the sense. (O.E.D.) Words are deliberately limited, often to the barest minimum, so that the hearer (or reader) is left to work out meaning and implications for himself. They also make occasional oblique references, using not the name but some identifying feature or incident. By this means, the poet establishes status or locality, evokes a complex web of associations and emotional responses, and calls to mind stories which reflect glory (or shame) on the poet, his listeners or his subject. Instead of doing all the work himself, the poet counts on the knowledge, quick wittedness, and emotions of his listeners to enrich and flesh out his poem. The allusions commonly fall into the following main categories: (a) supernatural

'A New Zealand war speech', drawn by Augustus Earle (engraved by J. Stewart), published by Longman & Co., London, May 1832, PUBL-0022-160, Alexander Turnbull Library, Wellington, New Zealand.

This image depicts Maori chief Wiremu Kingi Tarapipi Te Waharoa delivering a speech to an audience seated on the ground. Nowadays, it is still the orator who takes centre stage, but the audience sit on chairs. 'Punch in Canterbury . . . [Christchurch 1865]', artist unknown, PUBS-0078-44, Alexander Turnbull Library, Wellington, New Zealand.

'Unidentified Maori chief [from the Wanganui region?] holding a tewhatewha', photograph by Frank James Denton, [190-], Tesla Studios Collection, G-23308-1/1, Alexander Turnbull Library, Wellington, New Zealand.

Mita Taupopoki (1845?–1935), Chief of Te Arawa, shown here in ceremonial dress and wielding a *toki*, was renowned for the manner in which he delivered *whaikōrero*, [c. 1915], photographer unidentified, New Zealand Railways Collection, G-23794-1/2, Alexander Turnbull Library, Wellington, New Zealand.

'Chief Whatanui standing inside the porch at Hine-nui-tepo meeting house at Te Whaiti. He is wearing a kakahu (cloak) and holding a kotiate (violin-shaped patu, or club)', photograph by Albert Percy Godber, October 1930, A. P. Godber Collection, G-1675-1/2-APG, Alexander Turnbull Library, Wellington, New Zealand.

'Haka with tewhatewha at Parihaka', photographer unidentified, [c. 1930], G-17415-1/2, Alexander Turnbull Library, Wellington, New Zealand.

'Listening to a speech of welcome to Sir Peter and Lady Buck and their party, from the verandah of the Ikaroa-a-Maui carved meeting house, Waitara', photograph by Edward Percival Christensen, 10 March 1949, Archives New Zealand: National Publicity Studios Collection, 1/2 0400066 (AAQT 6401, A10998), Alexander Turnbull Library, Wellington, New Zealand.

'Mr Kareama Te Ngako, of Feilding, speaking during the visit of the ashes of Sir Peter Buck to Otaki', photograph by T. Ransfield, August 1954, National Publicity Studios Collection, 1/2 040123 (AAQT 6401, A36467), Alexander Turnbull Library, Wellington, New Zealand.

Opposite: *Tokotoko/tiripou* in hand, Kaumatua Simon Snowden speaks at a Waitangi Day ceremony at Waitangi. Photographer unidentified, February 1988, Dominion Post Collection, EP-Ethnology-Maori lands from 1976-05, Alexander Turnbull Library, Wellington, New Zealand.

This *pae* of Wairaka Marae, Whakatāne, shows a healthy row of speakers. The orator on this occasion is standing close to the *maihi/raparapa* to allow the spiritual emission of ancestral energies to flow through him from the ancestral house. Photographer unidentified, c. 11–14 May 1981, courtesy of the *Whakatane Beacon*.

beings; (b) ancestors; (c) kinsmen, living or recently dead; (d) places, especially within the tribal territory; (e) tribal and sub-tribal groups; (f) the moon, stars, and seasons; (g) valued cultural objects.[49]

In addition, these allusions serve as invaluable educational resources for anyone listening to *whaikōrero*. The example mentioned above of Te Pairi using gesture more than words was comparable in its effect. By gesturing towards the deceased, the audience conjured up memories, associations, emotions, sounds and images for themselves of the deceased and/or their family, tribe and wider associates.

Milroy raises the issue of the degree to which orators have maintained their knowledge capacity in terms of lexis, archaisms, colloquialisms, idiom and formal utterances. When concerted efforts were made by tertiary and private educational providers from around 1995 to 2005 to revitalise Māori language, culture, history and teachings, multiple approaches towards more effective and efficient teaching strategies were instituted, such as a strong push for mixed-mode teaching, web-based teaching and total immersion. The aim was to increase the number of speakers. Once a critical mass of speakers had been regenerated, the next shift was towards ensuring a high level of language proficiency. The focus on language quality was designed to address the decline that Milroy mentions, which would ameliorate the quality of *whaikōrero*. It is debatable whether extending knowledge of vocabulary, stock phrases and metaphor at a cerebral level will have the same depth of meaning as the organic immersion of Māori in Māori culture had before language suppression and loss started to occur from the 1860s onwards.

The Use of Formulaic Expressions

An obvious feature of *whaikōrero* is a reliance on formulaic expressions, regardless of the social setting or physical location. Schrempp underlines the fact that extemporaneous expression is usually bound to include formulaic content: it is part of the oral mnemonic as well as part of the tradition:

> Speed of *whaikoorero* delivery varies radically from speaker to speaker and occasion to occasion, but the ability demonstrated by some speakers to speak extemporaneously with rapid fire delivery, and yet maintain a regular cadence, strongly suggests that some degree of formulaic composition is involved. . . . there appear to be a number of stock phrases common to many speakers and one can pick out numerous instances of formulaic patterns even from within a single *whaikoorero* text.[50]

The following are some examples of commonly reiterated phrases:

te urunga tē taka [51]
te moenga tē whakaarahia [52]
haere ki te Pūtahi-nui-a-Rehua [53]
haere ki te poutūtanga o Pipiri [54]
nau mai, piki mai, kake mai [55]
Haere mai, haere mai . . . [56]
Tēnā koutou, tēnā koutou . . . [57]
haere ki te huinga o te kahurangi
haere ki te kāpunipunitanga o te hunga wairua
kua hinga te tōtara o te wao nui [58]

Although opinions may vary about the use of these types of phrases, Salmond explains:

'Te marae e takoto nei, te whare e tū nei, te wai e hora nei, ngā waka e tau nei, tēnā koutou, tēnā koutou, tēnā koutou' . . . . These phrases, along with the texts of the chants, illustrate one of the main stylistic themes of Maori oratory – the repetition of symmetrical structures. These repetitions give balance and sonority to the speech, and they are one of the reasons why Maori oratory seems so effortless.[59]

Sometimes the use of formulae can be seen as a skill and sometimes as a deficiency. The reason that I use the term deficiency is that as a bystander, you sometimes hear the audience muttering '*e, ko aua kōrero anō*', '*ko taua rite anō, ko aua kupu anō*', alluding in a derogatory way to the repetitive use of these stock phrases. There are also times, however, when an audience can be heard to respond positively.

Just how they are used can be viewed as evidence of oratorical development, either as evocative, fresh and entirely appropriate, or as staid, stale and with little power to evoke feeling in the listeners:

While certain formulae are shared among a number of singers, each singer's particular kit is yet highly specific to himself. More importantly, even though the acquisition of a large number of formulae and the ability to effectively combine them, constitute the most basic and necessary tasks in the apprenticeship of a new singer, the mark of the true master lies in a further step. This is to move from a strict use of fixed formulae, to the introduction of subtle variations and innovations within them, giving them a more highly individualized flavour. At this point, the singer is truly controlling the formulae rather than being controlled by them.[60]

By the same token, lacking the facility to manipulate these phrases, an orator would 'never become a singer'. That is, he would never be recognised as an orator of high proficiency since 'the more formalised and predictable speech becomes, the more powerful and provocative becomes any small or subtle variation that is introduced'.[61]

The Style of Delivery

One may be eloquent and one may be highly knowledgeable, but all of these things are fruitless if the orator is unable to project his voice so that the beauty can be experienced. Winiata says, 'I don't think there's much point in getting up if you're going to speak like a mouse'.[62] Hohepa recollected his elders who, while speaking on the *marae*, could be heard several kilometres away.[63]

Good voice projection is a must. I am not referring to an orator who merely yells, but an orator who can project his voice across the threshold of the *marae*, and is able to maintain optimum audibility. Audiences are quick to moan about the speaker who speaks to himself. If we add effective voice projection to the list of qualities that make a good orator, we will be also be alluding to 'audibility, clear enunciation, rich tone and vocal variety'.[64] Of course, when conducting oratorical exchanges inside or in a more confined space, there is less need for a strong voice.

Dramatic Delivery

Some magnificent speakers have been termed '*manu hakahaka*', which literally describes a bird that is animated and active. This is a term of endearment for an orator who enhances his *whaikōrero* with physical gesture and movement that on its own is a sight to behold. From witnessing such deliveries, says Salmond, 'People become connoisseurs of oratory, and take a real delight in spirited performances'.[65]

Pou Temara, who is himself a dynamic orator in word and movement, compares such orators to ballet dancers: they are agile, composed and commanding.[66] Their bodies speak. They brandish certain objects or *taonga* to invoke a cultural and spiritual presence. When used appropriately and effectively, these handheld props raise the authority and importance of the oration, the occasion and the orator, and ultimately serve to drive points home. Ward observed this in the mid-1800s whereby:

> The speaker generally roused himself into a strong passion, as he walked backwards and forwards before the audience, brandishing his weapon of war, striking his sides, and assuming a countenance so agitated and fierce, that a stranger from England would tremble for the consequences.[67]

One hundred years later, Salmond observes the Māori orator who:

> . . . strides towards the opposite party, chanting or calling out his greetings and gesticulating with a walking-stick, then abruptly spins upon his heel and walks back in thoughtful silence. He returns with the next few sentences, stressing each point with a stylized gesture, occasionally getting really carried away and making terrific faces. Tongue out and eyes rolling; but turning back as quietly as before.[68]

There is, however, generally a strong feeling that the performance must remain secondary so that the words are paramount. The uninitiated observer, or performer, may otherwise be mesmerised by the theatrical display and pay little attention to what is being said:

> Dramatic ability however found plenty of expression in the elaborate posture and pantomime that was part of Maori dancing and oratory. . . . Similarly oratory had customary forms, beginning with the intoned welcome to the dead and the living and interrupted by suitable songs, which are called the 'relish' of the speech. While the orator is delivering the more emotional parts of his speech, he walks or runs a short distance during each sentence, sometimes concluding the period by a leap to give emphasis, and accompanying his words with graceful motions of arms and body.[69]

Maning described the display of one chief who, in his oration, appeared to admonish members of his tribe and presented himself as being exceptionally vexed, probably more so than he actually was:

> He runs, gesticulating and flourishing his *mere*, about ten steps in one direction, in the course of which ten steps he delivers a sentence. He then turns and runs back the same distance, giving vent to his wrath in another sentence, and so back and forward, forward and back, till he has exhausted the subject and tired his legs.[70]

Such demonstrations of movement were also recorded by others of that period. These descriptions could just as well be applied to a large number of current speakers and the stances they use during their *whaikōrero*.

When *whaikōrero* are performed in full view of the public, for example, during ritual encounter, the orators are –

> . . . evaluated by the fire and drama of delivery, the appropriateness of content, and their general entertainment value. . . . The accomplished speaker wins prestige by demonstrating control over the formal devices of oratory, and the facility with which he can match the content of his speech to the immediate situation.[71]

It would be an injustice to criticise all other speakers as boring or dull because of their lack of movement. And it would be equally unjust to criticise someone for a paucity of words where movement may be all that is required. Ritchie documented an event that occurred around 1864 when Māori were in conflict with Pākehā. The British constabulary had arrived to determine whether the Māori people of a particular village would stand as allies or as adversaries. The chief at that time, he says, assembled his people and they listened to the discussions taking place for days. When asked to –

> . . . state his allegiance, the chief stood and, in silence, took the Colonial flag and draped it across his body. Standing there, wrapped in the flag, he declared himself and his people for the Crown, against the rebels.[72]

There are no hard and fast rules about the type of movements that can be used. Taiepa comments that 'Eastern martial arts movements can be used, as well as the traditional Māori martial arts movements.'[73] Mita Taupopoki, a famous speaker of Te Arawa, was a sight to behold, although he moved very little, basically just tilting his head. Video footage of him is still authoritative – not to mention regal and awe-inspiring – and makes highly recommended viewing.[74]

As Salmond explains, on occasion an orator set on enhancing his prestige would stand up and voice a loud and authoritative call, the *whakaaraara,* and stride the *marae* –

> . . . making humorous or controversial comments, everything demanding attention. The display is actively judged by the audience, and it has to meet the promise of its beginning. Some orators gain a reputation for this and even before they stand on marae the audience is alive with expectation.[75]

It is important, says Mahuta, that orators show 'aggressiveness of stance' when they *whaikōrero*.[76] Aggression in this case is synonymous with confidence and authority. Others use the term '*wana*' to describe this prestige, which may equally be derived from the knowledge content of the oration, proficiency in the Māori language, and animation of stance, gesture and movement. As Kruger explains: 'The qualities of Ihi, Wehi and Wana represent the highest form of praise any artistic performance can receive'.[77]

Generally speaking, there are three main styles with respect to movement. The most basic style is where the speaker merely stands in one position and may (or may not) use his hands to emphasise his words. The second style involves walking. The speaker rises from his seat and walks to the spot where he wishes to deliver his oration. He starts speaking, then stops, turns sideways and walks a few paces in one direction (usually in silence). He realigns himself with the opposing speakers, and continues to orate. He may stop speaking and head back from whence he came, continuing to move backwards and forwards like this several times until the oration is complete. The third style has the speaker positioning himself on the spot from where he wishes to give most of his oration. He then moves forward three or four metres then back, almost in a straight line. This style is called '*te pāpaka*', the crab, whose movements it resembles. The speaker may orate while standing, advancing forward, or while he is retreating. On walking backwards, individuals are usually advised not to turn their backs to the opposition – first, just in case an attack is made while their back is turned, and second, as a show of respect.

It would have been invaluable to film examples of these movements, but on a personal level, I have struggled with the issue of going to someone else's *marae* and video-recording the *whaikōrero*. It is even more challenging as a university employee because of the rigours one must go through in order to gain ethical consent. There is national television footage available, but many recordings have been cut and few capture entire *whaikōrero*. Unfortunately, therefore, evidence is largely confined to memory and to a few written descriptions, supplemented by the odd still photograph contained in a publication or private collection.

Perhaps in total contrast, Walker sees the capacity of a speaker to show modesty and deference to others as an admirable quality:[78]

> Rangatiratanga does not depend upon kaha or strength alone. A man's sense of spirituality, mauri, his capacity to put others in awe of him, wehi, and his ability to humble himself if need be, whakaiti, are all involved.[79]

Kāretu characterises Tainui speakers as being self-effacing with humble demeanours. He further observes that the younger generations are tending towards over-confidence and appear more self-indulgent, possibly as a side-effect of national speech competitions when young orators are coached to be confident.[80]

In observing some skilled, experienced, seasoned orators who have the ability to call on myriad dimensions in their orations, an observer needs to be attuned to whether a speaker is being an outright show-off or merely demonstrating a dramatic display out of sheer confidence.

The Use of Hand Props

Salmond gives one description of Māori orators who 'move like warriors, agile and strong'.[81] The term 'warrior' evokes images of someone wielding a weapon, and in fact a common sight is the speaker brandishing a hand prop of some form while he delivers *whaikōrero*:

> *Haere nei te whaikōrero, te rere o te mere, te mau tokotoko rānei, koirā, i kite i ērā momo tāngata e mau ana i te rākau me te whaikōrero, me te whiu i te rākau, te ātaahua o te tū. Mā te rere o te tinana e whakaū te tikanga o ngā kōrero.*[82]

The most common 'handpiece' during *whaikōrero* is the *tokotoko* – sometimes referred to as a 'common walking stick'. This may be functional, in that it is actually used to support, or it may be symbolic, in that it is employed primarily for use during *whaikōrero*. I seldom saw hand-held Māori weapons dating from the pre-contact period used through the 1980s and 1990s. Since then, however, I have noticed an increased use of weapons such as *mere, taiaha, tewhatewha, wahaika, kotiate, toki, pouwhenua* and *koikoi*. Both the *wahaika* and *kotiate* were prized weapons on the battlefield as well as being favoured by chiefs for use during speech-making, says Evans.[83] This duality of purpose in weapons is evident in Buddle's observations of Māori chiefs in the mid-1800s:

> In war as in peace, a Maori chief was more a leader than a commander.... the chiefs had people to 'lead – not control...'. The leaders generally exerted themselves to excite the passions of their army by addresses. The reasons of the conflict are set forth with all the peculiar powers of Maori oratory, and by the most impassioned appeals to the excited feelings of the untutored savage.[84]

I have heard accounts of various individuals, and seen recent photographs of those who have favoured the use of one type of weapon during their *whaikōrero*, but Pou Temara is the only orator I have seen employ a variety of different hand weapons. He has been training younger generations in the use of different types during *whaikōrero*. This could be viewed positively in terms of the revitalisation of weaponry and their use other than as decorative art pieces in homes and museums, and accoutrements for Maori performing arts.

Esteemed weapons are not, of course, the be all and end all of hand appendages used for *whaikōrero*:

> The carved walking-stick (*tokotoko*), a whalebone *kotiate* or a *mere* (hand weapons) are indispensable props for a dramatic performance, and some people say they repel *mākutu* (black magic) as well. They give the orator authority, and lend emphasis to his gestures. Sometimes the speaker has no walking stick, so he picks up an umbrella instead and uses that in his oration.[85]

In addition, speakers have used their jandals, hats and rolled-up newspapers as items to punctuate their remarks.

So exactly what is and is not acceptable to wield during *whaikōrero*? Is there a risk that the modern legal system will deem traditional hand-held Māori weapons dangerous and rule that they not be displayed in public? Will the objects themselves be relegated to powerlessness and be replaced by meaningless modern accoutrements?

Types of hand props

'Tiripou', 'turupou', 'tokotoko'

The *tokotoko* is sometimes referred to as a *'tiripou'*, *'turupou'* or *'rākau'* (a stick). When we talk of a walking stick, we refer directly to its main function as a support to help enable a person to stand and walk. Mehaka Herewini also extends its purpose, explaining that –

> . . . *he homai whakaaro ki roto i te kaikōrero. E kī ana rātou, mau ana koe i te rākau kua riro mai ngā āhua katoa o koro mā ki a koe. Pēnā ko koe te kaiwhakapapa, ngāhorohoro mai te whakapapa . . . .*[86]

When in possession of a *tokotoko* or *tiripou*, he says the orator is imbued with thoughts and ideas. The old people were of the belief that the speaker also received the spiritual support of his forebears and if he was a genealogist, for example, then genealogical recitations would come to him easily.

Pukepuke was advised by his father that the good thing about using a *tiripou* is that it does not carry the same sacredness or revered status as a *taiaha* or *patu*.[87] This rings true because the *taiaha* and *patu* were always employed for combat, and therefore associated with the shedding of blood, making their use very sacred from both an historic and contemporary Māori point of view. The full value of the *turupou* extends beyond the two spheres mentioned above, of spiritual support and cultural knowledge: Best explains that 'a priest, when travelling, sometimes used his walking staff (turupou) as a temporary shrine for his god when he wished to consult him'.[88]

Regardless of the symbolic meanings attached, there is no doubt that orators with mastery in manipulating hand accompaniments are truly a delight to watch. Whether it is a basic *rākau* being wielded majestically, or an intricately carved *rākau* that is a source of authority in its own right, the practice adds to the orator and their delivery. While there is a school of thought that hand accompaniments are not the *whaikōrero*, they do enhance and give life to the words being spoken.

The expression '*Kīhai koe i ākina ki te parāoa, i whiua ki te tao roa!*' announces that one has not been subjected to the wrath of the whalebone club, or the long spear. Kāretu regarded the possession of hand weapons on the *marae* as a precautionary practice by Māori chiefs of old in case visitors instigated a violent attack.[89] As Winiata states:

> . . . the use of weapons goes back to the battlefield and their primary role is protection. . . . when a speaker steps out from his *paepae* he is in effect in 'no man's land' and the weapon stays in front of him at all times so that it is always between the speaker and the opposing side.[90]

With physical confrontations now a thing of the past, there are at times oratorical battles, not necessarily contests of Māori language and knowledge, but of wit. As Taiepa says, the use of a Māori weapon of old in *whaikōrero* gives it a 'different sense' and changes it 'from a threatening thing to a means of allowing words and ideas to flow':[91]

> Elaborately decorated taiaha such as these were often held by chiefs and other important men when they made speeches at tribal gatherings and other important hui. They were seen as an emblem of rank at such events, and to challenge a rangatira out of turn while he was holding such a weapon was to take your life in your hands.[92]

Interestingly, Kruger of Tūhoe noted that while he was growing up, he saw speakers using the two-handed weapon, the *tewhatewha*, but in his adult years their use appeared to diminish, with speakers opting for *tokotoko/tiripou* instead.[93] In the Te Arawa area, Hohepa saw *patu pounamu, tokotoko, taiaha* and *toki* all being used.[94] Amongst Ngāti Porou, *tokotoko, mere* and firearms (but not in the combustible capacity) were employed during *whaikōrero*. There is also the suggestion that perhaps the occasion induces the oral artist to pull out all the tricks, including the most highly esteemed hand accompaniment. The more important the occasion, or the visitor, the more ornate and complex the hand accompaniment!

Some orators from Mātaatua are reluctant to use weapons, or *tokotoko*, while speaking inside an ancestral house. This probably aligns with the philosophy followed by Mātaatua people, that there are two separate domains with specific observances for each: Tū-mata-uenga – war that takes precedence on the open courtyard; and Rongo – peace – residing inside. From this position, there is no requirement for weaponry inside. The other view shared with me by Milroy is that wielding hand props such as *tokotoko* or other weapons inside a *wharenui*, which represents an ancestor from that area, is symbolic of cutting their insides.[95]

There does not appear to be a strong tribal preference for the employment of specific hand-held objects. Kruger says their increased use has perhaps been a direct result of speech competitions, *kapa haka* competitions and even television broadcasts.[96] Rangi, a tutor of Māori weaponry amongst Tūhoe, is a little concerned that the youth are very keen to learn to use hand-held weapons for the purpose of *whaikōrero*, but they do not want to learn the philosophy behind the weapons themselves.[97] There is, as indicated above, that tendency to elevate an orator because of his ability to wield a *tokotoko* or *patu*. Despite the criticism that some fledgling orators use *tokotoko* to give themselves an air of maturity that they do not in reality hold, there are indeed many orators who are both knowledgeable and skilled in weaponry and experienced in using them as oratorical enhancements.

Use of weaponry carries obligations, says Rangi, because 'ka mau patu ana koe, ka hāpai kē koe ki te kōrero o taua rākau, kaua ki tāu kōrero e whakarite ana'.[98] When you take up a weapon, he says, you also uplift all that the weapon represents. An orator can pick the time to use *tokotoko* or *patu* for *whaikōrero*, whether it be while they are beginning to orate, or even when they are older orators. How the weapon is held and manipulated, and when it is applied, are all considerations for the individual who decides to delve into this area.

Some observers question the employment of *tokotoko* when it is glaringly obvious that their legs are quite fit and able. Some experienced speakers say that they never had the desire to use *tokotoko* or *patu*. The good old, ever reliable, hand has always been a safe default option for the majority of speakers.

Conclusion

> Eloquence is held in much esteem among the New Zealanders; and they generally display, as orators, a remarkable ability.... But they have a certain native eloquence, enforced by readiness of speech and grace of action, which cannot but strike the listener with astonishment and admiration.[99]

So how is the grace described in this quotation effected? Temara says that in order to maintain the regal status of *whaikōrero*, a speaker must employ all parts of their body – the head, the hands, the eyes, the legs and the torso – to hammer home the words.[100] Mahuta describes such an exponent as:

> ... the polished, confident, witty speaker skilled in the use of classical Maori yet knowing when to add the common phrase to drive home a point or when to quote tradition and proverb to lend weight to his address. Because of his age his movements during whakoorero are seemingly slow and uninspiring. Occasionally he may stroll back and forward a few paces but gesticulation is kept at a minimum. On the other hand, there is the slightly younger man who is a master of the techniques of oratory even though the contents of his speech are not always striking. He commands good classical Maori with an apt use of chant, quotation, allusion and proverb. Holding a walking-stick lightly in his hands he runs back and forwards as he speaks with light hopping steps, pausing briefly at each turn. His is oratory of the old school, and his the pleasure in oratory that comes from control of a difficult and complicated art-form.[101]

Be like a bird, says Orbell:

> Eloquent orators and sweet singers were said to sound like the tui. . . . A performance by a good singer or a graceful speaker might be praised as being *he rite ki te kōpara e kō nei i te ata*, 'like a bellbird pealing at day-break' . . . . The tui was valued for its ability to imitate human speech, and the words it uttered were often thought to be meaningful.[102]

Salmond assesses quality *whaikōrero* from the creative skill of the orator:

> The first quality of a really good speech is creativity. . . . The second quality of a good speech is its erudition. . . . The 'third canon of good performance', appropriateness, is heavily dependent upon the second, for only if an orator has a wide repertoire of formal devices can he successfully match his speech to situational cues. Fourth, is the rapport that an orator can establish with his audience . . . from these *mana* can be won or lost.[103]

She comments further about the speaker having an extensive stock of *tauparapara* on call from which he can draw for the specific occasion, the particular district or his role in the *hui*:

> If a visitor recites a local *tau*, this is a great compliment to his hosts and a tribute to the range of his own knowledge. Most speakers use the same *tau* over and over again and perhaps know only one or two. The most precious chants are those passed down through the family, to which the orator has an indisputable right; the more common chants lose a lot of their impact by constant repetition.[104]

Not all observers favour the use of introductory recitations (*tauparapara*). Some actually regard them as time-wasting, rote-learnt aspects of *whaikōrero*, which can dominate and last longer than the main part of the *whaikōrero* that the people have congregated to hear.

In identifying some characteristics, we begin with the statement: 'an orator who excels at *whaikōrero* works on a number of levels, going beyond merely fulfilling the obligation to stand and greet visitors with formulaic expressions'.[105] First we focus on language, and Kāretu provides the following list of linguistic skills that an orator should possess:

- high Māori language proficiency;
- structures and formats their oration skilfully;

- adept at selecting lexis appropriate to the occasion and the period;
- has the ability to take a subject raised by a previous speaker and develop this topic within their own philosophies and knowledge;
- skilfully adapts an idea posed by another to conclude their own *whaikōrero*;
- after achieving the most out of the occasion they bring their speech to a thorough conclusion.

He adds that 'clear emphatic' use of voice is also important.[106]

Winiata elaborates and moves out into the realm of performance, saying that a speaker:

- has above average Māori language proficiency and can speak beyond the everyday language;
- can respond appropriately to comments made by others;
- has quality in the content of what they say, how they stand to deliver it, and the use of hand props and foot movement;
- speaks fairly and expresses comments that are representative of the entity who have chosen him as their spokesperson;
- knows what the right length is – not too long and not too short.[107]

Archer similarly identifies a good speaker as one who:

- speaks clearly;
- has the ability to impart knowledge and inform others;
- can entice an audience into thinking about issues he is raising;
- challenges the audience's current position/stance on issues;
- is vibrant and expressive with the ability to keep the audience engaged without becoming bored;
- prompts the audience to think;
- is an inspirational thinker;
- is emotive: can make them so sad that they cry;
- cleverly manipulates, adapts, develops something said and use this to delight the audience;
- is influential and persuasive;
- has new information to offer;
- shows consistency and originality in the content and constructions;

- has good voice projection, varies pitch and emphasis;
- is paronomastic, that is, employs pun.[108]

These are just some criteria which, if employed, will be effective and leave an everlasting impression in the minds of the audience, while enhancing the status of the orator and extending their popularity in this art form. To conclude this section, I leave you with a description of Te Pairi Tuterangi by academic and *tohunga* Pou Temara, a leading orator of national renown in his own right from the late 1980s to the early 2000s:

> Te Pairi Tuterangi's mastery of many skills made him a revered leader of Tuhoe, but he was best known for his distinctive style of oratory. He was an eloquent and charismatic speaker and this was enhanced by the way he used the marae as his stage. An impressive figure, with white hair and flowing beard, wearing long greenstone ear pendants and gesturing with his toki (adze), he would strut, run with short steps and leap into the air to give emphasis to his words. Immediately on landing he would flick his outside foot behind him and continue in the opposite direction. He never stood in one place, reasoning that it was more difficult for opposing tohunga to direct makutu at him. He usually wore a rapaki (kilt) when speaking, and if he was wearing European clothes he would deliberately remove his shoes, socks and trousers and wrap a blanket around his waist before starting. He was seemingly impervious to cold and pain. On one occasion after leaping in the air he landed on a piece of bone which pierced his foot. He sat down, removed the fragment and continued.[109]

Chapter Seven

The *Mana* of *Whaikōrero*

The Māori world has a powerful component known as *mana*, which generally refers to the authority, value and worth, status, importance, respect and acknowledgement of things animate and inanimate. The level or amount of *mana* afforded to anything may vary in accordance with its importance in the Māori world. This importance may be augmented by spiritual or religious association, genealogical affiliation, knowledge and expertise in specific areas, or by philosophical appropriateness. Māori have generic areas of *mana* associated with the individual people, locations, language forms, art forms and customary practices. This *mana* abounds in Māori cultural practices because it involves the interaction of people and location. *Whaikōrero*, therefore, has *mana* working around it, influencing it and being influenced by it.

The Sacred Provenance and Enactment of *Whaikōrero*

Mana of an esoteric nature permeates the Māori world and the Māori psyche. The role of Māori gods in Māori cosmogony and the descent of humanity from the very same gods across many generations imbue Māori behaviour and practice with this godly association. The ascription of specific roles and domains to different Māori gods places spiritual meaning and association at the forefront of Māori endeavours. '*Mana atua*' refers to the authority that Māori gods have in the lives and actions of Māori people. Māori afford this divine presence to occasions such as *whaikōrero* where the *marae* itself has different deities assigned to different parts and functions (we mention this in chapter 8).

Whaikōrero is inherently filled with *mana*, or at least, the speakers are imbued with *mana*, having so progressed in status as to be selected as orators – representative spokespeople on *marae*. Being a speaker may appear to have little significance to non-Māori, but in Māoridom it is a role of high importance, and in fact it gives status, identity and ascribed place within Māori society. The sanctity of this role is illustrated in the following example. Walker, in discussing the exploitation of Māori women, and in particular sexual abuse, describes one case whereby 'a group of innovative, action-oriented women in the Waikato put up the weights of seven kaumātua by denouncing them on the marae', and as punishment for their crimes the men 'were stripped of their speaking rights on the paepae'.[1] He draws the striking conclusion that the 'shame, the ignominy of being talked about, the denial of a prerogative so vital to male mana in a community of intense face-to-face relations with kith and kin is tantamount to living death'.[2]

Although this particular case was adjudicated under the Western legal system, punitive justice was most effectively imposed through cultural disempowerment. Limiting these men's ability to stand on the *marae* and orate diminished their sense of worth and belonging on what should have been their *tūrangawaewae*, their rightful place to stand. It stripped them of their roles and therefore to some extent made them outsiders, placeless people deprived of meaning and status.

Whaikōrero has a sanctity about it which sets the expectation that strictures will be upheld. *Whaikōrero* is a highly sacred practice, says Temara.[3] When *whaikōrero* are delivered, the level of language drawn on is raised and refined. During *whaikōrero*, a speaker also adopts a heightened physical and spiritual intensity and takes on a high formal register. This means that any denigration of the protocols afforded on the *marae* also impacts on the orator and the *whaikōrero*. Distracting, interruptive behaviour is therefore not tolerated while a speaker is delivering *whaikōrero*. Nor is it appropriate for adults, children or animals to walk across the *marae ātea* while a speaker is orating.

So why the sanctity around this ancient oral art form? Does the occasion require this? Does the composition of the people gathered require this? Does the time that the event is being held impact on this?

To some extent it can be argued that *whaikōrero* become a sacred ritual because many speakers preface their speeches with ancient chants, incantations and genealogical recitations, some of which link the oration and the speaker with the pre-contact period. Cutting across these utterances is, therefore, not viewed or received well by practitioners and observers alike. They are cloaked in what Māori refer to as *tapu*, an unparalleled respect for something because of its significance.

Because of the association with the dead, *tangihanga* (funeral ceremonies) always command the highest level of *tapu* (sacredness). Orations on these occasions are predominantly eulogies, relating past experiences of the deceased and commiserations to the bereaved families. These are emphasised with highly animated *whaikōrero* containing proverbs, song, *haka*, prophecy, allusion, historic narrative, cosmogony, cosmology and, on some occasions, lighthearted and respectful humour.

The event and object of *whaikōrero* are therefore multi-dimensional through time, as well as having genealogical and geographic connections, all of which are brought together through the orator in what is, in its finest form, a realisation of all that is essential and true in Māori custom, values and beliefs. The delivery and performance are embodiments of chronological reality, cultural meaning and personal role.

Mana Tangata: Influence and Authority Afforded to Humankind

Mana, and in particular, *mana* possessed by humanity may assume various forms that all play their own role in *whaikōrero*. The first of these is *mana whakatipu* that comes with attaining excellence in a chosen field. For example, poets specialise in their art, warriors commit to their profession and educators teach. The orator is highly proficient in Māori language, Māori history and Māori culture, and is knowledgeable about national and international events.

Mana tuku, is a particular *mana* that is endowed upon an individual when they are made the spokesperson for the family, the subtribe, the main tribe or an organisation. One function of *whaikōrero*, says Kruger,[4] is to acknowledge the *mana* of the opposing entity, and this is achieved by acknowledging their designated speaker. This also serves to acknowledge the ancestral lines of the speaker and the group they represent. As Binney says, 'On the *marae*, a man speaks in the name of his ancestors. His knowledge and *mana* are derived, at least in part, from them.'[5] Such a person, says Gudgeon,

> . . . is said to have *mana* when he possesses genius, audacity, and good fortune in a marked degree, for these are the signs of *mana*, and so long as he can retain these gifts he is regarded as a man altogether above the common herd, and one not lightly to be offended.[6]

Tupe describes *whaikōrero* as '*he mahi taumaha*', in other words, a practice heavily loaded with responsibility,[7] that is both psychologically and physically demanding. Most New Zealanders know that events such as *tangihanga* go on for a minimum of three days, which requires host speakers to provide oratorical services for some 20 to 25 hours. Tupe has Mātaatua affiliations and these tribes do not take the deceased inside. The orations and rituals normally take place outside, come rain, hail or snow – which is not only pschologically demanding but physically taxing as well.

The psychological demands are the pressure on the orator to represent their group to the best of their ability in protocol and delivery:

> *He nui nā āhuatana o te whaikōrero. Me hīmata atu e tāua i nā maunga e kīia ai e rātou ko koe ko te tangata te kākā tarahae o ngā maunga e tū, tā te mea, koirā ō maunga kārangaranga. Ka whai koe i ētahi kōrero māhau hei whakanui i tō maunga, i tō awa rānei, tō hapū rānei, tō iwi rānei. Tā te mea, ka tīkina e koe he kōrero māu i ō maunga, i ō awa, i ō iwi, i ō hapū, koirā ki a au rā te whaikōrero. He aha rā ngā kōrero o tērā maunga, o tērā awa? . . . Ko ō ihi, ko ō mana, ko ō āhuatanga katoa kei tō tūrangawaewae kei ō iwi, kei ō maunga, kei ō hiwi.*[8]

Pukepuke likens the orator to the land to which he has tribal ties – to the mountains and rivers, for example. He gets his very identity from these affiliations with the land, and it is this as well as his connections to tribes – his own and others – that give him his right to stand and orate.

Delivering *whaikōrero* constitutes a solo performance on the courtyard, sometimes with hundreds of spectators. Add on the expectations and critical assessment of that audience, and *whaikōrero* becomes anything but a stroll in the park. It is difficult to conceive, says Best, the shattering effect of a 'communistic society' on someone who fails to stay inside it, who is in some way recalcitrant or rebellious. Part of the glue that binds such societies is found in the sanctioned forms of communication and discourse that the tribal culture upholds and is expressed through. 'In the Maori community the powers of public opinion were remarkable, and had no small effect in the preservation of law and order. A marked feature of the social life of the people was that of public discussion of all proposals and activities . . . . Perhaps the Maori sense of dignity was seen to its greatest advantage at the clan or tribal assemblies, whereat speech-making was much indulged in.'[9]

It is here, says Salmond, that the *whaikōrero* or formal speeches 'establish relationships between groups and allow both groups and individuals to vie for prestige within a tightly controlled framework of rules'.[10] 'Oratory is the way for a man to win fame in Maori circles, and these men move about to a great many *hui* every year'.[11]

At the funeral of my grandfather,[12] one of my uncles was disgruntled about the choice of a final resting place, attributing the decision to some other family members and voicing his disapproval on the *marae* in front of everyone there. These were heavy words for my uncle as well as for the family accused of the misdemeanour. John Rangihau, an upcoming replacement leader and someone who had been mentored by the deceased, spoke in response. His words were along the lines '. . . *he wā tōna ka hoki mai koe ki te kohi i ngā kōhatu kua whiua e koe hei hoa mōu*': the time will come when you will have to pick up the stones that you have thrown, and take them as friends for yourself.

There are times when I think orators perhaps forget who and what they represent: they forget to uphold the *mana* of their people and stand instead as individuals with all the self-indulgence that that can impart. Perhaps if every speaker were to be more conscious of this and less focused on themselves, then they might seek to improve their own *whaikōrero*. Better *whaikōrero* means more credibility for the speaker, the tribe and the region. As Salmond notes, 'Oratory then acts as a ceremonial buffer against invasions of prestige, and the greater the *mana* of the visitors, the more oratory they should elicit'.[13] The more *mana* held by a visiting party, the more effort should be made by the host group to afford ritual that is commensurate. Māori tribal leaders, the Queen of England, Māori Party Ministers, for example, should receive a full welcome with a good number of the most eloquent speakers providing the *whaikōrero*. Persons of lesser importance might receive formalities of a lesser degree. There is a coded arrangement, and Mihipeka Edwards makes a similar comparison in terms of *karanga* during *pōhiri*. If, for instance, a young girl performs the ritual call of welcome on to the *marae*, then the response should come from a young girl of similar status.[14] Mihipeka cautions against the use of less important individuals to receive guests formally because this may be viewed as a lack of respect. The same came be said of uninitiated orators being employed to welcome or address dignatories. Tauroa mentions such a case when a young orator for a visiting group, which included a government minister, responded, much to the chagrin of his own elders.[15] 'Perfection expresses goodwill, imperfection brings insult, hurt, slight, to the one being challenged. Unless the slight is deliberate, intended, who wants to insult or hurt a visitor?'[16]

It is clear, then, that *whaikōrero* is the 'prime entry into the power game' for an individual, and their *mana* is an 'asset which rises and falls with their ceremonial performances, and is heavily dependent upon a cadre of seasoned orators'.[17]

Whaikōrero is actually laden both as performance and as entity, and its impact affects the *mana* of all present as well as that of the orator himself. And at the same time, its enactment confirms the prestige of those who take part, as *manuhiri* and as *tangata whenua*.

Protocol and Proficiency

All visitors to a host venue or *marae* must consider correct practice on arrival. But 'correct practice' from the perspective of visitor or host? According to Salmond, 'visitors should follow the local pattern.... Any attempts by a visiting group to impose their own rules of *marae* procedure on the host *marae* will be heartily resented.'[18] As Tauroa says: 'These are not arbitrary rules made up on the spur of the moment to thwart individuals. They have been determined by the people over generations and changes are made by the people to accommodate their own kawa and their own marae situation.'[19] Failure to conform on the part of the visitors could cause serious damage to the *mana* of the hosts who 'were often on the look-out for an insult and, so countless were the opportunities offered by the breaking of ceremonial laws or ancient customs, by innocent speeches that could be twisted into allusions about some past tribal defeat or some chief's conduct, that offence was almost sure to be taken and bloodshed to follow'.[20]

These days it is highly implausible that bloodshed will result from a breach of protocol, as it probably did in pre-contact times. There is no doubt, however, that verbal vilification, libel and slander have enormous potential to cause damage to the reputation of the people targeted.

Generally speaking, 'the strict traditions and protocol of marae visits must be honoured'.[21] Take, for example, the case of Te Taitokerau (northern tribes) visiting southern tribes. Some Te Taitokerau tribes allow visitors to come onto the *marae* regardless of whether or not there is currently a visiting group already being afforded the protocols of welcome. On one occasion, however, a group from Te Taitokerau visited a Te Arawa *marae* (some 600 kilometres or so to the south), and proceeded on to the *marae* while another visiting group was being formally received. As a result, Te Taitokerau were reprimanded by a Te Arawa elder and advised that they should have waited.[22]

Other breaches of protocol include cutting across the path of a speaker, talking loudly during an oration or even sleeping (which has been known to occur when ceremonials are taking place inside the meeting house).

Ignorance, in Kāretu's opinion, is no excuse.[23] He says everyone should make it their business to find out the protocols belonging to the host *marae* prior to making a visit – 'Do your homework!'[24] Host *marae* nowadays tend to take a more proactive approach by informing visitors of the correct procedure on their *marae*. Brief guidelines may be communicated in advance, Māori wardens sometimes advise visitors immediately before they descend on to the *marae* or may give indications while the first host speaker delivers his *whaikōrero*. These are means of avoiding an unwanted clash of etiquette, which would be received as a *takahi* on the *mana* of the host, damaging the relationship between the two entities and resulting in shame on the offender – diminishing *mana* once again. '*He tao kī tēnā me uaua ka kore*': The reputation of the offender also stands to be discredited.

Another caution, not restricted to *whaikōrero* alone, regards the issue of proficiency, and the ill-feeling and envy that may arise in someone not as proficient towards those who are skilled. This is more likely to be the case when the orator is relatively young. I have heard observers of a similar age group chastise such potential, probably more because these young individuals are doing what they cannot, or are not permitted to do. My own *pakeke* (elders) advised that an orator should always mentally safeguard themselves by asking their ancestors to spiritually support them. Offering up a prayer of sorts serves as a protective agent to ward off ill-feeling, whether this is intentionally or subconsciously directed by a spectator.

It is clear, therefore, that an orator must aspire not only to be proficient in language and performance, but also to develop a keen sense of propriety in order to minimise the risk of negative reaction such as *takahi* and the possibility of harm being done to *mana*. Any small error may allow the cynic to make criticism and to use this as a means of undoing all that is done well – unfortunately, there are people in every society who are prone to behave this way.

I always remember some comments made by one of my *pakeke* with regard to *mana*. His understanding was that when it appears that two people are not seeing eye to eye, this is actually a conflict of their *mana* rather than of the individuals themselves. The professional or the individual of high status and importance is a person with *mana* that has been built over many years and been constantly affirmed, reaffirmed and consolidated internally. This gives them *wehi*, an awe that almost makes them impervious to attacks on their personal *mana*. The dilemma for such authoritative people in the context of delivering *whaikōrero* is that when there is an attack on their *mana*, it has grave effects because of their status. This effect is likely to pass beyond the person being attacked to his people. The 'learning' orator, on the other hand, is still establishing his position or status, and is perhaps more cautious in every respect. There is less cause for envy. If he is corrected, either privately or in public, this may be interpreted or received as a learning experience, which can be added to his awareness of 'correct protocol'. Humility and diplomacy can play major roles in the maintenance of good relationships amongst speakers. They also help maintain decorum and prevent tension.

The heaviest attacks on *mana* usually occur during controversial clashes on *marae* or pseudo *marae*, but these have tended to be less frequent over the last two decades than they were, for example, up until the 1980s. Māori are now more accommodating and less confrontational in the main. A result of Western spiritual indoctrination? Perhaps. An acceptance of colonisation? Perhaps. Modernised conceptual thinking? Perhaps. Pacification? Perhaps. Assimilation? Perhaps. I am by no means saying that the possibility of confrontation no longer exists. This is always a possibility and I have witnessed two close calls in the last seven years.

Casting Judgement

'*Kia tika tonu tō whakanoho haere i ō kōrero. Kei waho te tangata e titiro mai ana ki a koe, te āhua o tō whakatakoto i ō kōrero, ka taunuhia koe*', says Tupe,[25] which means a speaker should be particular in the way he presents the *whaikōrero* because there are spectators judging him – looking for the opportunity to make disparaging comments or cast incantations of ill intent. Waiariki refers to one elder who had no qualms in questioning the validity of a speaker if he was incompetent. He tended to ask: '*He aha i tukuna mai ai ko te ihu hūpē nei hei kōrero?*' (Why was this snotty nose allowed to speak?)[26]

In a similar case documented by Salmond, a speaker from Te Aitanga-a-Hauiti delivering his *whaikōrero* of welcome to Te Whānau-a-Apanui referred to the visitors as '*he iwi kore waka*' (a tribe without a migrating vessel).[27] Eruera Stirling of Te Whānau-a-Apanui replied that it was they, Te Aitanga-a-Hauiti, who were a tribe without a vessel because '*he mea tiko rātou ki uta*' (a whale had deposited them ashore as faecal matter). This was a reference to Paikea, their ancestor, who according to tribal history landed atop a whale. Following Eruera's response, a leader from the

Gisborne area chastised the Te Aitanga-a-Hauiti speaker for firstly denigrating the visitors, and secondly, prompting Eruera to remark that they were 'whale shit'.

In extreme cases of disagreement, when a speaker has made an error, the women folk of Te Arawa have launched into a chant (*pōkeka*) so as to cut him off. Although I have not actually seen this with my own eyes, I have heard that the ultimate display of derision for an action or for the behaviour of a speaker was for the women present to show him their buttocks or their private parts. The act of exposing one's posterior, *whakapohane*, sends a message to the individual that they are no better than faecal matter which, during a time when human consumption amongst Māori was practised, inferred that a person would be eaten and eventually reconstituted as body waste. This might be exercised if, for example, a 'young or incompetent speaker pushes himself too far forward, or breaks an important rule, [and] the old women of the tribe stand before him, turn around and flip up their skirts by way of graphic comment. The same might occur to an accomplished speaker who insults his hosts'.[28]

Disrespect, in terms of *whaikōrero*, can take many forms as I have indicated: a female speaking on a *marae* which does not permit women to *whaikōrero*; *whaikōrero* being delivered by junior speakers to senior, high-ranking visitors; delivering *whaikōrero* in the English language; saying the wrong thing; or cutting across protocol.

The number of speakers presented by the host people might also come under scrutiny in some cases, because having five or six speakers is usually a strong indicator of the importance of the occasion and/or the visiting party. Salmond mentions a visit by East Coast elders to a Northland *marae* where they were 'met with a perfunctory welcome', probably in the form of too few hosts. When the East Coast speaker stood to reply, he addressed the cooking-fires, tea-kettles and oven stones. He also threatened to leave the *marae* and withhold the large monetary donation, *koha*, which they had brought with them. A member of the host *marae* apologised and the visitors stayed, though they did not hand over the monies.[29]

Even requesting that speeches be cut short can appear disrespectful. Salmond documented an instance when Waikato requested Te Arawa speakers to keep their *whaikōrero* short because the Governor General of New Zealand was outside waiting to come on to the *marae*. In response, Te Arawa drew their speeches out, probably making them longer than they would have originally intended.[30]

When *whaikōrero* do not go 'according to script', what happens? I have already mentioned some examples and there are others. On one occasion a speaker was alternating between speaking in Māori and in English. He also blurted expletives in English, after which an elderly *kuia* of the *marae* approached him. This should have been enough to tell him that what he was doing was inappropriate but he continued to speak. Those present were dumbfounded and the *marae* was silent with heads bowed low. When he finished speaking, he sat down all by himself. No one would sit with him, nor did anyone support him in song at the end of his *whaikōrero*. By the next morning, he had departed from the *marae*. A speaker knows that he has strong backing from members of his party when they break out in a song of support at the conclusion of his oration.

Another sign of disapproval is when negative comments are made within earshot of the speaker. Comments such as: '*E hoa,* what's that fellow talking about? He's not worth listening to!' may be overheard.[31] People may just call out '*E noho!*' (Be seated!). Some are told outright to keep the speech short if they go on too long. Some women actually pre-empt the oration and instruct their menfolk to be brief. Comments may be made as whispers, or be clearly audible, depending on the degree of disapproval. As in the previous example, body language can be another indicator that people do not support a *whaikōrero*. They turn their backs, they laugh and chatter, and move about. As an indication of even stronger disapproval, 'Women may demean a speaker – may terminate a man's speech with waiata, walking in front of a speaker'.[32] This brings the speech to a 'forced conclusion'.[33]

'On the marae, if you transgress and someone reprimands you, you sit down and your whole day is miserable. Your whole *mana* disappears'.[34]

Conclusion

The point I am making in this chapter is that the language of *whaikōrero*, whether it seems mere rhetoric or is akin to common speech, has the power to encapsulate, reaffirm and transmit *mana*. As Royal reiterates: 'The spoken word was very important to the old people. They believed in the power of language'.[35] The invitation to speak on a *marae*, says Tauroa, was a great honour.[36] In the words that follow, Āpirana Ngata, an eloquent and knowledgeable speaker in his own right, describes the orator:

I tū ia [te manu kōrero] ki te marae, ka whakapuaki i ngā whakaaro i takea mai i te hōhonutanga o tōna hinengaro, ka whakarongo te iwi ki aua kōrero, ā, mā ēnei ka taea e rātou te tatau ōna kārangaranga, te wāhi mōna i roto i te iwi. Ka rangatira te whakatakoto o āna kupu, ko ia anō hei rangatira whakatau mōna. Ko tēnei ko tōna mārama ki te reo, te

> *tāonga nāna i tā te rangatira ki tōna marae. Ka whakaritea ki te Korimako, he manu tino reka o te Wao Nui a Tāne. E āhei ai te tauira hei pū kōrero, i whāngaia ia ki taua manu kia whiwhi ai ki ōna painga. Ko te tangata i mātau ki te kōrero i huaina he korimako, ā, ka whakarongo te iwi ki te rangi, ki ngā kupu i taka mai i ōna ngutu. Ka ngaro ki te Manawa rawa, ka whakairotia kia hōhonu rawa mo ake tonu atu, ki te hinengaro o te tangata. Ko ngā kauhau e pūmau tonu. E uru ana ki ngā tomotanga o ngā whare hui ko ngā kōrero e tomo ana ki te ngākau tangata, e rewa ai rātou, anō he whai pari rawa, e takahi ai rātou i te ara o te tika, ko ēnei kauhau pono i whānau tonu mai i te whatumanawa o te tangata e whakapuaki ana i a rātou.[37]*

I have attempted to interpret Āpirana's description and hope that my translation captures the essence of what he had to say:

> The speaker stood on the forecourt and expressed ideas which stemmed from deep philosophies. The people listened and from those words were able to identify his multiple affiliations as well as his position in the tribe. By discharging these words with respect and integrity the speaker was in effect improving his own social standing. His knowledge of words was a treasure through which he would bestow honour upon his own *marae*. He was seen like the *korimako*, the bellbird, whose voice is a delight to hear in the native forests of New Zealand. So that a student could reach this level of eloquence, he would be fed this bird, and he could then, as an orator, be referred to as the *korimako* because of the fluency of his speech. The people would hang on his words which would permeate their inner beings, the centres of their minds, for eternity. Such deliveries would be remembered and reiterated. The words expressed inside the meeting houses would also enter the people's souls and uplift them, allowing them to pursue what is right. Such rhetoric as this was spawned in the very heart and soul of the orator.

Chapter Eight

Protocols of Place

A 'platform for speaking'[1]

Regardless of who the orator is, he needs a venue if he is to deliver a speech, and integral to this are the seating arrangements for the host and visiting speakers. In this chapter I address the question of whether the venue affects the positioning of speakers as well as the manner and substance of the *whaikōrero*.

This body of designated speakers is generally referred to as the *pae*, the *paepae* or the *taumata*. These words can mean either a platform for speaking (i.e. the actual seats) or the body of speakers themselves. I would translate *pae*, with respect to location, as a resting place or perch. *Paepae* may simply be the plural of *pae*, or a word derived from the name of the beam that stretches across the front of the traditional Māori meeting house and acts as a doorstop, or verandah stop, preventing debris from blowing inside. This type of doorstop is variously known as the *paepae kaiāwhā*, *paepae āwhā*, *paepae kainga āwhā* or *paepae roa*.[2] The Ngā Puhi tribe use the term *taumata* rather than *pae* or *paepae*.[3] Hohepa says this was a place inside the pallisaded village where the chiefs sat, and was also a place where individuals fought. People had to be given permission to go there. Hōri Tait refers to it as 'te paepae o Hou-mai-tawhiti'.[4]

> And in Te Arawa for instance, I find that the marae is very much the men's domain. And these men they sit on a paepae. But here the only time they used to speak of the paepae is when there is anyone lying on the veranda – when there is [a] tupapaku. They refer to that little bit, that front part of the meeting house, as the paepae and when anyone is dead we know that the area is quite special, at that particular time.[5]

As already discussed, *whaikōrero* is predominantly a male domain. Therefore it is not surprising that when we talk about the *pae* 'its speakers and senior members, usually the menfolk, occupy the front seats. Older women, and those who will support the kai korero with waiata sit close behind the speakers.'[6] The restriction on women seating themselves on the *pae* still prevails, but in the case of *pae* within the meeting house, this restriction has not gone unopposed. As Mead explains:

> But now these men are saying to us, 'Oh this is just for men only, this paepae'. I didn't think anything of it when our chairman said he was going to put a seat there, for whaikorero. I was quite happy for that to happen; but he made it a permanent seat, and I just couldn't accept it when we were told that it was for men only, and no women dare sit here. That puts a difference on it altogether. Because what they are saying to us - we are tapu men; we are so special that you women cannot come and sit here. That's never been a part of us.[7]

It is not clear what seating arrangements were customary in pre-contact times. Best wrote that from what he had observed, when a visiting group came onto the *marae* for a *tangi*, after the grieving, everyone would sit on the ground and only the current speaker would be upstanding.[8] John White in his 1888 work on the history, mythology and traditions of the Māori, described rituals of encounter that make it explicit that *tangata whenua* and *manuhiri* were seated on the ground during speeches of welcome on the marae.[9]

In the mid-late 1700s, 'Descriptions of whare were used back in Europe to help assess the extent to which Maori demonstrated a state of savagery or barbarism as opposed to the civilization' of the European.[10] Although there is no specific reference to *wharenui*, small dwellings about five metres long and three or four metres wide are described, which casts doubt on the notion that encounter rituals could be conducted inside. However, there are also early descriptions of structures that seem to resemble the *paepae kaiāwhā* (mentioned previously as the verandah stop, but literally meaning the 'beam that eats storms'). In about 1849, H. F. McKillop described the difficulty Māori apparently had when they attempted to sit on chairs rather than seating themselves on their ankles.[11] Because of these descriptions and the evidence of Māori material culture and oral tradition, it seems most likely that specific seating for orators is a post-contact development. As civilisation advanced and enculturation occurred, Māori were determined to adopt European practices, and sitting on chairs was one of these. In describing memorable orators, Hohepa Kereopa recollected Te

Pairi Tuterangi,[12] of Te Waimana, choosing to sit on the ground when he attended a funeral on a Te Arawa marae. When it was his time to orate, he stood up and did so. This would have been around the 1980s or 1990s.

Outside Rituals of Encounter: The Seating

The 'dichotomy of the sacred and the profane'[13] is a determining factor in the arrangement of buildings on *marae* and the placement of permanent fixtures for orators. We can look first at *marae* that host ritual encounters outside. 'The two groups stay spatially separate and opposite throughout the ritual, facing each other across the *marae*, and it is only when the ritual is over that they merge in the *hongi* line.'[14] Looking out from the meeting house, some *marae* have the *pae* to the left, some have it to the right, and at Te Rewarewa Marae, Rūātoki, it is located between the two *wharenui*.[15] Since around the late 1960s, some *marae* have constructed permanent *whare mate*.[16] Prior to these, many *marae* either had their dead lie outside on the verandah of the meeting house, or in temporary shelters which were removed immediately after the burial of the deceased.

There does not appear to be a set pattern to the positioning of seats. Some *marae* have the host and visitor seating on the same side of the *wharenui* as in figure 8.1.

The arrangement known as *pae whakawhiti* (figure 8.2) has the seating, and the discussion, travel across the front of the *wharenui* from the *noa* to the *tapu* side. Some

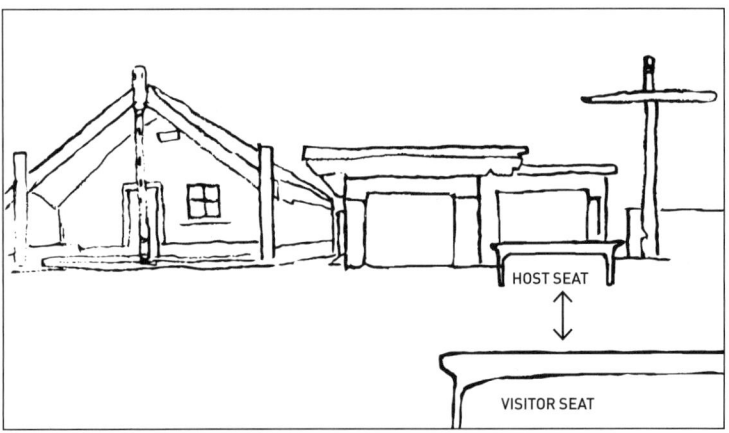

Figure 8.1 Some *marae* have the seating of the host and visitor arranged almost directly opposite each other.

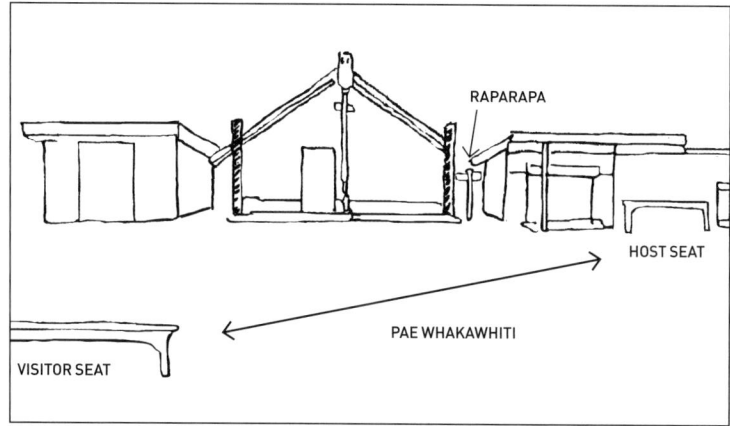

Figure 8.2 The *pae whakawhiti* arrangement seats hosts and visitors diagonally to each other. *Pae whakawhiti* may also cross from right to left.

of my informants have commented that Tūhoe and Te Arawa seating arrangements should be laid out diagonally to each other.

The philosophy amongst Mātaatua and Te Arawa is that the seats or chairs for the hosts should be situated close to or at the bottom end of the *maihi*, close to the *raparapa*, so that the emission of knowledge and spiritual power from the ancestral meeting house can extend into the line of speakers. As figure 8.2 shows, the seating for the host speakers is not close to the *raparapa*, because a *whare mate* has since been built where the seats would have been, therefore resulting in the relocation of the seats to the immediate left of the *whare mate*. There is a view held by some practitioners that when an orator speaks, he should be directly in front of the *wharenui* because this is the ancestor and contains representations of tribal descendants (in the form of carvings and/or photographs). The first speaker is the one who is closest to the *maihi/raparapa*. The order then moves outwards, away from the ancestral house.

Te Arawa tribes often welcome visitors inside their *wharenui*, especially if the occasion is a funeral. In the past, however, they also conducted their ceremonial welcomes outside. Winiata seems to think that formalities shifted inside some 200 years ago.[17]

As mentioned in the previous chapter, most visitors take time to seek information on protocols regarding the order of speaking on the particular *marae* they are visiting, or when they arrive they may observe the behaviour of the group before them or be advised by Māori wardens. The host speakers sometimes tell the visitors if they appear to be moving to the wrong place. A speaker should, therefore, be sure of where they are seated and the flow of speakers.

The order of speakers outside usually moves in a clockwise direction. Having guiding principles like this provides order, and eliminates *ad hoc* or incorrect positioning of speakers. To get up 'out of order' is usually met with some verbal instruction to stop speaking and sit down. Morehu mentions one case when a speaker started up out of turn. One of Morehu's elders told the man to wait but he continued to speak. After telling him two or three times to no avail, the elder of the host *marae* launched into a chant to cut off his oration.[18]

On another occasion, at a funeral at Mātaatua Marae, Rotorua, two men from a large visiting group got up at different ends of the *pae* to speak at the same time. Each was oblivious of the other. Directions were discretely passed along the row for the one who had begun to orate out of turn to sit down, and after a minute or so he finally conceded. Reedy explains that rules of order limit the 'ping-pong' mix up and uncertainty of speaking.[19]

Although it is only inferred, there is a 'clear spatial segregation between the locals and visitors'.[20] I am unsure of the origin of this special segregation, but it is alluded to by Buck as having a crucial function:[21]

> When engagements [of war] took place on the sea beach, a chief could stay his men by drawing a line with his club across the sand. His men stopped dead on their side of the line while the exhausted enemy could rest on the other side of the line in perfect safety.

In describing the *marae ātea*, Harawira refers to a similar division of space:

> The marae atea is used for welcoming guests and making speeches. The kaikorero or speaker moves back and forth or sideways across the marae atea, keeping a small distance between himself and the people he is talking to.[22]

Mātaatua people refer to it as the *pae kouka*, a term I have been unable to find an explanation for. As can be imagined, this division is more apparent on the *marae ātea* than it is inside the *wharenui*, where the hosts are in almost direct contact with the visitors, especially if the visiting group is large. On occasion I have heard visitors complain about such close encounters, presumably because the sanctity of separation is placed under threat and the safety offered by ritual segregation is eroded. In simple terms, the space between hosts and visitors symbolises a boundary behind which the hosts can govern the immediate area around them and beyond which the visitors can express themselves within the confines of protocol.

Hohepa asserts that, in former times, Ngā Puhi had no fixed rules about the positioning or order of speakers.[23] This would definitely have added spice to the events, leaving visitors in a state of uncertainty and the way open for clashes to occur.

Inside Ritual Encounters: Seating in the *Wharenui*

Some tribes, including Waikato, Te Arawa, Taitokerau and Rongowhakaata, often conduct formal welcomes inside the *wharenui*. The way they position the seating for hosts, visitors and designated speakers differs from one to another. During *tangihanga*, Ngāti Whakaue, namely Tūnohopū and Te Papaiouru, have the *pae* seats located across the back wall of the *wharenui*, with visitors seated along the left-hand side of the *wharenui*. During *tangihanga* on these Te Arawa *marae*, the women are seated to the right (looking in). The host speakers begin on the right-hand side (looking in) and then move across to the left (figure 8.3).

When the visitors are seated at the *kopaiti*, that quadrant of the meeting house immediately inside the doorway between the left-hand corner and the centre of the

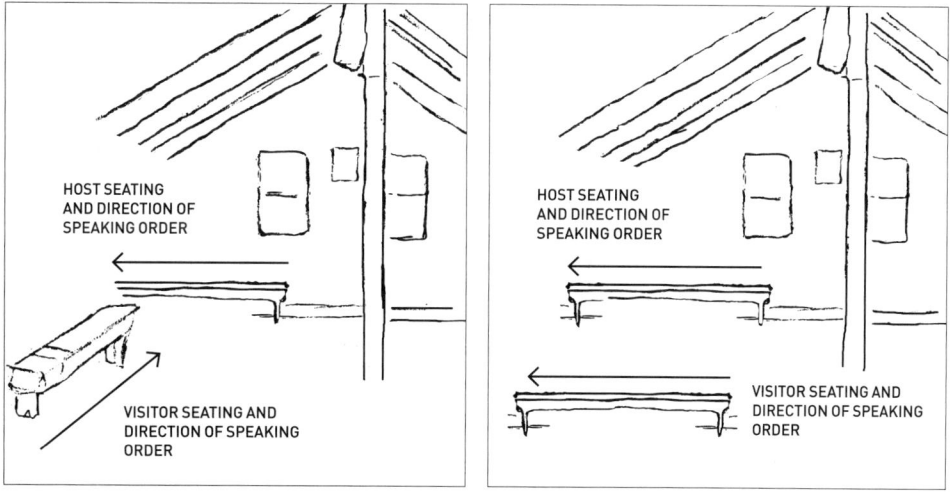

Figure 8.3 (LEFT) An example of a *pae* for visitors and hosts in the Te Arawa area during the *tangihanga*.
Figure 8.4 (RIGHT) An example of a *pae* for visitors and hosts in the Te Arawa area on occasions other than funerals.

house, there are two applications in regard to speaking order and the direction. If the occasion is a funeral, the speaking order, on many Te Arawa *marae*, begins with the speaker closest to the doorway, and works along the speakers heading in the direction of the host speakers at the far end of the *wharenui*.

For occasions other than *tangihanga*, the seating inside the *wharenui* has the visitors seated parallel, opposite the host speakers. Others have the first visiting speaker located innermost, with the direction of succeeding speakers moving towards the doorway (see figure 8.4).

On one work excursion in 2004 as I visited Kurahaupō, Tokomaru and Aotea in Taranaki, I observed different seating arrangements at different *marae*. Ōwae Marae had the host speakers seated to the left as you enter the *wharenui* with the visitors' seating parallel and opposite on the right-hand side. Urenui Marae had a similar set up. At Pariroa Marae, the hosts were seated on the right-hand side of the *wharenui* looking in and the visitors on the left-hand side. At Kairau (Parihaka), the visitors' seating was inside the door to the left. On a Ngā Puhi visit, at a *tangihanga*, the deceased was lying in state at the far end of the *wharenui*, with the seating flanking the centre line. The visitors were on the left (looking in) and the hosts seated to the right. In other words, there are intertribal and intratribal differences.

Speaking Patterns: Alternating or *En Bloc*

Regardless of place, it is common for the host people to open speaking exchanges. Beyond this, however, in Māori society there are two primary speaking arrangements, generically known as *tauutuutu* (alternating) and *pāeke* (*en bloc*). There is some discussion around the origins of these speaking styles. One theory is that they came from the very beginning of Māori existence when the Māori super deities discussed the future of their parents, Rangi-nui and Papa-tū-ā-nuku (discussed in chapter 2).[24] The order in which they spoke is seen to be the origin of these two models, that is, while some spoke progressively and cumulatively, others spoke dialogically, with the presentation of alternative arguments.

One of the first documented accounts of speaking order is given by White: 'The visitors had not been there long when an Awhitu chief rose and made a speech of welcome, and was followed by a Mount Eden chief'.[25] However, it is unclear whether this is an illustration of the *en bloc* or alternating pattern. I would hazard a guess that the Āwhitu chief was the host speaker, either on an Āwhitu *marae*[26] or another *marae* in the Auckland area, which are characterised by the *en bloc* pattern in which the host speakers orate first. McGuire describes the contrary pattern in which, when the host speakers had 'concluded their welcoming oratory, etiquette required that one or more of the elders among the guests reply'.[27]

While there are clearly geographic and tribal differences in speaking order, it is also possible that this may be determined sometimes by the nature of the encounter event. There are *marae*, in particular on the west coast of the North Island, for example, where at a *tangi* it is the visitors who are permitted 'to give vent to their feelings before being welcomed by the hosts. This may include speeches by the manuhiri',[28] as Pateriki (Pat) Rei explains. Whanganui, for one, allow such visitors to orate first,[29] which may be viewed as a fine gesture of consideration for the visitors who could well have travelled a great distance to farewell the deceased.

The alternating speaking pattern is known by several names, including *tauutuutu, utuutu, tauhokohoko, tau whakautuutu, whakawhitiwhiti* and *tū mai tū atu.*

> This alternating system of *whaikōrero* is used by tribes who claim descent from the people who migrated to Aotearoa on the *Tainui* and *Te Arawa* canoes, notably those of Waikato, the King Country, the Volcanic Plateau, and parts of the Bay of Plenty.[30]

As mentioned above, with the one exception of the West Coast, the host speaker is the first speaker, and usually the last. In other words, the host gets the first as well as the final say. There are differing views on how this privilege is used, however. Rather than give a full oration, as is expected to fulfil the oratorical exchange, often the last host speaker merely calls the visitors to physically engage after the speeches by way of *hongi*, or they simply announce the proceedings to follow after the physical engagement.

One theory about the origins of this alternating pattern is that it began with a formalisation of intertribal conflict amongst Māori. Buck speaks about war parties performing *haka* to each other. The first party would *haka*, and then sit down. The foe would then stand and *haka* in response:

> Sometimes the parties alternated with additional war dances in a competition to excel in rhythm, vigour, and sound. When the war-like demonstration ended, the visitors were welcomed in the orthodox manner, with wailing, speeches, and the concluding pressing of noses.[31]

The different terminology used for the alternating speaking pattern reveals something of its original function, if not its origin. *Tauutuutu*, for example, normally requires the host to have one more speaker than the visitors to allow them to alternate and still have someone to conclude the proceedings. Indeed, it was viewed as an expression of host *mana* when a *marae* could provide enough people to fulfil this speaking arrangement. Such ability indicates not only the health and robustness of a tribal group, but also a degree of co-operation with visitors which in itself is an enactment of encounter that is subsequently formalised through the delivery of *whaikōrero*. In addition, such a requirement would have also stimulated succession planning amongst tribes, encouraging them to upskill speakers so as to maintain their traditional speaking pattern without compromise or modification.

Kingi describes the slight variant of *tauutuutu* that is called *whakawhitiwhiti*. This involves an alternating speaking pattern with a diagonal seating arrangement (see figure 8.2, page 117)[32] that, because of its spatial complexity and patterning, underlines the importance of consent, order and protocol in the delivery of *whaikōrero*.

The majority of tribes adopt the *en bloc* speaking pattern commonly referred to as *pāeke*. It is also known in some parts as *pā harakeke* or *taiāwhiao*,[33] and *pā eke* in Taranaki.[34] Under this model, all of the host speakers orate first :

> The home speaker welcomed the visitors by their tribal name and prominent chiefs by their personal names . . . . He concluded with the orthodox welcoming phrase, 'Haere mai, haere mai, haere mai', Welcome, welcome, welcome. He was followed by all other local speakers.[35]

After the hosts temporarily relinquish the speaking podium to the visitors, they have it reinstated at the conclusion of all the visitors' speeches. As a general rule, visitors are not able to orate on the *marae* courtyard after this. A host speaker concludes all the orations, at least for that particular welcoming encounter. Hosts who use the *pāeke* format sometimes mention the term, 'keep a spare in the kitchen', or 'have a spare bullet'. The 'spares' and 'bullets' are metaphors for having a speaker available at short notice to finish off the speaking exchanges.

Tribes seldom question a preference for one model over the other and pay due respect to the pattern traditionally adopted and adhered to by each. However, it is clear that each style has certain characteristics and advantages. *Tauutuutu*, for example, has the advantage of extracting information from the visitors more quickly, whereas *pāeke* requires the designated host speakers to finish speaking before they hear what the visitors have to say. Probably the most advantageous aspect of *pāeke* is the ease with which the protocols can be upheld: that is, to have the host speakers begin and end if need be. The host *marae* can accomplish this with two speakers, as opposed to *tauutuutu* which requires one more speaker on the host side. This also makes *pāeke* a very efficient means of completing oratorical exchanges. *Pāeke* minimises distractions from the main theme because the visiting speakers are unable to respond immediately and shift the topic or the mood of the exchange. Under *pāeke*, the host speakers in particular are able to maintain the structure and presentation of their deliveries in the way that they intended. *Pāeke* tests the memory banks of the visiting speakers, because they must wait until all the host speakers have orated before they respond. A speaker who is further down the *paepae* may hear the very first host speaker make a point he wishes to pick up on, but by the time he actually stands to speak, he may have forgotten the point completely.

On the flip side, under *pāeke*, there is the potential for the visitors effectively to have the last say about the main theme because their last orator can speak as comprehensively as he wants to. As Temara says, it is difficult to reinvigorate a topic once it has gone cold.[36] If a long time has elapsed because of the number of speakers, the momentum can wane. Visitors can take a totally different approach to the topic and adopt another register because they have the 'podium'. The hosts are not really in a position to respond, unless something provocative or belittling is said or done – then a host speaker, that 'spare bullet', may be called upon to refute the point or challenge some action. Under *pāeke*, each speaker must present a solid argument because once he has finished orating and sat down, he is not usually allowed to speak again. If there are any arguments or comments left unresolved, succeeding speakers may pick up on them, possibly to the dismay of the previous speaker who may wish he had been more thorough in his delivery.

Conversely, the disadvantages that characterise *pāeke* work are transformed under the *tauutuutu* model. Because orations alternate between host and visitor, responses to comments are almost immediate. Energies and synergies between the speakers are exchanged and often lead to a vibrant atmosphere with memorable orations traded between them.

Another advantage of *tauutuutu* is that the hosts quickly become aware of the visitors' position as they do not have to wait too long to hear them speak. Responses to matters of importance can be contested or responded to by the hosts who will clearly have the last say on all that is raised.

The glaring difficulty with *tauutuutu* for hosts is in maintaining the capacity to provide the quantity of speakers required. The inability of the host *marae* to fulfil its speaking protocols lends itself to criticism. This adds pressure on the host *marae*. Kingi describes a situation under this practice where, for example, Te Arawa might have five speakers and the visitors ten. After the fourth host speaker has finished, the host will hand over speaking to all the remaining visitors. The last Te Arawa host speaker then finishes off the speaking. This, he says, is not *tauutuutu* and there is a failure by the host in this case to uphold their *mana* and reaffirm their practices.[37] Might this be a hybrid combination that begins with *tauutuutu (tau)*, with the *pāeke* style being applied midway through and then concluded with the host speaker rounding off with the *utu* (response)? This could then be coined a '*taupāekeutu*'.

Hohua Tutengāehe refers to this variation as '*pae whakakeke*'.[38] It sometimes leads to extra long welcoming ceremonies because hosts are motivated to uphold their speaking protocols, that is *tauutuutu*, and seek to provide the additional orator. As already mentioned, this is likely to have the effect of motivating those tribes that practise *tauutuutu* to focus on their oratorical capacity. With the potential for mischief, a visiting group may 'stock up on speakers so that the other side runs out of qualified men and is forced to break the alternation'.[39] All of this keeps oratory alive and gives it that vitality – that fresh breath – of a living art form.

Unlike all other *marae* that adopt either the *en bloc*, the alternating or the hybrid model, one particular *marae* with which I am affiliated interchanges the alternating and *en bloc* model, depending on who has governance over the event at the *marae*. The *marae* straddles the boundaries between Mātaatua and Te Arawa. A visitor may therefore encounter *pāeke*, in accordance with Mātaatua, or *tauutuutu*, in accordance with the practice of Te Arawa, especially if the event is a *tangihanga* and consideration is given to the genealogy of the deceased as to which oratorical exchange is applied. I have heard of another *marae* within the Mātaatua region that actually practised *tauutuutu*, but because this practice was not endorsed by the wider region, an elder advised them to align with Mātaatua and practise *pāeke*.

Some tribal areas are more accommodating than others and some tribes from the North – Te Taitokerau – will adopt the speaking protocols of the visitors if they have an esteemed person amongst them. An example given by Patu Hohepa concerns a visit by a Waikato contingent. In honouring the Kingship currently under the guardianship of Waikato, the Taitokerau hosts accommodated the *tauutuutu* style:

> The men will speak – usually about five speakers each side, depending how serious the topic is. The home people will open up the speechmaking and when the first speaker

finishes he might hand it over to the visitors, who might have about twenty men who might all want to speak.[40]

Some tribes are very particular about having their speaking protocols adhered to by all visitors. Rangi recollected the funeral of the late John Tūrei, who lay in state on Te Rewarewa Marae, Rūātoki. One visitor deviated from the normal clockwise speaking order and spoke out of turn. He was told to sit down or else his head would receive a blow from an adze, *'ka kore koe e noho . . . pakaru tō māhunga i te toki'*.[41] With the clockwise speaking order, as in Mātaatua, Iraia says that anyone who intends to speak should not dilly dally around, otherwise the next speaker may get up and cut them off.[42] Sometimes when this happens, it is due more to the eagerness of a speaker than the hesitation of another. At other times it is due to sheer ignorance of the speaking protocols on that particular *marae*.

Tribal Speaking Models

Generally, different areas follow known and predictable speaking protocols. There may be exceptions on some urban *marae* because of affiliations with areas outside of the town in which they are located. For example, there are Tūhoe-established '*marae*' beyond Tūhoe tribal boundaries; Te Tirahou Marae in Auckland has tribal boundaries that lie within Ngāti Whātua; and Mātaatua Marae, in Rotorua, is within the tribal boundaries of the Te Arawa people.

In the main, it is the tribes who are descended from the main fleet of migratory ocean-voyaging vessels to land in New Zealand – the Tainui and Te Arawa canoes – that adopt the alternating, *tauutuutu*, speaking pattern. The tribes that were formed from these two vessels cover part of the Bay of Plenty and the Waikato areas, and therefore it is possible to assert that 80–85 percent of Māori follow the *pāeke*, *en bloc* pattern.

The Speaker's Use of Space

There are guiding principles that govern the movement of an experienced orator. Turning movements, for example, either to the left or right, have their philosophical underpinnings. Some Tūhoe (Mātaatua) advise that, where possible, a speaker should stand and move to the left to speak. This means that he returns to his seat by turning to the right. Returning to the seated position in this way is termed *kōrapa*.[43] It may be coincidental, but Heuer describes how 'Before fighting, if a warrior moved to the left when avoiding an obstacle in his path, this was considered to be a bad omen'.[44] We might extrapolate then that this philosophy has transcended both time and practice of origin. Indeed, some, if not the majority of individuals, prefer not to stand in front of other speakers and deliver, possibly because it is considered rude to stand with one's back to another, and also because it renders one open to physical attack. Some speakers would rather stand and speak on the spot than feel the uncomfortable sensation of having their backs to their peers. There is a belief that the preference to return to one's seat from the right is related to what happened to the demi-god Māui who was injured on his left-hand side by a stone thrown at him by his father. The right-hand side of the body is considered the more sacred side of the body. Is the fact that most Māori are right-handed merely a coincidence?[45]

One routine adopted by the speaker is the *hīkoi whakapae*, which has an orator moving left and right, speaking at the pivot before walking back the other way. Another standard course is what Mātaatua refer to is the *pāpaka* (the crab), which sees the speaker move forward and back, always facing the opposite speakers. This may be adopted by either host or visiting speakers. A speaker should always face whomever he is addressing. When an orator does not have the space to locate himself appropriately – stuck, for example, in the middle of speakers – he may orate from a fixed position.

Exceptional individuals, such as Te Pairi of Te Waimana, rarely stood still and moved about considerably while orating. Being an ardent believer in the black arts, Te Pairi figured that by constantly moving about he made a less easy target.[46]

Tūhoe have a belief that a speaker should not venture too far from his group when he orates. There are two reasons for this: first, for the sake of unity and practicality; and second, because the link between the speaker and the people should be maintained and upheld. Close proximity enables the supporting group to 'support' the speaker in the provision of song or information which he can include in his delivery. In terms of practicality, if a speaker locates himself ten metres or more away, it takes too long for the group to reattach themselves to their speaker when the time comes to sing. Te Wharehuia makes the analogy that the speaker is like the Māori seafaring vessel, the *waka*, and the supporting group is the anchor. This alludes to familial structures in which the speaker must maintain the link. To voyage too far, that is, to create too much distance between the speaker and his group of supporters, affords the possibility of the anchor, the people, being cut away, leaving the speaker on his own.

The Specific Roles of the Speakers

While in the past, there were probably many speakers of high calibre, nowadays the number of eloquent and knowledgeable speakers has declined and hosts and visitors alike make concerted efforts to ensure that there is at least one experienced elder accompanying or representing them during formal welcoming ceremonies. This elder advises the less experienced about what their separate roles as subsequent speakers might be.

From the host's point of view, it is likely that there will be some understanding of the role of each speaker, which may be more specific to tribes operating under the *pāeke, en bloc*, speaking arrangement:

> The greater part of *te kawa o te marae* or *marae* etiquette centres upon the regulation of oratory – who may speak, in what order, and how they structure their remarks . . . . apart from the selection of speakers, the order of speech is also carefully governed . . .[47]

Senior speakers tend to take a lead role in arranging more junior speakers if they are recognised authorities in the field of oratory. When the congregation of speakers includes leaders of similar rank, then the speakers may discuss the order and reach some consensual agreement as to who should talk about what. The more prominent the gathering, the more prominent the attendees, therefore, it is likely that the number of speakers will vary accordingly. Tahuri refers to the funeral of Rangihau who drew large crowds because of his status.[48] Māori wardens were given the responsibility of organising who would speak for the visiting speakers and where they should sit, rather than taking an unpredictable, *laissez faire* approach.

The opening speaker is usually referred to as the *kākā kura*, which Salmond translates as the 'red parrot, the bird that leads the flock'.[49] Under the alternating speaking arrangement, Downes makes the point that the most senior speaker from each side acts as the first speaker.[50] Mahuta says that 'Speaking depends on rank, age, wisdom, and knowledge' and the chief may speak either first or last.[51]

The first speaker, says Kāretu, lays the foundation that the following speakers can complement.[52] With reference to Te Arawa, Kingi asserts that the role of speaker number one is to address genealogical links: this might be between the deceased and the visitors, or between the hosts and the visitors, after which speakers from the visiting group may wish to expand further.[53]

Tūhoe, in particular, agree that for visitors going on to *marae*, the speaker with the closest genealogical affiliation should speak first, or failing this, the person who lives closest by. Because those living closest by are normally most familiar with the host *marae*, its people and its practices, they are in a better position to inform and advise other visitors. I have, on occasion, heard some people voice their disapproval because a 'local' speaker has not commenced orations for the visitors. Although proximal affiliation is seen by some to be a determinant as to who should open the speechmaking for the visitors, it may not always be the case. It may very well be left to the most senior, the most knowledgeable or the most eloquent to begin orations. This is generally the preferred option for host speakers so that the opening speech is of the best possible quality, making it respectful of the occasion and the guest(s). Prominent speakers often have the ability to meet all these requirements. There appear to be some parallels with *karanga*, in as much as they are 'usually performed by senior women who have a good command of the [Māori] language – otherwise one could say the wrong word and that could be disastrous'.[54]

Amongst Tūhoe, there are varying opinions about who should align the genealogies between hosts and visitors – whether this be the first or the last speaker – but there is unanimity that the recitation of genealogies should be flawless. In the event that the *pae* is not totally composed of experts, Tūhoe prefer the more junior or less initiated speakers to start off the speeches so that the more experienced can finish off on a high note. This allows the more experienced orator to fix any errors, if necessary, and make closing summaries.

There does not appear to be one single practice that all tribes adopt with regard to the selection of who starts and who concludes, however. Some argue that inexperience should under no circumstances precede experience. There are times when age is a factor, but at other times those more senior may actually concede to someone more knowledgeable in the art of oratory and/or cultural practices. I have observed a younger, more established, orator direct older tribal members on how they should service the cultural requirements during the exchange of orations. The senior members did not appear to be put out by this.

Reedy, of Ngāti Porou, and Mahuta, of Waikato-Maniapoto, describe the role of 'middle order batsmen' as discussing what the opening speakers have delivered. They are sometimes termed *kaiwetewete* (Ngāti Porou) or *takawaenga* (Te Arawa).[55] Kereopa and Temara say that these people should be the ones who draw out the genealogical associations between the various representative groups that are in attendance.[56] According to some Ngāti Porou, Te Arawa and Ngā Puhi elders, they will be the less confident speakers who have been strategically positioned in the middle of the experts.

The closing speaker is known as the *tangata kōpani* (Te Arawa); the *kaiwhakakao*, *kaiwhakatepe*, *kaiwhakaoti* or the *tāoro* (Tūhoe); or the *kaiwhakawhāiti* or *kaiwhakamutunga* (Ngāti Porou). The role of this speaker is to bring the speeches to a healthy conclusion and to tie up any loose ends. Temara describes the last speaker's role as analogous to that of the builder who brings the building to full completion – the person who finally closes the door to the house, indicating that it is complete.[57]

For the host side, the closing speaker puts the finishing touches on the deliveries of all the speakers who have preceeded him, thereby minimising the potential for criticism or rebuttal. This appears to be a commonality amongst tribes from the North and South Islands. Barlow writes that in former times this role was performed by the chief, the *ariki*.[58] Reilly adds that this was a similar practice to other Polynesian communities where the *ariki* would spend the majority of his time listening and watching so as to be in a better position to comment on all the angles covered in the discussions.[59] They might, for instance, correct any errors or add additional commentary to an important aspect omitted by one of the previous speakers. For this reason, it makes sense that the last speaker on both the host and visitor sides is the most senior, astute, wise, knowledgeable and eloquent. Regardless of whether they start or finish the orations, it is still a bonus to have such proficient speakers participate.

In addition, the last speaker for the host side is deemed responsible for finishing off all the speeches for that formal part of the day. Māori sometimes refer to this as '*he whakahoki i te mauri*', or '*he whakahoki i te rākau*' – the 'handing back' of the 'stick'.[60] There is some debate, however, about the saying '*he whakahoki i te mauri*', which literally means handing back the 'life essence'. Older Māori do not agree that this is ever relinquished before death, and therefore do not support those of their colleagues who actually verbalise the idea that they are handing the *mauri* over to the speakers from the opposing side.[61] Kingi says that all the final speaker for the hosts needs to do is to bring the right to speak back into the control of the hosts,[62] to let the hosts have the last say:

> The *mauri* (ethos) of the marae is held by each speaker as he speaks. Thus the tangata whenua needs to speak last to take back the mauri of the marae so that it remains with the tangata whenua and is not taken from the marae by manuhiri.[63]

Comments like this were more applicable to Māori society prior to 1990, when there was a regular availability of speakers. From my own observations, travelling around during the 1980s and 1990s, some *marae* only had one, two or maybe three speakers. Because hosts initiate most of the oratory, under *pāeke* it is they who indicate to the visitors when it is time to orate. There are a number of ways that they do this, some verbal and some non-verbal. Phrases regarding the handover of speaking include '*ka huri*' (turn it over to you), '*kei a koutou*' (it's over to you), '*kei a koutou te rākau*' (you have the stick), '*kua pāhi tēnei taha*' (this side has passed), and '*kua mutu mātou*' (we have finished).[64] The handover may also be communicated by the raising of an eyebrow, eye contact between opposing speakers, a nod by the host speaker, pointing a finger or walking stick in the direction of the visitors, or by allowing an extended period of silence of perhaps 20–30 seconds.

'Save one quiet bullet in the barrel', says Pouwhare.[65] 'Keep a spare in the kitchen', says Winiata.[66] These comments refer to preparations by the host *marae* to ensure that 'One speaker remains silent, in case a challenge is issued.'[67] If there is no such affront, then the role of the closing host speaker may merely be to announce the order of proceedings following the welcome, giving the time and day of the burial, for example, or issuing an invitation for the visitors to shake hands and *hongi* with the hosts to end the formalities.

Hohepa says that Ngā Puhi's practice is to have at least two speakers if they are the hosts.[68] Rangi says that there were many speakers in former times but this has declined over the years.[69] There seems to be an expectation nowadays that there be a specific number of speakers.[70] The main role of the host speakers is to tend to the welfare of the visitors. Some Mātaatua orators do not believe that hosts should express acknowledgements to themselves, for example, by words of acknowledgement to ancestral buildings located in close proximity to the venue. Apropos of this, when the occasion is a funeral, host speakers often refrain from focusing too much of their oration on the deceased. They will have done this when the deceased first arrived at the venue to be laid in repose. Once again, in this situation, welcoming the visitors is the primary role of the host speaker who often speaks on behalf of the close relatives of the deceased because they respect a cultural stricture to refrain from orating while they are mourning one of their own. It is considered a slight on the bereaved family if the host speaker fails to discharge proper acknowledgements to the visitors on the family's behalf.

Visiting speakers may also have coordinated roles, if the visitors are all from one and the same tribe. If it is a pan-Māori occasion, then orations will be more spontaneous and specific to the entity each visiting speaker represents.

When Tūhoe orators are part of a visiting group, there is a common tendency for them to begin their speeches with a generic acknowledgement of any other visitors present because they may be strangers to each other. This provides a platform of common purpose, *kotahitanga*. Should they forget to do this at the beginning, they can do it at the conclusion of the speech. At funerals, an opening speaker may well be the most closely related person, perhaps two or three times removed from the deceased, or the tribe of the deceased. This speaker might otherwise be the one most familiar with the affiliations of the person lying in repose or the venue (as we mentioned earlier). In this way they are able to inform the other visitors of the practices adopted by the host people:

> Within the tribal region of Mātaatua in the Bay of Plenty the tikanga is that if Mātaatua speakers are present among the visitors they must speak first so that they can identify with the host speakers in welcoming the visitors who have appeared for the first time on a particular marae.[71]

With reference to Te Tairāwhiti, Salmond says that it is the role of the first visiting speaker to find genealogical ties between the visitors and the hosts.[72]

'Ko te rukuruku a Whakaotirangi':[73] Koha

'*Ko te rukuruku a Whakaotirangi*' is a phrase that Te Arawa use with reference to the gifts offered by visitors upon their arrival amongst the hosts. Te Hiko Hohepa explains that this custom derived from an ancestress, Whakaotirangi, who carried tubers with her on her travels to plant upon arrival in new lands.[74] Instead of the term '*rukuruku*',

Hohepa uses '*rokiroki*', which refers to a collection of articles or possessions, or to preserve, therefore it is likely that '*te rokiroki a Whakaotirangi*' describes the tubers Whakaotirangi brought as her 'gift' intended to help sustain the people.

The exchange of goods has long been a common practice amongst Māori, and it is likely that this custom began before Māori migration to New Zealand. It continues to play an important role in Māori *marae* ritual, and in fact, in all encounter rituals hosted by Māori both nationally and internationally. The significance of the practice in the context of this study is the fact that it normally signifies the near conclusion or end of an oration.

> Firth distinguished 'exchanges which were primarily economic' from 'ceremonial exchanges which served some wider social purpose', and 'intra-communal exchanges', which were relatively few, from 'extra-communal exchanges', which were fairly common and took place in the context of hospitality extended by hosts to visiting groups.[75]

Offerings by visitors during rituals of encounter have evolved over the years and take differing forms. They are known as *koha* or *takoha* (an unspecified gift), *kohi* (a gift of joint collected monies), *whakaaro* (literally a thought, usually a monetary donation), *kōkohu* or *kōkuhu* (a gift handed over in secrecy), *moni whakahoki* (a monetary reciprocation for monies given previously), *maunga-ā-ringa* (a gift presented in person), *whakapuru* (a gift of dried *kūmara*), *kai-whakapaepae* (the reciprocation of food), *āwhina* (assistance), *aroha* (a gift of genuine sympathy and consideration) and *kai-makamaka* (a food offering). Such exchanges often take place on the open courtyard or the pseudo courtyard, or inside the building where the welcoming ceremony is being conducted.

> The giving of koha stems from the tradition of bringing gifts when visiting a marae. For the Maori, generosity and hospitality is a matter of honour. Giving rather than receiving is very important. Money is a modern form of koha, but Maori often used food as koha. Tribes would give food that was plentiful in their area but in short supply in their hosts' district. For example a group that lived in the bush would take preserved pigeons as their koha, while other tribes who lived by the sea would offer dried fish or shellfish.[76]

A *koha* (gift or token of appreciation) is given by the *manuhiri* to the *tangata whenua*, usually at the end of the last *whaikōrero*. In traditional Māori society this was in the form of food, especially delicacies from the local area of the *manuhiri*, and/or *taonga* (treasured items), which could range from weapons to finely woven cloaks. Food is taken directly to the kitchen and not laid on the *marae*. Today the most common form of *koha* is a sum of money. *Koha* laid formally on the *marae* is intended to defray costs of the *marae*, but *koha* given quietly to the organiser of the *hui* is intended to help cover the expenses of the *hui*.[77]

The role of the orator begins well in advance of their actual oration. It may start with preliminary arrangements associated with attending or hosting the occasion, when they may undertake research about the people they are visiting or the people who are coming to visit them. The visitors may make enquiries regarding the purpose of the gathering, which will provide information that can be incorporated into their speeches. Upon arrival at the event, visiting orators often, but not always, congregate at the entrance for the formal welcome and organise *koha*.

Some areas, Mātaatua, Ngāti Porou, and Ngā Puhi,[78] for example, have the last speaker present all of the *koha*. In other areas, each speaker presents the *koha* on behalf of those they represent. There is sometimes confusion when mixed tribal practices operate. I have seen Mātaatua speakers feel denied the opportunity to speak because a visiting speaker has presented their *koha*, in accordance with their own tribal practice. For the Mātaatua speaker, this indicates that orations have finished. Henare Tuwhangai of Waikato referred to his role of placing the final *koha* down as the 'pack horse',[79] that is, his major responsibility during the encounter ritual was the handing over of the *koha* on behalf of the visitors.

It would appear that there is no strict convention for how an orator presents the *koha*. On the *marae*, the visiting speaker normally places it midpoint between the host and visiting speakers, the *pae kauka*. However, this is often an unmarked boundary that neither the host nor visiting speakers will venture beyond during their orations. It seems to be neutral ground for both parties. If formalities take place inside a meeting house, then a midpoint is normally ascribed and the *koha* placed there. I have seen one speaker go to the 'halfway' line, place a note on the floor and retreat gradually back to his seat leaving a trail of money behind. On another occasion, a single speaker put down the donations of different visiting groups with an announcement of who they were each from. I heard tell of one smart orator who placed the paper money on the ground on a blustery day, leaving the host person to chase the money about in the wind – a bit of light amusement for everyone who was there.

During one university recruitment and practical experience excursion for our international students to the west coast of the North Island, we were welcomed on to

Urenui Marae by Ngāti Mutunga. We were advised by the host people not to place our *koha* of money on the floor of the meeting house but rather to put it directly into the hands of the host receiver.

Some individuals prefer to hand the monies over privately to a member of the tribe or family, for example, during the formal handshake. During funerals, the monetary *koha* may be given to a family member at an opportune time. Again, the orator must be aware of the local significance attached to it when they hand the *koha* over on the *marae* or transfer it from person to person. Variations do exist amongst tribes and *whānau* as well. Edwards says of his own people,

> . . . Te Arawa do not lay a koha on the marae. It is given in a heavy handshake during the pōwhiri or on the day they leave to go home, when they poroporoaki to say goodbye . . . . The only time Te Arawa places a koha on the ground is when they travel with other tribes collectively as one ope. I have seen many envelopes put down together with each tribe's name written on individual envelopes.[80]

Koha placed on *marae*, says Morehu, is '*moni whakahoki*', that is, monies which the recipient might be expected to reciprocate at some stage in the future, either near or distant.[81]

There are just as many variations involved with exactly when a speaker presents the *koha*. Some speakers give it immediately prior to their song. Some present it while the supporting song is still being sung at the conclusion of their speech, and others present it immediately after the song before making some closing remarks. Other speakers place the *koha* with the closing words of their oration. It appears to be a stylistic variable adopted by different individuals. Tūhoe speakers do not stick to one particular moment. According to Te Hiko Hohepa, Te Arawa end with the *koha*, so it follows the supporting song.[82] Ngāti Awa also do it this way, according to Merito.[83] Ngāti Porou speakers may present *koha* before or after the song.[84]

It is often the case that a host member is delegated the role of receiving or fetching the *koha*. This function is commonly performed by a non-speaking member, unless there is a shortage of hosts available. If the *koha* is placed before the visitors have sung the accompanying song, the hosts usually wait until the song has ended before retrieving it.

While it is hoped that these examples may serve as models or guidelines, every individual speaker has to consider the value of his own practices while also recognising the cultural adherences enforced by tribes and subtribes of their hosts.

Chapter Nine

The Structure of *Whaikōrero*

There is unquestionably a particular structure attached to *whaikōrero* and, as Mahuta explains, it is this that 'differentiates it from other types of discourse'.[1] This set structure is linked with its formality. The following generic models are acceptable starting points for looking at the structure of *whaikōrero* that are delivered by a host or visiting speaker at any occasion, with the exception of a funeral.

Table 9.1 Model Whaikōrero Structure

HOST	**VISITOR**
Whakaaraara	*Whakaaraara*
Tauparapara/tau	*Tauparapara/tau*
Mihi ki te manuhiri	*Mihi ki te marae* and *whare tipuna*
	Mihi mate
	Mihi ora
Take	*Take*
Mōteatea, waiata, haka	*Mōteatea, waiata* and/or *haka*
Whakamutu	
(final speaker: explanation of detail regarding forum)	conclusion[2]

Although the differences listed in table 9.1 may not appear great, the models are markedly different. At the same time, they both retain the essential core components listed by Mahuta as:

Mihi mate (eulogies to the dead)
Mihi ora (acknowledgements to the living)
Take (the event).[3]

Māori speakers may approach their oration analogically, as in the following:

> Each part of the house [meeting house] has a specific symbolic significance and when a group of speakers, visitors, manuhiri, or local people, tangata whenua, engage in oratory, whaikorero, on the marae, they are said to be metaphorically constructing a meeting house. Firstly the basis for discussion, kaupapa, or floor, is laid down and then the speakers support one another in ways comparable to the holding up of the ridge-pole by the pou or the uprights within the house.[4]

Some speakers model their structure around the image of a Māori canoe on a voyage or draw on aspects of the natural world using the symbolism of a tree's growth, a bird's flight, or the lives and behavioural patterns of animals and insects.

A common introductory component for *whaikōrero* is the *tauparapara*, which may precede or follow the *whakaaraara*, a plosive verbal utterance by the speaker, signalling his intention to speak, to be discussed later. *Tauparapara* take the form of prayers or incantations composed for a variety of functions: protection, safe and unrestricted travel, rhythmic chants used while moving canoes across the land or for paddling in unison, dedicatory chants to assist in the acquisition of knowledge and genealogical recitations. Some have an esoteric association, for example, they are –

> ... a special prayer or chant to the gods which varies according to the purpose of the gathering. ... e.g. chants to dispel evil influences, to alert the people, to sanctify the people. Main chants are to invoke the protection of the gods, and to honour the visitors.[5]

Employing *tauparapara*, says Mahuta, 'sets the tone and indicates that it is a formal discourse'.[6] *Tauparapara* raise the awareness of the speaker and the audience, setting the scene for oratory. They inspire the speaker. Awatere makes the following comment about '*tau*', as they are known for short:

> *E ihi ai, e wana ai, e mana ai te kupu, e rangatira ai te kōrero: e tapu ai te tāuhu o te kōrero, tīmataina te whaikōrero ki te tau, arā ki tētahi o ngā momo waiata i runga ake nei.* <u>*Ki te kore he tau o tāu whaikōrero, e whakaiti ana koe i ō mātua, i ō tīpuna, i tō iwi, i tō waka, e whaaki ana koe ki te ao e kōhungahunga tonu ana koe engari kua kanewaha ki te mau i te rākau ā Tāne-i-te-wānanga, i te rākau ā Tū-te-ihiihi, ki ngā rākau i āta wehea e Koro mā mā te hunga i whāngaia ki te kaimārō o ngā kete Wānanga.*[7]</u>

Awatere talks about *whaikōrero* commencing with *tau* and their potential to influence the words and the topic. To omit or neglect to include a *tau*, he says, is a denigration of one's parents and ancestors – one's people. Such an omission indicates that a speaker still does not have the maturity in the area of oratory to take up the special knowledge espoused through the selected schools of learning, *wānanga*, and the speaking characteristics of Tāne-i-te-wānanga as the proprietor of knowledge, and the challenging aspects of Tū-te-ihiihi.

Tau is the generic name for a chant, prayer or incantation. McLean and Orbell describe *tauparapara* as ritual chants 'performed by orators (manu kōrero) before speaking on the marae'.[8] One interpretation of the term '*parapara*', says Mahuta, is in reference to the skids used to convey a canoe across the land.[9] Sample whaikōrero 11 by Pei Te Hurinui Jones, a eulogy to the fifth Māori king, Korokī Te Rata Mahuta Tāwhiao Pōtatau Te Wherowhero upon his death in 1966, is an example of this. Part of the chant is given in table 9.2.

Table 9.2

Ki okioki ē, ē hē, tōia te waka.	Should one rest? No. Keep pulling!
Ki okioki, ē hē, tōia te waka.	Should one rest? No. Keep pulling!
Ki runga ki te maunga e tū mai nei.	Pull it onto the mountain that stands yonder.
Whakatakotoria ki te ngaro parapara koa.	Place it on the skids.
Me he tētē waka, hei, me he tētē waka, hei,	Like the small canoe.
Me he pītau whakarei te tētē kura o te waka!	Like the carved figure, the ornamental fronds of the canoe.

In this example Pei uses the *tau* to conclude his oration rather than to open it, perhaps likening the end of his speech to a canoe finally coming to rest at its intended destination. The application of such chants and incantations is especially appreciated when they have a direct relationship to the rest of the speech or the purpose of the gathering. Merito assesses the gathering and, if this is a first-time visit for him to that particular *marae*, then he selects a chant that clears the way for him to speak.[10] If it is a funeral, he may select an opener that makes strong references to death. Temara of Tūhoe explains that *tauparapara* may include aspects that are not found in prayers (*karakia*), like references to Māori deities such as Tū-mata-uenga and Tāne, for example.[11] Te Hiko Hohepa of Te Arawa actually says that these introductory recitations are '*pōhuatau*' or prayers to the Māori deities of the spirit world.[12]

In terms of function, these *tau* or *tauparapara* are merely referred to as 'chants used as speech introductions'.[13] This perhaps infers that they have no function beyond being temporal markers, indicators that a speech is about to begin. Sometimes people call these introductory speech components *karakia*, a term that expresses the wish to use supernatural powers to effect events and beings in the natural world. For example, an online source describes *karakia* as –

> ... charms, incantations, spells, etc. Used for all manner of purpose; in hunting (luring birds to be snared or to drink), in fighting illness, in playing games (like encouraging darts to fly straight), in addressing weapons or asking gods to give strength to the weapon and wielder, in warfare (to render pursuer and pursued fleet of foot, to cause the enemy to lose strength), in choking on food (the victim was also slapped on the back), to draw in land and sea to make a journey shorter, or draw it out to discourage others, to delay the passage of the sun across the heavens. Karakia were based on sympathetic magic rather than direct requests.[14]

Just as *karakia* act as intermediary between the spiritual world and the temporal world, so does the *tauparapara* at the start of the *whaikōrero* bridge the gap between host and visitor, silence and speech, *noa* and *tapu*. Māori orators sometimes adopt biblical references and use them as the opening component of their speeches. Another traditional chant applied as a speech opener is a *kākāriki pōwhaitere*, originally used as a prayer chant when uplifting felled trees to make into canoes.[15] Milroy sees the derivation of the word *tauparapara* as a combination of *tau*, an incantation, and *parapara*, the blood that is shed during battle. The *tauparapara* was, therefore, a cleansing prayer of sorts, to free the returned warrior from the sanctity of the war field.[16] On the topic of warfare, Mahuta mentions *tau marae* as a *whaikōrero* starter.[17] These chants were employed to render the enemy weak.

Cleave and Salmond explain *tauparapara* as follows:

> When members of one tribe are visiting another a tauparapara or formal introduction to a speech is normally employed. This is a poetic and allegorical manner of introducing oneself tribally and proverbs like those above are alluded to in clever and sometimes cryptic ways.[18]

> The chants are full of archaic words and obscure historical references, and they have a distinctive 'spell' quality. The role of the voice and the mystery of the words lend the *tauparapara* its dignity, and the recitation conveys *mana* and *tapu* rather than specific information.[19]

So what appears to be a simple oratorical component contains more than mere rhetoric. *Tauparapara* add the formal dimension to oratory. They raise the ante and enhance the orator and the occasion. They make the occasion special and give it importance. Whaikōrero proper begins with a *tauparapara*. This puts you in a form of tapu, then you start the whaikōrero proper.[20] *Tauparapara* protect the speaker and his group from curses, says Mahuta, and help the speaker recall the words of his ancestors.[21] While addressing school teachers, Pat Rei said that *whaikōrero* should begin with a *karakia* of some form.[22]

It appears that particular tribes employ *tauparapara* as part of their orations more than others. Ngāti Porou, says Reedy, do not place a lot of emphasis on *tauparapara* since some of their elders view *tauparapara* as unnecessary and sometimes merely time consuming.[23] A friend engaged in research amongst his Taranaki relatives found evidence of a similar train of thought, with the comment that some *tauparapara* were lengthier than the main body of the oration. I have listened to some *whaikōrero* that did seem '*tauparapara* heavy', but in considering the content of those *tauparapara*, they have been particularly apt.

Other chants used as introductions for speeches are *manawa wera*, which are Tūhoe chants to vent anger. One such composition expresses the fury of Tūhoe women, some of whom became widows after the defeat of Tūhoe forces at Ōrākau. When Ngāi Tūhoe meet Waikato–Maniapoto people, the chances are that a Tūhoe orator will refer to the chant to make a historical connection to this event. The same chant acknowledges the deaths of those Tūhoe who died in the encounter between Tūhoe and Waikato-Maniapoto and the crown constabulary. It reminds Tūhoe of the disapproval of the Tūhoe womenfolk and the fact that they were cautioned against engaging in battle.

I have harboured a suspicion at times that some speakers are not fully aware of the significance of the chants they employ, in as much as I have struggled to find a link between the chant and the purpose of the gathering. There are competent users, however, who in employing chants and incantations have fulfilled all the requirements for Māori *whaikōrero*, such as acknowledging the divine gods, giving eulogies to the deceased and creating memoria to the departed. Te Hiko Hohepa says that if a Te Arawa speaker uses a *pōhuatau* or *karakia* at the beginning of his oration, then he may consciously omit separate acknowledgements to God because this is considered already covered by the *pōhuatau*.[24] I think there are times when, even if the speaker is not fully conversant with the *tauparapara* they employ, they may be using it for its protective purposes:

> Only the opening speaker would use *tauparapara* to initiate [his] *whaikōrero*. Successive speakers were increasingly unlikely to do so because they were cognisant that the use of

tauparapara by the opening speaker had initiated the *tapu* state into which all speakers enter into during the *whaikōrero* exchange.²⁵

Salmond writes that by employing *tau*, *tauparapara* and *pātere* (in Te Tairāwhiti), a speaker is demonstrating his higher knowledge.²⁶ Some speakers are able to craft their orations stringing three or four of these together. An oration might be interspersed with *tau* in order to drive an issue home. Their inclusion should be considered seriously because any misuse could have negative consequences for the speaker.

In general, *whaikōrero* may commence with any of the following so long as the form chosen is appropriate for the occasion:

tau
tauparapara
pōkeka
manawa wera
pātere
huatatau
kawa waka
karakia
whakaaraara
haka taparahi
ngeri
tohi
waiata
pepeha
whakataukī
whakatauākī

These introductory components serve many purposes, such as seeking support from Māori deities and tribal ancestors and affiliates, making genealogical ties, expressing rituals of welcome, intoning farewells to the deceased and lifting *tapu* (i.e. the desanctification of a heavy spiritual stricture).

Tait says that it was common practice for Te Arawa speakers to employ *tauparapara* when they were the visiting body.²⁷ Is there, perhaps, some inference here that as hosts, they may forgo this component? Employing the *tauparapara* at the outset also serves to inform the audience early about the tribal affiliation of the speaker or group.

Winiata says that a stylistic feature of Te Arawa is that, as a visiting speaker, he will not launch into the *tauparapara* until he has acknowledged the other visitors alongside him.[28]

Reedy is somewhat critical of the modern trend to accept the notion that the omission of the *tauparapara* is an indication that a *whaikōrero* is of lesser status.[29] This would definitely be of concern to Ngāti Porou orators if they endorse Reedy's comments that the *tauparapara* was formerly left for the opening speaker.

Merito uses *waerea* as the *tauparapara* because the function of a *waerea* is the 'clearing of the passage', or removal of any inferred intangible obstructions believed to hinder successful progress for the visitors.[30] The biblical expression '*he hōnore, he korōria ki te atua, he maunga-ā-rongo ki te whenua, he whakaaro pai ki ngā tāngata katoa*' ('honour and glory to God, peace and goodwill to people on earth') has been adopted by numerous speakers as their speech opener. Te Kapunga (Koro) Dewes recorded approximately twenty *tauparapara* in 1970, and there are innumerable others that speakers use and are as yet unpublished. There does not appear to be any set rule that a current speaker must use an archaic chant as the opening component of his speech.

Whakaaraara: The Call of Alert

The full form of *whakaaraara* is '*whakaaraara pā*', which Cowan refers to as the 'sentinel's chant'.[31] Another term for the *whakaaraara* is the *koko*.[32] *Whakaaraara* refers to the act of alerting people to the imminent appearance of someone, or something. It is often the primary indicator that a speaker will soon be upstanding. The call is often strong, and at a higher pitch than a normal speaking voice. It is intended to carry, as would any warning call. The word '*Tihei!*' or the full phrase '*Tihei mauri ora!*' are commonly used. Māori believe this exclamation originated from the earliest times when one of the primal gods, Tāne, fashioned the first woman. He breathed life into her and she sneezed (*tihei*) the sneeze of life: '*Tihei mauri ora!*'[33] Like the cry of a newborn baby announcing its arrival, the *whakaaraara* serves to announce the fresh breath of a new orator. Apart from psychologically preparing the speaker and the audience, these calls lessen the likelihood that another speaker will get up at the same time.

Different tribes and different individual speakers may use variant forms, like '*tihei!*', '*tihei mauri ora!*', '*tihere mauri ora!*', '*tihe mauri ora!*' and '*tihewa mauri ora!*' In essence, they all mean the same and have the same purpose. Another variation used at funerals in recent years is '*tihei mauri mate!*'. I have heard debate about this variation because '*mauri*' is synonymous with living entities, as opposed to dead ones. The most widely used phrase is '*Kia hiwa rā!*' ('Be watchful, be wakeful!').[34] *Kia hiwa rā* was a call exchanged between sentries throughout the hours of darkness to warn any would-be attackers that the fort was prepared and could not be caught 'napping'. The failure of a sentry to let fellow sentries know that they were likely to be under attack and the fort was in imminent danger was serious.[35] Many of these alarms, says Buck, 'have been handed down and give colour to speeches'.[36] These songs, these *whakaaraara pā*, also served the purpose of reassuring 'the occupants of the pā that they were not neglecting their duties'.[37] Some of these effusions are short and may have merely developed from their one-liner beginnings to lengthier watch songs.

A full example of the *whakaaraara pā* documented by Buck is:[38]

Kia hiwa ra e tenei tuku,	O hither terrace, be on the alert,
Kia hiwa ra e tera tuku,	O yonder terrace be on the alert,
Kei apurua koe ki te toto.	Lest ye be smothered in blood.

Ngāti Toa, on the West Coast of the North Island, have the following *whakaaraara*:

Whakaarahia!
Whakaarahia!
E tenei pa!
E tera pa!
Kei apitia koe ki te toto.
Whakapuru tonu,
Whakapuru tonu
Te tai ki Harihari.
Ka tangi tiere
Te tai ki Mokau.
Kaore ko au e kimi ana,
E hahau ana,
I nga pari ra
Piri nga hakoakoa,
E kau oma tera
Ki tua.
E-i-a ha-ha!

Ka ao mai te ra
Ki tua.
E-i-a ha-ha![39]

Two shorter examples of *whakaaraara* are:

E ara, e ara, e tēnei pā, e tērā pā,
Kei āpitia koe ki te toto,
Whakapuru tonu whakapuru tonu . . . .[40]

Moe araara, ka tau te manu ki te pae
Koheri, kohera, ka tiritiria, reareaia tama ki tona hiwa
Kia hiwa![41]

Both encourage the people inside the fort to be vigilant and 'sleep lightly' so as to avoid a surprise invasion and the possible loss of lives. The latter is recorded as having been used in 1852 by a watchman.[42] Here I provide loose translations:

Get up! Arise, people of the village.
Lest your blood be drawn (by the enemy)
Plug the gaps (Let there be no breach of security)

Be alert during sleep
When the bird sets to rest on the branch (perhaps the invader)
Gather from here and there
And keep the youth vigilant.

Another common *whakaaraara* compares the sentry to the eeler:[43] '*Ka moe te mata hī tuna, ka ara te mata hī taua*' ('If the eel does not bite the eeler will fall asleep, whereas the sentry must be vigilant throughout the night. He cannot afford to lose concentration.').

The call '*Taiaha hā, taiaha hā!*' exhorts the warrior to take up his arms (in this case, the long fighting staff known as the '*taiaha*') in readiness for combat. Other less formal alerts that a speaker may use to indicate that he is rising to speak are '*kei runga*' ('I'm getting up'), '*kei konei*' ('over here') or '*e tū ana*' ('I will stand').

Amongst Tūhoe, there does not appear to be one set practice about whether the *whakaaraara* precedes or succeeds the *tauparapara*. Some speakers do not use *tauparapara* per se, but employ *whakataukī*, *whakatauākī* (proverb) or *pepeha* (aphorisms of genealogical identity), strongly intonated to announce the beginning of the *whaikōrero*. With *pepeha*, the orator signals his tribal affiliation.[44] Historic reservoirs of knowledge such as *whakataukī* or *whakatauākī* can also serve to forecast the basis or central theme of a speech.

Mihi: Acknowledgements

In most cases, *mihi* (acknowledgements) play a prominent role in extolling the virtues of the opposite party, whether they be host or visitor. These *mihi* may include many aspects: acknowledgements of a divine entity, words of greeting to those who have congregated, references to the buildings that symbolise ancestors, recognition of the *marae*, words of farewell to those who have died and acknowledgement of the Māori monarchy.

Again there is no stricture about which *mihi* should take precedence: *mihi* to God, *mihi* to the visitors or *mihi* to the Kīngitanga. With Waikato speakers, it is highly likely that they will acknowledge their monarch, regardless of whether they are speaking in their own area or not. At times, speakers from other tribes may also make the same tribute to the Kīngitanga, especially if Waikato are the visitors. Tait says that it was common for Te Arawa speakers to acknowledge the biblical God of Western renown.[45]

Many Tūhoe are of the view that such acknowledgements of God are a more recent trend, especially amongst Tūhoe. I have been unable to ascertain when exactly this began and what prompted the inclusion of such acknowledgements in *whaikōrero*. An ambiguity surrounding this particular issue is that when Māori orators '*mihi ki te Atua*', it is not always 100 percent clear whether they are acknowledging a Pākehā God or Māori deities. My guess is that the origin dates back to the mid-1900s when senior Māori were ordained into Christian churches of various denominations and Māori religious movements, such as Ringatū, Paimārire and Iharaira took flight. Scripture may have been included as part of the orations by ordained Māori in Māori settings. Being speakers of repute, their sermons may have served as model *whaikōrero* for onlookers and learners alike. Another possibility is that acknowledgements were included in *whaikōrero* shortly after Pākehā established a New Zealand education system, which included religious teachings in the late nineteenth century. Reedy points out that it has almost become mandatory for speakers to include Christian references for fear of criticism if they do not.[46] Because of this, less established speakers will tend to conform.

One might also speculate that this Christian content became common and followed the path of the mission stations as they were established by Pompallier and other missionaries throughout the country:

> ... he [Pompallier] was able to establish the following mission stations: Hokianga 1838, Kororareka [Russell] 1839, Mangakahia, Kaipara, Tauranga, Akaroa 1840, Matamata, Opotiki, Maketu 1841, Auckland and Otago 1842, Wellington 1843, Otaki, Rangiaowhia and Whakatane 1844. In the course of setting up these missions Pompallier made 4 voyages down the East coasts of the North and South Islands.[47]

Whaikōrero numbers 3, 9, 10, 12 and 14 in the appendix give examples of acknowledgements to God in some form or another from almost the length and breadth of the North Island – Taitokerau, Taranaki, Te Arawa, Waikato and Mātaatua. Although there is no knowing the exact time or place when God became an integral component in *whaikōrero*, these examples indicate some of the tribal and individual expression of references to non-Māori deities in Māori orations. Further analysis of sample *whaikōrero* might provide more evidence of when actual acknowledgements to a Pākehā God became prominent.

Reedy makes the point that, perhaps with reference to Ngāti Porou, not all succeeding speakers will mention God in their orations, considering their first speaker to have discharged this service.[48] Iraia of Ngāti Whare (southern Bay of Plenty) stated that in his day from the 1960s through to the 1990s, acknowledgments to a biblical God became the primary opener of *whaikōrero*, followed immediately by *whakaaraara* and *tauparapara*.[49] Te Hiko Hohepa says that as a young man in the 1950s and 60s, he heard some of his Te Arawa elders give thanks to God for his blessings over the people, but again, not all speakers did so.[50]

Walker's simple explanation of the sequence of events is that speeches:

> ... follow a set pattern beginning with a tauparapara.... This is followed by a eulogy to the dead, which may contain mythological illusions and a statement of philosophy of life and death. The eulogy culminates in a farewell to the dead, passing them on to the ancestors. Once the separation between the living and the dead has been stated the living are then addressed and welcomed.[51]

Kāretu is quick to state that the primary focus of orations by host speakers is acknowledgement of the visitors.[52] I think that he is probably expressing his own disagreement with host speakers at funerals who sometimes launch into farewell speeches directed at their own deceased lying in repose. Dewes supports the primary focus being on the visitors, as he states, '*tā te tangata whenua he manaaki i te manuhiri*' (the role of the host is to look after the visitors) so that they feel as comfortable and at ease as possible amongst the hosts rather than as if they are still visitors or strangers throughout the duration of the event.[53]

When visitors acknowledge the living, some speakers begin with acknowledgements to the *kaikaranga* (the female caller). This appears to be a new trend, which I have come across only in the last decade. Acknowledging the *kaikaranga* appears to be prevalent amongst southern Māori in Otago and Southland. Most visitors acknowledge the host orators, and in doing so, says Kāretu, they are paying tribute to all the tribal and subtribal entities that those host speakers represent.[54]

In a general forum, other than a funeral, the visiting speakers might focus their orations on the subject of the event that has brought them all together before directing acknowledgements to the hosts (speakers and those assembled). At funerals, they might prefer to begin their orations with eulogies to the deceased, prior to redirecting their words to the host people. One variation, according to Tahuri, is for people to be acknowledged before mention of the *marae* and physical representation of an ancestor in the form of the meeting house.[55] After the formalities, speakers often focus comments on individuals they know who are seated amongst the hosts, or affiliated to the hosts. I have been cautioned that there are times when this practice makes important attendees feel uncomfortable because it singles out some and omits others. *Kei mahue ētahi.*

It is often the case that visiting speakers, especially those from Mātaatua, Ngāti Porou and Te Arawa, will quietly and respectfully acknowledge fellow visitors who have accompanied them onto the *marae* before delivering their full oration for all to hear. If, however, there are multiple speakers from one tribe on the host side, they may designate this role to the opening speaker, rather than have each speaker reitererate the acknowledgements of the former speaker.

In general, host speakers seldom make acknowledgements to their own *marae* because it is considered audacious and possibly self-indulgent. Similarly, speakers may avoid acknowledging the *marae* and its buildings if they themselves have some genealogical affiliation to that *marae*. The general assertion in such cases is '*waiho mā tētahi kē atu koe e kōrero*' ('let someone else pay the tributes').

Kaumātua Pateriki Rei of Te Arawa and Ngāti Toarangatira explains the role of visiting speakers as follows:

Ka haere ngā whaikōrero, me [he] waewae tapu koe kua mea koe, tuatahi o ō kōrero he mihi ki te tupuna whare, ki a Tāne-whakapiripiri, ka mihi hoki te marae, ngā waihonga ake o rātou, a te hunga kua mate . . . me ehara koe i te waewae tapu, mihi tuatahi ki te tūpāpaku, koia nei te kaupapa i haere mai ai, kātahi ka mihi ki te kiri mate . . . i muri iho ka mihi ki ngā kuia ki ngā wāhine ko rātou nei hoki te puna o te roimata, ngā whare tangata. Mā rātou hoki e tika ai ō tātou tangihanga. Auē tonu ana, auē tonu ana, ka mutu, ka mihi ki ngā koroua o runga i te paepae. I muri i tēnā, kua mihi ki ngā iwi kua whakaeke mai i mua i a koe, ngā rangatira kei reira e noho mai ana. [Ka] mihi ki ētahi atu iwi kua whakaeke mai.[56]

If the visit is the first by the visiting speaker, the first greeting should go to the ancestral house, to Tāne-whakapiripiri, then to the *marae* as symbolic reminders of those who belong there and have since passed on. If the visiting speaker has actually set foot on that *marae* on a previous occasion, and the occasion on this revisit is a funeral, then eulogies to the deceased should take precedence, followed by the bereaved family and the womenfolk, the repositories of sorrow and the perpetuators of generations, because of whom the funeral meets all expectations in a Māori sense. Following this are the greetings to the host speakers and those who have arrived on the *marae* prior to them.[57]

Te Arawa and Tūhoe appear to follow the practice of making such acknowledgements only when the visiting speakers are first-timers. Dewes says that when Ngāti Porou speakers venture outside their ward, they pay homage to the *marae* as a matter of respect.[58]

When speakers acknowledge the *marae*, they often include buildings permanently affixed to the *marae*: the main meeting house(s), the dining hall, or the purpose-built shelter for the bodies of the deceased. There are various names used to describe main meeting houses: *wharenui* (a large house), *tipuna whare* (a house rightfully named after an ancestor), *whare tipuna* (a house with pictorial or carved representations of ancestors contained within), *whare puni* (sleeping quarters) or *whare rūnanga* (a house where discussion forums take place). The use of these names highlights the importance of the building and the significant role that it plays. Acknowledging the building is an acknowledgement of all the Māori philosophies, histories and cultural underpinnings as well as the ancestors they represent.

Complementary to the *wharenui* is the *wharekai*, the dining room. Where *wharenui* in Mātaatua and Te Arawa represent an eponymous male ancestor, the *wharekai* is usually named after an eponymous female of the tribe. Some Ngāti Porou *marae* also have the *whare nui* named after an eponymous female ancestor. Some orators, therefore, pay homage to the *wharekai*, depending on whom it represents. We must note, however, that not all *wharenui* and *wharekai* are named after ancestors. Some are named after significant events.[59]

Acknowledging the *marae* ultimately pays tribute to Papa-tū-ā-nuku, the deital represenation of mother earth, provider of sustenance and the spiritual connection with Māori cosmogony. Other physical structures on the *marae* such as the *whare mate*, the *pou haki* (flagpole) and *kōhatu whakamaumahara* (memorial stones) may also be afforded greetings.

Eulogies

In as much as references to the ancestral house effectively acknowledge a spiritual entity, Māori always acknowledge the spirit world when they pay homage to the recent passing of people affiliated with the hosts and visitors and popular or influential individuals elsewhere, Māori and non-Māori alike. 'The dead are eulogised because they are an essential part of the Maori community, i.e. the living and the dead are the community, and a belief in the physical and symbolic existence of the world of the dead.'[60]

Just as a speaker would be seen to be praising himself if he were to acknowledge his own *marae*, it is deemed inappropriate for a host speaker to make lengthy eulogies to the deceased on his *marae*. It is, however, acceptable and common practice for a host speaker to recognise the bereavements suffered by the visitors in the recent past, and even in the distant past.

If the funeral is that of a nationally esteemed Māori, it is common for all orations to include the most eloquent and animated eulogies one is likely to hear anywhere. They will extend to every possible aspect of the individual and of death itself. It is a biased narrative whereby the life of the deceased is recapitulated: everything affirmative is accentuated and the negative left forgotten. Some orations, on the other hand, are very frank and focus their words on the less positive attributes or actions of an individual. While some of these comments may appear pernicious, they may in fact honour the deceased because they are just that, 'frank and honest', which sometimes lingers on in the memories of those present.

Where host speakers may keep tributes to the dead brief, it is expected that visitors speak elaborately and at length:

> They ever speak in eulogy of the deceased, of his good qualities, his generosity, hospitality, courage, &c., frequently crying him farewell and using many peculiar expressions, figurative, mytho-poetical; quotations from ancient myths, proverbial sayings, and aphorisms. Extracts of an allegorical nature called from old-time lore, dirges and laments for the dead, are all introduced into their speeches.[61]

Indeed, it is sometimes commented that even the average person is farewelled like a god. The deviances of youth and any ill-gotten ways seem to fade and are replaced with tributes as if the person was angelic and truly an example of a fine being. I suppose this bodes well for every one of us.

Whereas some speakers prioritise the farewells to the dead above all else, for example, among Ngāti Porou,[62] speakers from different tribes might acknowledge the hosts and the buildings before focusing their orations on the deceased. Tūhoe and Te Arawa, for example, tend to address the deceased immediately following the *tauparapara*, and then move on to toothier topics for discussion.[63] If an observer actually listens to multiple *whaikōrero* at the same *tangi*, it is easy to become sceptical about whether any fresh material is being introduced by each successive speaker. I agree that repetitiously eulogising the deceased pays them honour, but I doubt that it raises the profile of those speakers whose orations are repetitive.

In chapter 5, I mentioned that people are prohibited from speaking when the deceased is a close relative. However, there are ways around this. Woodard describes how she has heard men actually uttering words of farewell as they advance onto the *marae*, because they are not permitted, as close relatives, to orate. This *karanga-like* oration enables them to express their feelings without transgressing inhibiting protocols, and to deliver a eulogy of sorts but in an indirect way:

> *Mo te 'reo tāne', ae, kua rongo au [i] te tāne e poroporoaki ana [i] te wā e piki mai ana ki runga [i] te marae. Te nuinga o ēnei, he tino tata ki te tūpāpaku, no reira, na te mea kāre rātau e āhei ki te tū ki te whaikōrero, ma tēnei ka taea te whakaputa mai o ngā korero kai roto, [i] a rātau e mau ana.*[64]

The Event of the Day: The *Take*, the *Kaupapa*

Apart from at a *tangihanga*, speakers adopt myriad stylistic ways in which to talk about the event of the day, the *kaupapa* or the *take*. Some introduce the subject with a proverb; others use prophecy, a biblical utterance, a song, *haka*, genealogies, historical narratives or a combination of any of these. The ability of an orator to link these introductory components to the theme of the day and then develop them serves as an indicator of the speaker's proficiency. A great thing about *whaikōrero* is that an audience can never predict what issues an orator might raise, apart from when the occasion is a *tangihanga*. The orator has a 'speaking licence' that allows him to introduce any new topic; follow up on previously mentioned topics; and talk about historical narratives, politics, law, health and education amongst many others. The main goal for the orator should be to ensure that the *kaupapa* of his delivery dominates the oration rather than the peripheral material.

The Complementary Song: The *Waiata*

The most accurate indicator that a speech is drawing to an end is the commencement of the complementary song. Not all of the *whaikōrero* samples provided (only nine in fact) have a complementary song as such. Two have *haka* instead. Again, we can only ponder the period when, as some informants say, song forms were first used to finish off an oration, especially in the absence of recordings prior to the early 1900s. Because these informants are now aged in their mid-fifties and sixties, they are recalling times when they would have been in their teens. They saw their elders orating around 1950, and eventually became practitioners themselves. The use of song to conclude orations appears to be less sanctioned than other components of *whaikōrero*, and practices vary even within single tribes. It would be fair to say, however, that it is rare nowadays for an oration not to be complemented with a *waiata*, *haka* or *ngeri*. In addition to enhancing the oration, occasions that incorporate a song of some kind help ensure the continued transmission of knowledge and historical events contained within those compositions – compositions not specifically composed to support speeches. In addition, the song allows participation by the group. Because members of the supporting group are represented by the speaker and do not get to speak as individuals, performing a supporting song affords them the opportunity to express the way they feel about the occasion. They can share in the joy, anger or poignancy of the event through their vocal and physical participation.

Nevertheless, there are variations in the delivery of songs and the explicitness of any rules surrounding their delivery. For example, Kāretu states that in his opinion, regardless of the direction an oration takes, the traditional chant-like song form known as *waiata koroua*, *waiata tahito* or *mōteatea* should be employed to conclude a speech:

> *Ko au hoki kei te kī inā tū te tangata ki te whaikōrero, ahakoa pēhea nei te piki, te heke, te kotiti noa rānei o te kōrero, me whai atu ko te waiata koroua, kaua ko tētahi waiata-ā-ringa.*[65]

Mahuta concurs: 'Even though two or three waiata may have occurred in a speech to illustrate different points, a speaker will still try to end his speech with a waiata.'[66] Hohepa, in commenting about Te Taitokerau, notes that – as with other components of *whaikōrero* – songs are becoming a given, and rules are starting to emerge about where they should be included, who should sing them and which songs should be performed.[67] But there is clearly room for flexibility and creativity: Moorfield observed Wiremu Tawhai of Te Whānau-a-Apanui including parts of songs after different sections of his oration.[68] With reference to northern tribes, Te Patu Hohepa says that it is not necessary to have one complementary song for each speaker – having one song after five speeches is acceptable practice.[69] Of course, this would apply to tribes that adhere to the *pāeke*, follow-on, speaking pattern.

'*Kei nga waiata nei ka kitea te tohungatanga o o tatau tipuna ki te whakatakoto i nga kupu o te reo Maori*'.[70] In this statement, Ngata reiterates that it is in the traditional song forms mentioned by Kāretu above that the eloquence of Māori of former times can be clearly heard. The songs contain the ideologies, philosophies and viewpoints of the particular periods in which they were composed. With reference to the *mōteatea* series of traditional Māori songs collated by Sir Āpirana Ngata, Bruce Biggs comments that all 'New Zealanders will be grateful for Te Hurinui's translations, which open to them the portals of another way of life, now gone forever'.[71] As an extension of a learning forum, individuals who are specialists in song are usually assigned or expected to lead in the supporting song. Some speakers actually use song to begin their orations in place of *tauparapara* because of the appropriateness of the lyrics to the event and to what the experienced orator intends to say. Mahuta makes the point that a Waikato elder, Ngapaka Kukutai, held the opinion that including a song early in the *whaikōrero* indicated a shift away from eulogies to speaking about the living.[72]

The following comments by Tauroa and McLean espouse the benefit of including *waiata* in *whaikōrero*, explaining that –

> . . . when the waiata is appropriate to what has been referred to in the whai kōrero, the mana of the group and the speaker is heightened.[73]

> A European would think it most strange if a guest speaker were to burst into song before, after or during a speech, but on the marae the reverse is true. In days past it would have been unusual for a speaker not to do this. And today, particularly amongst the older speakers, it is still custom to follow it with a waiata (song) of relevance to the subject, in which the speaker will generally take the lead and will be helped by his supporters. Often there will be several waiata or pao during the course of a speech.[74]

Unless poorly or erroneously performed, the supporting song should add to the overall quality of the speech. Just recently, during a *pōhiri*, I heard the designated speakers proposing that a certain number of songs would be required for a certain number of speakers. Someone quipped that 'if the oration is of quality it will be aptly supported with a song', a polite hint that should the oration fall short, then perhaps it would not receive a song, and some jovial discussion ensued amongst the womenfolk. At other times it is possible for a great oration to be finished off anticlimatically with a 'dead' song of support: lacking in thematic relevance or simply sung without any enthusiasm.

There is a strong assertion that when a speaker launches into his oration with words such as '*tihei mauri ora!*', he is establishing this particular setting as *tapu*, imbedding it with all the sanctity, formality, spirituality and revere of the Māori world. Conversely, the complementary song is the means by which this *tapu* is removed from the oration: '*ka riro mā te waiata e whakanoa*'.[75] Kereopa follows on by saying that women are more able to lift this *tapu* than their male counterparts.[76] The men (of Tūhoe) effect the same lifting of the *tapu* by launching into a chant, or *haka*.[77] Hohepa Kereopa put it like this:

> Males need to *waiata* and *haka* at the end to get out of the *tapu*. Women, because they have the power of *noa*, need only *waiata*. The women should start the *waiata*, not the men. Nowadays, we all do the *waiata*, and don't *haka* at the end. . . . if I was to stand up and *whaikōrero*, and not go through the proper process, then straight after, when I sit down, I am open to challenge. If I go through the correct process, then there is no ground for anyone to challenge me.[78]

Again, this highlights the complementarity of roles between Māori men and women, and the particular power of women in traditional Māori belief systems to maintain equilibrium. It is not only Tūhoe who believe that a *waiata* should finish off the oration to lift the *tapu*. The belief is also shared by Te Whakatōhea and Ngāti Porou.

Song during *whaikōrero* has other functions. It can be used to crystallise the *take* of a speaker, or to end a speech that the group accompanying the speaker feels does not do them or their cause justice. Melbourne remembered an occasion when a speaker failed to verbalise the issues his group wanted him to express, and spoke his own mind instead. As a consequence, the elderly women of the group told him to sing his own song – '*Māna anō e waiata tāna ake waiata.*'[79] This was a clear indication that he and his group were not unanimous in their thinking. The group did not own what he said and it was a disclaimer of sorts.

I have been present on occasions where the women have launched into a song in order to end the oration of their representative speaker who was detracting from the positive spirit of the assembly and airing his criticism of what had transpired. This is a mechanism by which host people are able to salvage the dignity of their *marae* and to protect their *mana*. This may not constitute an outright disagreement about what the speaker is saying, but rather a recognition that the time and place are inappropriate.

On another occasion, on my own *marae* of Painoaiho, a visiting group from Waikato arrived to mourn a person recently deceased. The speaker sounded like a scratched record, repeatedly going over things he had already said. His repetitiveness seemed to be more of a cover up for having nothing else to say rather than a conscious oratorical technique to reinforce what he had said. He did not appear to have reached the end of his oration when one of the women from his entourage stood up and started singing a song of conclusion. The group had obviously become embarrassed because of his failure to represent them eloquently.

Choosing an accompanying song to complement a speech requires careful thought and should be considered well in advance of the actual oration so that the speaker, and the group, do not appear disorganised while they debate what to sing. Dewes draws a parallel between orations and the composition of songs because they both enable a person to express his or her feelings about current events.[80] The selection of appropriate songs is a finishing touch that can be viewed as the ultimate demonstration of an orator's ability to enhance the meaning and maximise the drama of his oration overall.

It would be a tricky task for somebody to assess just how many speakers have the knowledge to make this type of evaluation, because one would need to possess an extraordinary working knowledge of tribal songs throughout the land. Song forms vary and include *waiata tangi* (laments), *waiata aroha* (love songs), *oriori* (lullabies), *pao* (topical songs), *pātere* (songs mapping a route and events of significance), *waiata-ā-ringa* (action songs), *hīmene* (hymns), *waiata karakia* (prayers in song form) and *waiata ngahau* (songs of enjoyment).

Waea Mauriohooho's advice to Moorfield was that the accompanying song should fit the occasion. For example, a funeral should be accompanied by a poignant song.[81] Reality, however, often falls short of the ideal. When secondary school groups act as hosts or are out visiting, for example, they often perform an action song, hymn or modern group song. At times an orator might compromise their position on the appropriateness of the song and indulge the majority by allowing his supporting group to sing a song known by most of them. This shows unity and respect for all. When the occasion is one of joy or celebration, a speaker may take the opportunity to share his repertoire of music and his singing prowess by including songs of a more entertaining nature. From the late 1990s through to the present, there has been a resurgence in the use of the traditional Māori song form known as *mōteatea*. Pupils of Kura Kaupapa Māori (Māori Immersion Schools) and Reo Rua (Bilingual Units) are proactive users of traditional Māori songs because of the passionate belief that these provide the ultimate complement to orations.

Dewes notes that in former times Ngāti Porou performed *mōteatea*, but have subsequently moved to more modern songs and *haka*.[82] An example of a *mōteatea* that a Ngāti Porou group of old might have sung includes the words '*Tūhoe moumou kai, moumou taonga, moumou tangata ki te pō*'. This is a respectful salutation by Ngāti Porou to the Tūhoe people. Dewes explains that Ngāti Porou also use action songs. The themes of many action songs, especially those written during the era of World War II, express hatred for Hitler, encourage their soldiers to return home and mourn those who did not.[83]

There has been concern about the substitution of traditional Māori song with entites such as action song: 'If the use of the tauparapara and the waiata should ever lapse on the marae or if action song is allowed to take its place, the Maori people will have lost a vital part of their heritage'.[84] Such an erosion has been taking place for some time, however. In the mid-1800s, Wilson observed that Christian hymns had become substitutes for traditional Māori song.[85]

More recently there have been claims that Māori youth are more interested in modern Māori compositions than the comparatively monotone 'trad' *mōteatea*. Kāretu has no reservation in defending the *mōteatea*, however, arguing that even teenagers can be encouraged to adopt the traditional song type rather than reverting to the action song and hymn.[86]

In terms of song selection, a major *faux pas* is to duplicate a song that has already been sung. I have seen it happen and the comments about the group who repeated the song were negative, to say the least. It reflects an undereducated group who obviously have only one song to their name.

It is unlikely that one tribe will use a song of another to complement their *whaikōrero*, but it has been known. Haupeke Piripi, a northern speaker, once sang a song associated with the visiting group in jest (see Sample whaikōrero 5 on p. 190), with reference to Ngāti Awa having 'stolen' a Ngāti Porou *haka*. Capitalising on historic accusations that Ngā Puhi stole the Mātaatua canoe, Haupeke said that he would now steal their song as well.[87] Some orators, especially those who are first up to speak, take the opportunity to 'get in first' and sing a song they know before anyone else does – a song which might potentially be sung by the visitors – forcing the guests to reach further into their repertoire to find a fresh, unsung song. Some orators cheekily do this on purpose to challenge their friends on the opposing bench. If the latter speakers are able to answer the call, they are duly acknowledged (without being openly credited of course). If the succeeding speaker(s) are unable to produce a new song, they may wittily reply with some excuse or confession to fuel the banter.

Despite all the song forms available, the traditional form remains the most favoured. Forty years ago Mead noted reasons for the continued appreciation of old songs. The same holds true today:

> It now becomes a little clearer why Maori chant has persisted so long and why devotees of it are so dedicated to its perpetuation. First and foremost, it is an art form, an aesthetic activity of the highest order, which delights the senses. Performers of old chant are able to share the aesthetic experience of the original composers and of the generations who have passed on. At the same time they can give pleasure to the present devoted public with such beautifully contrived illusions . . . .[88]

There is flexibility as to who should start off the complementary song. Because most orators and their groups have come to some prior agreement as to what the song will be, there is normally also an understanding as to who will start it off. Some orators prefer to launch their own songs, while others are prepared to let their groups do so. There is a degree of complementarity involved now only in the subject matter of the oration and the song, but also in the delivery of each. While Pukepuke heard his elders comment that if an orator does not have a song, he should not speak[89] – perhaps inferring that the orator should be prepared to sing his own song – some men will defer to the women when it comes to starting the song even if they are accomplished speakers and singers.

Some Tūhoe speakers maintain that the orator himself should start the song. Malcolm of Te Arawa says that Te Arawa formerly had the speaker himself or a male supporter begin the accompanying song, whereas nowadays it is the women, the son or a designated songster. Women are better singers, he says.[90] Ngāti Pikiao, another subtribe amongst Te Arawa, have a male lead in the song.[91]

At the funeral of Percy Murphy, which I attended in 2009 at Rangitahi Marae in Murupara, I observed a speaker from a neighbouring *marae* assisting with the orations of the host Rangitahi Marae. Upon his first delivery, the local school launched into a tribal composition, less specific to the *marae* from whence the orator came, but strongly advocated by Rangitahi Marae and the songsters there. When the speaker stood for the second time, he quickly launched into a song more suited to the genealogical affiliations of his own *marae*. Complementary songs can carry political undertones. In this case, songs were used to assert the autonomy of *marae* and individuals and the maintenance of identity. Another speaker might have been quite comfortable in accommodating an appropriate song known by the majority rather than performing a solo.

Ngāti Porou seem to vary their practice in that the women sometimes start off the song and sometimes a particular singer – male or female – is responsible for this.[92] 'Married couples often co-operate where the husband orates and the wife assists with the waiata'.[93] Some orators cunningly –

> . . . circumvent the expectation of others to conclude their *whaikōrero* with *waiata* by jovially 'passing on' the prospect to successive speakers, with a statement like: 'Mā te mea i muri i ahau te waiata' (the next speaker has the *waiata*). Thus, there are times when not all speakers will conclude with *waiata*, but rather one *waiata* is performed to encompass all. Often this arrangement occurs when the visitors are from the same area and/or belong to the same organisation and, therefore, have come as a unified entity.[94]

There is no simple, one-size-fits-all model of where the song should be performed on the *marae* because of the diverse locations in which *whaikōrero* now take place. As older *marae* were more spacious, the positioning of the speakers, and consequently the singers, was more fixed.

> At no time should any speaker – whether on the marae-atea or in the whare – turn his back on the opposite paepae. When a marae-atea speech is concluded, the kai korero should be standing in such a position that those who support him or her for the waiata do not have to walk any distance to join them.[95]

As a general rule, the singers avoid positioning themselves in front of the orator. They may be beside him, but typically stay slightly behind. Again, the orator can be considerate and locate himself in a position that allows the supporting singers to situate themselves appropriately.

At times I have observed indecision amongst some supporting singers about whether to sit down straight after they have sung, or to remain standing while the orator makes his closing comments. Tūhoe often sit down immediately, allowing the orator to finish on the 'podium', but Kāretu and Tait have noticed an increasing tendency for support groups to remain standing after they have sung.[96] Temara cautions against this, just in case the speaker draws out his speech, leaving them standing foolishly behind.[97] For example, Kruger refers to Arapeta Awatere including more than three songs in his speech, which would have left the singers looking very out of place if they had stood throughout.[98] Tait observes that the practice of supporting speakers remaining standing after they have sung is more a Te Arawa practice, reiterating that the supporting song denotes the ultimate conclusion of the *whaikōrero*.[99] From the audience's point of view, there is more freedom for people to shuffle, whisper or reorganise themselves during a song. While the speaker is in full cry, he should be the focal point for everyone.

After the main body of the *whaikōrero* has finished and the concluding song has been sung, the speaker might make some final closing statements. Some speakers make their concluding remarks prior to the song. These comments may be short, medium or, in some cases, long, if the orator decides to embark on another almost new chapter, even when they have just said that they would keep the 'pipe' short. This sometimes leaves the audience feeling bewildered and wondering when the *whaikōrero* will actually finish. And it can lead to more embarrassment for the singers if they are standing waiting for the speaker to end.

Concluding remarks come in various forms. If they occur prior to the concluding song, the speaker may use the words '*he wai*' (a song). After the song, he may say '*ka huri*' (I turn), as he heads back to his seat, or else, '(*e*) *tau ana*', '*tau ana ki raro*' or '*kei raro*', all of which indicate that the speaker has finished.

The national anthem of concluding remarks has '*Āpiti hono, tātai hono*' imbedded in some variant form – for reasons we shall discuss shortly. Frequently, the concluding comments express the belief that hosts and visitors are the living embodiment of all their ancestors and extended families. When the hosts and visitors meet in these formal settings on *marae*, it is viewed as a unification of all the genealogical relationships of the living and those who have passed. Put simply, when the two entities meet, 'the association of the visitor and host at the physical level is paralleled at the spiritual level . . . the dead are joined to the dead and the living are joined to the living'.[100]

A generic form that expresses this belief is:

Āpiti hono, tātai hono.
Te hunga mate, ki te hunga mate.
Āpiti hono, tātai hono.
Te hunga ora, ki te hunga ora.

Join the genealogical bonds
That unify the dead in the spiritual world
And so shall the familial bonds of the living be intertwined
As we meet in this tangible realm.[101]

Some speakers, either consciously or erroneously, substitute the words '*āpiti hono, tātai hono*' with '*tawhiti hono, tātai hono*', '*tāpiti hono, tātai hono*', or '*āwhiti hono, tātai hono*'. One can only surmise that these are tribal and/or individual variant forms, but the message, or the intent, still seems to be the same. The following are a few examples of its application.

Āpiti hono, tātai hono, rātou te hunga mate ki a rātou, tātou hoki te hunga ora, tēnā koutou, tēnā koutou, kia huihui mai tātou katoa.[102]
He poto noa iho rā hoki te kōrero mō rātou, kāti anō, ko tēnei, āpiti hono, tātai hono, koutou te hunga wairua kua wehe atu nei, kua takahia atu te ara whānui e ngā mātua, e ngā tūpuna, nā reira, moe mai koutou, moe mai koutou, moe mai koutou.[103]

I have heard this form being used by speakers from Waikato, Te Arawa, Ngāti Manawa, Ngāti Porou, Raukawa and Taurangamoana, and some of the samples provided have speakers from Rongowhakaata and Te Taitokerau using it as well.[104]

There are mixed views about the widespread use of such utterances. They are sometimes viewed positively for the fact that they identify the speaker's tribal affiliations, or demonstrate the knowledge a speaker has for the tribe with whom the turn of phrase is synonymous. Using powerful stock phrases such as these can add authority to the oration and credibility to the budding orator. On the flip side, the use of such phrases can be taken as showing a speaker's lack of creativity or knowledge.

After hearing this utterance over and over, it was refreshing to hear Te Wharehuia Milroy add a fresh spin and use the words '*Waiho ake te aka o te rangi ki a rātou mā, Ko te aka o te whenua ki a tātou nei . . .*'.[105] The meaning is similar in that it asserts the link between the spirit world and the material world and that we, the living, continue our social relationship(s) with each other.

Another stock phrase used to conclude *whaikōrero* is

Eke, eke	She lifts, she ascends
Eke, panuku!	She glides into safety!
Hui e –	O unity –
Taiki e –	O victory –

To this day, the descendants of the Te Arawa canoe use this chant to round off speeches of welcome. The concluding words, raised in a thunderous chorus, express the wish that all will be well with the tribe and its guests.[106]

Although Buck asserts that this is a Te Arawa phrase, it is also a phrase that is widely used.

It may be that speakers with dual or multiple affiliations, due to intertribal marriage, include such phrases in their *whaikōrero*. The younger generation of speakers appears to employ stock phrases more than experienced and/or aged orators. It seems likely that in this age of information technology and ease of travel, trainee orators now have access to wide-ranging oratorical examples on which to model their own *whaikōrero*.

Another probable reason for the general adoption of stock phrases originally specific to one tribe is the education system. Prominent indigenous Māori language and culture teachers often come from specific tribes. As they educate Māori youth nationwide, their tribally linked knowledge becomes Māori knowledge for their students who, when their time comes, use utterances that are more particular to the tribal affiliations of their tutors rather than their own.

Aside from finishing with a song or some closing comments, another means to end *whaikōrero* is by handing over the *koha*. Te Hiko Hohepa says that, in fact, the *koha* is the last component of the *whaikōrero*.[107] Some hand the *koha* over before the song, some do it during the song and some do it after. The only real consistency is that it normally happens after the main body of the oration (see also chapter 8).

Variant Structures of *Whaikōrero*

Whaikōrero inside the *wharenui* may take a variety of forms. Some speakers do not give *tauparapara*.[108] Little has been written about the differences between the structure of *whaikōrero* conducted out on the open courtyard and those performed inside the meeting house. The following are merely possible structures appropriate for *whaikōrero* whether inside or out, as revealed by researchers, historians, ethnographers, exponents and the samples which they provide.

Barlow gives the following:

> tauparapara (ritual chant) + mihi ki te hunga mate + mihi ki te whare tūpuna + mihi ki a Papa-tū-ā-nuku + mihi ki te hunga ora + pūtake kōrero i runga i ngā whakaritenga o te hui + waiata.[109]

Salmond's model is similar:

> *whakaaraara + tau + mihi mate + mihi ora + (take) + waiata*
> call + chant + greet dead + greet living + topic + song.[110]

Tauroa's model is:

> tauparapara + mihi marae / whare + mihi hunga mate + take (reason for gathering) + waiata + closing comments[111]

Salmond describes a variation on the structure by describing an occasion 'where the boundaries of typical *whaikōrero* were broken. A speaker, who was infuriated by events, demonstrated his disapproval by "ditch[ing] all preliminaries," launching himself straight into the *take* and, later . . . refus[ing] to sing an accompanying *waiata*.'[112]

Mahuta says 'Any formal speech worthy of the name whaikoorero will contain an introduction, a central part or body, and a conclusion.'[113]

In the sample structures in the appendix, the '*' denotes that a section may be shifted and is not in a fixed position.

It is worth considering whether there is an apparent move towards standardisation of the structure of *whāikorero*. Variant structures provide uniqueness, freshness and vitality. Reedy says that with standardisation, the 'creative dimension of *whaikōrero* is lost' and *whaikōrero* are monotonous.[114] Kruger asks how *whaikōrero* can be entertaining and enticing when they follow standardised structures and orators seem to copy or seek to emulate others.[115] Mahuta comments that some orators are possibly scared to deviate in case they are reprimanded. Consequently,

> during *whaikōrero*, a speaker may confine himself to traditional patterns and to certain stereotyped phrases that have come to be used for particular types of whaikōrero. Nevertheless, he is still free to develop a personal style in terms of his ingenuity in selecting appropriate phrases and chants for his speech.[116]

When the *whāikorero* is rote-learned and standardised, the womenfolk get bored, Mahuta says. Variation and uniqueness, says Te Patu Hohepa, are what separate the elite speakers from the mainstream:[117]

> The *take* is optional, and many speeches follow through the ritual greetings without ever launching into general discussion. . . . Orators do abandon this sequence in moments of particular inspiration, but usually they follow it closely, and address their inventiveness to its poetic embroidery instead.[118]

Personally, I believe that there is a strong correlation between standardisation and the *mana* of the speaker. That is, the more expert and knowledgeable the speaker, the greater chance there is that he will avoid repetition and/or standardisation. The dilemma that young orators face is 'whether or not they should conform to the standards of contemporary *whaikōrero*, or test the boundaries. Whatever they choose, they still risk meeting with the support or rejection of their elders.'[119]

Kruger firmly believes that the goal should not be to imitate others, but to pursue oratory at its best.[120] If this means an orator includes ten songs, ten proverbs and ten tribal mottos, so be it.

Wide-ranging descriptions of *whaikōrero* from the perspective of numerous *kaumātua* suggest that speakers should be conscious of the impact (or lack of it) of their *whaikōrero* on the audience. While *whaikōrero* should remain within the boundaries of etiquette, there should be space for innovation. When conscious deviations from *whaikōrero* norms occur due to the speaker's knowledge and understanding, then *whaikōrero* will be more interesting, elaborate and reach the quintessence of *whaikōrero*, that is, quality oration as opposed to prototypical oration. With only slight deviations in mind at this stage, I look forward to a future when *whaikōrero* are alive, and not limited to rigid and predictable structures; a future where *whaikōrero* can hold the attention of listeners purely because individual speakers are creative enough to apply their 'personal touch'. Tragically, the art of *whaikōrero* has been undermined and, possibly through ignorance, arrogance or complacency, a sense of impiety has developed regarding the true value of *whaikōrero*. The effect of such impiety has been to the detriment of quality *whaikōrero*, as Kāretu outlines in chapter 10 (see page 167).

Does having a 'system' of *whaikōrero* strengthen or weaken the art of *whaikōrero*? Are *whaikōrero* formulae made formulaic only because they have been noted by researchers and thus fixed as cultural tags? And why should an orator who chooses to deviate from the system or structure of *whaikōrero* be deemed arrogant, ambitious, ignorant or naive, as opposed to innovative and/or inspiring? Is the system of *whaikōrero* nothing but a 'psychological fence' of behavioural normalisation, whereby an orator who tests its boundaries is wounded by the 'barbs' of conformity. Are there orators, or potential orators, courageous enough to shift the 'fence', and are there elders who will allow the 'fence' to be moved by the orator, so that it may better encapsulate the vast and beautiful landscape of oratorical potential?[121]

Chapter Ten

The Future of *Whaikōrero*

Whaikōrero is a survivor – well, at least the art form has outlived the *moa* and the musket wars. It survived the phases of suspicion of educated Māori who, up until the late 1900s, were reluctant to share their knowledge outside of Māori constructs and paradigms. It survived the decline and suppression of the Māori language, and it has survived Eurocentrism. It has not, however, survived without undergoing changes, some of which have been a direct result of the very things mentioned above. With the changes, some of the traditional processes of selection, succession, acquisition and knowledge, and even the forums that allowed this practice to survive and remain integral to *whaikōrero*, have had to be reconsidered by Māori. From being a highly valued practice, because it was restricted to a select group in the past, does *whaikōrero* still have this status that, in effect, makes it a privilege? Has the language of *whaikōrero* changed? Has the learning process changed? Has its application changed? I look at some changes and play visionary to see what changes, if any, lie on the oratorical horizon.

Changes in *Whaikōrero*

It seems to me that *whaikōrero* is not appreciated as a privilege nowadays. Whereas *whaikōrero* was once a life-learned experience and what I view as part of a social progression in the course of a man's lifetime, it has since been fast-tracked, as a corollary to the renaissance efforts to revitalise the Māori language, to the point that an adult individual can potentially practise as an orator within four years of beginning to learn the language. The Māori language itself is the critical ingredient here. Through colonisation and one of its most pernicious practices, language suppression, the Māori language by the early twentieth century was in a state of erosion and potential death. Then, around the 1930s, there was a shift in thinking and educationalists adopted the view that cultural traditions had a valid place in the education of a people. The world wars, particularly World War II, made an impact by removing many Māori speakers from their homes and communities. Around the 1950s, Māori viewed the Western world and its practices favourably to such a degree that they encouraged their children to speak English. Post-war urbanisation saw the continued exit of Māori from rural communities, the sanctuaries of Māori language and custom, through to the mid-1970s. This contributed to the greatest loss of language. Around the same period, Māori lobbied for the Māori language to be taught in schools.

One of the effects of this lobbying was that the Māori language became an asset and an advantage for individuals, whether they were Māori or not. It propelled younger Māori at a faster rate to the status normally reserved for elders with years of experience, knowledge and language, and did so prematurely in some cases. Educational providers, in championing the cause for Māori language revitalisation, equipped students with the linguistic means to orate, so that what might have taken forty years or so to learn was now compressed into just four or five. This has basically given rise to two different types of orator: the orator who focuses his learning with the primary intention of being an eloquent orator, and the 'homegrown' Māori who acquires his knowledge from wherever he can find it, collecting like a magpie gems of histories, genealogies, utterances and experiences that can be used in a context that is normally associated with knowledge and authority, and the generational transmission of these.

How recognisably different is an oration by the 'roots orator' from that of the scholar? The language itself is still distinctly Māori. As in former times, *whaikōrero* of today still include genealogies, proverbs, historic narratives, songs, allusions, metaphors and similes amongst the myriad linguistic devices. I doubt that any empirical data has been quantified to make concrete comparisons on the usage of such devices between recent decades, let alone the nineteenth and twentieth centuries.

In my view, the learning process of *whaikōrero* has changed over the years in accordance with the state of the Māori language, Māori culture and national government commitments to things Māori. The future of *whaikōrero* will adjust similarly as these aspects change. The major developments in the learning process of *whaikōrero* are two-fold, the first being Māori language acquisition, and the second being the utilisation of electronic resources to acquire *whaikōrero* samples and Māori knowledge for incorporating into actual *whaikōrero*. This will happen over the next 50 years or so. By 2100 we might expect to see an increasing number of Māori language speakers. Therefore, all things going to plan, there will be less emphasis on Māori language acquisition. Māori knowledge, however, will continue to be accessed through Western forms of knowledge dissemination as the greater Māori population continues to reside in major cities, away from the more traditional *marae*-styled education forums specific to tribal entities. Māori knowledge will become more pan-Māori because of the increased access to information shared across the internet. I doubt that technology will automate *marae* participants out of existence during formal *marae* protocols, but perhaps we will see Māori knowledge (Māori language included) acquired through contemporary media with the fine tuning provided by traditional *marae* forums.

I believe the application of *whaikōrero* will continue as it does today, but I say this with a hint of pessimism. There is a risk that the invitation to *whaikōrero* will increasingly become a highly tokenistic means to meet a Treaty of Waitangi commitment by mainstream entities increasingly engaging with Māori. As Māori, we avail ourselves to add importance to formal proceedings with the full appreciation that the cultural obligations start with the preparation of the venue, such as the *marae*, and requirement that hosts be physically engaged throughout the duration of the proceedings, including packing up after the visitors have departed. Non-Māori, however, do not experience the same obligation and even as hosts, may depart immediately after eating with the visitors. Cultural tokenism also occurs when Western entities invite Māori to participate solely as speakers, fulfilling the formal exchange of speeches, and then open the proceedings up, for example, to the Vice-Chancellor to discuss the purpose of the forum. In this sense, *whaikōrero* has become the access key to dialogue with Māori that, while being important, is contrary to the dialogic tradition of *whaikōrero*.

What would make these oratorical exchanges less tokenistic, in my opinion, would be for non-Māori to acquire an understanding of the language to appreciate the richness of verbal exchanges between speakers. An eloquent orator might wonder whether it is worth their while orating to the best of their ability when the non-Māori hosts they might be representing or the visitors are none the wiser about what is being said. A waste of eloquence. A waste of richness. A waste of knowledge imparted. The value of *whaikōrero*, therefore, would depend on who the participants are and/or the nature of the exchanges. I doubt that non-Māori CEOs or government dignitaries will take the time to become conversant in Māori to a level that will enable them to engage with Māori in Māori. Māori will continue to be employed to undertake this role (token or otherwise) for some time yet and probably forever.

Will Tū-mata-uenga,[1] the principal Māori deity of war and the confrontational essence he represents, continue to be afforded a place on the *marae* during *whaikōrero*? Will he still assume a presence during *whaikōrero*, or merely exist as a romanticised, inferred potential of a bygone era within this new world?

There are perhaps three governing philosophies of old imbued in the position of the orator. First, they may have had the right to orate passed down to them through bloodlines; second, they may have had authority conferred upon them from the people they have served appropriately; or third, they may have been elevated to that status because of what they have achieved through their own self-determination. All of these give credence to the individual in establishing his right to orate, but it does not end there because the individual then needs to prove his worthiness as a recipient of that privilege. As Kāretu says, '*He tokomaha ngā tāngata kōrero, engari ngā tāngata whaikōrero!*' (Speakers of Māori are a dime a dozen, but eloquent orators are more scarcely sought).[2] One might read into this that orators should aspire and endeavour to be more than a mere speaker with Māori language fluency. That which is rote learned should take second place to the spontaneous and the creative.

A Glance Back in Time

To see the shift in *whaikōrero*, let us first draw some comparisons regarding *whaikōrero* as observed by informants and authors from 1844 to 2002. The first recorded description was made by George French Angas. He wrote that one *whaikōrero* he heard at a funeral in Ngāhuruhuru in 1844 was one of the 'finest and most impassioned bursts of eloquence he had ever heard'.[3]

Reedy observes that orators, probably up until around 1975, were proficient in the art with a comprehensive command of speaking, total body movement and use of hand accompaniments.[4] Milroy, in drawing comparisons, says that he had not seen anyone with such a command during the late 1980s and mid-1990s.[5] A salient difference observed by Kruger of Tūhoe and Malcolm of Te Arawa is that later speakers lacked the philosophical depth that former speakers engaged in.[6] Kruger opines that some speakers are mistakenly viewed as expert orators on the basis of their stance, posture, body movement and use of hand accompaniments, when in fact they fail to address any issues with serious depth or breadth.[7] Sir George Grey, as documented by Ward, noted during one of his terms as Governor of New Zealand (1845–1853, 1861–1868) that –

> ... according to the custom of the nation, the most effective speeches were invariably principally made up from recitations of portions of ancient poems. . . . the art of the orator was shewn by his selecting a quotation from an ancient poem, which figuratively, but dimly, shadowed forth his intentions and opinions. As he spoke, the people were pleased at the beauty of the poetry, and at his knowledge of their ancient poets, whilst their ingenuity was excited to endeavour to detect, from his figurative language, what were his intentions and designs. Quotation after quotation were rapidly and forcibly chanted, and made his meaning clearer and clearer; curiosity and attention were by degrees riveted upon the speaker, and if his sentiments were in unison with the great mass of assembly, and he were a man of influence, as each succeeding quotation gradually removed the doubts from the minds of the attentive group who were seated upon the ground around him, murmur of applause rose after murmur of applause, until, at some closing quotation, which left no doubt as to his real meaning, the whole assembly gave way to tumults of delight, and applauded equally the determination he had formed, his poetic knowledge, and his oratorical art, by which, under images beautiful to them, he had, for so long a time, and at least so perfectly, manifested his real opinion.[8]

Around the same period, McGuire wrote: 'The wit and common sense of the Maori were often shown by the proverbs he treasured and used both in daily speech and formal utterances'.[9] Kāretu makes strong his views on *whaikōrero* delivered between 1970 and 1990 in the following:

> What was once a noble and lofty art is fast degenerating into a perfunctory, platitudinous, recited litany of rote-learned words and phrases. The occasions are becoming fewer when one could be moved and stirred by the command of rhetoric, of metaphor, of mythical allusion, of pithy and apposite aphorism, of wit and candour, of subtlety and nuance interspersed with chant where appropriate and concluded with haka.[10]

Kāretu's comments are critical and conscience-provoking, but over and above this, they should be motivating for current and aspiring orators. After I read these words, I became more observant of *whaikōrero*. Unintentionally, I became audaciously judgmental. I was not, and still am not, an orator myself. Nor was I qualified to pass such judgement without being present at the multitude of occasions where *whaikōrero* were being performed. However, I was not alone. You had only to be present to hear spectators criticise the orations being made as substandard.

Changes Brought About by Colonisation, Christianity and Relocation

Societal, technological and cultural changes are inevitable and one major consideration has been how to establish a balance between cultural maintenance and compromise. As well as the maintenance of culture, how do Māori keep young people interested and inspired by traditional practices in a contemporary and rapidly evolving world?

> A superior race may conquer and impose its speech and its worship to a considerable extent upon the vanquished, but many of the old customs still remain ages after conquerors and conquered have been fused into one race.[11]

This statement by Newman is applicable in the case of Māori cultural practices because *whaikōrero* is just one of many that have survived colonisation, assimilation, bi-racial and multi-racial marriage, religious influence and legislation. Māori never lost sight of their Māori cultural practices but changes have happened. Time constraints and urbanisation have played a part in the modification of *marae* practices. *Whaikōrero* are getting shorter and shorter, as a mere formality that people want to get through as quick as possible, says Kereopa.[12] At Te Hiko Hohepa's funeral in Rotorua, I remember seeing two orators remove themselves from the *marae* after presenting their *koha* but without seeing the welcome process through to its conclusion. My eyebrows were raised in wonder as to the reason, or possible reasons for this. Was it a show of arrogance or ignorance, or both? Or was it a glaring example of the pressure of the times when time was indeed of the essence?

One unassailable influence has been the introduction of the English language. 'In this modern day speech making is still considered an art and follows, at least in part, many of the old forms. Mercifully, however, speeches are usually much shorter and will sometimes be bi-lingual with a truncated English version following the Maori.'[13] Malcolm concurs that in former times English was not acceptable during *whaikōrero*, primarily because Pākehā were not in strong attendance at Māori forums where *whaikōrero* was a formality.[14] Over time, however, Pākehā have been more of a presence at Māori funerals, and consequently, have been afforded the opportunity to speak, usually in English. Some of the sample *whaikōrero* provided have English included. Some Māori take the time to paraphrase the essence of their *whaikōrero* in English, albeit a 'filtered' version. Nevertheless, as Salmond found, Māori is still regarded as the only proper language to use on the *marae ātea*. Two old men were cried down for compromising and doing *whaikōrero* in English so that the Minister of Māori Affairs could understand. People 'would rather provide an interpreter and continue to conduct the proceedings in Māori'.[15]

When the ocean-voyaging vessels of the Europeans arrived in the early 1800s, some of the most influential cargo on board came in the form of the Bible and the cross. Evidence of this influence is highly apparent through the opening acknowledgements in *whaikōrero* to a super being, the 'alpha' and 'omega' and God Almighty. Even as far back as 1905, Gudgeon documented the introduction of non-Māori deities into Māori speech forms.[16] Ngāti Porou speakers, says Dewes, have taken to commencing their *whaikōrero* with Christian prayers, translated into Māori.[17] Similarly, Te Taitokerau, who were rapidly colonised in the early 1800s, adopted Christian prayers in place of *tauparapara* and employed hymns as the accompanying songs to conclude orations, at the expense of the traditional Māori.[18] I often find it challenging to interpret whether Māori orators refer to this divine entity monotheistically or polytheistically.

Another critical point in the development of Māori and the evolution of Māori culture has been urbanisation when 'the pressure of population provided the push; the pull came from the towns where labour was in great demand and where wages-money gave opportunities for a fuller life'.[19]

With regard to *whaikōrero*, the urban shift that occurred around 1945–65 had two major effects. The first was on the link between speakers and their *marae*. With diminishing numbers on rural *marae*, the number of speakers also declined. Collegiality amongst neighbouring *marae* resulted in speakers attending other *marae* in order to lend support by being additional personnel for their oratorical seats, so to speak, something that occurred less in the past, says Tahuri.[20] Māori have since begun contingency and succession planning so as to equip their own *marae* with speakers (*kaikōrero*) and callers (*kaikaranga*) and to lessen their dependency upon borrowed speakers. This seems a more appropriate way to safeguard the dissemination of knowledge.

Urban drift also resulted in the establishment of pan-Māori *marae*, educational facilities and Māori organisations such as Hoani Waititi Marae, Te Tira Hou and

Ngāti Pōneke. Although these urban *marae* afforded some autonomy to the group hiring the facilities, *whaikōrero* and the *tauutuutu* or *pāeke* style had already been established as the cultural practice for oratorical exchanges. The movement by young and old to live in different tribal areas also impacted on the practices of their home *marae* because whenever these people returned home, they translocated some of the cultural practices they had been exposed to and become familiar with from beyond their own tribal boundaries.[21] Some Māori cultural observances have had to be made offshore where Māori have established themselves, sometimes over two or three generations. For example, Ngāti Rānana are based in London and Poipiripiri are an Australian-based group. This has, to a large extent, been prompted by the need for a sense of psychological and social belonging or identity. Such cultural adaptations sometimes come under scrutiny, nonetheless, as various groups of Māori strive to maintain the inklings of culture that reaffirm and define them as Māori.

Changes in Language and Knowledge

I have already mentioned the effect of Māori language loss in New Zealand on *whaikōrero*, one difference being the quality of language used by orators. The language of oratory is distinct from that used in day-to-day conversation.[22] In 1997, Milroy opined that there has been a decline in Māori language use and, as a consequence of this, the quantum of highly proficient Māori language speakers has also decreased:

> *Nā te kore e whakamahia o te reo ia rā, nā te ngaro haere o te reo, kāre he kupu katakata, ngahau, kīwaha, kīrehu, whakataukī. Kāre te reo Māori i kōrerohia ia rā, kāre i āta mōhiotia te tikanga ake o ētahi kupu me te wā e tika ana kia kōrerotia tērā kupu. Kāre o ināianei kaikōrero e ōrite ki ō nga wā o mua i te mea ko te puna kupu kua mimiti haere kē, te puna kupu hei whakaahua, hei whakaari i te whakaaro. Ahakoa pēhea, kei te haumate haere te reo ka kaha atu te ngaro haere o te reo, ngā puna kupu, i te tangata, me ngā kupu hei whakaahua i ō whakaaro, hei whakaari i ō whakaaro, ka rerekē haere atu te āhua o te takoto mai o tēnei mea, te whaikōrero, ka noho noa iho ko te mihi noa iho, he mihi noa iho, [he] mihi te mea nui o roto. Ka ihi kore tēnei mea te whaikōrero ka pērā, ka hapa ana.*[23]

I will not delve into the myriad reasons surrounding language loss as there are ample reports on the Māori language renaissance, which provide detailed accounts and statistical data. The critical point, perhaps, is that the Māori language was seen as 'the touchstone of an identity and self-respect already in jeopardy',[24] and still remains the touchstone today, minus the 'jeopardy'. Throughout the fluctuating fortune of the Māori language, it is still, says Dewes, 'the most essential feature of Maori culture, which as a way of life continues to be dynamic.... language proficiency is the goal for those aspiring to excellence in Maori ceremonial and general leadership.'[25]

Hohua Tutengāehe powerfully describes the vitality of the Māori language as the one entity that demonstrates the epitome of Māori spirituality, history, genealogy, ethos, respect, value and cultural values. Māori language, he continues, is the breath of the Māori people:

> *Nā te kī rā o te reo i te wairua Māori koia nei te taonga e kōrero nei ki a tāua. Ko te reo Māori hoki mōku te tikitiki o tōku māhunga upoko tapu, te kuru pounamu o tōku manawa, te taumata o tōku wairua. Koia te taonga e mōhiotia ai tātou, āe, he Māori, ... I roto i te reo ka mau te ia o te tangata, ... Ko te kanohi o te Māori te reo, ko tōna hanga te reo, ko tōna wairua te reo, ko ōna tikanga katoa te reo e horahia ai ki te ao ngā taonga me ngā atua Māori o tuawhakarere.... Koia hoki au i kī ai ko te reo te wairua o te iwi Māori, i te mea ko te hā ko te hauora tēnā. Ka kore he hauora ka mate te tangata.*[26]

Morehu is critical of younger generations who vehemently aspire to be orators but do not have a great command of the Māori language and try to compensate for this by rote-learning Māori incantations.[27] Add a touch of theatrical performance to this and there you have it. Over the period from the mid-1980s to the 1990s, Milroy was so pessimistic about the dearth of highly proficient speakers that he thought *marae* oral formalities might become automated.[28] One can only thank initiatives such as Kura Reo, Te Panekiretanga and some tertiary providers that this has not befallen us – yet.[29]

One cannot deny that languages struggle to maintain the same linguistic qualities that they had in former times, and Māori is no exception. Tupe notes that the language of the old people is no longer heard. What is heard instead is a new generational language.[30]

I will never forget the disappointment expressed by one fluent speaker from the East Coast (Ngāti Porou) about the issue of rote-learnt speaking. At a *pōhiri*, he welcomed the visiting group to the host university of which he was a part. Two young gentlemen responded in kind. He was excited to hear them orate so fluently, and after the formalities, he continued to follow up with this eloquent duo. To his dismay, they spoke to him in English, apparently having limited knowledge of the

Māori language. *Ka rūrū tana māhunga.* He was shocked. The point here is that, while elders also rote-learned stock phrases, chants and incantations, they had the capacity to modify these in accordance with the situation, and they already had a command of the language. The stock phrases were part of a vocabulary and a context: they were not the vocabulary and context themselves.

Merito makes the comment that his elders were knowledgeable about the principles of *whaikōrero*, as opposed to merely knowing how to speak Māori.[31] Oratory was not purely and simply oratory, but rather a critical component of the cultural observations of Māori as a whole. This knowledge base was affected by the prohibition of the Māori language at school, which denied younger generations the knowledge their parents or grandparents might have handed on by word of mouth with Māori as the medium of transfer. It threatened the position of the language at the heart of the culture and in the souls of the people.

The diminishing knowledge facility, says Merito, is a result of changing social systems. When Māori proliferated in concentrated masses, they would readily engage in sharing knowledge on a regular basis, wherever they would meet. More recently, however, this form of exchange has been prevalent only at forums specifically designed for this purpose.[32] The fact that younger generations moved away from *marae* to live in towns also compounded matters in terms of succession planning.

I attended an uncle's funeral in 2008 and, during the course of the orations, my fourteen-year-old daughter had questions. Impressed by the orator, she asked who the speaker was and to what he was referring. The orator was progressing through his *tauparapara* at the time, albeit in the form of a *pātere*, traversing the landscape and reciting names of particular local places. Having grown up humbly as a hunter and shepherd, he was reciting the names of places which, I believe, he would actually have traversed, as opposed to some orators who mention well-known locations but may never have set foot there. Here was an individual who had lived life as a Māori and lived Māori knowledge purely as part of life itself. This knowledge became beneficial as he progressed to the rank of orator. Of course, I relayed his information on to my daughter.

There is a proverb, '*ko te tangata kāre he kai i tōna whata ā-pakapaka, ko tāna he whānako, ka whakamā*', which means, the person without food in his stocks is inclined to pilfer from elsewhere, only to live in shame. I find this analogous to oratory. Orators who are fluent in the Māori language but lack a strong cultural, genealogical or historical narrative base appear to me to borrow, repeat and regurgitate what others have already said incessantly. They borrow from the oratorical pantries of others. The embarrassment, however, is experienced most by the group represented by the orator because nothing new is effectively being said on their behalf. As Milroy points out, if *whaikōrero* become repetitive then we might as well train parrots or press the button on a recording.[33] To regress beyond that would mean delivering orations in English.

Perhaps tongue in cheek, Eruera Manuera alluded in one of his *whaikōrero* to the repetitive nature of Māori oratory and the fact that Māori tend to accept this regurgitation *ad nauseum*. If a speaker were to adopt this manner in a court of law, they would be pulled up for being repetitive.[34] After admitting that he was struggling to provide new information, Eruera quickly sat down, lest he be guilty of exactly what he had just charged. Some speakers stand there at a loss, with nothing to say. They look stupid and their supporting group feel embarrassed. Even worse, some speakers openly confess that they have nothing to say and announce that they are finished, but continue to stand as if the gods will rain down some additional rhetoric.

There seem to be fewer occasions of humorous oratorical exchanges, or it may be that I am primarily disposed to attending *tangihanga*. Hohepa says that his elders did not condone humorous antics during *whaikōrero* and they would chastise a person for joking around.[35] We might wonder whether these occasions were all funerals. Ironically, when Te Hiko himself received his honorary doctorate, many of the orations, including those made by his fellow Te Arawa speakers, were interspersed with humour: the speakers taking full advantage of the opportunity to develop comments by others in a cheeky, but respectful, manner. The point I am raising is whether *whaikōrero* are now a more serious business.

Some posit the idea that it was the Māori academic forums of old that provided the knowledge base for orators. These forums were less available in their traditional form during the 1980s and 1990s. The provision of this knowledge-sharing was then devolved, in the main, to government-funded tertiary providers such as private training enterprises, polytechnics and universities. Around the mid-to-late 1990s, tribes began to revive their own *wānanga* and educational providers with strong tribal bases, such as Anamata (Tūhoe-based) and Te Whare Wānanga o Awanuiārangi (Ngāti Awa-based) and Te Wānanga o Raukawa (Raukawa-based), that emerged to address the cultural knowledge of their people, *whaikōrero* included.[36] The Wānanga o Aotearoa established itself as a major knowledge provider on a national scale and we might now be justified in feeling more assured about the survival of the Māori language and culture, and better educated as indigenous people in general.

How Far Can Tradition Go to Accept Change?

There is another Māori proverb, *Te marangaitanga, he kōawa kē* (From a deluge the stream changes direction). The deluge referred to here is the evolving world. Just as one can never be one hundred per cent certain of the path waterways might take, so it is with the future of Māori customs as Māori seek to retain foundation philosophies, all the while feeling the pressure to adapt to changes in the world at large. With *whaikōrero*, what might the proverbial future hold?

I recall one day tuning into the Māori television channel 'Whakaaturanga Māori' and seeing a formal welcome ceremony for a group of mostly mute visitors.[37] Some of the hosts also appeared to be mute. They seemed to be practising all of the formalities of *whaikōrero*, only they were communicating in sign language. There was an interpreter for the host speaker to give an explanation in English. A visitor responded accordingly, but he was actually speaking Māori. I assume that an interpreter was converting the host's *whaikōrero* into sign language. Is this still *whaikōrero* if there is no actual exchange of words by the orators? And does the provision of a translation in English call into question the whole issue of Māori being the agreed language of *whaikōrero*?

Maintaining the theme of disabilities, let us consider the blind orator. I have not seen or heard of any accounts whereby a blind orator has taken a stand to *whaikōrero*. Hypothetically speaking, the greatest challenge would be having to perform in the presence of the deity Tū-mata-uenga, where speaking might present a physical challenge. A blind orator could have a bodyguard of sorts. If, however, the orations proceeded under the auspices of Tāne-i-te-wānanga, then words and concepts would be all that were required.

One elder of repute was Kepa Hamuera Anaha Ehau (c. 1885–1970) of Ngāti Tarāwhai and Ngāti Whakaue. He was a Māori leader, a law clerk, a tri-lingual interpreter, a soldier, and a historian, and he has been hailed by some as the greatest Te Arawa orator.[38] In his later years, services during the war took their toll and he was confined to a wheelchair. His orations were still admired regardless.

I myself have witnessed *whaikōrero* from wheelchairs on two occasions. The first of these was Te Kurapa Rangiaho (Ranapia) at Waiohau Marae in the 1990s. The second was at a funeral at Maungapōhatu in 2008. There were no physical challenges issued at either of these speakers. The orator at Maungapōhatu faced an 'earthly' obstacle in that the pathways on the *marae ātea* at the time were in the initial stages of development. Having just been dug, they merely prompted the orator to reassess where he should best position himself for the *whaikōrero* exchange and still be audible.

Rather than be caught short for orators, Kruger hoped that his own tribe of Tūhoe would take a more proactive approach in future to ensure that they have an ample supply of proficient speakers:

> . . . *kaua tēnā iwi, tēnā hapū e waiho mā te waimarie noa e hari mai he tānata whaikōrero ki runa i tō marae, enari, māna tonu e whakatipu ōna rangatira whaikōrero.*[39]

In Kruger's comment he says that tribal and subtribal entities should not leave the provision of orators up to 'lady luck' and they should make some investment in developing their own.

Reedy notes that a major difference between the past and the present is that orators of old had a physical presence on a par with their verbal delivery. They employed their bodies to full effect in what he describes as 'drama in its own making'.[40] Straddling these two aspects, of being eloquent and dramatic, Morehu adds that an orator who does not present himself confidently has difficulty enhancing his verbal delivery.[41] Māori-focused knowledge forums, especially those looking at *whaikōrero*, have seen a resurgence in dramatic *whaikōrero*, particularly amongst younger speakers in the 30-to-40-year age bracket. If there is one major change in the way speakers from these groups carry themselves, it is that they now have commonalities as a result of emulating their tutors. Over time, these fortunate orators will continue to develop their stance and alter them on an individual level, so evolving as exemplars for generations after them. This should see physical displays that are on a par with verbal deliveries well into the future.

Whaikōrero for Women?

Pou Temara, staunch though he is on the issue of women delivering *whaikōrero*, threw a curve ball during an interview I had with him when he said that perhaps in the distant future, 60 or 70 years hence, women might actually grace Tūhoe *marae* but this would not happen during his lifetime.[42] He is not the only Tūhoe elder I have heard express this possibility. It remains a possibility until the future reveals itself. Temara gave a glaring example extolling the knowledge and eloquence of Tūhoe women as being equal to or better than some of their male counterparts:

> *Ka hangaia he paepae wāhine, he paepae tāne, kātahi ka hoatutia e māua nei ngā kaupapa. Tū mai ki te whaikōrero, kātahi ka tū mai, karawhiuwhiu rawahia e ngā wāhine ngā tāne rā ki te whaikōrero, ki te tauparapara, ki ngā kōrero o nehe, ki te mau i te rākau, nā te tāne kē rā tērā mahi . . . mamae tonu pea ngā tāne i tērā tauira. I pērā te expose i a rātou, i kitea ai tō rātou tino hē. Kei te pērā anō ki te taha whakararo o Tūhoe ki roto o Rūātoki. He nui ngā kuia pai atu i ngā tāne koroua rā ki te kōrero. Kei te mātau rātou ki ngā āhuatanga, kaupapa o te wā. Ngā koroua rā, i tua atu i te whai-ā-kākā nei, i kō atu i tērā, kua kore e aro i a rātou, nā reira, nā te mātauranga titiro tawhiti, ā tōna wā, e tū ai ngā wāhine o Tūhoe ki te whaikōrero, e kore e taea e koe, e kore e taea e au te kati, engari, te wā i a au e ora nei.*[43]

Haami Piripi of Te Taura Whiri i te Reo Māori (the Māori language Commission) also speaks highly of women:

> Maori communities would have to consider letting women speak on the marae. . . . after the survey showed young women to be the saviours of the language. . . . Young women in particular had a high level of proficiency in the language. . . . 9 per cent spoke it 'well' or 'very well'. . . . If we've got a whole new generation of speakers coming through who are predominantly women, then what will this mean for our communities, our marae?[44]

At a gathering at Mangatoatoa, Henare Tuwhangai (of Waikato-Maniapoto) heard a visiting orator declare that if a woman were to stand on the *marae*, her neck would be snapped – '*ka heriheria koe ki te tū i te marae, ka kōwarihia te māhunga*'. Henare Tuwhangai responded saying, '*Whakarongo mai koutou, aku mātua. E Kohi, kōrua ko Tūranga, kia kopi ō kōrua waha. Mehemea he oranga mō tātou, mō te iwi Māori, kei te kōrero o te wahine, tukua kia kōrero.*' He appealed to his elders, Kohi and Turanga, to listen and not say a thing. He said that if women have something of benefit to say for the people, then they should be allowed to speak. He then redirected his words to the woman at hand who had given rise to the initial comment, saying:

> *E kui, kaua koe hei hopī, e tū koe ki te kōrero. Kei te haere ō kōrero i runga i ngā kaupapa tika e puta ai tātou te iwi Māori. Ka whia tekau tau, rau tau, ngā kaumātua nei e tū ana kia kitea he hua i roto, kārekau ana. Koinā ka kōrerotia e au te kawa o Waikato, kia ngāwari te kawa o Waikato, koutou wāhine mā, ko taku kōrero tēnei, kaua koutou e hopī, e tū ki te kōrero. Hei aha noa iho ngā kawa o Te Arawa e kōrero nei, waiho atu rā rātou, engari, ka tae mai koutou ki ahau, a Hēnare, Tū mai! Kōrero!*[45]

Henare explained the flexibility of Waikato, that authorised the woman to stand and speak, and said she should take no heed of the Te Arawa demand that she remain seated. A long time has passed, said Henare, and there has been little value in what they, Kohi and Turanga, have said. He was giving her licence to address the forum, but not, however, to *whaikōrero*.

With regard to the position held by some tribes, that denying women the right to *whaikōrero* is for their own protection and especially their facility to reproduce, could a case be made for an exemption if the woman is post-menopausal or barren? Her capacity to reproduce is not an issue and the argument against her ability to speak is therefore null and void. Others argue that because of women's unique potential to render sacred acts common, they are not permitted to sit on the speaking platforms. But could a *tohunga* not return the *mana* to those places? If a woman is prepared to risk her potential to reproduce and makes a conscious decision to accept the consequences, should she be allowed to *whaikōrero*?

Is transgender an issue? Are men who have sex changes recognised as men or women on the *marae* and in Māori protocol? If a female from birth has a male appendage surgically added, does (s)he now forfeit the right to *karanga* and now accept the right to *whaikōrero* as a man? Similarly, does the male who has his phallus surgically removed now adopt all the roles traditionally performed by women? The Māori cultural purist needs to have acute vision to identify such persons on their physical appearance alone. At twenty-five metres distance, the application of cosmetics and female dress makes it challenging, for the untrained eye anyway, to make a sound judgement on this gender issue. In order for those tribes with gender-specific strictures to maintain their culturally prescribed protocols as the host tribe, they need to be exceptionally alert and vigilant to these types of changes.

Women are powerful in the Māori world, as of right from birth. This is undeniable, and may not be retracted. In this modern day, women are establishing themselves as powerful individuals at all levels and across all disciplines. 'Maori women have taken over leading our people, not from choice but from need. I don't know what's happening to our men, but I hope eventually they will come back with us.'[46]

Henare foresees a future where Māori women are fully appreciated:

> The status of Maori women and the future of Maori society lies with Maori women and we will not see a strengthened Maori society without that recognition. . . . I believe that we are forgetting to look at our kuia. It is easy to think that ideas spring only from the young, that our elders may have nothing new or visionary about them, but there are many who do. I'm

always astonished at the radical insights of our older women. At times they are far more profound than we are because at the stage they have reached, they've been knocked about sufficiently to have maintained a firm and unalterable hold on their vision. They fear nothing. They do not prevaricate. They are committed to principles, not power.[47]

Robb explains that in 'the oldest Maori traditions, men and women take independent but mutually supportive roles in a welcoming ceremony'.[48] But is the application of the 'oldest Maori traditions' now outdated? Is there a new tradition in the making that will see role swaps and *whaikōrero* by women?

Whaikōrero for Māori Only?

Prior to 1995, Kāretu observed Pākehā assuming the role of orator in the *whaikōrero* setting. He was not entirely pleased with their attempts to *whaikōrero* in Māori, or rather, in a Māori language 'sour to the ear'.[49] There are, nowadays, Pākehā recognisably fluent in the language and knowledgeable in Māori affairs. If Pākehā are highly conversant in Māori, should they then be allowed to *whaikōrero*? Perhaps the most appropriate question is whether or not they should be denied the right to speak. Where I have seen Pākehā permitted to *whaikōrero* I have been unsure whether this latitude was due to their command of the Māori language or their social standing. Individuals of high status all tend to be afforded more leeway in cultural settings.

Notable Pākehā have been acknowledged since the early 1800s. These men have included early missionaries such as Bishop Jean Baptiste Francois Pompallier;[50] authors and writers such as William Colenso,[51] H. Williams,[52] Elsdon Best, George Grey, John White and John Moorfield. It appears that Māori themselves have acknowledged the contribution of such Pākehā and rewarded them with the right to *whaikōrero*. Reilly notes:

> I've often thought when Crown agencies, for example, visit *marae* it would be best if they did their own *whaikōrero* rather than 'employ' a Māori to do it for them (a kind of token face). I've seen Pākehā dominated organisations virtually 'require' one of their Māori members to speak even when it's clear that they are not skilled either at language or *whaikōrero*. I think this rather cruel . . . . as if Pākehā expect all Māori to be able to *whaikōrero*. Yet perhaps Māori prefer that than a Pākehā speaking?[53]

What accommodation, if any, should be made for international visitors? How do they fit into the oratorical sphere of Māori? As they involve themselves in the culture, it is highly probable that they will also want to participate in oratorical exchanges. Some Māori are exceedingly considerate and under the guise of *manaakitanga*, make allowances. Although there is a tendency by Māori, in their thoughtfulness, selflessness, empathy or political correctness to accommodate non-Māori, Tahuri cautions that once we, as Māori, begin to compromise our cultural practices, there is no knowing just where it will end.[54]

The Way to the Future

The whole issue of cultural change, evolution, development, accommodation or whatever variant form change might take, is a topic worthy of extensive debate, but I will not attempt to do it here. Biculturalism could prove challenging in future as New Zealanders juggle with the question of what actually constitutes a bicultural New Zealand. 'To try to live in the past was to show unrealistic defeatism, but to abandon the heritage of their ancestors completely in the attempt to acquire pakeha culture was like starting to cross a dangerous mountain river without a rope.'[55]

Who can actually initiate the changes when we look at *whaikōrero*? Or maybe the bigger question is whether anything can be done to stem the change. Are changes happening purely as a mistake or, as Kereopa says, has *whaikōrero* been breaking down because of a lack of understanding?[56] Tauroa directs his comments at Māori who have not been raised within the culture:

> A culture cannot be learned from a textbook. True understanding and appreciation are possible only from first-hand experience. This has been recognised by both Maori and Pakeha; so, since many Pakeha people have expressed the desire to take part in a 'marae experience', Maori people, aware of their sincerity, are now making special efforts to make marae more widely available to visitors seeking to learn. . . . the Maori has made few concessions to the presence of non-Maori visitors. Maori have continued to maintain customs that they have developed and nurtured for many, many generations. It is essential for all New Zealanders that the Maori maintain the integrity of their culture rather than permit adjustments that are simply intended to make it easier for the non-Maori to fit in.[57]

As we can see, it is not Pākehā who have initiated changes on *marae*. Māori bodies, themselves, have been responsible. This fact led Kāretu to comment:

> It is in recent times that kawa has degenerated in some areas into confusion. The fact that tribes are now actively trying to revive and retain their kawa with as little compromise as possible means that people feel again that there is something of value in such observance. . . .
>
> Many tribes are now settling for convenience rather than what is considered to be correct, and it is this aspect that worries people like myself. It makes all observance of kawa meaningless and useless. . . .
>
> What is the ideal situation? . . . . The experts are still here to teach those who wish to learn, the experts are still here to encourage the keen, the experts are still here to show people how, if only they are prepared to listen and learn. What should be avoided is further compromise and further watering down of kawa to suit the ignorant and the people who say it is anachronistic and time-consuming.[58]

The passive, accommodating nature of Māori, in general, means that many Māori elders are willing to make compromises. Whereas, perhaps, leaders were once prepared to warn a transgressor that their throat would be slit, or their neck trampled, it is now more likely that we only hear the interjectory mutterings of disapproval, or else the three simple, powerful Māori words: '*Kei te pai*' (That's alright. Don't worry about it.). Does the concept of *manaaki* now test the maintenance of culture? There are numerous cases where some compromise has been made, for example, in this account by Awatere:

> *I runga i ngā whaikōrero, i aroha a Ngāti Pikiao ki a mātou, kore rawa mātou, i āritatia mō te tae pō. Ko ngā tikanga me ngā kōrero, e tika ana ki te marae mahia ai, i mauria katoatia a i whakaotia ki roto o te whare nui. I muri o te tuatoru o o mātou kai-kōrero, ka karangatia kia haere ki te kai.*[59]

Here Awatere explains that in terms of *whaikōrero*, the Ngāti Pikiao people were considerate towards Awatere and others and were not offended when they arrived at night. The protocols that normally took place outside on the *marae* were conducted inside the meeting house. The host initiated these proceedings, which indicates to me that the essence of traditional practices is often more important than the way events take place. If meaning is not compromised, actual behaviour and events can be:

> It is a measure of the strength of Maori culture that it has survived five generations or more of active suppression.... The Maoris have a strong sense of cultural identity which they have a determination to preserve. If it were not so, Maoritanga would long ago have succumbed to the pressures to which it has been, and is being, constantly subjected....[60]

Kāretu, writing on customary practices in general asserts:

> Kawa to me epitomises the role of the tangata whenua and the manuhiri in the marae situation with the great respect that it demands of each for the other. To welcome someone, and to be welcomed warmly with all the attendant rituals, is a moving experience. To never again be drawn forward with the karanga, to never again hear the kuia call farewell to the dead, to never again hear the eloquence and excitement of the whaikōrero and waiata, to never again enjoy the warmth of the whare nui, a warmth engendered by all these elements – all this would be to witness the death of part of the justification for human life.[61]

Unfortunately, I do not know anyone who has the prophetic powers to say what course *whaikōrero* and Māori customary practices will take. I am convinced, however, that *whaikōrero* will not cease to exist, unless the Māori people themselves cease to exist or identify as Māori. I take this position because *whaikōrero* is more than a mere speech, as Koro Dewes explains:

> Maori ceremonial (te kawa o te marae) and Maori oratory (te kawa o te whaikorero) best display the integration of individuals and groups, male and female, young and old, noise, speech, chant and melody, gestures, dance and musical accompaniment, traditional and spontaneous renditions, weeping, wailing and laughter. Maori oratory, which is quite dissimilar to Pakeha public speaking, is fused together to give the speaker diverse ways of expressing thoughts and feelings, and its mastery is the pinnacle reached by one well-versed in the oral arts in all their aspects.[62]

Whaikōrero is Māori language. *Whaikōrero* is Māori spirituality. It includes deities from Māori and non-Māori realms, Māori knowledge, Māori history, Māori people, Māori lands, Māori successes, Māori losses, Māori art, performance, individual status, group status, geomentality, social interaction, attitudes and behaviour. This is why I refer to it as *Te Ao o te Whaikōrero*. It has its own world. It is a nomadic art form. It is a proud art form. It is a transient school of education. It is transgenerational and intergenerational.

> I believe that the speakers have more than just the one primary function of welcoming visitors. As I observe speakers on marae I view my own role as the teacher in a learning institution as actually being reversed. I observe and learn, as do innumerable others who have assembled, and I and they must appreciate the free education offered by the marae institution. The marae has become the classroom and those who have the right to speak its educators, and those who have not yet earned that right are the passive students who have attended because of a form of 'voluntary obligation'.[63]

Whaikōrero is not stagnant.

> In traditional Māori thought there is a continuing dialogue between the past and the present. . . . Ancestors appear to the living, the living assume the actions of the ancestors, and history is thereby renewed. . . . On the *marae*, a man speaks in the name of his ancestors. His knowledge and *mana* are derived, at least in part, from them. The past, then, conveys the wisdom which lies before him and is thereby brought into the present. The *tikanga* 'correct ways' come from the past. The myths and the historical narratives, by their telling and retelling, keep alive the exploits of the cultural heroes and so provide the cultural presuppositions which structure human action. They convey social 'messages' and warnings[64] but, as in all oral traditions, also allow new meanings to be brought forth.[65]

'Ko te reo te waka wairua o ō tātou mātua tūpuna e rere nei i te ao'.[66] Language transcends time and generations of people. The physical entity of our ancestors might have remained fixed within their lifetime, but the spirit in which they voiced their thoughts and views and the visual images of them performing *whaikōrero* were able to be transferred from one generation to the next.

The school of oratory is enriched and enculturated because of its ability to reside within fixed parameters while having ample space to twist and create new space. Belief in these boundaries ensures its survival and its uniqueness. Perhaps this individualism is what gives *whaikōrero* its signature introduction – an introduction that announces to the world that what is about to happen is a new beginning of an old art form. This signature introduction initiates a rebirth on every formal occasion of speech, whereby the living essence of Māoridom is affirmed and reaffirmed, vitalised and revitalised. *Kia tihei te mauri ora!*

Appendix

Sample *Whaikōrero*

The following transcriptions have been taken from audio files held by Radio New Zealand, Auckland, in the form of Digital Audio Files (DAT); sample *whaikōrero* accompanying Brooke-White, *Whaikoorero: Ceremonial Farewells to the Dead*; and *Māori Programme Tapes* (MPT) that recorded Māori subject broadcasts on National Radio known at the time as 'Te Reo o te Māori' and 'Te Reo o te Pīpīwharauroa'.

Where possible I have provided data on each sample, including the tribal affiliation(s) of the orator, the location, the forum to which the oration was delivered, a title, and whether the orator was visitor or host.

The date of delivery, if known, has also been provided. I have attempted to transcribe as accurately as possible and apply orthographic conventions appropriately with the aim of representing the intended meaning of the oral delivery. This results in verbatim transcriptions for some parts. Attempts have also been made to respect and maintain the dialectal enunciations specific to each speaker. Where orators have aspirated or dropped particular consonants in accordance with their tribal dialects, for example, *h* and *w*, these have been reinserted by the author as [h] or [w]. This collection is not intended to be representative of high quality orations. They are merely samples to demonstrate the stylistic, lexical and content range of *whaikōrero*. Some of the orators are fledglings where others are more established orators.

Sub-categories for parts of the oration have been included: these include *whakaaraara* – the call to alert: *tauparapara* – an incantation or chant-like recitation; *mihi ki te whare* – verbal acknowledgements to physical buildings; *mihi ki te marae* – verbal acknowledgements to the *marae*; *mihi ki te pae* – verbal acknowledgements to the speakers on the opposing side; *mihi/poroporoaki i ngā mate* – eulogies; *mihi ki te hunga ora, mihi ki (t)ētahi* – verbal acknowledgement(s) to individual(s); *kōrero whakararata* – placatory acknowledgements; *whakataukī* – proverbs; *kaupapa* – main theme of the delivery; *waiata* – complementary song; *haka* – male performance item; *pepeha* – tribal aphorism; *kōrero whakakapi* – summary comments; and *whakamutunga* – sign-off line to end oration.

SAMPLE WHAIKŌRERO 1

a) Orator	Haimona Snowden
e) Tribal affiliation	Te Taitokerau
i) Location/venue	
o) Forum	
u) Source	Radio New Zealand, Dat Tape, Dat275-1, Side A (3'21"–11'50")
	Ngā Taonga Kōrero (Te Reo o Aotearoa Archives) Vol. 4
ha) Visitor/host	Tangata whenua/host
he) Sections	
Whakaaraara	Tihei mauri ora ki te whaiao, ki te ao mārama
Tau(parapara)	Ka nukunuuku, ka nekeneke
	Ka nukunuuku, ka nekeneke
	Titiro ki ngā wai o Tokerau e hora nei
	me he pīpīwharauroa ki tua, takoto te pae, takoto te pae.
	Papā te whatitiri
	hikohiko te uira, i kanapu ki te rangi,
	whetū ki raro rā
	rū ana te whenua e
Mihi ki te mōrehu kaiārahi (acknowledgement to a tribal leader)	Te whaea o te motu, e Kui, e Whina, e tū ana i runga i te wehi, ko te hiahia ko tō mana hei konei au nei hei tautoko i te kaupapa whakatau i tō tāua iwi.
Mihi ki Te Kāhui Ariki (acknowledgements to the Māori Queen)	Te Atairangikāhu, te ariki nui, kōurua ko tō hoa rangatira, tēnā koutou, tēnā koutou, tau atu anō hoki te kāhui ariki nui tonu.
	Te mana, te tapu, te wehi, te ihi.
Kaupapa	Haramai anō rā i tēnei tau whakamaharatanga ki te hāinatanga o Te Tiriti o Waitangi. Haere mai i ngā āhuatanga o te wā. Haramai anō hoki i raro i ēnā maunga whakahī o ō tātou mātua tūpuna. Ngā mātāwaka e tau nei, ngā hau e whā, ngā iwi o te motu katoa.
	Nau mai, piki mai, kake mai.
Whakaraara	Nā reira, kia hiwa rā, kia hiwa rā.
	Kia hiwa rā i tērā tuku, kia hiwa i tēnei tuku, kia whakahiwaia hoki te papa tapu e hora nei hei pikinga mai mō taku manu, hei kakenga mai mō taku manu, nā reira, piki mai, kake mai, nau mai.
Mihi/poroporoaki i ngā mate	Ahakoa he kaupapa tapu tēnei, ka maumahara ki a rātou te kāhui wairua kua wehe atu nei i mua i a tātou, i raro i ō tātou maunga whakahī, i roto i ō tātou whare tangihanga. He poto noa iho rā hoki te kōrero mō rātou, kāti anō, ko tēnei, āpiti hono, tātai hono, koutou te hunga wairua kua wehe atu nei, kua takahia atu te ara whānui e ngā mātua, e ngā tūpuna, nā reira, moe mai koutou, moe mai koutou, moe mai koutou.

Mihi ki te hunga ora	Tātou, ngā mahuetanga iho, tēnei anō tātou ka huihui mai ki tēnei papa tapu o ō tātou mātua tūpuna, nā rātou nei tēnei taonga, Te Tiriti i hāina, hei whakawhanaunga i a tātou ngā iwi o Aotearoa, nā reira, ngā rangatira o ēnā o ō tātou marae maha kua tatū mai nei, kua tae mai nei i runga i tēnei kaupapa i tēnei rā, heoi anō rā ka whakapakari ake ki te whakatau atu i a koutou kua tae mai nei. Ka hoki ki ngā mahara, tō tātou rangatira matua i tūria ai tēnei marae tapu o ō tātou mātua i ngā tau kua pahure ake nei, i te rā, i te rā nei, ahakoa kua ngaro ia, kei te mahara tonu kei konei ia i roto i te wairua hei tautoko i ngā kaupapa e whakahaeretia nei e tātou i tēnei rā, te manaaki e Te Tiriti o Waitangi. Nā reira, koia nei ko te reo o Te Taitokerau ki a koutou katoa e tau mai nā, e ngā iwi, e ngā hau e whā, e Kui mā, e Koro mā, e tama mā, e hine mā, te rangatahi, tau atu anō hoki ki taku [w]hānau i heke mai nei i Te Aupōuri, Te Rarawa, Te Kawariki, ahakoa kei hea koutou haramai, haramai, haramai. Kei te mōhio tonu ki tā koutou tono i ngā tau kua pahure ake nei, heoi anō rā, ko tēnei, haramai koutou, ahakoa ngā [w]hakaaro, he maha tātou kei konei, he maha ngā [w]hakaaro, he maha ngā kaupapa. Nō reira, kua tae mai koutou ahakoa nō hea koutou, nō hea koutou, i hīkoi mai nei me ō koutou [w]hakaaro, hare mai. Te reo tēnei o Te Taitokerau e mihi ana nei ki a koutou, ki te iwi whānui tonu i te rā nei, nō reira, hare mai, hare mai, hare mai.
Kaupapa	Nō reira, e te whānau, e kore e maha atu ngā mihi, e te rangatahi, i ā koutou tono he tono kia huihui tātou te iwi Māori ki te marae o ō tātou mātou tūpuna i raro nei i ngā tau, ā te tau ā tū mai nei i te whā me te rima o ngā rā o Pēpuere. Hoinō tēnei, he tono nā koutou. Hoinō tāku he whakaatu mehemea kua tutuki tērā kaupapa, kei te pai tonu. Ki ngā rangatira, ki ngā kaumātua o Te Taitokerau, nā reira, hoinō tēnei he whakaatu i tā koutou tono, e mihi ana i a koutou, Ngāti Awa, e mihi ana ki a koutou, nā te mea, i tērā tau rā, i konei anō koutou e manaaki ana i tērā o ō tātou marae, hāunga te [tērā], i runga i te kaupapa o ō tātou waka, engari ko te manaaki i te manuhiri i tērā [o] ō tātou marae, nā reira, tēnā koutou. Ngā mihi whānui ki a koutou, kua oti te mihi ki a koutou, hoianō he tautoko tēnei. Nā reira, e te whānau, ahakoa pēhea ngā whakaaro me hoki anō ki tērā tau, 1990, ngā kaupapa i tutuki i tērā tau. Te rangatahi, nā koutou ngā kaupapa i tutuki ai, nā mātou ngā kaumātua i hora te whakaaro ki mua i a koutou, nā koutou i whakatinana, nā, tū ana tērā hui rangatira i tērā tau. Mai i tērā tau ki tēnei, kei te haere tonu, kei te mana tonu, nā reira, te hiahia kia pēnei tonu ā ngā tau e tū mai nei, nā reira, kāhore rā e whānui atu te mihi atu ki a koutou te whānau, hoianō, te whakawhaitai [whakawhētai] tonu ki te wāhi ngaro mōna i pai ki te manaaki, te tiaki i a tātou, nā reira, huri noa, huri noa, te whānau
Kōrero whakakapi	Tēnā koutou, tēnā koutou, kia ora huihui tātou.
Waiata	(action song performed by a secondary school)

SAMPLE WHAIKŌRERO 2

a) Orator	Tā Himi Henare (Sir James Henare)
e) Tribal affiliation	Te Taitokerau
i) Location/venue	Waitangi (author's deduction)
o) Forum	Religious Occasion (author's deduction)
u) Source	Radio New Zealand, Dat Tape, Dat275-1, Side A (16'27"-29'50") Ngā Taonga Kōrero (Te Reo o Aotearoa Archives) Vol. 4
ha) Visitor/host	Tangata whenua/host
he) Sections	

Mihi ki te hunga ora	Tēnā koutou i hāpai ai i te amorangi ki runga hei whāinga atu mō mātou mō te hāpai ō o muri.
	Ngā minita o te taha kikokiko, tēnā koutou, me ngā mema o te whare pāremata. Tēnā koutou ngā kaihautū o te iwi Māori. He mea whakamīharo tēnei, ko ngā minita o te taha wairua, ko ngā minita o te taha kikokiko me ōna kaihautū, kei konei katoa.
Mihi ki (t)ētahi	Tēnā koe te minita mō ō kōrero ātaahua, kua whakaatutia nei e koe i tēnei rūnanga, i tēnei huihuinga nui rawa atu. Tēnā koe mō ngā whakamārama, mō ngā whakaaro ōu ake, o te minita Māori, me ō te kāwanatanga hoki. I karangatia ai ahau kia tū atu ki te kōrero, kei aku rangatira e tau nei, puta noa o te motu, koutou katoa. He kūare nōku ki te kōrero Pākehā, ka karangatia tēnei hui. Whakaaro ahau he Māori ahau, me kōrero Māori au. Ko wētahi kei te kī mai, kāo, he Pākehā ētahi o tātou, me kōrero Pākehā koe, kia ahatia. Poto noa ake tēnei kōrero, ko te tono mai ki a au kia whakamārama ake au i te hītōria o tēnei marae e tau nei tātou. Ki te huri atu koutou ki muri nā i te hanga tamariki e noho mai nā, i ngā papa kōhatu e tū mai nā, ko te wāhi tēnā i hui ai ngā āriki o Ngā Puhi, i wānanga ai me hāina rānei Te Tiriti, kāore rānei. He wāhi tino tapu i ōna rā. Tōna ingoa, ko Te Taurangatira. Hei ingoa tēnā ngā papa kōhatu. Ka pātai ngā tamariki nei ki a au ki hea, te whare hui nei tū ai? Ka whakaatu au ki konei, te taha o Te Taurangatira. I te rima o ngā rā o Pēpuere, i te tau whā tekau te tau, ka whakawhiti mai Kāwana Hopihana i runga i tana manuao, whakawhiti mai ki konei i tāwāhi nei. Ka tūtaki ki ngā rangatira o Ngā Puhi i reira ka whakatakoto i tana kaupapa, i tana whakaaro kia hāinatia Te Tiriti o Waitangi. Nō te ahiahi ka hoki iho ngā rangatira o Ngā Puhi ki konei ka wānanga rātou, āe rānei me hāina Te Tiriti o Waitangi, kāore rānei. Ko te wāhi i noho ai rātou, i kōrero ai, kei konā tonu i te hanga tamariki e noho mai ana. Ka kīia ko Te Taurangatira, he tapu i ōna rā, i konei ahau i te wā i hikitia ai te tapu e ngā kaumātua kua mate atu.
	Koia nā i tohungia ko te tāima hui mō tātou ki konei, ko te wāhi i noho ai ngā rangatira o Ngā Puhi ki te whiriwhiri 'āe rānei me hāina Te Tiriti o Waitangi, kāore rānei'. Nō te pō, i te ata pōuri o te ono o ngā rā o Pēpuere ka whakaaetia rātou ki konei kia hāinatia Te Tiriti o Waitangi. Ka whakawhiti i te awa o Waitangi, ka piki ki runga te whare o Te Tiriti, ka hāinatia e rātou Te Tiriti i reira. Ko te wāhi i whakaaetia ai e rātou, nā, kei konā te hanga tamariki e noho mai ana. Ko ngā ariki o Ngā Puhi e wānanga ana, ka kīia e rātou ko te Taurangatira. Kāore i te marae rā, engari i konei. He pai rawa atu tēnei hui wānangatanga mā tātou. I rongo ai hoki i hui ai rātou ngā mana, ngā wehi me te ihi o Ngā Puhi i konei. I kōrero ake au i tēnei kōrero kāore hoki i roto i ngā pukapuka hītōria i tuhia ai i tērā wā. Ko kōrero anō te whakaaro nui o te tangata i runga ake i ō rātou papakāinga hāinatia Te Tiriti, Kāo, i konei. Ka tohungia e rātou ētahi o ngā rangatira, ā, nō rātou, tokoono pea. Tokoiwa rātou ki runga ki te tū atu ki te kōrero ki a Kāwana Hopihana, 'Kāre mātou e whakaae ki a koe kia noho mai i konei'. Nā rātou anō i whakarite atu i konei. Nōku tonu pea ētahi o ngā tupuna i tū ake. Kāore tātou, te iwi nei tonu, kei te mōhio koia nei tēnei o tā rātou kaupapa. Ka tae ki runga i te ono o ngā rā o Pēpuere, i te ata o te ono o ngā rā o Pēpuere, ka tae mai a Hopihana, he mea tono atu nā rātou kia whakawhiti mai Hopihana, kua whakaae rātou ki te hāina i Te Tiriti. Ka tae mai Kāwana Hopihana ka tohungia ngā rangatira ki te tū atu te kī atu i a Kāwana Hopihana, 'E hoki koe. Kāore mātou e whakaae ki a koe ka noho mai hei matua mō mātou'. Engari ka mutu te tū atu o tērā ariki ka hīkoi atu ka hāina i Te Tiriti o Waitangi, ka hongi ki a Kāwana Hopihana. Tukuna a Kawiti, ka tū atu, 'Kāore mātou e whakaae ki a koe kia noho mai hei kāwana. Hoehoe noa au o runga o ōku waka, ka puhipuhia au e te Pākehā. Engari ngā mihinare, waiho ake ngā mihinare i konei'. Ka mutu, ka hīkoi atu te kaumātua rā, ka hāina i Te Tiriti, ka hongi i a Kāwana Hopihana. Nā rātou anō i whakarite atu i konei. I kōrero ake au, he wāhi tēnei kia mōhio ai tātou i te nui o tēnei wāhi e wānanga nei tātou i roto o Ngā Puhi. Koia nei ko ngā papa kōhatu i tūngia mai, e tū mai nei hei tohu whakamaharatanga ki te wāhi i hui ai te rūnanga o ngā ariki o Ngā Puhi i tērā wā. Tā rātou manuhiri, tō rātou hoa i konei, ko Iwikau Te Heuheu, nō Ngāti Tūwharetoa. Kāti taku whakamārama mō te wāhi nei. Poto noa ake. Nō te tau kotahi mano, e iwa rau, e toru tekau, te tau ka whakaurua ngā kaumātua nei i roto i te rūnanga o ngā rangatira o Ngā Puhi, ko Te Tiriti o Waitangi.

Mihi ki (t)ētahi (cont'd)	I tērā wā, tekau mā waru anō ōku tau ka uru au i konei. Mātou e hui ana ko te rūnanga o ngā rangatira o Ngā Puhi, Tiriti o Waitangi, ki konā tonu. Ko māua ko Eru Pou ngā tamariki a ngā kaumātua i konei. Ka mōhio mai koutou ka rima tekau mā whā tau, i a au e tū atu nei ko hau anake te mōrehu o ngā rangatira o te rūnanga o ngā rangatira o Te Tiriti o Waitangi. Ko hau anake mea puru atu nei, nā taku kaha tamariki i tērā wā taku whakaurunga atu e rātou i runga i te rūnanga o ngā rangatira o Te Tiriti o Waitangi. Ā te ono o Pēpuere, a te Wenerei, ka pau te whā tekau mā rima tau ōku i te pōari whakahaere i Te Tiriti o Waitangi. I kōrero ake i ahau i tupu ake ahau i roto i ngā kōrero mō Te Tiriti o Waitangi. . . . , ō mātou kaumātua kua ngaro ake nei, kāti, ko au anake anō te mōrehu i te rā nei. Ka haere hoki ki te pakanga me ngā kuia o Ngā Puhi ko rātou te komiti wahine o Te Tiriti o Waitangi, nā rātou ko te whare kōhatu e tū mai nei. I kōrero ake i a au ēnei kōrero, whakatū poto atu ki a koutou. Kōrero a te heamana, i whakamārama ahau mō te rā o Waitangi. Poto noa. Tēnei whenua, Te Tiriti o Waitangi e kīia nei ko Te Tiriti o Waitangi. Nā Kāwana Bledisloe, nāna i hoko mai i te Pākehā tērā whenua, te wāhi kei reira nei Te Tiriti kei runga. Nā Kāwana Bledisloe i te wā i a ia, koia te Kāwana Tianara o Niu Tireni. I te tau toru tekau mā rua te tau, ka hokona mai e ia i tētahi Pākehā mahi pāmu, mahi ahuwhenua, tērā whenua. Nā ngā tūpuna anō o Ngā Puhi i hoko ki te Pākehā, engari nā Kāwana Bledisloe, nāna i hoko, kātahi ka tukua e ia mō te iwi Māori, Pākehā katoa o ēnei moutere. Ka tīmata mai i reira te whakanui i te rā whakamaharatanga ki te hāinatanga o Te Tiriti o Waitangi. Ka whakatūngia hoki Te Pōari Kaitiaki o Te Tiriti o Waitangi. Nā Kāwana Bledisloe anō, nāna i whakakaupapa te ture. Nō te tau whā tekau mā tau ka whakatika tonu ki te haere ki te pakanga mātou. Ka whakauru au i mua o te whare rūnanga e tū iho raka e Te Taitokerau katoa hei whiriwhiri mō rātou i roto i te pōari whakahaere i Te Tiriti o Waitangi. Ka mōhio mai koutou, ā te ono o ngā rā o Pēpuere, ā te Wenerei, ka whā tekau mā rima ōku tau ki te pōari whakahaere i Te Tiriti o Waitangi.
Kaupapa	Nō reira, kei te mōhio ki ngā whakahaere o te rā o Waitangi. I tērā wā, i te tekau mā tahi o te ata, ka noho te wāhi huihui ki reira, mehemea ki te tae ake he minita o te Kāwanatanga o tērā wā me ētahi mema pāremete, ko ngā Pākehā torutoru me ngā Māori torutoru, ko mātou ki reira me taku whakaatu atu ki a koutou ka tū ahau ki te pōari. Ko mātou tokotoru ngā mema Māori te pōari o Te Tiriti o Waitangi. Ko Korokī, ko Te Riri Kawiti, ko hau. Ko mātou ngā whiriwhiri o te iwi Māori puta noa ki te pōari whakahaere i Te Tiriti o Waitangi. Ka mate a Korokī, ka tohungia ko Hepi Te Heuheu hei whiriwhiri i muri a Korokī he whakahaere mātou i te pōari o Te Tiriti o Waitangi. Nā Kāwana Bledisloe i whakauru ki runga i te ture mō Waitangi kia kotahi whiriwhiri mō ēnei rangatira ariki o Ngā Puhi, mō Waka Nene, mō Hōne Heke, mō Pōmare, me Kawiti. I tēnei rā ko te uri o Pōmare, ko Tūreiti Pōmare, ko Hepi Te Heuheu, me ahau hoki. Koia nei ngā Māori kei mua i te pōari whakahaere i Te Tiriti o Waitangi. Kāti nei rā ōku whakamārama atu ki a koutou, i te mea, ā te ata māua ko Minita, kei te noho te pōari o Waitangi kua riro ko ia te kaiwhakahaere ināianei i te pōari o Waitangi. Ko te minita Māori, ko te minita o ngā whenua e noho nei ko Koro Wetere. Nō reira, kāore e taea āpōpō, ā te ata āpōpō konei māua kia mutu mai te hui a te pōari, nā, ka hoki mai anō māua ki konei āpōpō.

Kāti nei rā ēnei whakamārama, kei ōku rau rangatira mā, ehara i te mea whakahāwea atu koutou i kore ai e kōrero Pākehā ki a koutou, hoianō, kia whakatutuki atu i tēnei wā, he kōrero atu anō wāku mō ōku whakaaro mō te rā o Waitangi me Te Tiriti o Waitangi hoki, tae noa ki te take i kōrerotia ai e te Minita Māori mō te Tiripiunara o Te Tiriti rā, o Te Tiriti o Waitangi. |
| Kōrero whakakapi | Kāti nei rā he kōrero māku mō tēnei wā, tēnā koutou, tēnā koutou, e heke iho ana ki raro, kia ora huihui mai anō tātou. |

SAMPLE WHAIKŌRERO 3

a) Orator	Haimona Snowden
e) Tribal affiliation	Te Taitokerau
i) Location/venue	
o) Forum	
u) Source	Radio New Zealand, Dat Tape, Dat275-2, Side B (0-7'41")
	Ngā Taonga Kōrero (Te Reo o Aotearoa Archives) Vol. 4
ha) Visitor/host	Tangata whenua/host
he) Sections	
Tauparapara	Nau mai, piki mai, kake mai, kua tae mai, kua tae mai, kua tae mai.
Mihi ki ngā atua Mihi ki te whare	Ko te mea tuatahi tonu, ko te whakawhetai ki te wāhi ngaro mō ngā manaakitanga maha i manaakitia ai tātou, nā, i āhei ai tātou ki te huihui mai anō ki tēnei marae ki tēnei tau. Nā reira, korōria, he hōnore ki te runga rawa, he maunga-ā-rongo ki te mata o te whenua, te whānau kua tae pai nei i te rā nei, nā reira, te tupuna whare e tū nei, koia tēnei ko te whakamanatanga o Te Tiriti o Waitangi, nā reira, tū mai koe. Ko Ranginui ia e tū iho nei, te papa e hora nei, tēnā kōrua.
Mihi ki te hunga ora	Ngāti Wai, rau rangatira mā, koutou kua tae mai nei te reo whakahuihui i a tātou, te reo o te rā, haramai, haere mai, haere mai.
Kaupapa	Haere mai, ahakoa he kaupapa kē anō tēnei i tae mai ai, i tau mai ai ki tēnei papa tapu o ō tātou mātua, me hoki ngā maumahara ki a rātou mā, ki te kāhui wairua kua ngaro i runga i ō tātou marae maha. E kore e taea te hipa tēnei kaupapa i waenganui i a tāua, ahakoa kei hea tāua e hui ana me hoki ki te kāhui wairua, me maumahara ki a rātou. I ngā tau maha ko ngā tino taniwha o Te Taitokerau ngā kaikōrero o konei. I te rā nei, heoi anō, he hohopu noa iho hei whakatau atu i a koutou. Taea te pēhea? Taea te pēhea i ēnei rā? Heoi anō, i pai ai, i māia ai te tū ake he tāne kei muri i a mātou hei whakatikatika i ēnei āhuatanga, nā reira, ka whakapakari ake ki te tū ake, e te whānau, haere mai, aratakina mai tā koutou tamaiti, te tamaiti āpōpō nei ka tūkinotia e tāua e te iwi Māori. Ākina, ākina ki te kōrero. Nā reira, hare mai, haere mai, haere mai. I te taenga mai o te Kāwana Tianara ki tērā o ō tātou marae ko te kōrero ki a au, wāku nei kōrero, me kōrero i te reo Māori. Ka tū atu au, nā, kua [w]hakarerekē. Tā tātou tamaiti e kore kē e mōhio ki tōku reo, nā reira, me huri au ki te reo o tā tātou tamaiti, nā reira, kia manawanui mai.
	Mr Minister, Winston, a privilege, an honour to stand here on behalf of our people. Taitokerau welcome you on this sacred marae of our tūpuna. All I want to say is I would like to endorse the remarks of the previous speaker where he mentioned something about the pūtea, or a huruhuru e rere ai te manu. Whatever that means. All I want to say Mr Minister is simply this, if you were here last year you'd recall the tremendous, the greatest festival in the history of Māoridom, to see so many wakas floating on Waitangi harbour here. Today we are lonely because there are only three wakas down there, what I'm trying to say is simply this, perhaps you can help us with some way that you might be able to bring back a few more wakas next year down here, whatever source you might be able to tap Mr Minister, will be very grateful. We have representatives of some of the wakas which are not here today, but we like to see them come up with their wakas. We have not . . . stand up, they were coming up under their own steam, but fortunately we had a man here, not from your department, somebody else who offered to pay for the transport of the wakas. That Mr Minister is all I'm trying to say, perhaps next year we'll be able to see a few more wakas floating down here, nā reira, koutou, e Himi mā, koutou, tēnā, mā koutou e āwhina tēnei take. E Kui mā, e Koro, . . . hāpai, arataki mai tā tātou whānau e mihi atu nei ki a koe, ngā karakia o ō tātou mātua i a koe e hīkoi nei ki tēnei papa tapu.

Kōrero whakakapi	E Kui mā, e Koro mā, kāti anō mō tēnei wā, huri noa, tātou i huihui nei, tēnā koutou, tēnā koutou, kia ora e huihui tātou.
Haka	(A haka performed by Ngāti Awa boys)
Kōrero whakakapi	. . . mā tātou ā rātou kaupapa e pīkau, e hāpai, tēnā koutou, kia ora.

SAMPLE WHAIKŌRERO 4

a) Orator	Bruce Gregory (mema Māori mō te rohe o Te Taitokerau) (author's deduction)
e) Tribal affiliation	Te Taitokerau
i) Location/venue	
o) Forum	Pōhiri : Bruce Gregory (mema Māori mō te rohe o Te Taitokerau) (author's deduction)
u) Source	Radio New Zealand, Dat Tape, Dat275-2, Side B (8'06"-11'34") Ngā Taonga Kōrero (Te Reo o Aotearoa Archives) Vol. 4
ha) Visitor/host	Tangata whenua/host
he) Sections	
Mihi ki ngā kaikōrero	He tū tautoko tēnei i ngā mihi, i ngā kōrero o ngā rangatira tū i mua i ahau. Kei a rātau, i ngā kupu tahito, i ngā mātauranga i ō tātou nei tūpuna he tāora i runga i tēnei, tō tātou marae, i waenganui i a . . .
Mihi ki (t)ētahi	E Te Au, i a koe ki roto i te whareāinga, i te wharemiere *parliament*, ināianei, e kite ahau i runga i tēnei teheina, o te marae o tō iwi. Ahakoa kei kō he rongo atu au i ngā kōrero nō koe mō ngā take e pā ana i ngā iwi kei runga i a mātou, he tangata tino kaha ki te tū ki roto i te ao o tērā whare. Ināianei he titiro i a tātou he aha te āhua o tēnei tangata ki runga i, o roto rā? Nō reira, kei roto i a koe te kaha mō tō iwi. He rongo atu i ngā iwi puta o te motu, ko wai tēnei tangata e tū mai nei, e tū mai nei, e tū mai nei? Nō reira, nau mai, haere mai. Haere mai ki raro i te pū tūhākari e rere mai ki runga rā, Haere mai i mua o tēnei, tō whare, Te Tiriti o Waitangi. Mauria mai ki te [w]hakaaro o tēnei tiriti. Ko te mahi he rongo atu i a tātou, ngā kōrero kei roto i a koe, o Te Tiriti. Kei konei hei rongo atu i a tātou i ngā whakaaro kei roto i a koe, nō reira, e Ngāti Wai, haere mai, haere mai. I te wiki kua pahure ake nei he kite i a koutou ki runga i te marae o Rātana, nā, ka tū ana koe ki reira, kei kōrero mō ngā mea katoa. I tēnei hāora, tā, he rongo atu i ngā kōrero pērā, nō reira, e tātou mā, kāhore he kumea o ēnei nā kōrero, engari, e tū ki te tautoko i ngā kōrero i ōku nei kaumātua rangatira e tū mai ki mua i ahau, nō reira, nau mai, haere mai, haere mai, haere mai.
Haka	(The haka 'Kura Tīwaka' is performed by Ngāti Awa boys)
Kōrero whakakapi	Nō reira, e te minita me tō rōpū, whakatau nei ki runga i tēnei tō tātou nei marae, tēnā koe, tēnā koutou, tēnā koutou.

SAMPLE WHAIKŌRERO 5

a) Orator	Haupeke Piripi
e) Tribal affiliation	Ngāti Wai
i) Location/venue	Waitangi (?)
o) Forum	
u) Source	Radio New Zealand, Dat Tape, Dat275-2, Side B 12'20"-23'36") Ngā Taonga Kōrero (Te Reo o Aotearoa Archives) Vol. 4
ha) Visitor/host	
he) Sections	
Whakaaraara	Kia hiwa rā, kia hiwa rā Kia hiwa rā i tēnei tuku, kia hiwa rā i tēnā tuku Kia tū, kia oho, kia mataara.
Kōrero whakararata	Ko te kaupapa tuatahi mōku, kia tae au ki kō rānei kia pai ai taku huri atu ki a koutou ki te kōrero ki a koutou katoa kia kite ai waku kanohi, kanohi parori nei, i a koutou katoa.
Tauparapara	Te tai rā, te tai rā Timu ana, e pari ana ki tawhiti nui, ki tawhiti roa, ki Hawaiki rā anō. He tai tapu nā Tangaroa, tērā whaitiri te awa o Mātaatua i haramai ai i te nuku rā, i te ngaru whatiwhati, ka hoki nei koe ki te pō tūāuriuri. He kuru tongarerewa taku ika poutapu nā Te Oro, nā Puhi-kai-ariki, ngā hoehoe o te pō, te whetū rere ata ko Tāne-mahuta ka tau . . . . Hui e, tāiki e.
Kaupapa	Nō reira, kua tae mai rā, kua tae mai rā, kua tae mai rā. Kua tae mai rā te tamaiti nei i tatari ai koe me eke kia tae mai ki konei iāianei. Kua tae mai, kua tae mai, kua tae mai. E Haimana tamaiti, tō pānga ki a Ngāti Kurī e noho nei. Ko te whānau Paro, ko Te Ākitai, ko Maniapoto, ko [a]hau e tū atu nei ko Ngāti Wai, ko te uri o Hikihiki e noho nei, e noho nei, e noho nei. Engari ngā kino o ngā mahi o Ngāti Weko, kore au e pai i tērā ingoa, nā te mea, e hiahia ana koutou ki a koutou anake ngā moni e kōrero nā koutou. Kua kore koutou e pai kia mōhiotia a Ngāti Wai hei iwi, nō reira, te taumata tapu o ōku mātua tūpuna, karanga mai rā, karanga mai rā, karanga mai rā. Kia huri ake taku titiro ki konei, ki te iwi e mea nei ehara tana maunga i te maunga nekeneke e huna mai rā i raro i te tōtara. Ngāti *Blow*, koia nā rā te tōtara i kōrerotia ai he peka wai rā kei konā atu nei. Nei nā, e huna ana te pouaka me te hāinatanga o Te Tiriti i roto, nā reira, takoto mai i te rae o te rākau i kōrerongia ai e Peta Wairua ki a au. Takoto mai, noho mai. Noho mai koutou ki te taha o te tuhituhi nā, o te pānui nā. I kōrerotia ai e tō koutou tupuna, e Te Kooti, i roto i ana waiata 'E pā tō reo,' mā ngā rangatira anō te matua o te iwi Māori e ārahi te iwi ki te hē. Ko te kōrero a Āperahama Taonui e pēnei ana, 'E Ngā Puhi. Hīpokina Te Tiriti o Waitangi ki tōna ake kākahu, kāhore ki te kākahu, ki te kara o Ingarangi.' Kīhai a Ngā Puhi i whakarongo, kīhai i whakarongo. E Ngā Puhi, hei Tā Āperahama Taonui, mōu, kīhai i whakarongo. E kore e tika Te Tiriti. Ko tēnei whare hei pūngāwerewere te kainoho i roto, koia nei ngā poropiti o rātou mā e moe mai rā, e moe mai rā, e moe mai rā. Tēnā titiro ake tātou ki ngā waiata a Waikato e pēnei ana, 'Te Tiriti o Waitangi kei roto i te moana e'. He aha te take i roto i te moana? Tēnā, kia hoki tātou te kōrero a Āpirana Ngata, 'Ko koutou, e te iwi Māori, he para whenua, he para whenua, he para whenua. Ahakoa pēhea tō koutou haere atu ki roto i te moana, te mātauranga o te iwi tauiwi, ka tuhaina mai koutou ki uta, nā te mea, he para whenua koutou, he para whenua koutou.' Nō reira, e Peke, ko koe anake te mea hora nei me ngā tauiwi nei, kia tā koe kia mangu, ka pērā me Haimona rā. Pērā me te korokē e noho mai nei i te taha ki a Haimona, nā, kua tāngia, kua mangu atu i te mea nei, heoi anō te take e puta tērā haupū o Te Aupōuri

Kaupapa (cont'd)	e noho nei, e noho nei te au [ao] mārama. Ahakoa nō Ngāti Kurī, ko te au [ao] mārama tēnei, titiro mai nei, kitea mai ngā niho kua kite au i ngā wāhine rā kua hiahia katoa i taku tamaiti, tā koutou tamaiti mokopuna. Nō reira, karanga mai, e te taumata tapu o ōku mātua tūpuna, karanga mai, karanga mai, karanga mai. Kei te hari atu, kei te koa te ngākau kua puta mai te rangatira nei, tētahi taha ōna nō Te Waipounamu, i te ātaahua o tā mātou tamaiti i Whanganui. Peke mai te whetū, harawana kē koia mātou rā, koia kē a Ngāti Wai. Nā wai i kī, koia kē a Ngāti Wai? Koinei i tika, a, nā te mea, e pā ana hoki ki tā tāua kōtiro. Ka tika i tēnā, kua mākutungia a Gail. Hei tāku rā, nā reira, karanga mai ō tātou tini mate, o ngā tau, o ngā marama, o ngā wiki, o ngā rā o nanahi nei e korekore . . . e hoki mai, ahakoa ko wai he tauiwi nā te mea whanaunga katoa nō tātou ā tātou hunaonga, ō tātou hungawai i ētahi tāima. I ētahi wā, he tauiwi, he tauiwi, he tauiwi. Nā reira, ka hari hei hakarongotanga mai mā Ngāti *Blow* e tāhae ana nā Ngāti Awa nei i wā rātou haka, pēnei i a Ngāti Awa i mea nei, 'E Ngā Puhi, nā koutou i tāhae tō mātou waka.' Nā tū ake ana a mātou whaikōrero, 'Taku rākau e. . . .' Ka pai ana hoki tāku nei tāhae mea kē. Homai taku tāhae, māku e kī ake ngā korokē nei, korokē koretake. Tukuna e rātou tō rātou tuahine, tō rātou whaea tupuna kia kauria te waka nei a Mātaatua, 'Kia whakatāne hoki au i a au.' Koretake ana wērā korokē. Ka pai ki te [w]hakapai a te korikori kai o te tinana, engari, māngere riro atu i a Puhi-kai-ariki te waka. Ka nuihia atu ki Tākou, huri ana, hei kōhatu, hei kōhatu, hei kōhatu. Nō reira, i roto i te rā nei ka mahia e rātou he waka hou mō rātou, Mātaatua, ka piri mai ai ki tēnei o ngā waka. E toru kē ō tātou nei waka. Nā, koretake ngā korokē nei te tiaki i tō rātou waka, mā tātou anō e tāhae, kei te pai, kei te pai, kei te pai. Nā, karanga mai koutou, karanga mai koutou, karanga mai koutou. Nō reira, e hoa mā, kua nui rawa rā ngā mihi, kua nui rawa kōrero. Heoi nei, tū i te kaitautoko i ngā tokorua nei, i ngā rangatira i mua ake i a au nei.
Waiata	'. . . he maunga rongonui e tū mai nei i te marae ko te rerenga kupu a ngā tūpuna, nō Hawaiki mai tuku iho i . . .'

SAMPLE WHAIKŌRERO 6

a) Orator	
e) Tribal affiliation	Te Rarawa
i) Location/venue	Ahipara
o) Forum	Welcome to Governor General Bernard Ferguson for the opening of of a new building.
u) Source	Radio New Zealand, Dat Tape 3, Dat341-2, Side A (5'00"-12'52")
ha) Visitor/host	Tangata whenua/host
he) Sections	
Tauparapara	Waiwai te moana i haerea Puta ki te whaiao, puta ki te ao mārama Tēnei ka unuhia te rito o te harakeke Ui mai ki ahau he aha te mea pai? Māku e kī atu he tangata.

Mihi ki te hunga ora	Haere mai te manuhiri tūārangi, haere mai, haere mai, haere mai. Haere mai te Kāwana Tianara, te reo o te Kuīni me tō hoa rangatira, me tā kōrua whānau. Me tō rōpū whiriwhiri, haere mai, haere mai, haere mai. Haere mai, e te Kāwana Tianara. Haere mai ki te aituā i pā ki a tātou i ngā rā tata ake kua pahure nei. I te mate o tō tātou matua, o Sir Winston Churchill, tētahi o ngā tangata i whakatakotoria ai ngā whakahaere i te wā Pakanga Tuarua, i kore ai te kapua pōuri e tau iho ki te whenua, ki runga anō hoki ki ngā tāngata kaipupuri nei te tika. I te rā nei e noho nei tātou i runga i te rangimārie. Nā reira, haere mai, haere mai, haere mai. Haere mai, e te Kāwana Tianara me tō hoa rangatira. Haere mai.
Pepeha	Haere mai ki Ahipara kāmehameha. Ko Whangatauatia[?] te maunga, ko Toakai te tangata. Te moana o Ngā Tai a Paroro [?], te one, Te Oneroa-a-Tohe. Haere mai te Kāwana Tianara, kōrua ko tō hoa rangatira. Takahi nei i ngā marae e hoe nei ō kōrua iwi Māori. I te rā nei kua takahia e kōrua ngā marae maha o te motu mai i Te Rerenga Wairua, Te Hiku, tae atu ki Te Upoko-o-te-Ika. Ka whiti ki Te Waipounamu, ka tae atu ki Wharekauri, nā reira, haere mai, haere mai, haere mai.
Kaupapa	Tēnei te nui o te mihi, te hari, me te koa mōu kua tae mai i te rā nei i tā mātou īnoi i tae atu nā ki a koe kia haere mai koe ki Ahipara, ki te whakapuare i tō mātou whare e tū nei. He tau whakamahara nā mātou mō te ōhākī o ō mātou tūpuna. E te whānau i muri nei, kia mau ki te whakapono, kia manaaki, kia atawhai te tangata. He whakamārama. Ko 'Te Ōhākī' tuatahi i kōrerotia ki tēnei whenua, nā tō mātou tupuna, nā Poroa. E te whānau, hei tāku mātāika whenua, hei tāku mātāika tangata, hei tāku pukepuke whenua, hei tāku pukepuke tangata. [Ki] te whakarāpopoto katoatia ēnei whakataukī i kōrerotia e ō mātou tūpuna, ko te ingoa o te whare e tū nei, Te Ōhākī, nā reira, haere mai te Kāwana Tianara, haere mai. Tēnei, e te Kāwana Tianara, hei taupoki mō ēnei mihi i tēnei pōwhiri ki a koe, te Kāwana Tianara, kōrua ko tō hoa rangatira, tēnei ahau kei te tuku atu i te koha a Te Rarawa, a ēnei iwi e pae nei me te marae nei. [*The orator is encouraged to speak in English and does so.*]

SAMPLE WHAIKŌRERO 7

a) Orator	
e) Tribal affiliation	
i) Location/venue	
o) Forum	Welcome to the Governor General
u) Source	Radio New Zealand, Dat Tape 3, Dat341-2, Side A (14'38"-17'51")
ha) Visitor/host	Manuhiri/visitor
he) Sections	
Kōrero whakararata	*Your grace, members of parliament, other visitors, ladies and gentlemen, Mr Wickham said that in this valley you are all one people, therefore you paler members of this unified race will pardon me if I talk in the language of this one valley to which you belong.*

Mihi ki te pae	Tēnā koutou e mihi mai nei ki a au. Tēnā koutou i runga i te āhuatanga o ngā aituā e hinga mai nei, e hinga mai nā i ngā marae maha o te motu, huri mai ki ngā aituā o tēnei marae o tātou.
Mihi/poroporoaki i ngā mate	Haere e pā mā, e kui mā, haere. Haere ki te pō, ki te pō nui, ki te pō roa, ki te pō tarauri, ki te pō tangotango, ki te pō whēkerekere, ki te pō tē kitea, haere, haere, haere ki ngā tūpuna maha kua rehu atu nā ki te hunga i ngaro i te tangata.
Mihi ki te hunga ora	Kāti. Tēnā koutou e noho mai nei i te ao tūroa nei.
Mihi ki te marae Mihi ki te whare	Inā, he waewae tapu ahau, ka mihi atu au ki tēnei marae, tēnā koe e te marae e takoto mai nā, tēnā koe e te whare e tū mai nei.
Kaupapa	Kia pai anō rā ki a tātau katoa, kua tutuki mai nei koutou i te rā o tēnei rangi. Mōhio katoa koutou katoa, tātau katoa, te reo o tēnei rangi nō ngā mea mate, ngā mea mate o ngā Māori, ngā mea i mate o ngā Pākehā, i tērā o wai, te wai i ngā whare i mua atu nei. Nā, tuarua, kua kōrero, kaua e waiho tērā kōrero, ā, ko wai ake ngā toto o ō mātou kuia, me ō mātou tūpuna i konei. Kāore mātou i te māharahara mō tērā kōrero, nā, i roto i tēnei wā, *Dunkyou [thankyou]* ana au ki a koutou katoa, Māori, Pākehā, o ngā takiwā katoa nei kua tatū mai nei i kōnei. Ka nui tēnei, pērā atu tō mātou nui, tō ngā Māori, me koutou i tēnei rangi. Ngā mea kōrero, koutou i muri ake i tā tātau kōrero, tō mātou matua, tutuki mai nā koe i roto i tēnei rangi me tāu rōpū katoa te [h]uaki te kō[h] atu i waenganui i a mātau katoa, moumou toa, nō reira, e mō[h]io ana mātau katoa ngā Māori, kua kōrero nei, nā ngā Māori . . .
Kōrero whakakapi	Nō reira, tau . . . koutou katoa, ngā rau rangatira e awhi nei, e tū nei au i mua i a koutou, tēnā koutou, tēnā koutou, *thankyou*. *Thankyou* koutou.

SAMPLE WHAIKŌRERO 8

a) Orator	
e) Tribal affiliation	Taranaki
i) Location/venue	
o) Forum	Tangihanga/Funeral
u) Source	Radio New Zealand, Dat Tape 3, Dat362-2, Side B (2'45")
ha) Visitor/host	Manuhiri/visitor
he) Sections	
Tauparapara	. . . ē..ī, taku mate, taku mate ki taku rōpū tāne, ki taku rōpū wāhine, ka riro pai koutou, karapitia iho ki te papa o te waka, ka hutia te kuha, ka hāpainga te kakau o te hoe, tipua horonuku, tipua hororangi. He aha i rāhoto ki tai o te moana, whakangaro atu ai taku kura ki a au e? Taukiri te mamae.
Mihi i te Kīngitanga Poroporoaki i ngā mate	Nō reira, e pāpā, he kupu whakamutunga atu ki a koe. Haere, haere, haere. Haere ki ō tau, ki ō mātua tīpuna. Haere ki ngā Kīngitanga, haere ki a Pōtatau, haere ki a Tāwhiao, haere ki a Mahuta, i hoatu ai ēnei kōrero ki mua i a koe. Ko koe, kāre koe e wareware nei i tō mokopuna, kāre koe e wareware i tō mokopuna mai rā anō, ā, tae mai ki tō aituā. Āhua ngoikore tō tinana, kātahi kua okioki, i roto i tēnei rā kua moe rā, kua mate i roto i tēnei rā, nō reira, takoto. Takoto te takotoranga o tō Tauweke, o tōu matua, o tōu hākari rāua ko . . . homai. Nō reira, haere, haere, haere, haere pāpā. Haere haere ki a rātou. Haere haere. Haere ki te tini, ki te mano, kei konā katoa i mua i tō aroaro. Nāna, nāna te kata, me āna tuāhine i haere mai i te aroaro o tō mokopuna ki te hari mai i te roimata ki runga ki a koe, ki runga i te tipuna, tō mokopuna kua hoki.

Pepeha	Nāna. Tāmaki ki raro, Mōkau ki runga, Mangatoatoa ki waenganui. Nāna, te pāpā. Nāna, kua tae mai ki te riringi i te roimata ki runga ki a koe, ki te hari mai i te aroha.
Poroporoaki i ngā mate	Nō reira, takoto, takoto, takoto, takoto. Takoto, māu e karanga, māua [h]e wā, ka tae mai. Ka tae mai. Ka haramai ki te hari mai i te roimata, ngā [h]au e whā kua takoto mai ki mua ki tō aroaro. Kei te tangi ki a koe. Inā, nā te wā o Tauweke, a Te Rauwera. Tukuna mai e ia, e rātou o . . . kōrerotia ake e au ngā Kīngitanga, tekau mā rua. Nānā, e Tonga, kua tae mai te mōrehu o Tauweke, o Tauweke. Nō reira, takoto, takoto. Takoto e pāpā.
Poroporoaki	I karea anō rā i kotia te ara ki Te Reinga i tūhera tonu mai i te pō ka kī te tangata nō mua mai ia nō Ara, nō Mai. Karekau ana he toa i te ao nei hei kuru i te mate kotahi anō ia e mano ki te hinganga i . . . Nō reira, te pāpā, mai rā anō i ērā wā, mai rānō ā, kāore anō i kotia noatia te ara ki Te Reinga. E tū ana tonu mai i te wā i ara mātou ki roto i tēnei rā e eke nei, e eke nei, e eke nei. Nō reira, takoto. Takoto, kei te eke mai ērā karangatanga, ērā karangatanga, ērā karangatanga. Inā, nā te kati. Wai[h]otia atu e ia te tini mate i muri, engari te mamae o te tangata kua tae mai ki tōu aroaro. Ko tae mai, nāna, ngā aituā, nō reira, he w[h]akanui tō koutou, he w[h]akakī tō koutou, e ara nei koutou i roto i tēnei marama.
Waiata	
Kōrero whakakapi	Nō reira, [h]aere, [h]aere e koro, [h]aere. Nō reira, tēnā anō tātou katoa. Tēnā anō tātou katoa kua tae mai tātou ki te mihi ki tō tātou tau wehe, ki tō tātou matua. Te kōpura whakamutunga mai i Wharenui ki Waitōtara . . ., nō reira, tēnā anō tātou, kia ora tātou.

SAMPLE WHAIKŌRERO 9

a) Orator	
e) Tribal affiliation	Taranaki
i) Location/venue	
o) Forum	Tangihanga/funeral (author's deduction)
u) Source	Radio New Zealand, Dat Tape 3, Dat341-2, Side A (8'21"-18'43")
ha) Visitor/host	
he) Sections	
Mihi/poroporoaki i ngā mate	A[h]akoa kua wa[h]angū koe, e koro, e [a]hakoa, nā ngā ao ka kīia ō tūpuna, ō mātua, e tēina atu nei ki mua i a koe. Ko te mea nui rawa, e . . . . . ., Maniapoto-Waikato, taka[h]ia atu ana e koe ō aituā, [h]aringia mai ana e koe, ka tika kē ērā kupu. Ka tika kē ngā mihi i konā. [H]aere mai Waikato, [h]aere mai Maniapoto, [h]aere mai me te aro[h]a, o te pikitanga mai, o te eketanga mai, ngā pikitanga, o . . . mai.
Pepeha	Nāna te w[h]akamutunga o tō mātou . . . nāna kē i whakaeke mai. Ka tika kei ngā [h]ui e piri atu nei ki a koe, ki a koutou, e Kāti, a[h]akoa kua tae koe, kei runga i a koe te Nehenehenui. Waikato-Maniapoto, kei runga i a koe. Āmine, Āmine ngā kupu kōrero me ngā mihi. Tēnā koutou, nā runga i ēnei rangi, Parinini[h]i ki Waitōtara, Te Āti Awa, Ngāti Ruanui, kia ora e [h]ui[h]ui tātou.
Tauparapara	Ka [h]ura rā tana tau ki te atua rā kia tuki tana tātai ka [h]ura rā tana tātai te tura kē . . . tana tāuta ka rā hoki te koroko nui, te korokoro a . . . ko Tū, ko Tū, ko Rongo, ko Rongo.

Kaupapa – poroporoaki i te mate

Hāngai tonu aku kōrero, e Tonga, ki a koe i tēnei mēneti, mēneti korokoro nō tō whānau, o tō whānau, i te mihi ki a koe, nā, ko tae mai inanahi, inapō, kāre e wareware ki āu kōrero ki a au, 'He tamaiti koe nāku, he tamaiti koe nāku, he tamariki koe nāku, he tamaiti koe nāku.' Ka tika tonu ētahi kōrero, e Tonga. . . . Mōhio mai anō au te wā e ora ana taku matua, nā, hei aha, ki a au, i haere mai ai, pēnei au, ka tūtaki mai au ki tō mokopuna i te huarahi, ā, tae noa mai i te ata nei, ka pēnei au kei te waru karaka nei e tae mai tō mokopuna ki te riringi i ngā roimata Kīngitanga ki runga ki a koe. Hei aha noa, me tukuna atu nei kātahi au ka mōhio, kāre tō mokopuna e tae. Kāore ērā o [ōu] whanaunga, ērā kārangarangatanga ōu i runga i tērā o ka, ko Mōkau ki runga, ko Mangatoatoa ki Tāmaki, ki te pou Kīngitanga o Pōtatau e karanga mai nei e te. Ka uru ki roto o Pare Waikato, ki roto o Pare Hauraki, ērā karanga kātoa mōu i whīkoi ai koe i roto i ngā whīkoitanga heke iho. Ka huri mai ki Te Kaokaoroa o Pātetere, ki a Ngāti Hauā, ēnā nohonga tangata nunui e. . . . e tā i ngā kawa, ko koe anō te kaihautū o te Kīngitanga i roto i a rātou. Huri mai koe, Wharepūhunga ki roto o Ngāti Raukawa. Ēnā manu nunui, ēnā kārangarangatanga nunui, ko koe anō te kaumātua o te Kīngitanga e haere i roto i a koe.

Puta mai ki roto o . . . ko Te Nehenehenui, . . . pā mai te kaumātuatanga takataka i waenganui, e, ki tō mokopuna, ā, ki te Kīngitanga, nō reira, ki a au, kei konei, kei te mōhio koe kei te tangi mai tō mokopuna ki a koe i runga i te torona o ōna tūpuna e noho mai rā i te riu o Waikato. Kei te tangi mai a Waikato ki a au, nō reira, koutou te whānau ake, kauaka e whakahuahuatia ake, ko wai ko Te Rangi, Parininihi, ko te tapoto te whetū ake nei i runga anō i ō tātou mokopuna, ... mate o Tonga. [H]e kōrero nui, me tangi nui a tēnei kōrero ki runga ki a koe, e Tonga, ā, me te tangata haere ake te wā, a wai ake? Kāre au e pēnei noa i pai māku ēnei kōrero, pēnei au, ka mau mai i a au tō mokopuna, ka mau mai i a au aku mātua, aku tūpuna i te huarahi, mā rātou e ringingia ēnei kōrero ki runga ki a koe. Hei aha. Kei te mōhio, ka ora mai ō rātou ngākau, tomo mai rātou, . . . mai he kanohi o roto o Waikato ki roto, i runga i tēnei o . . . i mua i a koe. Me mutu e au aku kōrero i konei. Ngā mate katoa kua eke mai ki runga ki a Tonga, i roto i Te Nehenehenui, te mate nui rawa ia, te mate o tērā mokopuna o koutou i te ata, nā reira, haere atu, haere atu ki a Dat. Haere atu ki te rārangi Kīngitanga kei konā e moe mai. Kua mutu aku mihi i konei, kia ora katoa tātou.

Ko te pare kōmutunga tēnei o te ākau, te pāpātanga me te tauhekenga, kua taka ki hea? Ka[h]ore, a[h]akoa ka eke tōna wā [h]ei [h]aerenga a ia. Kei te pai. Kei te tika tonu tana [h]aere. Te w[h]īkoi mutunga tēnā mō tātou mō te tangata, te mate. Kei te [h]aere a ia ki te ringa o te kai[h]anga, koia [h]oki te mea māna e *okayo* te ā[h]uatanga o tātou, o te tangata, ki raro, nō reira, [h]aere, [h]aere ki tō tātou ariki. E ngā karangatanga maha, e ngā [h]au e w[h]ā o te motu, o te kopinga mai o tō tātou pāpā, tō tātou tūeke. Te [h]aerenga mai o ngā aituā ma[h]a i runga i a koutou, ki runga i tā tātou tauira. Tēnā koutou, tēnā koutou, tēnā koutou, nō reira, kia ora tātou.

. . ., takoto, . . . ngā tangamoana i wai[h]o ake ai i ō tūpuna . . . ka whā ia koutou i te wā i aku tūpuna, tēnā koe. Takoto, te tangata nāna i tono, nā ngā whārua e karangatia nei, ngā hau e whā. He aha, e taku tupuna, koia anō noa te aroha, koia e whakamā i a Whiri, e mihi ki a koe i tēnei wā, i roto i ō kura. Mō[h]io ana koe, ko koe anō tēnā kua [h]aramai rā ki ahau, taku mokopuna, hopukia ō mātou kōrero, tēnei wā, e taku tipuna, nā te tino kaha o te aroha, ka kahakina mai . . . kua tū ki mua i a koe. Koia e au ana te ua i tēnei wā, hei ahakoa rā, e taku tupuna, kua [h]aere i tēnei wā, kua tae anō ki ngā wā i to[h]ua mai hei wehe atu i mua i a mātou. Taku māmā i a Tui, taku māmā i a Tamaho, i wā i a Kaa, taku māmā. Koia anō ngā mea kei te mahara ake au, e mau rā ki a rātou, homai i tēnei wā, i te wā i mate ai te Atua. Ko taku kōrero anō tēnei, kia haere mai au i ēnei rā kua taha ake nei. He hauā taku kōrero ki a koe, ka kōrero Pākehā, otirā ko taku tupuna, haere, haere, haere. Haere ki te nui, ki te tini. Haere ki tō tamaiti, ki a . . . nāna nei i karanga te ao. Haere, kua ea e taku tupuna.

Kōrero whakakapi	Kāre e nui rā ngā kōrero, ngā mihi ki a koe, haere, haere, haere.
	Kia ora e huihui anō tātou . . . tēnā koutou. Kāre au i mōhio ki tō huhua kārangaranga i a koutou, ka mahue i a au tētahi, hoki koutou. Kāre hoki au [i] karanga tēnā. Tēnā tātou katoa.

SAMPLE WHAIKŌRERO 10

a) Orator	Kepa Ehau
e) Tribal affiliation	Te Arawa (Ngāti Tarāwhai)
i) Location/venue	Tama-te-kapua marae
o) Forum	Tangihanga/funeral: eulogy to Frederick Augustus Bennett (1950)
u) Source	Brooke-White, *Whaikoorero: Ceremonial Farewells to the Dead*, pp. 5–9
ha) Visitor/host	Tangata whenua/host
he) Sections	
Kōrero whakaratarata	My Lord Bishop, Frederick Augustus Bennett, Commander of the Order of St Michael and St George, Licentiate of Theology.
Mihi/poroporoaki i ngā mate	Te matua i roto i te Ariki, ahakoa kua rangona atu kei te hoki mai koe a tōna rā, nā ngā hau e whā i kōrero tētehi reo o te kāinga ki te whakatau atu i a koe i mua i tō maunutanga mai. Kei te hahae te tau o te ate, kei te hotu te whatumanawa, kei te pātuki te tārāuma, kei te mōteatea ngā mahara mō koutou, mō ngā tāngata o te motu ka huri kāweka nei. Inanahi tata, whakatika te matua o te iwi Māori, a Tā Āpirana Ngata, haere atu ana ki a koro mā. Pō rua mai, ka whakaoma atu hoki tō Tūwharetoa, a Tūpara Maniapoto. Nō te rā nei, ko koe kei taku ariki, kua whai atu koe i te ia, i te oru o tō koutou tira. He aha rā tēnei hanga? Koia rānei he pukenga wai, he pukenga tangata? Koia kē pea ko te heke o Maruiwi i toremi ai ki Te Reinga? He parekura, he aituā! Heoi rā, e Pā mā, haere i te ringa kaha o te mate! Ngā tōtara haemata, ngā totara whakahīhī o te wao tapu nui a Tāne Mahuta. Ngā tāngata hautū, ngā haumi, ngā whakatakere o ngā waka. Ngā toka tū moana ākinga ā-tai, ākinga ā-hau, ākinga ā-ngaru tūātea. Aku parepare, aku whakaruruhau. Te mūrau a te tini, te wenerau a te mano. Aku manu tīoriori, aku manu hōnenga, ngā kākā waha nui o te pae, ngā kākā haetara ki te iwi i ana rā. Ngā tamariki o ngā whare tapu, ngā whare wānanga, ngā whare maire, ngā whare whakairo, ngā whare kōrero, haere koutou ki te wā kāinga. Te Pīhopa Māori tuatahi o te Hāhi o Ingarangi i whānau, i nānātia, i whakatupuria koe i te wā kāinga, i whakatangatatia atu koe ki Te Waipounamu. Nō reira, ka tāpaea e koe tōu tinana ki te para ki te ngaki i te māra a tō tātou Matua. Nōu ka hoki mai, ka ūhia ki runga i a koe te Pīhopatanga o Aotearoa. Kua whawhaitia e koe te whawhai pai, kua omakia e koe te oma pai. 'Kua mōai koa a Taupiri, a Te Rewarewa, e tū tai ana rā, te kauika taramea i te mātārae i waho o Muruika.' Takoto, e moe, okioki te 'Tamarahi-pāriri, tītoko o te rangi whakawhiti o te rā, whakaaio whenua.' Te pononga a Te Atua, haere, e hoe i runga i tō waka i te whakapono. E tae koe ki ngā rire o ngā rangi, ki te tauranga i tō Atua, tēnā te reo pōwhiri whakatau i a koe:

Mihi ki te hunga ora, mihi whānui	'Haere mai e te hunga whakapai a tōku Matua, nohoia te rangatiratanga o te rangi, kua rite noa atu mō koutou nō te ōrokohanganga mai rā anō te ao.' Kahungunu! Kei te hira rawa tāku whakamoemiti ki a koe mō tōu aroha, whakaaro rangatira ki te whakahoki mai i a Pēneti ki te hau kāinga. Kei te whakawhetai a Te Arawa mō tēnei koha nui whakaharahara. William Boyle Bennett, kei te mihi atu ki a koutou ko ō tāina, tuāhine i tō tātou tuakana ka moe. Taku tamāhine kahurangi, a Arihia Ngārangi-o-Ue, te oha pouaru ā taku rangatira, kei te tangi atu ki a koutou ko te pōkai kura me te whānau pani. Samuel Marsden Bennett, kei te oha ki a koutou ko ō tāina, tuāhine. Pōuritia, mamaetia, tangihia te matua ka wehe, ka riro i mua ki te taka, ki te whakapai mai i te kāinga hei tukunga atu mō tātou.
Kōrero whakakapi	Noho mai i roto i tō tātou whare mate, whare pōuri, whare tauā. Mā te Atua koutou e manāki, e tiaki. Māna e mea tōna mata kia tīaho iho ki runga ki a koutou, māna koutou e atawhai. Māna e whakaara ake te māramatanga o tōna kanohi ki a koutou, māna e homai te rangimārie ki a koutou, āianei, ā ake, ake, ake.
Whakamutunga	Pererika! Nau mai, hoki mai ki te wā kāinga, ki ō maunga, ki ō kōhatu, ki ō moana, ki ō kārangarangatanga e tauwhanga atu nei, e apakura nei mōu. Ki konei koe tukua atu ai ki tōu hono tātai, ki a Taipōrotu Te Mapu-o-te-rangi. Kōrua ngā puhi kākākura o runga i a Te Arawa – ki a Te Arawa iwi, ki a Te Arawa tangata, ki te Hono-i-wairua, ki te Pūtahi-nui-a-Rehua, ki te tini, ki te mano, ki te ngia o te mātoru i te Pō!

SAMPLE WHAIKŌRERO 11

a) Orator	Pei Te Hurinui Jones
e) Tribal affiliation	Ngāti Maniapoto
i) Location/venue	Tūrangawaewae marae
o) Forum	Tangihanga/funeral: eulogy to Kingi Korokī (1966)
u) Source	Brooke-White, *Whaikoorero: Ceremonial Farewells to the Dead*, pp. 12–14
ha) Visitor/host	Radio New Zealand broadcast.
he) Sections	
Mihi/poroporoaki i ngā mate	Haere, e te Kīngi, ki tua o Paerau. Haere i runga i ō waka, haere i runga i ngā maunga kōrero ā ō tūpuna e moe nei i te whenua. Kua rewa atu tō waka, e te Ariki, mā roto i tō awa i Waikato. he wai pounga hoe mai nā ō mātua.
He rangaranga	E huri tō kanohi ki te Hauāuru ki Whāingaroa, ki Aotea, ki Kāwhia. Ka ahu mai ai, e Tama, tō tira ki te ara mauī ki runga o Maungatautari, ki te hikonga uira i runga o Wharepūhunga i Rangitoto. Ngā tohu ēnā a ō tūpuna. Takahia ē koe, e Tama, te ara ki Rotorua-nui-a-Kahu. Ka tae atu ai koe ki Te Rotoiti, kei konā, e Tama, ngā wai kaukau a ō tūpuna o Ngāti Pikiao o runga i a Te Arawa, i tō ara tāne, mai i a Tamatekapua.

APPENDIX 197

He rangaranga (cont'd)	Taiāwhio te haere i runga i ō waka i a Mātaatua, Horouta, Tākitimu kia mihia mai koe e ngā uri a ō tūpuna a Toroa, a Porourangi, a Kahungunu. Whakamau mai mā te Upoko-o-te-Ika ki ō kāwai maha, ki a Raukawa, ā, ka piki mai mā runga i ō waka i a Kurahaupō, i a Aotea, i a Tokomaru. Kei Parininihi, māu e maianga mai ki Mōkau, ki Mangatoatoa, ki Tāmaki-makau-rau. E huri tō kanohi ki Te Taitokerau ki ō tūpuna o roto i ngā toronga maha, i a Rongopatutaonga, ka whakangaro atu ai koe, e Tama, ki tua o Mōriānuku. Haere, te Puhi o Tainui, moe mai i runga i a Taupiri, i te urunga o te kahurangi ka oti atu koutou te rārangi kīngi ki te Pō.
Kōrero whakakapi	Kī okioki ē, ē hē, tōia te waka. Kī okioki, ē hē, tōia te waka. Ki runga ki te maunga e tū mai nei. Whakatakotoria ki te ngaro parapara koa. Me he tētē waka, hei me he tētē waka, hei, Me he pītau whakarei te tētē kura o te waka!

SAMPLE WHAIKŌRERO 12

a) Orator	Whati Tamati
e) Tribal affiliation	Waikato (Ngāti Māhanga)
i) Location/venue	Tūnohopū marae
o) Forum	Tangihanga/funeral: eulogy to Kepa Ehau (1970)
u) Source	Brooke-White, *Whaikoorero: Ceremonial Farewells to the Dead*, pp. 25–29
ha) Visitor/host	Manuhiri/visitor
he) Sections	
Tauparapara Mihi/poroporoaki i ngā mate	Tēnei, tēnei manawa e hē nei, e Kepa! Ko kōpū parapara ko tāu urunga. Te kurī mitimiti i te hinu a Houmai, kā whati. Ko Rehua. Ko te hou koe a wai? Ko te hou koe a te tini. Ko te hou koe a Houmaitawhiti! Nā Houmaitawhiti ko te tianara o runga i te waka nei i a Te Arawa i purutia ai te mauri ora o rātou mai o tērā rangi tae mai ana ki tēnei rangi, takoto nei.
Pepeha	Nō Maketū ki Tongariro. Nō Maketū ki Tongariro. I pupū mai ai te wai i te take o Tongariro ki te moana o Rotorua, ki te awa o Waikato tōna puianga paengahuru ki Te Moana-nui-a-Kiwa. Nōu te reo, e Kepa, mōu, ki runga ki a Tainui waka mai i Tāmaki ki Mōkau, Hauraki ki Pare Waikato, Mangatoatoa ki waenganui ki Te Kaokaoroa-a-Pātetere.
Mihi ki te kāhui ariki	Kua tatū mai. Kua tatū mai. Kua tatū mai. Kua tatū mai te mokopuna a te motu. Kua tatū mai te Kāhui Ariki. Kua tatū mai ana kuia, koroua. Ka tere pipi whakaao ki mua ki a koe, ki tō reo. Tēnei te tau nei! Tēnei te tau nei! Tēnei te tau nei! Me ngā waka o te motu mai i te maunga hauhunga ki reira, ki Taranaki, kua tatū mai.

Kaupapa	Tēnei wāhanga, tēnā wāhanga, nāu i karanga kua tatū mai. Tēnei te kawe mai nei i ngā taonga whakamirimiri a ō kuia, a ō koroua i waiho ake ai.
Te takitaki o tēnei hanga o te mate te roimata, te hūpē, i roto i te rārangi e kīia rā, 'Whāia te kotahitanga o te wairua,
Nā te aroha me te rangimārie i paihere'. Ō taonga tēneki whakamirimiri i a koe e ora ana, waihotia ake.
Nō reira, kua tatū mai. Kua tatū mai. Kua tatū mai.
Kepa Ehau ā te tini, ā te mano. Ahakoa ō hoa i te taha Māori, ahakoa i te taha Pākehā. Kei te mōhio atu ki te rā o Tūmatauenga ko koe te kaihautū; ko koe i roto i te mura o te ahi. I a koe ngā manaakitanga a te Runga Rawa tatū mai ai koe ki tēnei rā. I meingatia ai e ia tēnei wehenga mōu i runga i tō marae, i roto i te iwi huri noa i ngā hau e whā.
E Kepa, haere! Haere! Haere! Haere! E haere atu ana, e mōhio atu ana, i eke koe ki runga ki ngā taumata i kōrerotia ai, he whitu tekau, he waru tekau he mahi māuiui. Mahue mai i a koe ēnei, ēnei taumata.
Nō reira, he ahakoa ngā taonga katoa i a koe, ā, kua waihotia iho rā e koe ki te hunga i mahue ake. Nō reira, haere te pou tōtara. Haere te waha kōrero ki runga ki ngā marae maha, puta atu ki roto ki ngā whare wānanga rapu i te ora mō te iwi,
Ko koe. Nō reira, haere i te rā i tohungia ai e te Atua. Haere ki te tīmatanga. Haere ki te whakamutunga. Haere ki ō tātou mātua me te iwi. Ehara i te huarahi hou, nō ngā whakatupuranga. Ahakoa poropititanga, ko te takotoranga tēnā; ahakoa Kīngitanga, ko te takotoranga tēnā; ahakoa tohunga, ko te takotoranga tēnā.
Nō reira, kua takotoria e koe i roto i tēnei rangi.
Haere! Haere! Haere!
Nā, kua eke mai. Kua eke mai.
He ahakoa ngā aituā i runga i a Tainui waka kua tau tahi ki a koe ki a Te Arawa i tēnei rangi. Ahakoa ngā mate kua whetūrangitia, kua tatū mai te pito ora, e kōrerotia rā te hunga mate.
Ka kīia ka ea, ka ea, ka ea te wāhi ki a rātou. Kei te hoa, haere. Pōtiki, haere. Haere ki te Pūtahi-nui-a-Rehua. Ki te poutūtanga nui o Pipiri, ki te urunga tē taka, ki te moenga tē whakaarahia. Waiho mā te hunga i mahue i muri e whai atu i ō tapuwae.
Nō reira, haere ki te tīmatanga, haere ki te whakamutunga.
Waiata	Takoto ana mai te marama i te pae te tara ki Te Uruhi.
He ripa tauārai ki te iwi ka ngaro.
Ki te pō uriuri, ki te pō tangotango, ki te pō oti atu.
Hei whare kōrero, hei whare wānanga
mā Hine-Nui-i-Te-Pō e kuku nei i te tangata.
Te hinganga o te tini, te moenga o te mano.
Mau tonu iho nei ngā whakataukī a Tūpaengarau.
I tūtuki ō wae, ngā hauata,
taka i te rākau, taka te wai – ngā hauata . . . i.
Wera i te ahi, hinga ki te whare – ngā hauata.
Whakatūtū ai te kapua i te rangi me he ko Kaiwaka.
I tohia iho nei ki te tohi o Uenuku
ki te tohi tāngaengae,
te whatu o te āhuru nā . . . ē!

SAMPLE WHAIKŌRERO 13

a) Orator	Mane Tatare
e) Tribal affiliation	Te Tairawhiti
i) Location/venue	Te Poho-o-Rawiri Marae, Tūranga-nui-a-Kiwa
o) Forum	
u) Source	MPT 2
ha) Visitor/host	Tangata whenua/host
he) Sections	

Tauparapara	Takatū ana ngā tai ki te ākau, e whakanukunukuhia, kia whakanekeneke whiua rerehia rātou ki te wai, ki tai wiwī, ki tai wawā. Toia te hau marangai kia kaha rongo taku kiri i te kikini o rehutai, o ngā tai whatiwhati e haruru nei mō koutou i te rā nei.
Rangaranga whenua	Tū ana tā a runga o Hikurau o Titirangi. Ka titiro a Tūmai awa, ka tū ki Te Aitanga-a-Māhaki. Ko te maunga haumi tērā. Ka huri ki Rongowhakaata. Ka huri ki Tāmanuhiri, ka huri ki te koroua nei, ki a Taharākau nōna nei te kōrero, 'Te kai a taku kāinga, he ahi kouka i te awatea, he ai i te pō.'
Whakataukī	
Mihi ki te marae	Tihei mauri ora. E tika ana, Papa-tū-ā-nuku takoto. Tawini [Tawiri], te tipuna awhi i te hunga haere. Whakaoi anō tēnei e karanga nei, e kaupapa nei ki te hunga haere ki te hunga whakaeke ki runga i a koe.
Mihi ki te hunga ora	Haere mai, haere mai, haere mai. Haere mai ngā koroua, haere mai te āhuatanga kei runga i a koutou i tatū mai ai koutou ki tēnei marae e mōhiongia ana e te ao Pā[kehā], e te ao Māori, Te Poho-o-Rawiri. Nō reira, haere mai koutou.
	Nā te mea, he uaua tonu ki a au tēnei mea te kōrero, engari, ka kore au e mōhio kei te kōrero au ki a wai, ka tino uaua rawa atu. A, heoi anō, haere mai te mea nui, haere mai te mea nui. Kei te pai noa iho ki ahau tā koutou tae mai i tēnei wā, nō te mea hoki, he ao kē tēnei. Nāwai i kī kia pū anake, ko mahi tangata. He whakaputa atu tērā kōrero, nō reira, he pai noa iho tā koutou tae mai i tēnei wā. Ngā āhuatanga pea o te wā i tae mai ai koutou i tēnei. Ko te mea nui kē, me kī pēnei. Kua tae mai koutou, kua hāwhe tutuki ō koutou whakaaro, ākuni roroa ake, kua kī whakaaro nei, ā, nā, kātahi ka tīmata ngā painga o tā koutou haere mai. Kei te kāpō tonu au i tā koutou haere, engari, ko te mea nui kē, he taonga waiho i runga i a rātou, whakataungia, mihingia te ope haere, te ope haere. Koia nei nā taku tū kai konei, e aku rangatira, hei kōrero ki a koutou. Haere mai ngā mate o Tākitimu rāua ko Horouta, kei ngā marae huhua o Te Tairāwhiti, o Te Poho-o-Rawiri e ono, o ētahi ake o ngā marae nei. Kua kōrerongia [e] mātou. Kua tangihia mātou i ōnā rā, engari, te wā nei, ko koutou e whakahua rā i ngā mate o Te Tairāwhiti, ngā mate kei runga i a koutou haria mai, haria mai.
Kōrero whakakapi	Kimihia, rangahau kei whea rā koutou ka ngaro kē. Kei ngā pakanga i paerau pea. I paheke i Whiro te pūpū ai tō hekeroa i te pō [nō noa nei]. Haere koutou, kua huri koutou i te ārai takoto mai, koutou rau rangatira mā o ngā marae o ngā rohe i takahia mai e koutou. Nau mai ki runga o, ki Te Poho-o-Rawiri. Kei konei ngā kārangarangatanga o te rohe, o te rohe. Mai Te Paritū ki Te Taumata-o-Apanui, ka huri ki Ōrapāpārua. Kei konei, haere mai, haere mai koutou kia tūtakitaki koutou i ngā uri a rātou kua ngaro ki te pō, [i tau ki raro].

SAMPLE WHAIKŌRERO 14

a) Orator	Hare Reniti
e) Tribal affiliation	Ngāti Awa
i) Location/venue	
o) Forum	
u) Source	MPT 2
ha) Visitor/host	Tangata whenua/host
he) Sections	

Mihi ki te atua

Me hua pēnei ake au, te kōrero tuatahi nā, ko tērā kōrero, mā te whakahua ake, ko te wehi ki a Ihowa te tīmatanga o te mātauranga. Ko ia te tīmatanga me te whakamutunga. Ko ia anō hoki te tīmatanga me te whakaotiotitanga.

Mihi ki te hunga ora

Kei roto i tērā kupu te āhuatanga mō tātou, i roto i te kupu o tō tātou matua i te rangi. Kia tae mai ki runga i te āhuatanga o tō koutou reo i karanga ai e whai haere nei i ngā tapuwae o te Ringatū.

Kaupapa

Ko tēnei rā, koinei te rā o te okiokitanga. Kei roto nā hoki ōna kupu katoa, te whakamāramatanga o ngā wāhi o te reo o ngā uri o te tangata. Kāre au i te whakahoki ake ahau i te kōrero ki rō inanahi haere mai ai i runga i tā koutou reo ki te whakatutuki i te rangatiratanga, i te tapu, i te mana ake kei roto i tō koutou reo. Te uri e kōrerotia ake nei i roto i tēnei rā, i haere mai ki a Rawiri, ki tana marae i mua atu hoki ki Te Poho-o-Rawiri. Kia oti ko tēnei rā, ko te hāpati e kōrerotia ake nei, koinā te whakaotiotitanga o te kupu tuatahi i runga kē i ngā taumata e tohi ai ki tēnā wāhi, ki tēnā wāhi. Kua hoki mai tēnei ki te rāwhiti. Nō koutou te rā oti i tēnei. Kua tae mai kia oti ki a koe te Rongopai. Kei konei te whakaotiotitanga i runga i te tangata o te rangimārie, i roto i te ngākau o te aroha. E mōhio te hunga tātou, te hunga e whakapono ana. Engari, me pēnei, ko taku kōrero, tēnā koe te Rongopai e whakahuritia nei e koe, te kaumātua, te kōhatutanga o ngā whakaaro i roto i te whakapono, i te tikanga. . . . Haere mai i ngā whare, amuamutanga i ngā marae kia tae mai koutou ki roto ki a koutou i tēnei rā. Kia tae tōmuri mai ki roto i a koe kia uru mai ko te whānau ki roto. Māku e tae mai e whakahua ake i tana kupu kāre i roto i tēnei. Korekore ake nei au te haeretanga o ngā tāngata i runga i te whakaaro Māori e haere mai ai taua kupu i mahara ai rātou he wairua poke, engari kei koneki. Waiho tonu i reira te takototanga o taua kōrero e whakahoki ake ana ki te okiokitanga.

Ko wāna mahi katoa, ko koutou tēnei, ko ngā uri Māori e whai nei i te hokitanga tē tutakahia. Kei roto, kei tēnei kupu e kōrero ake au, kotahi tonu, kotahi tonu te kupu. I te tīmatanga te kupu, mā te Atua te kupu, ko te Atua anō taua kupu. Kei konei e huna ana te āhuatanga o taua wairua ora. Engari, kei a koutou, kei a koutou. Āe, he whānuitanga atu o aku kōrero, waiho mā te kaumātua nei e whakaotioti ngā mihi me mihingia nei ki ō tātou mate, ngā mihi ki ō tātou māuiui mā tō tātou koroua e whakahoki. Nā reira, koinei hei kupu kōrero ake, nā, kei waenganui i a tātou, Tūpai, tēnā koe e noho ake nei i runga i te taumata.

APPENDIX 201

Mihi ki te hunga ora	E pūpū ake nei te wāhī nā tātou kua hoki mai, hoki rangatira mai e mā, ki roto i tēnei āhuatanga. Ka āhei, tō tātou tēnei, ko te whakawhirinakitanga i runga i te whakaaro kotahi ki taua kupu e kōrerotia ake nei. Koia nei te taonga o tō koutou koroua, o tō koutou tipuna i tīhae rā i ngā whatumanawa ki runga ki te whenua, ki te tangata kia maringi rawa te toto kia kitea ai i te ao māramatanga i roto e kōrero nei koutou te āhuatanga katoa e whakahua haere nei i ngā tau. Āe, e hoatu ki a ia, nāna hoki i whakahua te hōnoretanga, te korōria hei painga ki runga maunga-ā-rongo ki runga i te whenua hei painga mō ngā tāngata katoa i roto i a Waikato, te Rohe Pōtae o ngā Kīngitanga, ngā Kīngitanga kē a te Atua. Nā reira, kua tae mai rā tēneki, koneki tō koutou whakaaro hei ngā tamariki. Nā te hunga e hauhautia ai te āhuatanga mātauranga. Kei a koutou e titiro ake nei i roto i te whare nei ngā whakapikopikotanga. Ngā āhua katoa kei koneki, kei konā katoa ngā tohungatanga a ō koutou tīpuna e whakaoioi i a koutou. Hei aha? Hei painga mō wai? Hei painga mō ngā tāngata katoa huri noa i te ao.
Kōrero whakakapi	Nā reira, koinei te whakapaingia i te ingoa o tō tātou Atua, o ngā mea pai katoa kua whakawhiwhia ki a tātou. Waiho i reira. Te [awherotanga] hei whakaranea atu i te āhuatanga o te reo.
Whakamutunga	Nō reira, tēnā koutou, tēnā koutou, ki a tātou katoa.

SAMPLE WHAIKŌRERO 15

a) Orator	Eruera Manuera
e) Tribal affiliation	Ngāti Awa
i) Location/venue	
o) Forum	
u) Source	MPT 2
ha) Visitor/host	Tangata whenua/host
he) Sections	
Whakaaraara	Tihei mauri ora.
Kōrero whakarata	Kei te kimi noa ake i ētahi kōrero kē, kē atu i wā wēnei kua tū ake nei i mua i awau, kāre e kitea e au. Ko aua kōrero rā anō kua kōrerotia ake nei ināianei. Heoi anō i te pai ko tāua te Māori kāre e riri ki te pērā, ahakoa kōrero atu, kōrero mai, ko aua kōrero rā anō, kāre tāua te Māori e kī, e kī e pupuri. Engari, pērā kei roto i Te Kooti Whenua Māori, kāre e kore ka panaia, ā, karanga mai, kua kōrerotia anō ēnā, wēnei o ngā āhuatanga e tētahi o ngā tāngata kua mutu ake nei.
Mihi ki te hunga ora	Nā reira rā, whakatau mai rā, whakatau mai rā ki a tātou, ki ngā mōrehu o tēnei wā. Kei reira, kua tae mai i te āhua o ngā tikanga ērā āhuatanga katoa i whakaarohia ai, nā, kia mauria mai ki konei tirotiro ai me kore e kitea he wāhi pai hei tūtūtanga mō tēnā wāhi, mō tēnā mea, mō tēnā mea. Nā reira, tēnā koutou, tēnā koutou, te hunga i puta ngā mahara pēnei. Anei, ka kitea ēnei āhua, ēnei whakaaro. Anei koutou ka kitea, me pēnei. Nā reira, tēnā koutou, tēnā koutou te hunga kaha ki te titiro i ngā āhuatanga katoa o tātou, o tātou o roto o tēnei rā, ahakoa kei whea noa atu e haere rā. Kāre kau he kōrero kē atu, kāre kau he kōrero kē atu.
Mihi/poroporoaki i ngā mate	Heoi anō, he mihi tonu ki a koutou, ā, ki ētahi o ō tātou aituā hoki, ngā aituā kua whetūrangingia, kua tukua ki te taura whenua, kua mihia, tangihia.
Kōrero whakakapi	Engari ko tātou ngā pare kawakawa o wērā mate, katoa koutou, tātou, rātou rā ko te hunga ora, nā reira, ka mihi atu ki a koutou, tēnā koutou, tēnā koutou, tēnā koutou.

SAMPLE WHAIKŌRERO 16

a) Orator	Waha Stirling
e) Tribal affiliation	
i) Location/venue	
o) Forum	Pōhiri: South Island Secondary School *Kapa Haka* Competition
u) Source	MPT 2
ha) Visitor/host	Tangata whenua/host
he) Sections	
Tauparapara	Tihei uriuri, tihei nakonako. Tau hā whakatau hā ko te marae whakatau hā, ko te rangi kei runga. Whakatau hā, whakatau hā, ko te Papa-tū-whenua. Whakatau hā, ko te matuku i heke mai i Rarotaka [Rarotonga] i rukuhia ai a manawa pou roto, i rukuhia ai a manawa pou waho. [Tina], whakatina kia tina, te matuku i heke mai e pūpū ana e wāwau ana. Tārewa tū ki te rangi. Eke, eke panuku, eke Takaroa, eke, eke ki te wheiao, ki te ao mārama. Whano, whano, haere mai (i) te toki, haumi e, hui e, tāiki e!
Mihi ki te hunga ora	Ngā hau, ngā waka, haere mai, haere mai, haere mai. Haere mai i runga i te karanga. Haere mai i runga i te karanga o tō mātou rangatira kua tīraha ake nei, haere ki . . ., haere mai koutou, ngā mōrehu o ngā marae. Haere mai me ngā aituā maha i pani atu rā koutou i te tau i te paunga o te tau. Nau mai, haere mai, haere mai i te karanga o te koroua nei, ahakoa kua tīraha rā tō mātau rangatira, kei konei tonu, kei konei tonu.
Mihi/poroporoaki i ngā mate	Nō reira, haere mai koutou, haere mai koutou me ngā āhuatanga o ngā aituā kei runga i a koutou. Nā koutou i tangi, nā tātou katoa. Nō reira, kia oti te wāhi ki a rātou mā, haere, haere, haere.
Kaupapa	Kei te rangatahi, kei ngā putiputi ātaahua puta noa, puta noa, puta noa. Ko koutou ngā putiputi o āpōpō. Tēnā koutou, tēnā koutou. Inā ka manuhirihia mātou i a koutou i tēnei wā. Ngā manu kōrero, ngā kōhanga reo, koutou. Kia ora ki a koutou tamāhine mā, e tama mā, koutou. Nau mai, haere mai i tēnei rā. Haere mai i runga i ngā āhuatanga hei whāwhā, hei whāwhā i ngā mea tapu o ō koutou tīpuna, hei takoto i te kōrero o tētahi koroua:
Kōrero whakakapi	E tipu e rea i tōu ao- *grow up healthy child, in your years*, ō ringaringa ki ngā mea a te Pākehā, *those hands of yours to those things of the white man*, hei ara mō tō tinana, *so that you may survive*. Ko tō wairua ki ngā mea tapu o ō koutou tīpuna hei tikitiki mō tō rae, *those sacred things of your ancestors, be there ever, that is be a guardian to your forehead for the days ahead. Last but not least*, ko tōu wairua, kia aroha ki te Atua nāna i hanga ngā mea katoa, *your love for the maker, God, the father āmine*.
Whakamutunga	Ka mutu ēnei kōrero pakupaku, kei te makariri hoki ā tātou tamariki, kei te patua e te huka o Papa. Nō reira, kei te whakapotopoto ēnei, aku kōrero. E ngā rangatira o ngā marae, tēnā katoa koutou.
Waiata	Haere ki te . . . . . . ehara taku maunga i te maunga nekeneke, he maunga tū tonu eee.

SAMPLE WHAIKŌRERO 17

a) Orator	Hohua Tutengaehe
e) Tribal affiliation	Mātaatua (author's deduction)
i) Location/venue	Christchurch
o) Forum	Pōhiri: *Kapa haka*
u) Source	MPT 2
ha) Visitor/host	Tangata whenua/host
he) Sections	

Tauparapara	Purapura whetū ki te rangi, he mārama ki te ao, takahia te whenua, takahia te tangata, taku kuru tangiwai ka ngaro. Kia hiwa rā, kia hiwa rā ki tēnei tuku. Kia hiwa rā ki tēnā tuku kei whakaekeekehia koe e te tangata whakaeke. E whakaeke tonu ana ngā tai ki Ōtautahi. Karangatia te tangi a te manu ki Hawaiki e kimi ana, e hahau ana i tana piringa, i taku piringa ki te whaiao, ki te ao mārama, kia kī ake au, tihei mauri ora!
Mihi ki te hunga ora Rangaranga whenua	Te Waipounamu huri noa e pā nei kotahi tonu te kōrero ki a tātou. Kei ngā rangatira, kei ngā kuia, kei ngā uri tātou, tātou, e eke rā mai ki uta ki te Whānau-o-[Tairongo]. Ka whakarangi pūkohu au ki Te Aitanga-o-Whetūroa. kia noho au ki Puhinui ki te maunga[-a-Rongo] o te rangiāniwaniwa. Ki te tihi tapu o Maungapōhatu, kua tae ki Turakina kia tiro atu ai ki raro ko Hamuera, ko Rang[i]tāne, ko Muaupoko, ka huri taku haere ki te tai hau-ā-uru, ki te pūwaha a Tamanui, ko Te Āti Haunui-ā-Paparangi. Piki ana au ki te rā nei, ko Te Āti Awa e mātaki [kau] ake au ki te tihi o Tongariro, e ko Tūkino. Ka rere tika taku haere ki Te Rerenga Wairua ki a Ngā Puhi noa e noho mai na i te Hiku-o-te-Ika. Ākina mai au e te hau marangai, tū ana au i Te Pūwaha o Waikato, e ko Tainui. Kia titiro ake au ki Taupiri, ki a Kīngi Pōtatau, ko te mauri o te motu, he tipua, he taniwha. Me huri noa ake au rā ki a Raukawa, ki Hauraki, ki a Marutūahu. Tāpapa ana au ki te [hiwi] o Moehau kia mārama tonu taku titiro ki Tauranga, e ko Ranginui, ko Te Rangihouhiri ki Rangataua, ko . . . . Tū rangatira tonu au i Rangataua, ko Tauriwakanui. Piki ana au i Te Arakaura [Koura] Noho ana au i runga i te Taumata i Te Riu-o-Tama-a-Waho. Ka titiro atu au ki Te Mauri-o-Waitaha. Ko Mātaatua, ko Ngāti Awa, ki te Mānuka-tū-tahi, ki Whakatane, ki a Apanui ki te Ngutuawa-o-[Mōtu], e piki ai au ki Hikurangi, ko Te Kani-a-Takirau. Ka titiro ki raro ki Ngā-Tukemata-o-Kahungunu hei taka, maumahara mai ki a au ki a Tākitimu ki Te Waipounamu kia tiro noa ake au ki tōna maunga whakahirahira, ki Te Aorangi. Ki te tonga, ko Ngāi Tahu, ko Ngāti Māmoe. Kia whakataukī ake ahau, 'He Whetū te whare, Waihora te moana, Te Rehua te papa marae e takoto nei, te tangata ko Riki Te Maraki Taiaroa, hiki mai, kake mai!
Mihi ki te hunga ora	Kei ngā rangatira kei te hiki te mana, kei te tapu, kei te wehi e haere mai rā, haere mai rā, haere mai aku rangatira o Ngāi Tāua e haere nei. Haere mai i te rā i pāoho ai tō mātou koroua. I tēnei wā kua wairuatia ia, kua tae ki te Ariki, ki tōna matua nui ki te Tonga o Whare Tapu i kaingākautia ai e ia i te wā i a ia.
Kōrero whakakapi Whakamutunga	Nō reira, kei ngā maunga, kei ngā maunga karawa, kei ngā moana parapara, ki a rātou, haere mai, haere mai, haere mai. Ngā mātā waka, ngā mana kōrero o ia taumata, haria mai rā ngā pare kawakawa, whārikihia, haria mai tēnei taonga ātaahua ki taku titiro, ki te kanohi kāre ka kite anō, engari, ki a rātou oti atu, oti atu, oti atu. Kei te pēhi tonutia mātou e ēnei rangatira i katohia nei e Aituā [i riro ai i te ao] tūroa, i pēhia ai e aituā ki roto i te repo e kore nei e kī i te tangata. Nō reira, kei te aroha, haria mai te rangatahi o te tau rangatira hei whāwhā i ngā māuiui i ngā rā kei mua i a rātou. Haere mai, anei rā, kua hinga nei. Kotahi tonu o Te Karetai, haere mai rā ki ngā taonga, ki te tangata whenua.

SAMPLE WHAIKŌRERO 18

a) Orator	Nikora Ngaropo
e) Tribal affiliation	Ngāti Awa/Hato Pētera
i) Location/venue	
o) Forum	Secondary School Speech Competitions (author's deduction)
u) Source	MPT 2
ha) Visitor/host	
he) Sections	
Whakaaraara	Tihei mauri ora.
Tauparapara	He pō, he pō, he pō, he ao, he ao, he ao. Tākiri mai te ata, korihi te manu tino awatea, ka ao, ka ao, ka ao te rā.
Mihi ki te hunga ora Rangaranga whenua	Te Arawa, Te Arawa mai o Maketu ki Tongariro. Ko tā tana karangatanga tēnā, ko Te Arawa. Ko tēnei rā nāu, nāu tēnei rā, nō reira, ka mihi atu ki a koutou Te Arawa.
Mihi ki te hunga ora	Te Arawa, tēnā koutou, tēnā koutou. Nā koutou i karanga tēnei hui kia tū ki a tātou, tēnā koutou, tēnā koutou, tēnā koutou. Ngāti Porou, haere mai, haere mai, haere mai. Haere mai ki Te Ata-o- Taura. Ahakoa nāku i karanga i te rā nei, kua āwhinangia mai au e koe, nō reira, ka hari te ngākau, haere mai, haere mai, haere mai. Te Whakatōhea, haere mai, haere mai, haere mai. Haere mai i runga i Te Ata-o-Taura. Haria mai ngā āhuatanga katoa o ō tātou mate hinga atu ki konā. Ka nui te hari o te ngākau ki a koutou ka huihui mai tātou ki konei i te rā nei ki te whakanui i te kotahi rau tau o ngā kura Māori i tīmatangia ai.
Kōrero whakakapi	Nō reira, ka mihi, ka mihi ki a koutou, tēnā koutou, tēnā koutou. Ngāti Raukawa, haere mai, haere mai, ahakoa kotahi tōu tira, hai aha, he kotahi nō Mōtai tērā te ao nei a . . . te haere, nō reira, haere mai, haere mai, haere mai. Ngā Puhi, haere mai. Haere mai ki Te Ata-o-Taura. Ko koe te tangata tawhiti kia haere mai. I haere mai hoki koe i Te Rerenga Wairua rā anō.
Whakamutunga	Nō reira, ka mihi atu ki a koe, haere mai, haere mai, haere mai. Tēnā koutou, tēnā koutou, tēnā koutou. He wai, kua mutu ahau.
Haka	. . . utaina . . . utaina mai ngā iwi o te motu . . . auē, auē, auē ha hi . . . Nau mai, e ngā iwi.

SAMPLE WHAIKŌRERO 19

a) Orator	Selwyn Muru
e) Tribal affiliation	Ngāti Kurī, Te Aupōuri, Te Pātū, Ngāti Rehia, Murikahara, Te Whakatōhea.
i) Location/venue	
o) Forum	
u) Source	MPT 2
ha) Visitor/host	
he) Sections	
Whakaaraara	Tihei mauri ora ki te whaiao, ki te ao mārama.

Tauparapara	Auē, ka tū rā kei runga ko wai koe kua tū koe? Rangi-nui i runga, Papa-tū-ā-nuku i raro. Ka whakawehea kōrua, pūpū ki raro ko te ira tangata. Ka rangohia rūrū ana te ruru e kai mai ana te kai haere.
Rangaranga whenua	Kāore koa ko au ko Māui-tikitiki-a-Taranga i whakanukunukuhia ai, i whakanekenekehia ai ō tātou waka tapu mai i Hawaiki. Ka tere mai, ka tangi, ka tere mai ka tangi, eke Tangaroa, eke panuku ui e, tāiki e! He pukepuke maunga he piki e te tangata, he pukepuke moana e tēnei, te waka. He mana tangata e kore rā e taea te takahi, nō te mea, he tapu, he tapu, he tapu, he tapu.
Mihi ki te hunga ora	Nō reira, haere mai te tapu, haere mai te ihi, haere mai te mana, haere mai koutou, ngā mana waha nui, ngā manu tīoriori o ō tātou marae. Haere mai ngā maunga, haere mai ngā moana, ngā moana tapu i hoehoengia ai e ō tātou mātua tīpuna . Haere mai ngā toka tū moana, ākina e tai, ākina e hau, akiaki a Tāwhiri-matea. Ka tika te kōrero a tō mātou rangatira nei, kīhai te iwi nei i karanga i tētahi whaea hei mihi ki te motu. Mā mātou anō mātou e hari mai. Mā wai ō mātou mana e takatakahi, mā wai e takatakahi? Kia riro mā ngā pepa o te Pākehā nei? Kāo. Nō reira, ka noho atu ki te pae, ki te mihi ki te karanga i a koutou ō mātou rangatira i te rā . Nō reira, haere mai, haere mai, haere mai. Haere mai Murihiku . . . . Mauria mai rā ngā mana tūhaua o Tūhawaiki mā.

Karitai, koirā toki kia āta koikoi ai ngā mātua tīpuna hei hāpai i ō rātou tokinga nui, pai rawa. Haere mai ngā maunga teitei kei konā. Kāre ō mātou maunga o Te Taitokerau. Pāpaku noa iho ngā maunga o Te Taitokerau. Engari he kōrero rā kei runga, he kōrero katoa kei runga. Ahakoa te pāpaku, nō reira, haere mai ngā maunga teitei a Aorangi, te waka nui o te ao Māori, ko Te Waka-a-Māui. Nō reira, haere mai, haere mai ō mātou rangatira. Haere mai Tahu- pōtiki. Ka tika anō koutou kia haere tahi mai i a Porourangi. Nō reira, haere mai o mātou rangatira. Ko Hikurangi maunga te maunga e kore nei e nekeneke. Engari kua neke katoa mai, mai i te rā nei. |
Kōrero whakakapi	Nō reira, haere mai ō mātou rangatira kua neke katoa mai i te rā nei. Nō reira, Te Ariki Tapairu, whaea, te Kuīni o Ngāti Porou, haere mai ki tō mātou, nā, hei kuīni ki te kuīni. Nō reira, mihia tonu, mihia tonu ngā mana kei runga i a koutou. Ō tātou aituā maha kei runga i a koutou, haria mai rā te pūtaketake. Heoi, ko te whakataukī māku, he kaumātua anō te kaumātua, he kau anō te kau. He kāhui noa iho tēnei e mihi atu ki a koutou. Nō reira, haere mai e koro tangata, whakaporo nui i te rākau. E Mōni, haere mai rā. Ka tika anō māua e ārahi mai te tira nei, māua e ārahi mai. Ko koe te kanohi o Pine Taiepa, ngā tāngata i [w]hakakōrero ai i tō mātou whare i roto i te rākau. Nō reira, haere mai. Ārahia mai tō tira i roto i te rā nei, koutou, e Tame mā, ngā pū kōrero huri noa e mōhio tonu kei muri nā noa ētahi, koinā e tū, e reri ki te tautoko i tō rātou rangatira. Nō reira, haere mai rā, haere mai, haere mai. Nō reira, he koretaketake nā tātou te iwi, he . . . ka hau mai i te pō nei. Kāre e tika mō te pae, kore e taea nā. He kararehe nohinohi ka tingitingi, koinā te take i whakakararehengia ai mātou. Nō reira, kāhore noa i tuku mahi tika, nā te mea, he kararehe noa iho te pae. Koirā rā te whakamahi a ngā iwi ki a tātou tīrarirari i a tātou. Ko te mea nui nā i ngā taonga, nā tātou i tuitui, i herehere ki te . . . . kotahi i runga i te aroha, i runga i te rangimārie.
Whakamutunga	Nō reira, haere mai ō mātou rangatira, haere mai. Nā reira . . .
Waiata	Mā wai rā e taurima mai te marae. . . . . . me te aroha e
Kōrero whakakapi	. . .Āpiti hono, tātai hono, rātou te hunga mate ki a rātou tātou hoki te hunga ora. Tēnā koutou, tēnā koutou, kia huihui mai tātou katoa.

SAMPLE WHAIKŌRERO 20

a) Orator	Pou Temara
e) Tribal affiliation	Ngāi Tūhoe
i) Location/venue	
o) Forum	
u) Source	MPT 2
ha) Visitor/host	Manuhiri/visitor
he) Sections	
Tauparapara Rangaranga whenua	Me whakarangipūkohu e au ki Tititangiao, ki te Aitanga-a-Whetūroa kia whītikiria taku hope ki te maurea whiritoi. [Heke] ana iho au ki Puhinui ki te maunga-ā-rongo o te rangi āniwaniwa. Ka mawhiti rā taku haere ki ngā tihi tapu ki Maungapōhatu. Ka tae ake taku titiro i hoki i Ruatāhuna nā ki Manawatū e, ko te aitanga a Tūhoe Pōtiki puta noa hanga rā o te tipua. A, eke ana au ki Huiarau. Kei te titiro atu au ki te Tai- rāwhiti, ki Hikurangi, ki te maunga e kore nei e nekeneke. Ko Waiapu e rere rā e. Ko Porourangi tēnei. Kia huri mai au ki Te Kani-a-Takirau, ko Hinematioro, ko Rongowhakaata. Ka titiro atu au ki Whakapunake, ki Nukutaurua e. Ira rā, ko te Aitanga-a-Kahungunu. Ka tiawhe rā taku haere ki te pūtake rā o Kahuranaki, ko Te Whatuiāpiti, Tākitimu. Me whakairi tēnei ki konei, ināhoki kua ū ki runga i a koe. Te uri a Te Whatuiāpiti, te uri a Tamatea-Arikinui, te uri a Kahungunu, tēnei koutou te whakaeke i runga i te karanga a ngā taonga nei, i runga i te karanga a te iwi, te hunga kua eke ki te pō, ina rā, kua hoki mai rātou ki te wā kāinga. Kua pau i a rātou te ao te huri. Engari [i] tēnei rā ka mutu tā rātou rā, kua hoki mai rātou ki te kāinga. Hei aha? Hei tirohanga kanohi mā koutou, mā ngā uri o ngā taonga nei.
Mihi ki te hunga ora	Nā reira, e hika mā, nō rātou te reo karanga i tēnei wā, nō rātou te reo karanga ki a koutou ki ngā uri. Nā reira, e hika mā, nau mai te tapu, te mana, te ihi ngā iho i hoatu ai ngā maunga kua tae mai koutou i tēnei rā ki eke ai te whakataukī a ngā tīpuna he pā-tikapu e kitea te tangata, he pā-harakeke kāre e kitea, he tapu, he tapu, he tapu. Nō reira, koutou te tapu, te ihi, te ariā o rātou mā kua huri ki te pō oti ai, ngā karanga ki a koutou. Nāu te āhuatanga ki ō tātou mate i kīia ai ko rātou ki a rātou, ko tātou, ko te hunga ora ki a tātou. Ko tātou nei te uri o rātou mā kua heke ki te pō i ngā rā whakatata nei. Te hunga ora e tau nei, e mihi tātou ki a tātou. Nō reira, i runga i tērā kōrero Ngāti Kahungunu, kāre i taea te kōrero. Haere mai, haere mai, haere mai.
Waiata	Kāore te mokemoke, te tuohu noa . . . . . . ka hoki tāua ki te whare huri ai e.
Kōrero whakakapi	Nō reira, tuia te kawa, tāia te kawa, ko te kawa o te haere, nau mai, nau mai, mihi mai ki Tāmatua.

SAMPLE WHAIKŌRERO 21

a) Orator	
e) Tribal affiliation	
i) Location/venue	
o) Forum	

u) Source	MPT 2
ha) Visitor/host	Manuhiri/visitor
he) Sections	
Whakaaraara	Tihei mauri ora.
Tauparapara	Timotimo te pō, timotimo te ao. Nō Rangi-tū koe, nā Rangi-roa, nā Tāne rā koe, nā Wharehihi, me te Whare-i-rarapa tuki ai Wharerangi.... Tihei mauri ora! Karanga tapu te mauri tū, tū te whiwhi i waho. Puritia mai i waho. Tēnei te Māori e whakakīkī tēnei te mauri. He mauri kei runga, he mauri kei raro. Ka puta ki waho, ki taiao, ki te whaiao, ki te ao mārama, tihei mauri ora!
Mihi ki te whare	E koe, te whare tipuna e tū nei, e tū.
Mihi ki te marae	E te marae e tahora rā, takoto.
Mihi/poroaki i ngā mate	Ko ngā tini mate o tātou, ngā tini aituā, nā koutou i tangi, nā tātou i tangi i tō mātou nei rohe. Nā mātou i tangi, nā tātou i tangi, tēnā koutou, tenā koutou e mihi mai ki a mātou.
Mihi ki te hunga ora	Eritinia. He nui nō te kōrero, he aha rānei? Engari i runga i te kaupapa, i runga i te kaupapa i tae mai ki konei. Kāre i kō atu, kārekau. He aha te kaupapa i . . .??. . . . Ko au tētahi o ngā mea i heipū te haere ki rāwāhi ki te haerenga o tēnei, te tira, o Te Māori ki roto i te ao haere ai. Kua oti tētahi haere. Nō reira, i whai haere nei, i whai haere nei. Nā reira, i haere mai i tapu ai. Kāre he haruru i taku tapuwae i reira, kare e taea e au te kaute.

Nā reira, kei te ora mai koutou i te āhuatanga o Te Māori i roto i tōu ake whakaaro o tēnei i tēnei rā. Hoki ana au ki te kāinga nei i te kōrero o Ngāti Porou, ko aua iwi, iwi e noho nei nā, he aha te mea nui i kitea e koe i tō haere? Nā, hei a rātou tērā pātai rawa atu, te nui pea, o terā pātai. Anei taku kōrero ki a rātou, e waru hāora mātou e rere mai ana, e huri ana ngā mihini a te Pākehā. Kei te titiro [a]hau ki raro. I haramai ō tātou tīpuna, kāre i kitea te aroaro whenua. Nō aku pokohiwi tonu i tae mai ki konei. Kia aha ai? I whiwhi ai tāua, ngā tāngata i tēnei rā he . . . . Nāwai rā, ka tae ki konei. Kāre au e mōhio nā ngā āwhina a te Pākehā. Kātahi *no more*! Ko Te Māori anō tēneki kua kitea e te ao. Kei konei ngā mea e rua hei kōrero māku, he kōrero whakahīhī māku ki ngā mea kāre i haere ki rāwāhi, karanga a te rā, tā Te Māori. Nō reira, kia haere mai nei, haere mai i runga i te kaupapa i rangatiratia ai. E pātai ana au, he aha te kaupapa nei i haere mai koutou ki te āwhina? Nau mai, haere mai. Ehara taku toa i te takitahi, engari he takitini. Whakakotahi kia haere, kia rangatira i tā tēnei rā. Nā reira, tēnā koutou, haramai. He aha te mea, te nui o te kōrero, he aha? Engari he kōrero kē nāu tēnei mō Te Māori nā tātou e noho nei, koutou kei runga i te paepae mai te hokitanga mai i roto o Ākarana nei. Ko koutou ō mātou rangatira i haramai nei mō te tutuki, te āwhina, whakatau. He aha tā mātou, mātou i haere mai mātou ki konei? He aha te kōrero kei te mōhio koutou? He aha mātou tē noho i runga i tō mātou maunga? Ehara i te maunga haere. Koinei rā ngā wero ki a mātou. Patua mātou o Ngāti Porou. Panuku kē i ō mātou wāhine, haere mai ki te rapa haere i ngā uri ka kī mai koutou kia tēnā koutou, he Ngāti Porou koutou, he Ngāti Porou mātou nei i tēnei rā. E wehe ana tāua, i tēnei rā kua kotahi tāua. Nō reira, ko aku kōrero. Me pēnei, ko ngā waka kia haere ki runga i Te Tini-o-Takirau. |
| Kōrero whakakapi | Tēnā koutou, tēnā koutou, kia ora tātou kātoa huri noa i te whare. |
| Waiata | Kāti rā e hika. . .e auē mai rā |

Whakamutunga

Te hokinga mai o ngā taonga ki te wā kāinga. Ngā manuhiri whakaeke ki te whare whakaata taonga o Te Whanganui-a-Tara, arā, nā te waka o Aotea rātou i whakatau, i mihi, i karakia, arā, i uhia ki te taonga nei, ki te aroha i te wā i whakapiri atu ai rātou ki taua wā e whakatūwheratia ana ngā taonga nei ki Aotearoa tonu. Heoi anō rā, ko tētahi o ngā kaumātua māngai kōrero, arā, rongonui o roto o Āti Awa, ko Hoani Heremaia. Ko tēnei tangata, nā rātou rā i whakatutuki ngā whakanekeneke me ngā whakairi i te kōrero ki runga i ngā manuhiri whakaeke. Anei a Hoani Heremaia. Hei a Taranaki te pōhiri tuatahi, ērā e noho ana mātou, nā, mā Mātaatua mā atu i nāianei, ana, ngā ope e whakaeke i tēnei wā, āe. Ko tēnei Ngāti Kahungunu, ko Ngāti Raukawa.

Hei a koutou e mihi nei te roroa o ngā kōrero. Te nunui, te hōhonu o ngā kōrero. Āe, me nunui noa rā, me roroa anō hoki rā i te roa o tō tātou taonga e ngaro atu ana, he roa rawa ngā tau ka whakahokia mai. Ō whakaaro mō te whakahaere i ngā mahi i te atapō nei, i te ono o ngā hāora, ā, tatū mai ināianei i muri i te tekau o ngā hāora. Ā mā tērā hoki rā e oti tōtika ai i te mea kua mahara hou te tinana, ngā whakaaro i te moenga rā i te pō nei, ana, kua pakari te wairua hei manaaki, hei whakatau [i a] koutou ngā kaumātua o te ao Māori i mua i ngā tīpuna tipua nei. Nā i tēnei rangi, āe, i konei hoki te Kāwana Tianara. Nā koutou i mau mai rā i tērā o ō tātou rangatira, ā, koia rā te rangatira o roto o tēnei rā, āe, ana, e whakanui ai hoki tātou, e nui ai tātou i ō mātou manuhiri.

Ka pēhea ngā whakahaere mō tēnei rangi, mō āpōpō, ā, tae noa ki te whakamutunga o te whakairi, whakaataata o ngā taonga Māori ki roto i tēnei whare? Mō ngā wiki tokoiwa, mō ngā wiki tokoiwa kua tuaringia ki ngā iwi o te motu o Te Ika-a-Māui. Kua wātea mai a mea, a Tāmaki-makau-rau, Ngāti W'ātua me Te Taitokerau. Muri atu i konei ki Ōtautahi, ki Ōtakau, ki Tāmaki-makau-rau, ana, mā rātou ko te pēwheatanga. Engari, ko te whakaaro me mutu i reira, ā, ki te pai rawa te tuari haere a ō tātou taonga ki a tātou o kō atu o Pōneke, ko Karaitiati, Ōtakau me Tāmaki-makau-rau. Hoani Heremaia, tēnā rā koe e whakatau nei, e whakatinana nei, e whakakaupapa nei i te manaaki i te tangata. Heoi anō, he mihi kei a koe ki te motu e whakarongo mai nei, kāre anō rātou i tae mai ki tēnei whakaata whakahirahira kei waenganui i a tāua. Āe, rongonui rawa nei pea ki tōku nei mōhio. Ki konei te rongonui o te motu o kō atu rawa o ētahi kē atu e noho ora rā ko ngā taonga nei i ngaro, ā, kua kitea. Heoi anō rā, e Hoani, mihi atu ki te iwi e whakarongo mai nei. Tēnā koutou, tēnā koutou e whakarongo mai nei.

Notes

Chapter One: Introduction

1. Reilly, 'He Kōrero Nehe Māori History', p. 2.
2. E. T. Durie, 'Ethics and Values in Māori Research', p. 65.
3. Cox, *Kotahitanga*, p. 12.
4. There are others who advocate strongly for oral traditions such as McRae (in Thornton, *Māori Oral Literature as Seen by a Classicist*, p. 2); Thornton, ibid, p. 4; Shortland, *Traditions and Superstitions of the New Zealanders*, pp. vii–viii; Reilly, 'He Kōrero Nehe Māori History', p. 18.
5. Cox, *Kotahitanga*, p. 13.
6. Royal, *Te Haurapa*, p. 13.
7. King, *Te Ao Hurihuri*, p. 18.

Chapter Two: What is Whaikōrero?

1. Barlow, *Tikanga Whakaaro*, p. 165.
2. Ibid.
3. The separation of Rangi-nui and Papa-tū-ā-nuku is explained in more detail by Buck, *The Coming of the Maori*, pp. 443–9.
4. Barlow, *Tikanga Whakaaro*, p. 184.
5. Te Kei Merito, interview, 1997.
6. The term *atua* refers to the 'gods responsible for the creation of the universe: the planets, stars, the sun and every living thing on earth, including mankind' (Barlow, *Tikanga Whakaaro*, p. 11).
7. Kimoro Pukepuke, interview, 1997.
8. Literally, the 'female fashioned from the earth'.
9. Wīhapi Winiata, discussion, 2002; Patu Hohepa, interview, 1998.
10. Rangiātea Church, http://rangiatea.natlib.govt.nz/RinAotearoaE.htm, accessed 16 June 2009.
11. Io-matua-te-kore is viewed as the most senior *atua*, from which worldly creation owes its existence.
12. Raiatea, http://en.wikipedia.org/wiki/Raiatea, accessed 16 June 2009.
13. Hue Rangi of Tūhoe and Joseph Malcolm of Te Arawa.
14. Joseph Malcolm, interview, 2003.
15. Mauriora Kingi, interview, 1998.
16. Includes the Te Whāiti–Minginui areas, situated approximately 20 km south-east of Murupara.
17. A tribe in the Murupara district.
18. A tribe in the Waiohau district.
19. A tribe in the Waiohau district.
20. Hieke Tupe, interview, 1996.
21. Ward, *Life Among the Maories of New Zealand*, p. 91.
22. Smith, 'Some Personal Habits or Mannerisms of the Polynesians', p. 458.
23. McGuire, *The Maoris of New Zealand*, p. 165.
24. Mataira, *Pukapuka Pānui*.
25. Mahuta, 'Whaikōrero', p. 4.
26. Hiwi and Pat Tauroa, *Te Marae*, p. 77.
27. White, *The Ancient History of the Maori*, p. 122.
28. Ibid, p. 165.
29. James Milroy, interview, 1997.
30. Salmond, 'Mana Makes the Man', p. 176.
31. Mahuta, 'Whaikōrero', p. 3.
32. Ryan, *The Reed Dictionary of Modern Māori*, pp. 520, 591, 294; and Ngata, *English–Maori Dictionary*, p. 311.
33. Williams, *A Dictionary of the Maori Language*, p. 485; and see http://www.reotupu.co.nz/wakareo/.
34. Schwimmer, *The World of the Māori*, p. 127.
35. Salmond, 'Mana Makes the Man', p. 167.
36. Salmond, *Hui*, p. 130.
37. Kernot, *People of Four Winds*.
38. Hiwi and Pat Tauroa, *Te Marae*, p. 72.
39. Mataira, *Pukapuka Pānui*.
40. Pou Temara, interview, 1997.
41. Hohepa Kereopa, interview, 1997.
42. Kāretu, 'E Aku Raukaura'.
43. James Milroy, interview, 1997.
44. Mataira (*Pukapuka Pānui*) also states that discussions must follow up on what has already said before them during welcoming ceremonies at funerals and all types of gatherings.
45. Tāmati Reedy, interview, 1996.

Chapter Three: How to Learn Whaikōrero

1. Te Uira Manihera in King, *Te Ao Hurihuri*, pp. 7–8.
2. Rangihau in King, *Te Ao Hurihuri*, p. 10.
3. Royal, *Te Haurapa*, pp. 21–22.
4. Orbell, *Hawaiki*, Preface.
5. Best, *The Maori School of Learning*, p. 9.
6. Ibid. Additional descriptions of the *whare maire* include its being referred to as 'a house of witchcraft; men are therein taught the ritual for man-slaying, destruction of food, blasting of trees or the land, spells for [retarding] men's footsteps, and spells said over weapons in war, or the ritual for divorce' (http://sacred-texts.com/pac/lww/lww1.htm).
7. The *whare pōrukuruku* is used for 'the same sort of teaching as in the Whare-maire, but it pertains to a single family, while the Whare-maire is used by all the neighbouring tribes' (http://sacred-texts.com/pac/lww/lww1.htm).
8. Perhaps the preference for night teaching and teaching across the colder part of the year assisted in the students' learning because there would have been fewer distractions during the longer winter nights. Such practices differ from the current opinion of educationalists who prefer morning

classes when the minds and bodies of students are fresh and alert.
9. Best, *The Maori School of Learning*, p. 10.
10. Royal, *Te Haurapa*, p. 41.
11. Best, *The Maori School of Learning*, p. 10.
12. Ibid., p. 6.
13. Dr Tīmoti Kāretu was Head of Department and Professor of Māori Studies at Waikato University in the early 1990s.
14. Best, *The Māori School of Learning*, p. 5.
15. McGuire, *The Maoris of New Zealand*, p. 37.
16. Cox, *Kotahitanga*, p. 12.
17. Salmond, 'Mana Makes the Man', p. 51.
18. Moon, *Tohunga Hohepa Kereopa*, p. 75.
19. Salmond, 'Mana Makes the Man', p. 51.
20. Ngā Manu Kōrero, online.
21. Te Hui Ahurei a Tūhoe was formerly known as Te Whetiwara o Tūhoe, the Tūhoe Festival.
22. Study at Massey, 2004, online.
23. Te Toi Hou, online.
24. Shirres, 'Mana Atua: Power from the Spiritual Powers', online.
25. Ka'ai, Moorfield, Reilly & Mosely (eds), *Ki te Whaiao*, p. 105.
26. Orbell, *The Natural World of the Māori*, p. 193.
27. John Tahuri, explanatory note, 1996.
28. Salmond, *Eruera*, p. 88.
29. Royal, *Te Haurapa*, p. 88.
30. In terms of Tūhoe, Te Hue Rangi and Kimoro Pukepuke also support the idea that a person did not ask to be taught, but that it was purely through the recognition of potential in young boys by Tūhoe elders that they were educated.
31. Ngoi Pewhairangi in King, *Te Ao Hurihuri*, p. 8.
32. Royal, *Te Haurapa*, p. 88.
33. Salmond, *Hui*, p. 123.
34. Ibid, p. 122.
35. Beaglehole, *Some Modern Maoris*, pp. 274–6; Mahuta, 'Whaikōrero', pp. 7–8.
36. Milroy, 'Ko te Āhuatanga Ā-Iwi', pp. 1–2.
37. Salmond, 'Mana Makes the Man', p. 50.
38. Heuer, *Maori Women*, p. 31.
39. Hiwi and Pat Tauroa, *Te Marae*, p. 41.
40. Siers, *The Maori People of New Zealand*, n.p.
41. Royal, *Te Haurapa*, p. 15.
42. Te Kotahitanga Tait, interview, 1996; and Kimoro Pukepuke, interview, 1997.
43. Sydney Melbourne, interview, 1997; Te Kei Merito, interview, 1997; Te Hue Rangi, interview, 2003.
44. Salmond, *Hui*, p. 122.
45. Schrempp, 'Introduction', p. 4.
46. 'Lord also utilises the notion of the formula to develop very fine discussions of the process of acquiring skills within the Yugoslav oral epic tradition, tracing some novices through the process of building up their skills of formulae. Beyond this, by comparing the songs of various performers, or of the same performer on different occasions or at different points in his career, Lord develops a fascinating account of the interplay between tradition and individual innovation. While certain formulae are shared among a number of singers, each singer's particular kit is yet highly specific to himself' (ibid).
47. Ranginui Walker, interview, 1998; Te Hue Rangi, interview, 2003.
48. Salmond, *Hui*, p. 122.
49. Tāmati Reedy, interview, 1996.
50. Te Hiko Hohepa, interview, 1997.
51. Mauriora Kingi, interview, 1998.
52. Robert Mahuta, discussion, 1997.
53. Eric Waiariki, interview, 1996.
54. Salmond, *Hui*, p. 130.
55. Awanui Timutimu (interview, 1995) mentioned one person who has just begun to learn cultural practices recently.
56. Mahuta, 'Whaikōrero', p. 19.
57. Salmond, *Hui*, p. 124.
58. Joseph Malcolm, interview, 2003.
59. Kimoro Pukepuke, interview, 1997.
60. Derek Morehu, interview, 1998.
61. Salmond, *Hui*, p. 130.
62. Pita Iraia, interview, 1997.
63. Salmond, *Hui*, p. 122.
64. Te Kei Merito, interview, 1997.
65. Education authorities took a hard line against the Māori language, which was forbidden in the playground. Corporal punishment was administered to children who disobeyed (Ka'ai, Lecture, 2005) and 'it was not until after 1900 with the banning of the Māori language in school playgrounds that the use of the language began to decline, leading to generations of Māori being deprived of one of their cultural taonga' (Ka'ai, 'Te Mana o te Reo', p. 204).

Chapter Four: Whaikōrero *as Rituals of Encounter*

1. Hanson, *Counterpoint in Maori Culture*, p. 107.
2. Salmond, *Hui*, p. 148.
3. Takino, 'Dying to be Counted', p. 287.
4. D. Sinclair, 'Marae: Land', pp. 89–92.
5. Kāretu, 'Turanga Waewae', p. 2.
6. Melbourne, '/First Encounters/', p. 2.
7. H. Tauroa, *A Guide to Marae*, p. 11.
8. Barlow, *Tikanga Whakaaro*, p. 68.
9. Ibid.
10. H. Tauroa, *A Guide to Marae*, p. 11.
11. Awatere and Dewes, *Maori Literature*, p. 1.
12. Interpretation and translation by author.
13. Hiwi and Pat Tauroa, *Te Marae*, p. 18.
14. Mead, *Tikanga Māori*, p. 110.
15. Salmond, *Hui*, p. 31.
16. Armstrong, *Maori Customs and Crafts*, p. 35.
17. Firth, *Economics of the New Zealand Māori*, p. 96.
18. Walsh, *More and More Maoris*, p. 47.
19. 'Other nucleus pas, permanently occupied, became social and ceremonial centres for the many smaller pas and villages round about' (Mitcalfe, *Maori*, p. 36).
20. Salmond, *Hui*, p. 31.

21 Koro Tihema, pers. com., 2008.
22 Walker, 'Marae', in King, *Te Ao Hurihuri*, p. 21.
23 Robb, *Kawa Marae*, p. 42.
24 Hazlehurst, *Political Expression and Ethnicity*, p. 3.
25 Mataira, *Pukapuka Pānui*, p. 18.
26 Patu Hohepa, interview, 1998.
27 Walker, *Ka Whawhai Tonu Matou*, p. 200.
28 Pou Temara, interview, 1997.
29 Walker, 'Marae', p. 26.
30 Mauriora Kingi, interview, 1998.
31 Te Kei Merito, interview, 1997.
32 Pou Temara, interview, 1997.
33 John Tahuri, explanatory note, 7 May 1996; Pita Iraia, interview, 1997; James Milroy, interview, 1997.
34 James Milroy, interview, 1997.
35 Pou Temara, interview, 1997.
36 Walker, 'Opening the Fiscal Envelope', pp. 122–3.
37 Pou Temara, interview, 1997.
38 Hohepa Kereopa, interview, 1997; Hieke Tupe, interview, 1996; Te Kei Merito, interview, 1997.
39 Derek Morehu, interview, 1998.
40 Mataira, *Pukapuka Pānui*, p. 17.
41 Bloch, *Political Language and Oratory*, p. 16.
42 Yoon, *Maori Mind, Maori Land*, p. 45.
43 J. Sinclair, *Collins Cobuild Dictionary*, p. 570.
44 Tāmati Kruger, interview, 2003.
45 Ibid.
46 Bloch, *Political Language and Oratory*, p. 13.
47 J. Sinclair, *Collins Cobuild Dictionary*, p. 570.
48 Best, *The Maori as He Was*, p. 65.
49 Thomson (*A World Awakens*, p. 6) and Shirres (*Tu Tangata*, p. 27) refer to Rongo as 'Rongo-maa-Taane', but Tautahi asserts that Rongo-mā-tāne is Tāne-mahuta, whereas Prytz-Johansen (*Studies in Maori Rites*, p. 182) asserts that Rongo-mā-tāne is also known as Rongo-marae-roa.
50 Māori Culture – Legends, online.
51 Tū-mata-uenga is the Māori god generally attributed with war. 'Ko Tu-mata-uenga anake i toa ki te whawhai ki a Rangi raua ko ana uri, a oma ana a Rongo te kumara, a Tane te manu, a Hau-mia-tiketike te roi, a kainga ratou e Tu. A ko Tu te atua nana i hanga te tangata a ko Tu te atua o te tangata' (Ms Papers 75, John White B36, Envelope 35). 'Only Tuu-mata-uenga was successful in the battle against Rangi and his progeny. Rongo the kumara, Taane birds, and haumia-tiketike fernroot fled and were eaten by Tuu. Tuu is the spiritual power who made man. Tuu is the spiritual power of man' (White in Shirres, 'Tapu', pp. 38–39).
52 Tregear (*The Maori-Polynesian Dictionary*, p. 461) refers to Tāne as 'one of the greatest divinities of Polynesia'. In terms of Māori, Buck (*The Coming of the Maori*, pp. 454–5) refers to Tāne as the most important of the departmental gods in New Zealand: 'He had been the leader among the sons of the primary parents (Rangi-nui and Papatūānuku) during the creation period. . . . As the greatest son of the Sky-father, he was Tanenuiarangi; as proper-up-of-the-sky, Tane-tokorangi; as the parent of man and other progeny, Tanematua; as the producer of life, Tanetewaiora; and because of his association with knowledge, Tanetewananga and Tanetepukenga.' According to other traditions, including those of Ngā Puhi, Kahungunu and Kāi Tahu, we owe our existence to the *mana*, power, of Tāne. It 'was Taane who made the first woman from whom we are all descended, Taane who brought light into our world by separating Ranginui and Papatuanuku, Taane who climbed up into the highest heavens and brought back for us the three baskets of knowledge. The meeting house is also referred to as Taane, Taane-whakapiripiri, "the trees of Taane bound together", and the house itself has a Maori cosmic significance. On a cosmic level the roof signifies Rangi, the heavens, the floor signifies Papa-tuanuku, the earth and the poles which hold up the roof, represent the poles used by Taane, helped by his brothers, to separate Rangi and Papa and make it possible for us to move into the light' (Shirres, 'Mana and the Human Person', online).
53 Marae, online.
54 Tregear, *The Maori-Polynesian Dictionary*, p. 461.
55 Buck, *The Coming of the Maori*, p. 454.
56 Ibid, p. 455. According to Best (*Tuhoe, the Children of the Mist*, p. 760), 'Paia-te-rangi is another name that Tāne is known by'; however, Mahupuku in Moorfield (*Te Whanake*, p. 42) applies the name Rangi-hāpainga in reference to Paia-nui-a-Rangi-e-tū-iho-nei during the separation period of Rangi-nui and Papa-tū-ā-nuku.
57 Best, *Maori Religion and Mythology*, p. 169.
58 Also known as Rongotau (Tautahi, 'A Religious Narrative', p. 16).
59 Buck, *The Coming of the Maori*, p. 457.
60 Taua Pouwhare, discussion, 1996; Te Hue Rangi, interview, 2003; Tāmati Kruger, interview, 2003.
61 Salmond, 'Mana Makes the Man', pp. 58, 59.
62 Tāmati Kruger, interview, 2003.
63 Awanui Timutimu, interview, 1995.
64 Buck, *The Coming of the Maori*, p. 389.
65 Robert Mahuta, discussion, 1997.
66 Derek Morehu, interview, 1998.
67 James Milroy, interview, 1997; Sydney Melbourne, interview, 1997.
68 Walker, 'Marae', p. 23.
69 Te Kapunga Dewes, interview, 1997; Te Hiko-o-te-rangi Hohepa, interview, 1997; Pita Iraia, interview, 1997; Kuia Te Rangi, discussion, 2001; Joseph Malcolm, interview, 2003.
70 Salmond, 'Mana Makes the Man', p. 45.
71 Robert Mahuta, discussion, 1997.

Chapter Five: Who Can Perform Whaikōrero?

1 Mahuta, 'Whaikōrero', pp. 18–19.
2 H. Tauroa, *A Guide to Marae*, p. 21.
3 Wīhapi Winiata, discussion, 2002.
4 King, *Te Ao Hurihuri*, p. 9.
5 Kāretu, *Haka*, pp. 84–85.

6. Tāmati Reedy, interview, 1996; Te Kei Merito, interview, 1997.
7. Pita Iraia, interview, 1997.
8. Awanui Timutimu, interview, 1995.
9. Te Hue Rangi, interview, 2003.
10. Moihi Te Mātorohanga in Joseph, *He Reo Pōwhiri/Te Karanga*, p. 17.
11. Hiwi and Pat Tauroa, *Te Marae*, p. 80.
12. Schwimmer, *The World of the Māori*, p. 139.
13. Harawira, *Te Kawa o te Marae*, p. 7.
14. Archer, 'Some Key Aspects of Māori Oratory', p. 13.
15. Kāretu, 'Kawa in Crisis', p. 76.
16. Kernot, *People of the Four Winds*, p. 60.
17. Tāmati Reedy, interview, 1996.
18. Ibid.
19. Armstrong, *Maori Customs and Crafts*, p. 40.
20. Salmond, 'Mana Makes the Man', p. 47.
21. Salmond, *Hui*, p. 148.
22. Te Kotahitanga Tait, interview, 1996.
23. Te Hue Rangi, interview, 2003.
24. Anecdote by Rangihau in King, *Te Ao Hurihuri*, p. 10.
25. Joseph Malcolm, interview, 2003.
26. Te Hiko-o-te-rangi Hohepa, interview, 1997.
27. Salmond, *Hui*, p. 149.
28. Mataira, *Pukapuka Pānui*.
29. Taua Pouwhare, discussion, 1996.
30. Sydney Melbourne, interview, 1997.
31. Pita Iraia, interview, 1997.
32. Metge, *In and Out of Touch*, p. 43.
33. Hiwi and Pat Tauroa, *Te Marae*, pp. 73, 40.
34. Salmond, *Hui*, p. 149.
35. MASPAC = Māori and South Pacific Arts Council. They would call meetings to discuss issues regarding Māori. Participants at this particular forum included Pat Rei, Hohua Tutengaehe, Hamuera Mitchell, Henare Tuwhangai and others.
36. MASPAC video (n.d: 39'48").
37. Koro Tihema, explanatory comment, 2004.
38. Salmond, 'Mana Makes the Man', p. 51.
39. Māori adze.
40. John Tahuri, explanatory comment, 1996.
41. A town in the Bay of Plenty, North Island.
42. Te Hiko-o-te-rangi Hohepa, interview, 1997.
43. Salmond, 'Mana Makes the Man', p. 59.
44. Michael Reilly, explanatory comment, 2005.
45. Salmond, *Hui*, p. 149.
46. Cleave, *The Maori State*, p. 16.
47. Te Hue Rangi, interview, 2003.
48. Taua Pouwhare, discussion, 1996; Te Kotahitanga Tait, interview, 1996.
49. H. Tauroa, *A Guide to Marae*, p. 40.
50. Tāmati Reedy, interview, 1996.
51. Michael Reilly, explanatory comment, 2005.
52. Tāmati Kruger, interview, 2003.
53. Douglas, *Across the Great Divide*, p. 55.
54. J. Smith, 'Tapu Removal', p. 67.
55. Te Kei Merito, interview, 1997.
56. Derek Morehu, interview, 1998.
57. Te Kapunga Dewes, interview, 1997.
58. Hohepa Kereopa, interview, 1997.
59. Derek Morehu, interview, 1998; Tīmoti Kāretu, interview, 1995.
60. Kimoro Pukepuke, interview, 1997.
61. Kāretu, *Kawa in Crisis*, p. 73.
62. Salmond, *Hui*, p. 127.
63. Ibid.
64. Interestingly, Roka Paora, a noted female elder of Te Whānau-a-Apanui, opined that women of Te Whānau-a-Apanui do not *whaikōrero*, but they do stand to support the male speaker (Paora, 'Te Kawa', p. 12).
65. Mahuta, 'Whaikōrero', p. 21.
66. Archer, 'Some Key Aspects of Māori Oratory', p. 8.
67. Hiwi and Pat Tauroa, *Te Marae*, p. 79.
68. Ibid.
69. Mataira, *Pukapuka Pānui*, p. 16.
70. Michael Reilly, explanatory comment, 2005.
71. Hiwi and Pat Tauroa, *Te Marae*, pp. 78, 80.
72. Ani Mikaere, Maori Women, online.
73. Te Kotahitanga Tait, interview, 1996.
74. Hohepa Kereopa in Moon, *Tohunga Hohepa Kereopa*, p. 28.
75. Hieke Tupe (interview, 1996) endorses the knowledge women possess in modern society. 'Engari ka titiro iho tātou i tēnei rā, kua kaha kē te mātauranga, te puta o te wahine i tēnei wā. Ka kite koe ināianei, ngā mahi katoa, [ahakoa] he aha te mahi, kei te wahine.'
76. Mauriora Kingi, interview, 1998; Ranginui Walker, interview, 1998.
77. Sydney Melbourne, interview, 1997.
78. Tāmati Reedy, interview, 1996.
79. Reilly, 'He Kōrero', p. 3.
80. Hohua Tutengaehe (MASPAC n.d., 48'30").
81. Te Kotahitanga Tait, interview, 1996.
82. H. Tauroa, *A Guide to Marae*, p. 78.
83. Rangihau (cassette, 1978) at Te Waimako, 1978, said 'kāre e tika te wahine ki te kōrero i te mea, koia te kōpū tuku mai i ngā rangatira ki waho. . . . Koirā kāre e whakaaetia ki te kōrero.' Women are the progenitors of chiefs . . . that is why they are not permitted to *whaikōrero*.
84. Kāretu, 'Kawa in Crisis', p. 71; Taua Pouwhare, discussion, 1996; Te Hue Rangi, interview, 2003.
85. Higgins and Moorfield, 'Ngā Tikanga o te Marae', p. 80.
86. Mataira, *Pukapuka Pānui*.
87. Te Awekotuku, 'He Ngangahu', p. 30.
88. Harawira, *Te Kawa o te Marae*, p. 17.
89. Best, *Notes on the Art of War*, pp. 68–69.
90. Edwards, *Mihipeka*, p. 18.
91. Shirres, 'Noa', online.
92. Mataira, *Pukapuka Pānui*.
93. Metge, *In and Out of Touch*, pp. 57–58.
94. Te Kapunga Dewes, interview, 1997.
95. Kuia Te Wai, discussion, 2001.
96. Famous accounts by Salmond of women speaking on *marae* include Hine Matioro, Materoa Reedy and Whaia McClutchie of Ngāti Porou; Mihi Kotukutuku of Te Whānau-a-Apanui; and Hine Katorangi of Ngāti Kahungunu.

97 Tāmati Reedy, interview, 1996.
98 Te Awekotuku, 'He Ngangahu', p. 31.
99 Tāmati Kruger, interview, 2003.

Chapter Six: What Skills are Required for Oratory?

1   Mahuta, 'Whaikōrero', p. 2.
2   Ibid, p. 20.
3   Tīmoti Kāretu, interview, 1995.
4   James Milroy, interview, 1997.
5   '. . . in a given society, there are two (often closely-related) languages, one of high prestige, which is generally used by the government and in formal texts, and one of low prestige, which is usually the spoken vernacular tongue. The high-prestige language tends to be the more formalised, and its forms and vocabulary often "filter down" into the vernacular, though often in a changed form' (http://en.wikipedia.org/wiki/Diglossia).
6   Ibid, pp. 41–42.
7   Mataira, *Pukapuka Pānui*, p. 16.
8   Schrempp, 'Introduction', p. 9.
9   Colenso, *Contributions Towards a Better Knowledge of the Māori Race*, pp. 29–30.
10 Tīmoti Kāretu, interview, 1995; and Wīhapi Winiata, discussion, 2002.
11 James Milroy, interview, 1997; Hieke Tupe, interview, 1996.
12 Te Hue Rangi, interview, 2003.
13 Winiata in Archer, 'Some Key Aspects of Māori Oratory', p. 14.
14 Mahuta, 'Whaikōrero', p. 2.
15 Kāretu , 'Whaikōrero', lecture notes
16 *Introduction to Whaikōrero* (coursebook), p. 35.
17 Hohepa Kereopa, interview, 1997.
18 Salmond, *Hui*, p. 176.
19 Te Hiko-o-te-rangi Hohepa and Hohepa Kereopa.
20 Tīmoti Kāretu, interview, 1995.
21 Ibid.
22 Mahuta, 'Whaikōrero', p. 14.
23 John Tahuri, explanatory comment, 1996.
24 Schrempp, 'Introduction', pp. 5–6.
25 Michael Reilly, explanatory comment, 2005.
26 Shortland, *Traditions and Superstitions of the New Zealanders*, p. 187.
27 See Sample whaikōrero 5, Appendix.
28 Tāmati Reedy, interview, 1996.
29 Pei Te Hurinui Jones in Ngata, *Ngā Mōteatea*, p. xxi.
30 Grove, *Ngā Pēpeha a ngā Tūpuna*, cover.
31 J. Prytz-Johansen in Reilly et al (eds), *Ki te Whaiao*, p. 61.
32 Brooke-White (ed.), *Whaikoorero*, pp. 12–14.
33 I am unsure if Pei is referring to Te Moana-o-Raukawa (Cook Strait) which would then link up with the South Island tribes; or whether he is referring to Raukawa-ki-te-tonga, the Raukawa people of the south located around the Ōtaki–Levin areas north of Wellington. If he intended the former, then this would align with the philosophy that the Kīngitanga is representative of all Māori in New Zealand. If he is referring to the latter, Raukawa-in-the-south, then this would reaffirm tribal connections with the Raukawa people to the south-west of the Waikato area.
34 Buck, *The Coming of the Maori*, p. 80.
35 Tāmati Reedy, interview, 1996.
36 Shortland, *Traditions and Superstitions of the New Zealanders*, p. 189.
37 Mahuta, 'Whaikōrero', p. 25.
38 Tāmati Reedy, interview, 1996.
39 McGuire, *The Maoris of New Zealand*, p. 38.
40 Haupeke Piripi, see Sample whaikōrero 5, Appendix.
41 Frederick Bennett, himself, was an orator of renown described as 'An essentially kindly and approachable man, the Bishop in bearing was a rangatira of the old school – the personification of simple dignity. The melodious voice that entranced many a congregation was, undoubtedly, a gift from his Polynesian forbears. In English his speech was slow and deliberate. But in Māori, words often poured torrentially from his lips. He loved to take an old Māori saying and use it as a text. There were few men, in a generation of orators, who could equal him' (http://209.85.141.104/search?q=cache:yMIdaOosbEcJ:www.anglican.org.nz/Liturgical%2520Resources/Other%2520Liturgical%2520Resources/FATSweb/2305.rtf+honenga&hl=en&ct=clnk&cd=5&gl=nz 0).
42 Brooke-White (ed.), *Whaikoorero*, pp. 6–7; see Sample whaikōrero 10 on p. 196.
43 Mahuta, 'Whaikōrero', p. 1.
44 Mead and Grove, *Nga Pepeha a nga Tupuna*, cover.
45 Yoon, *Maori Mind, Maori Land*, p. 48.
46 Ibid, p. 55.
47 Dewes, 'The Case for Oral Arts', in King, *Te Ao Hurihuri*, p. 57.
48 McGuire, *The Maoris of New Zealand*, p. 85.
49 *Introduction to Whaikōrero* (coursebook), p. 62.
50 Schrempp, 'Introduction', p. 5.
51 See Sample whaikōrero 12, Appendix.
52 Ibid.
53 See Sample whaikōrero 10, 12, Appendix.
54 See Sample whaikōrero 12, Appendix.
55 See Sample whaikōrero 1, 3, 4, Appendix.
56 See Sample whaikōrero 1, 4, 6, 13, 16–20, Appendix.
57 See Sample whaikōrero 2–4, 14, 15, 17, 18, Appendix.
58 See Sample whaikōrero 10, 12, Appendix.
59 Salmond, *Hui*, p. 164.
60 Schrempp, 'Introduction', p. 4.
61 Ibid, pp. 4, 6.
62 Winiata in Archer, 'Some Key Aspects of Māori Oratory', p. 22.
63 Te Hiko-o-te-rangi Hohepa, interview: an exaggerated description, 1997.
64 Archer, 'Some Key Aspects of Māori Oratory', p. 21.
65 Salmond, *Hui*, p. 130.
66 Pou Temara, interview, 1997.
67 Ward, *Life Among the Maories of New Zealand*, p. 91.
68 Salmond, 'Mana Makes the Man', p. 56.
69 Schwimmer, *The World of the Māori*, p. 86.

70 Maning, *Old New Zealand*, p. 34.
71 Salmond, 'Mana Makes the Man', pp. 52, 55.
72 Ritchie, *The Making of a Māori*, p. 27.
73 Archer, 'Some Key Aspects of Māori Oratory', p. 28.
74 Video-cassette screened during the wānanga. Current location of the resource unknown.
75 Salmond, 'Mana Makes the Man', p. 52.
76 Mahuta, 'Whaikōrero', p. 15.
77 Kruger, 'The Qualities of Ihi, Wehi and Wana', p. 92.
78 Ranginui Walker, interview, 1998.
79 Cleave, *The Maori State*, p. 17.
80 Tīmoti Kāretu, interview, 1995.
81 Salmond, *Hui*, p. 172.
82 Tāmati Reedy, interview, 1996.
83 Evans, *Māori Weapons in Pre-European New Zealand*, pp. 38, 42.
84 Buddle in Vayda, *Maori Warfare*, pp. 25, 62.
85 Salmond, *Hui*, p. 172.
86 Tony Herewini, discussion, 1997.
87 Kimoro Pukepuke, interview, 1997.
88 Best, *Maori Eschatology*, p. 10.
89 Tīmoti Kāretu, interview, 1995.
90 Winiata in Archer, 'Some Key Aspects of Māori Oratory', p. 27.
91 Archer, 'Some Key Aspects of Māori Oratory', pp. 27–28.
92 Evans, *Māori Weapons in Pre-European New Zealand*, p. 22.
93 Tāmati Kruger, interview, 2003.
94 Te Hiko-o-te-rangi Hohepa, interview, 1997.
95 Te Wharehuia Milroy, interview, 1997.
96 Tāmati Kruger, interview, 2003
97 Te Hue Rangi, interview, 2003
98 Ibid.
99 Shortland, *Traditions and Superstitions of the New Zealanders*, p. 186.
100 Pou Temara, interview, 1997
101 Mahuta, 'Whaikōrero', p. 6.
102 Orbell, *The Natural World of the Māori*, pp. 137, 183, 193.
103 Salmond, 'Mana Makes the Man', pp. 52, 55–56.
104 Salmond, *Hui*, p. 164.
105 Rewi in Archer, 'Some Key Aspects of Māori Oratory', p. 28.
106 Tīmoti Kāretu, interview, 1995.
107 Winiata in Archer, 'Some Key Aspects of Māori Oratory', p. 29.
108 Archer, 'Some Key Aspects of Māori Oratory', pp. 29–30.
109 Temara, online, 2007.

Chapter Seven: The Mana of Whaikōrero

1 Walker, 'Opening the Fiscal Envelope', p. 134.
2 Ibid.
3 Pou Temara, interview, 1997
4 Tāmati Kruger, interview, 2003.
5 Binney, 'Myth and Explanation in the Ringatū Tradition', p. 346.
6 Gudgeon, 'Mana Tangata', p. 4.
7 Hieke Tupe, interview, 1996.
8 Kimoro Pukepuke, interview, 1997.
9 Best, *The Maori as He Was*, pp. 97–98.
10 Salmond, 'Mana Makes the Man', p. 58.
11 Salmond, *Hui*, p. 148.
12 The funeral of Sonny White at Mātaatua marae, Rotorua, 1980.
13 Salmond, 'Mana Makes the Man', p. 49.
14 Edwards, *Mihipeka*, p. 26.
15 Hiwi and Pat Tauroa, *Te Marae*, p. 76.
16 Awatere, *Awatere*, p. 232.
17 Salmond, 'Mana Makes the Man', p. 50.
18 Salmond, *Hui*, p. 157.
19 H. Tauroa, *A Guide to Marae*, p. 21.
20 Tregear, *The Maori Race*, p. 37.
21 Robb, *Kawa Marae*, p. 23.
22 Salmond, 'Mana Makes the Man', p. 49.
23 Kāretu, 'Kawa in Crisis', p. 68.
24 Tīmoti Kāretu, passing comment.
25 Hieke Tupe, interview, 1996.
26 Whitu Waiariki, interview, 1996.
27 Salmond, *Eruera*, pp. 27–29.
28 Salmond, 'Mana Makes the Man', p. 47.
29 Ibid, p. 49.
30 Salmond, *Hui*, p. 152.
31 Metge, *In and Out of Touch*, p. 35.
32 Hiwi and Pat Tauroa, *Te Marae*, p. 79.
33 Salmond, *Hui*, p. 127.
34 Manawa Arahi in Metge, *In and Out of Touch*, p. 61.
35 Royal, *Te Haurapa*, p. 40.
36 Hiwi and Pat Tauroa, *Te Marae*, p. 73.
37 Apirana Ngata in Joseph, *Te Reo Pōwhiri*, p. 13.

Chapter Eight: Protocols of Place

1 Barlow, *Tikanga Whakaaro*, p. 85.
2 Williams, *A Dictionary of the Maori Language*, pp. 244–5. When referring to the *paepae kaiaawhaa*, the beam stretched across the front of the meeting house, the term *kaiaawhaa*, or *kai + aawhaa* was a partition of maybe 30 to 60 cm in height whose function was to 'eat' the 'storm'.
3 '*Ko te taumata ko te wāhi nohoanga. He wāhi i hangā ki roto tonu i te pā tūwatawata hei wāhi okiokinga mō te rangatira. Ka mahia e tētahi rangatira tōna, ka mahia e tētahi atu tōna, ahakoa he wahine, he tāne rānei. Ko ēnā hei wāhi kōrero mō rātou, hei wāhi hei haerenga mō te toenga o te whānau mehemea kei te raupatutia. Ka peke atu rātou ki runga i te taumata ki reira whawhai ai, ko tēnei te āhuatanga o te taumata i mua. E*

kore e āhei kia haere atu tētahi atu ki runga i te taumata kia pātaitia rā anō, kia tukuna rā anō, haere ki reira. Nā, ināianei kua kīi ko te pae, o roto o Ngā Puhi ko te taumata' (Te Patu Hohepa, interview, 1998).
4. Melbourne, *Ngā Kura Huna a Tūhoe Pōtiki*, p. 11.
5. Mead, *Tikanga Māori*, p. 115.
6. Hiwi and Pat Tauroa, *Te Marae*, p. 57.
7. Mead, *Tikanga Māori*, p. 115.
8. Best, *Maori Eschatology*, p. 170. Elsdon Best based much of his ethnographical fieldwork on the Tūhoe people.
9. White, *The Ancient History of the Maori*, p. 122.
10. Petersen, 'Signs of Higher Life', p. 13.
11. Ibid, p. 23.
12. Also known as Te Pairi Tarapekepeke (Te Pairi the leaper), a nickname afforded him by Tūhourangi chief Mita Taupopoki, because of his oratorical style and volatility (DNZB: http://www.dnzb.govt.nz/dnzb/, accessed 15 January 2010).
13. Walker, *Marae*, p. 24.
14. Salmond, *Hui*, p. 127.
15. Note: most *marae* have only one *wharenui*.
16. *Whare mate* are permanent fixtures to accommodate the dead during funerals.
17. Wihapi Winiata, pers. com., 2002.
18. 'Ka tū tēnā rangatira ki te kōrero ka tū tēnā rangatira ki te . . . kōrero, kāore anō kia tae ki te wā hei kōrerotanga mō te koroua, a 'Mea'. Ka tū ki te kōrero, ka mea atu ō mātou pāpā, ka tīwaha atu, 'ā taihoa koe' . . . . kāore i rongo te koroua, kāore i noho, ka haere tonu ngā kōrero. E toru ngā tīwahatanga atu ki a ia, 'e ka hē, ka hē,' arā, mō te tuatoru kāore rawa i noho ki raro, he turi rānei, he aha rānei, kāore tonu i noho ki raro. Kātahi ka tū tō mātou pāpā a [Mea] ki te whakahua i tana pōhuatau, ā, i tana pōkeka' (Derek Morehu, interview, 1998).
19. Tāmati Reedy, interview, 1996.
20. Salmond, 'Mana Makes the Man', p. 49.
21. Buck, *The Coming of the Maori*, p. 400.
22. Harawira, *Te Kawa o te Marae*, p. 16.
23. Te Patu Hohepa, interview, 1998.
24. 'E ai ki ngā kōrero a aku koroua, i tīmata mai te kōrero, te whakatakoto i ngā kupu i reira. I te wā i whakaarotia ai e Tāne me Pai, me Tū-mata-uenga kia whakawehetia ō rātou pakeke, engari, i roto i ngā whakaaro o ētahi atu, pērā i a Whiro, me Tāwhiri-mātea, me ētahi atu o ngā tuākana o te hunga nei, kāore rātou i manako, kāre rātou i whakaae, anā, i tērā tonu ka tautohetohe, ana, i roto i te tautohetohe koirā te tīmatatanga o te whaikōrero e mōhiotia nei e tāua' (Te Kei Merito, interview, 1997).
25. White, *The Ancient History of the Maori*, p. 165.
26. Āwhitu is some 60 minutes drive from Mt Eden, although in the period when this event was documented, it may have been the case that Māori paddled between the two areas.
27. McGuire, *The Maoris of New Zealand*, p. 85.
28. Kāretu, 'Kawa in Crisis', p. 78.
29. Pat Rei is a *kaumātua* of Te Arawa and Ngāti Toarangitira (Ngā Pū Kōrero, 1987, cassette tape).
30. Higgins and Moorfield, 'Ngā Tikanga o te Marae', p. 80.
31. Buck, *The Coming of the Maori*, p. 391.
32. Mauriora Kingi, interview, 1998.
33. Salmond, *Hui*, p. 153.
34. Edwards, *Mihipeka*, p. 153.
35. Buck, *The Coming of the Maori*, p. 419.
36. Pou Temara, interview, 1997.
37. Mauriora Kingi, interview, 1998.
38. Koro Tihema, pers. com., 2004.
39. Salmond, 'Mana Makes the Man', p. 48.
40. Edwards, *Mihipeka*, p. 27.
41. Te Hue Rangi, interview, 2003.
42. Pita Iraia, interview, 1997.
43. Kāretu adds, 'The concept of "korapa" so important in whaikorero applies here. With whaikorero, the speaker should move out to the left so that when he has finished he heads back to his seat with his right shoulder' (Kāretu, 'Kawa in Crisis', p. 69).
44. Heuer, *Maori Women*, p. 10.
45. In relation to this, I was told that the positioning of mourners around the deceased, i.e., by sitting alongside the left shoulder, is possibly connected to the Māui narrative. Williams (*A Dictionary of the Maori Language*, p. 140) also explains the negative perception of the left. 'Turn to the left instead of to the right after casting the mutu, look back when advancing for the purpose, flinch in a duel, or pass by the dwelling of friends through shyness: all these are aituā.'
46. Hohepa Kereopa, interview, 1997.
47. Salmond, *Hui*, pp. 47, 147, 153.
48. John Tahuri, pers. com., 1996. John Rangihau was a famous Tūhoe statesman who died in 1987. His funeral was held at Mātaatua Marae in Rotorua.
49. Salmond, *Hui*, p. 153: The opening speaker may also be called the *kaiwaahi*, the *tangata wāhi*, the *tangata whakatuwhera*, the *kaiwāhi* or the *kaitātaki*.
50. Downes, 'Maori Etiquette', p. 153.
51. Mahuta, 'Whaikōrero', p. 17.
52. Tīmoti Kāretu, interview, 1995.
53. Mauriora Kingi, interview, 1998.
54. Edwards, *Mihipeka*, p. 17.
55. Tāmati Reedy, interview, 1996; Mahuta, 'Whaikōrero', p. 18.
56. Hohepa Kereopa, interview, 1997; Pou Temara, interview, 1997.
57. 'E ai ki te tauira a Ngāti Tūhoe, kua whakarāpopotohia e ia [e te kaikōrero whakamutunga] ngā kōrero. Kua oti i a ia te whare rā. Kua uhia e ia te tuanui, kua oti i a ia te whakapuru i ngā puare o te whare rā, ko te mahi whakamutunga māna he tō i te tatau, he tō i te puta auahi o te whare rā kia kati' (Pou Temara, interview, 1997). Interpreted, this means the orator, the builder, adds the roof, gibstops any openings, and then closes the door and the window. This means the building is complete.
58. Barlow, *Tikanga Whakaaro*, p. 84.
59. Michael Reilly, pers. com., 2005.
60. The stick is symbolic of the right to speak, and consequently, it is a common sight to see speakers brandishing a walking stick or some form of hand prop during their orations (as mentioned in chapter 6).

61 Robert Mahuta (pers. com., 1997) commented that in terms of Waikato, the *mauri* is imbedded in Tūrangawaewae with the Kīngitanga,
62 Mauriora Kingi, interview, 1998.
63 H. Tauroa, *A Guide to the Marae*, p. 20.
64 The latter two phrases are cited in Salmond, *Hui*, p. 158.
65 Taua Pouwhare, discussion, 1996.
66 Wihapi Winiata, pers. com., 2002.
67 Kereopa in Moon, *Tohunga Hohepa Kereopa*, p. 114.
68 Te Patu Hohepa, interview, 1998.
69 Te Hue Rangi, interview, 2003.
70 Ibid.
71 Mead, *Tikanga Māori*, p. 123.
72 Salmond, *Hui*, p. 153.
73 Williams, *A Dictionary of the Maori Language*, p. 345. Mead and Grove (*Nga Pepeha o Nga Tupuna*, p. 148) explain that Whakaotirangi was a chieftainess on board the Te Arawa canoe and a variant expression reads 'Ko te pūtiki a Whakaotirangi', which refers to Whakaotirangi's tying of *kūmara* in bunches so that they would not be lost from the kit when Te Arawa was caught in Te Korokoro-a-Te-Parata (a great whirlpool) during its voyage from Polynesian homelands to New Zealand. Brougham and Reed, *The Reed Book of Māori Proverbs*, pp. 60–61; and Williams, *A Dictionary of the Maori Language*, p. 351 have another variant: 'Te Kete Rukuruku a Whakaotirangi'.
74 'Ko te kōrero a Te Arawa i te whakatakototanga i te koha, "anei te rokiroki a Whakaotirangi." Te rokiroki, ko terā te kete i roto āna kai, te kūmara nēi. Te whakaaro o taua kuia nei, a Whakaotirangi, ka tau ana rātou ki te whenua hou, ki Aotearoa, māna hei whakatipu i ngā kūmara rarā, i runga i te whenua hou hei whāngai i te iwi katoa, ahakoa iti noa iho, tana rokiroki, tana kete me ana kūmara i roto' (Te Hiko-o-te-rangi Hopepa, interview, 1997).
75 Metge, 'Returning the Gift – *Utu* in Intergroup Relations', p. 312.
76 Harawira, *Te Kawa o te Marae*, p. 9.
77 Higgins and Moorfield, 'Ngā Tikanga o te Marae', p. 81.
78 'The last speaker for the manuhiri will generally place the koha on the marae at the conclusion of his mihi, immediately before returning to his seat. This is an indication to the tangata whenua that there will b[e] no further manuhiri speakers' (H. Tauroa, *A Guide to the Marae*, p. 20).
79 Mahuta, 'Whaikōrero', p. 18.
80 Edwards, *Mihipeka*, pp. 40–41.
81 Te Ariki Morehu, interview, 1998.
82 Te Hiko-o-te-rangi Hohepa, interview, 1997.
83 Te Kei Merito, interview, 1997.
84 Mate Kaiwai, pers. com., 2001; Kuia Te Rangi, pers. com., 2001; Tāmati Reedy, interview, 1996.

Chapter Nine: The Structure of Whaikōrero

1 Mahuta, 'Whaikōrero', p. 27.
2 Modelled on Higgins and Moorfield, 'Ngā Tikanga o te Marae', p. 81.
3 Mahuta, 'Whaikōrero', p. 31.
4 Cleave, *The Maori State*, p. 7.
5 Barlow, *Tikanga Whakaaro*, p. 167.
6 Mahuta, 'Whaikōrero', p. 27.
7 Awatere, 'Te Kawa o te Marae', p. 20.
8 McLean and Orbell, *Songs of a Kaumātua*, p. 15.
9 Mahuta, 'Whaikōrero', p. 28.
10 Te Kei Merito, interview, 1997.
11 Pou Temara, interview, 1997.
12 Te Hiko-o-te-rangi Hōhepa, interview, 1997.
13 Mahuta, 'Whaikōrero', p. 28.
14 Unknown author (Karakia: Pae tukutuku).
15 Stafford, *Te Arawa*, pp. 5–6.
16 Te Wharehuia Milroy, interview, 1997.
17 Mahuta, 'Whaikōrero', p. 28.
18 Cleave, *The Maori State*, p. 10.
19 Salmond, *Hui*, p. 160.
20 Hohepa Kereopa in Moon, *Tohunga Hohepa Kereopa*, p. 113.
21 Mahuta, 'Whaikōrero', p. 31.
22 Pat Rei (MASPAC Video: n.d).
23 Tāmati Reedy, interview, 1996.
24 Te Hiko-o-te-rangi Hōhepa, interview, 1997.
25 Rewi, 'Ko te Waihanga me Ngā Wehewehenga', p. 21.
26 Salmond, *Hui*, p. 160.
27 Te Kotahitanga Tait, interview, 1996.
28 Wihapi Winiata, pers. com., 2002.
29 Tāmati Reedy, interview, 1996.
30 Te Kei Merito, interview, 1997.
31 Cowan, *The Maori Yesterday and To-Day*, p. 103.
32 NZETC Online, http://www.nzetc.org/tm/scholarly/tei-Bes02Maor-t1-body-d7.html. p. 333, accessed 23 November 2009.
33 '. . . in the light of the mythological origin of women. Tāne, eldest son of Rangi-nui (Sky-father) and Papa-tua-nuku (Earth-mother), sought to create a race of mortals to dwell on earth; this necessitated his finding a non-supernatural woman. Legend tells of his search for the female element (*uha*) in all realms and regions. . . . After many unsuccessful attempts Tāne journeyed to the twelfth heaven to seek assistance from Io, the supreme god. He was sent by Io's supernatural female attendants to form a woman from the earth at Kurawaka, the pubic region of his mother Papa. In some versions with his brothers, in others alone, Tāne returned and created woman from the mud and earth, breathing on the completed inanimate figure until it came to life' (Heuer, *Maori Women*, pp. 9–10). Further reading: Best, *The Maori School of Learning*, pp. 58, 60, 110, 111; Ka'ai et al, *Ki te Whaiao*, p. 6. Gudgeon's ('Mana Tangata', p. 126) version is that it was the Māori god of war, Tū, who breathed life into the first human after which he uttered the words 'tihe mauri ora ki te Whei-ao ki te Ao-marama'.
34 See Sample whaikōrero 17, Appendix.
35 'Most attacks were made at dawn when there was enough light to see the battlements. The rising of the sun ended the watchman's vigil and ushered in a day of peace and light. Kia hiwa rā is a very popular tauparapara and is used

extensively by Māori speakers especially by members of the Arawa Tribe' (Dewes, Cassette-tape, 1970). Sometimes the sentry would strike a gong to inform the other sentries that he is alert and on duty.
36 Buck, *The Coming of the Maori*, p. 388.
37 McLean and Orbell, *Songs of a Kaumātua*, p. 19.
38 Buck, *The Coming of the Maori*, p. 388.
39 Cowan, *The Maori Yesterday and To-Day*, p. 103.
40 Simmons, *Ngā Tau Rere*, p. 63.
41 Best, *Te Whare Kohanga*, p. 26.
42 NZETC Online, http://www.nzetc.org/tm/scholarly/tei-Bes02Maor-t1-body-d7.html.p. 341, accessed 23 November 2009.
43 '*Ka noho te tangata ki te hii tuna, a kore noa iho e kai ake te tuna. Ka warea noa tia iho a ia e te moe. Tena ko te mata hi taua e kore e moe he haere tonu ka tata ki te taupahi ka noho ka whanga (tatari) ki te haparatanga mai u[o] te ata, na reira i kore ai e moe*' (White, *The Ancient History of the Maori*, p. 60).
44 'Motto-maxims are used mainly by Maori orators in their formal speech on a marae . . . to introduce the speaker, and secondly, to acknowledge and compliment the host people in terms of their territory and ancestral heritage. With their motto-maxims, orators announce where they are from and in so doing imply their relationship, whether host, guest, friend or opponent. From the listeners side, the speaker's reciting his motto-maxim allows them to evaluate who the person is' (Yoon, *Maori Mind, Maori Land*, p. 55).
45 Te Kotahitanga Tait, interview, 1996.
46 Tāmati Reedy, interview, 1996.
47 Bishop Pompallier, online.
48 Tāmati Reedy, interview, 1996.
49 Pita Iraia, interview, 1997.
50 Te Hiko-o-te-rangi Hōhepa, interview, 1997.
51 Walker, *Marae*, p. 23.
52 Tīmoti Kāretu, interview, 1995.
53 Te Kapunga Dewes, interview, 1997.
54 Tīmoti Kāretu, interview, 1995.
55 John Tahuri, explanatory note, 1996.
56 MASPAC Video (n.d.).
57 Interpretation of Maspac Video comments by the author.
58 Te Kapunga Dewes, interview, 1997.
59 The *wharekai* of my home *marae* is named 'Ko Te Parekura' in recognition of the services rendered by *hapū* members during the war.
60 Mahuta, 'Whaikōrero', p. 34.
61 Best, *Maori Eschatology*, p. 23.
62 Tāmati Reedy, interview, 1996.
63 Tīmoti Kāretu, interview, 1995; and Te Kotahitanga Tait, interview, 1996.
64 Woodard, 'Karanga', p. 30.
65 Kāretu, 'Ngā Waiata o te Ao Tawhito', p. 3.
66 Mahuta, 'Whaikōrero', p. 37.
67 Te Patu Hohepa, interview, 1998.
68 Moorfield, explanatory note, 2004.
69 Te Patu Hohepa, interview, 1998.
70 Ngata, *Nga Moteatea*, Part I, p. xv.
71 Ngata, *Nga Moteatea*, Part III, p. v.
72 Mahuta, 'Whaikōrero', p. 36.
73 Hiwi and Pat Tauroa, *Te Marae*, p. 68.
74 McLean, *Māori Literature*, pp. 23–24.
75 Hohepa Kereopa, interview, 1997; and Pou Temara, interview, 1997.
76 Hohepa Kereopa, interview, 1997.
77 Hohepa Kereopa, interview, 1997; and Tīmoti Kāretu, interview, 1995.
78 Moon, *Tohunga Hohepa Kereopa*, p. 112–13.
79 Hirini Melbourne, interview, 1997.
80 Te Kapunga Dewes, interview, 1997.
81 John Moorfield, explanatory note, 2004. The late Te Waea Mauriohooho Murray was the *kaumātua*, resident elder, for Te Whare Wānanga o Waikato in the 1980s and 1990s.
82 Te Kapunga Dewes, interview, 1997.
83 Ibid.
84 McLean, *Māori Literature*, p. 24.
85 Wilson, *From Hongi Hika to Hone Heke*, p. 142.
86 '*Kua kite au i roto i āku nā mahi whakaako kapa haka nei nā, ka taea te hunga tamariki te whakapakepake kia tahuri mai ki ēnei tongarewa a tātou, a te Māori. Ka uru ana te pārekareka ki roto i a rātou ki ēnei mahi kore rawa atu e pīrangi ā muri atu kia hoki anō ki te waiata-ā-ringa, ki te hīmene rānei hei waiata whai mai i te whaikōrero*' (Kāretu, 'Ngā Waiata o te Ao Tawhito', p. 3).
87 '. . . *nā reira, ka hari, hei hakarongotanga mai mā Ngāti Blow e tāhae ana nā Ngāti Awa nei i wā rātou haka, pēnei i a Ngāti Awa i mea nei, e Ngā Puhi, nā koutou i tāhae tō mātou waka. Nā tū ake ana ā mātou whaikōrero, 'Taku rākau e . . .'* (see Sample whaikōrero 5, Appendix).
88 Mead, 'Imagery, Symbolism and Social Values in Maori Chants', p. 401.
89 Kimoro Pukepuke, interview, 1997.
90 Te Poroa Malcolm, interview, 2003.
91 Te Ariki Morehu, interview, 1998.
92 Kuia Te Wai, discussion, 2001; and Kuia Te Rangi, discussion, 2001.
93 Mahuta, 'Whaikōrero', p. 37.
94 Rewi, 'Te Reo o Whaikōrero', p. 26.
95 Hiwi and Pat Tauroa, *Te Marae*, p. 155.
96 Tīmoti Kāretu, interview, 1995; and Te Kotahitanga Tait, interview, 1996.
97 Pou Temara, interview, 1997.
98 Tāmati Kruger, interview, 2003.
99 Te Kotahitanga Tait, interview, 1996.
100 Mahuta, 'Whaikōrero', p. 34.
101 Translation by author.
102 Selwyn Muru: see Sample whaikōrero 19, Appendix.
103 Haimona Snowden: see Sample whaikōrero 1, Appendix.
104 Hoera Ruru, from Rongowhakaata, Te Aitanga-a-Māhaki and Ngāi Tāmanuhiri; Haimona Snowden.
105 Te Wharehuia Milroy, passing comment, n.d.
106 Buck, *The Coming of the Maori*, p. 47.
107 Te Hiko-o-te-rangi Hohepa, interview, 1997.
108 Hohepa Kereopa, interview, 1997, with reference to Tūhoe speakers. Awatere ('Te Kawa o Te Marae', p. 22) concurs: '*kaore e hē ki te kore he tau[parapara] o te whaikōrero,*

engari, me tino whakaoti ki te waiata. Ko ia nei te wāhi me whakaoti ngā whaikōrero katoa ki te waiata' (It is not wrongful if the *tau* is omitted, but here should be a concluding song).
109 Barlow, *Tikanga Whakaaro*, pp. 165–8.
110 Salmond, 'Mana Makes the Man', p. 52.
111 Hiwi and Pat Tauroa, *Te Marae*, pp. 64–67.
112 Salmond, 'Mana Makes the Man', p. 55.
113 Mahuta, 'Whaikōrero', p. 38.
114 'Kua rite katoa, pēnei i te standardised nei tēnei mea o te whaikōrero. Kua ngaro, e kī ana, te rerenga noa iho o te whakaaro. The creative dimension of whaikōrero is lost i tēnei wā, nō te mea, kua mārō katoa ngā ture me pēnei. Ki te kore koe e tīmata mai me tō tauparapara, kāre he painga o tō whaikōrero. Ki te kore koe e mihi ki ngā mate, kua wareware i a koe ngā mate, kua pērā. Ki te kore koe e mihi ki te runga rawa, kua mea. Nō muri noa nei te runga rawa i mihia i roto i ngā kōrero a te ao Māori. Kua hoki katoa wērā āhuatanga ki runga i ēnei momo tauira, me kī, kua stylised, standardised, *kua ōrite noa iho te whakaaoto o te kōrero*. Ka roa te tangata e whakarongo ana ki ngā kōrero kua hokihoki noa i aua kōrero rā, and its become monotonous. Kua takeo, kua rutua te tangata i te moe i runga i ērā tū momo whakatakoto i te whaikōrero. Kua ngaro te ia o tēnei mea o te rere o te kōrero, he whakaoho i te hinengaro, he whakaoho i te tangata e pai ai hoki te whakarongo ki ngā kōrero' (Tāmati Reedy, interview, 1996).
115 Tāmati Kruger, interview, 2003.
116 Robert Mahuta, pers. com., 1997.
117 '... ko ngā tino tohunga e kore e whakakūiti i ō rātou nei mahi kia pēnei, kia pēnei, kia pēnei. Ka whakarerekētia, mā te rerekē ka kitea te ātaahua o te reo' (Te Patu Hohepa, interview, 1998).
118 Salmond, *Hui*, p. 171.
119 Rewi, 'Ko te Waihanga me Ngā Weheweheanga', p. 28.
120 'Me te whakaaro ake anō, i tōku whatumanawa, āe, ki a au nā, kāre i whāia kia ōrite katoa tātou, enari ko te mea kia whāia kia tau, kia tau rawa atu te whakatakoto kōrero, kia eke ki tā tātou e hiahia ai. Tēnā mā te tekau waiata e eke ana ki ngā kōrero e hiahia ana tātou kia rongo mai ērā nā, mahia. Tēnā, kia toru tekau nā whakataukī, pepeha hai kauwhata atu mā tātou kia ū ai tēnā e whakaarohia ana e tātou ki uta, hai wetewete rānei i ā rātou kōrero e kōrero ana, kua mahia' (Tāmati Kruger, interview, 2003).
121 Rewi, 'Ko te Waihanga me Ngā Weheweheanga', pp. 28–29.

Chapter Ten: The Future of Whaikōrero

1 The Māori equivalent of Ares, of Greek mythology.
2 Tīmoti Kāretu, interview, 1995.
3 Angas, cited in Mahuta, 'Whaikōrero', p. 1. George French Angas (25 April 1822 Newcastle-on-Tyne – 8 October 1886 London) was an English explorer, naturalist and painter. He travelled through Australia and South Africa, visiting New Zealand in between, publishing books on Australia and Polynesia (Wikipedia, http://en.wikipedia.org/wiki/George_French_Angas, accessed 2 March 2009).
4 Tāmati Reedy, interview, 1996.
5 Te Wharehuia Milroy, interview, 1997.
6 Tāmati Kruger, interview, 2003; and Te Poroa Malcolm, interview, 2003.
7 Tāmati Kruger, interview 2003.
8 Ward, *Life Among the Maories of NZ*, pp. 91–92.
9 McGuire, *The Maoris of New Zealand*, p. 38.
10 Kāretu, 'Whaikōrero'.
11 Newman, *Who are the Maoris?*, p. 240.
12 Kereopa in Moon, *Tohunga Hohepa Kereopa*, pp. 115.
13 Armstrong, *Maori Customs and Crafts*, p. 40.
14 'I mua, kāre e whakaaetia te reo Pākehā, he kore tonu nō te Pākehā e taetae ana ki ō tātou marae, ā, nō nāianei, kaha ana te haere mai a te Pākehā ki ngā tangihanga, ki ngā hui Māori. Koirā ka ngāwari te Māori kia tū mai te Pākehā me tōna reo, engari, i mua kāre e whakaaetia' (Te Poroa Malcolm, interview, 2003).
15 Salmond, *Hui*, pp. 128–9.
16 Gudgeon, 'Mana Tangata', pp. 108–9.
17 Te Kapunga Dewes, interview, 1997.
18 Salmond, *Hui*, p. 157.
19 Pearce, *The Story of the Maori People*, p. 137.
20 John Tahuri, pers. com., 1996.
21 Tony Herewini, interview, 1997.
22 'Ka āhua heahea tonu ki te whakarongo atu ki ngā kōrero ināianei, e tama, kua kaipāipa noho ngā kōrero ināianei' (Hieke Tupe, interview, 1996).
23 Te Wharehuia Milroy, interview, 1997.
24 Kawharu, 'Maori Sociology', p. 244.
25 Dewes, 'The Case for Oral Arts', p. 47.
26 J. Moorfield [video cassette], 'Te Reo', *Te Whanake 3: Te Māhuri*, Cassette 2, Te Whare Wānanga o Waikato, TVNZ Archive, n.d. b.
27 Te Ariki Morehu, interview, 1998.
28 Te Wharehuia Milroy, interview, 1997.
29 'Nō konā, i roto i te rau tau e tū mai nei, ki te kore e mau te reo, kāre he take o te kōrero whaikōrero. Ki te mau te reo me hoki anō ki te titiro ki te whakamahi o te reo i roto i te āhua i whakamahia ai e koro mā, e kui mā. Kua tīmata kē tātou ki te whakatangitangi tapes i runga i te marae. Kua tīmata kē tātou ki te whakamahi i ngā rorohiko hei powerpoint. Ahakoa te ongaonga, te tiotio o te tangata ki tērā mea, e tama, kei te haere mai te wā' (Te Wharehuia Milroy, interview, 1997).
30 '... te mita o te reo i tēnei wā. Kāre i rite ki te tuatahi, rerekē te mita i te tuatahi i ināianei. Kua āhua pēnei noho te reo o te tangata i tēnei wā, he reo tamariki ki te kōrero. Kua kore te hā o ngā koroua o te ao tawhito, o te wā i a rātou' (Hieke Tupe, interview, 1996).
31 Te Kei Merito, interview, 1997.
32 '... i ngā wā o mua, ahakoa kei hea tāua te Māori, ō tāua koroua, ō tāua kuia, he kōrero te kai ...' (Te Kei Merito, interview, 1997).
33 '... he pai ake tō whakatūtū i ngā porete mā rātou e kōrero, he pai pai ake rānei tō whakatū i tō mīhini pēnā i ēnā nā ka tuku atu mā tērā e pānui atu ki te marae tū mai tētahi ka hoatu ki tētahi atu anō he wā kei te haere mai whakatakotohia ngā whaikōrero ki runga i te mea rā kua

34   *pēhia atu anei te whakautu ki tērā*' (Te Wharehuia Milroy, interview, 1997).
34   The following is a portion extracted from his speech. '*Tihei mauri ora. Kei te kimi noa ake i ētahi kōrero kē, kē atu i wā wēnei kua tū ake nei i mua i awau, kāre e kitea e au. Ko aua kōrero rā anō kua kōrerotia ake nei ināianei. Heoi anō, i te pai. Ko tāua te Māori kāre e riri ki te pērā, ahakoa kōrero atu, kōrero mai, ko aua kōrero rā anō. Kāre tāua te Māori e kī, e kī e pupuri. Engari, pērā kei roto i Te Kōti Whenua Māori, kāre e kore ka panaia, ā, karanga mai, kua kōrerotia ano ēnā, wēnei o ngā āhuatanga e tētahi o ngā tāngata kua mutu ake nei*' (Eruera Manuera, TW15).
35   '*Kāre e pai a Te Arawa ki ngā kōrero whakakatakata nei. Kāre rātou e pai, ōku nā koroua o mua, kia katakata te tangata i te wā e whaikōrero ana, engari, kua āhua rerekē ināianei, kua pai noa iho te tū mai a tētehi, werowero i a rātou anō, hei whakakatakata i a rātou anō, engari i mua, kāo, ka riri ngā koroua, aku pāpā, i ngā kōrero paki nei [a] ngā tāngata i roto i wā rātou nā whaikōrero*' (Te Hiko-o-te-rangi Hohepa, interview, 1997).
36   Te Arawa, Ngāti Porou, Tūhoe, Te Āti Awa and Ngāi Tahu.
37   'Whakaata Māori' (Māori Channel) broadcast on Friday afternoon, 15 January 2004.
38   NZETC, http://www.nzetc.org/tm/scholarly/name-207885.html (1885?–1970), accessed 5 March 2009.
39   Tāmati Kruger, interview, 2003.
40   '. . . *ko te tū a te tangata. Tuatoru ko te mau. Kua ngaro hoki te iwi e takahi ana i te marae ināianei e whiu ana i tēnei mea, te kōrero, e rere ana te rākau, e rere ana te tinana, te hope, te rere a te waewae, te takahi i runga i te marae, kua rerekē noa iho ināianei, engari, koirā katoa ngā kīnaki, ngā kawenga o tēnei mea o te whaikōrero, a ngā koroua o mua. Hei reira ka kitea te tohungatanga o te tangata ki tēnei mea te whaikōrero ki tāna mau i tana tinana, i te rere a tana ringa, ngā ringa, te rere o te waewae, te mau o te rākau, te haere o te kōrero. Was drama of its own making. Ruarua ngā tāngata e kite ana koe i runga marae e kawe ana tēnei āhua ināianei. As a youth. I kite ana rā i ēnei momo tāngata e kanikani haere ana i runga i te marae. Haere nei te whaikōrero, te rere o te mere, te mau tokotoko rānei, koirā, i kite i ērā momo tāngata e mau ana i te rākau me te whaikōrero, me te whiu i te rākau, te ātaahua o te tū. Mā te rere o te tinana e whakaū te tikanga o ngā kōrero*' (Tāmati Reedy, interview, 1996).
41   Te Ariki Morehu, interview, 1998.
42   Pou Temara, interview, 1997.
43   Ibid.
44   Haami Piripi, email correspondence, 2001.
45   Henare Tuwhangai (MASPAC Video n.d.: 43'30").
46   Te Hemara, 'Tikanga', p. 48.
47   Henare, 'He Whakataki', pp. 16, 22–23.
48   Robb, *Kawa Marae*, p. 26.
49   Tīmoti Kāretu, interview, 1995.
50   'He arrived early January 1838 in Aotearoa New Zealand and worked for thirty years to bring the Catholic faith to the people of this land. He was helped by Maori won to the faith before his arrival, priests and brothers of the Society of Mary, immigrant Catholic families from England and Ireland, Sisters of Mercy, and other Religious. He was quick to learn both English and Maori. He founded missions in 16 different places throughout the length of our country. He had a close relationship with many Maori leaders. Few New Zealanders, including Catholics, know about the contribution made by Bishop Pompallier at the signing of the Treaty of Waitangi. There he insisted that a clause be added which would guarantee the right of religious freedom for all. . . . Since his arrival in 1838 he had a close relationship with many Maori leaders' (The Return of the Remains of Bishop Pompallier, online).
51   Mackay, online.
52   'However, Herbert will be best remembered for his scholarship in the field of Maori language. His grandfather, William, had published the first substantial Maori-to-English dictionary in 1844. Enlarged editions, edited by Leonard, appeared in 1871 and 1892. For 15 years Herbert worked on a further revision. In January 1906 he had the opportunity of examining the collection of Maori manuscripts deposited in the South African Public Library at Cape Town by Sir George Grey (and he was responsible for their eventual return to New Zealand). Finally, in 1917, the greatly enlarged fifth edition of A dictionary of the Maori language was published under the auspices of the Polynesian Society by the Government Printer. This meticulously edited enhancement of earlier editions established the dictionary as the unsurpassed record of a Polynesian language, and Williams as the major Maori linguist of his day. It earned him honorary doctorates in literature from the Universities of New Zealand (1924) and Cambridge (1925)' (Bruce Biggs, online).
53   Michael Reilly, pers. com., 2005.
54   John Tāhuri, pers. com., 1996.
55   Pearce, *The Story of the Maori People*, p. 118.
56   Kereopa in Moon, *Tohunga Hohepa Kereopa*, p. 113.
57   Hiwi and Pat Tauroa, *Te Marae*, p. 13.
58   Kāretu, 'Kawa in Crisis', pp. 67, 69, 72.
59   Awatere, 'Te Kawa o Te Marae', p. 34.
60   Walsh, *More and More Maoris*, p. 45.
61   Kāretu, 'Kawa in Crisis', p. 78.
62   Dewes, 'The Case for Oral Arts', in King, *Te Ao Hurihuri*, pp. 55–56.
63   Rewi, 'Te Reo o Whaikōrero', p. 3.
64   Walker, 'The Relevance of Maori Myth and Tradition', pp. 31–32.
65   Binney, 'Myth and Explanation in the Ringatū Tradition', pp. 346–7.
66   Te Kepa Stirling, pers. com., 2005.

Bibliography

Literary Sources

Archer, C., 'Some Key Aspects of Māori Oratory: How They Compare With European Oratory, and Implications for the Teacher of Public Speaking', a thesis submitted in partial fulfillment of the requirements for the Fellowship of Speech New Zealand in Teaching Public Speaking and Communication, 2003.
Armstrong, A., *Maori Customs and Crafts*, Seven Seas Publishing, Wellington, 1973.
Awatere, A., 'Te Kawa o Te Marae: Adult Educational Lectures', Council of Adult Education, University of Auckland, n.d.
Awatere, A. and T. Dewes, *Maori Literature*, Department of Anthropology, Victoria University of Wellington, n.d. (reprint).
Awatere, H. (ed.), *Awatere: A Soldier's Story*, Huia Publishers, Wellington, 2003.
Barlow, C., *Tikanga Whakaaro*, Oxford University Press, Auckland, 1991.
Beaglehole, E., *Some Modern Maoris*, New Zealand Council for Educational Research, Wellington, 1946.
Best, E., 'Maori Medical Lore', *Journal of the Polynesian Society*, vol. xiv, no. 53, 1905, pp. 1–23.
——, *The Maori School of Learning*, Government Printer, Wellington, 1923.
——, *Polynesian Voyagers: The Maori as a Deep-sea Navigator, Explorer & Colonizer*, Government Printer, Wellington, 1954.
——, *The Maori as He Was*, A. R. Shearer, Government Printer, Wellington, 1974 [first printed 1924].
——, *The Whare Kohanga (the 'Nest House') and its Lore: Comprising Data Pertaining to Procreation, Baptism, and Infant Betrothal, & C., Contributed By Members of the Ngati-Kahungunu Tribe of the North Island of New Zealand*, A. R. Shearer, Government Printer, Wellington, 1975.
——, *Maori Religion and Mythology Part 1*, Government Printer, Wellington, 1976 [first printed 1924].
——, *Tuhoe, the Children of the Mist: A Sketch of the Origin, History, Myths, and Beliefs of the Tuhoe Tribe of the Maori of New Zealand; With Some Account of Other Early Tribes of the Bay of Plenty District*, 3rd ed., printed by A. H. & A. W. Reed for the Polynesian Society, Wellington, 1977.
——, *Maori Eschatology*, Kiwi Publishers, Christchurch, 1998 [first printed in *Transactions and Proceedings of the New Zealand Institute*, vol. 38, 1906, pp. 77–106].
——, *Notes on the Art of War*, printed by Reed for the Polynesian Society, Auckland, 2001.
Bevan-Brown, J., 'By Māori, For Māori – Is that Enough?', *Proceedings of Te Oru Rangahau Māori Research and Development Conference, 1998*, School of Māori Studies, Massey University, 7–9 July 1998, pp. 231–45.
Binney, J., 'Myth and Explanation in the Ringatū Tradition', *Journal of the Polynesian Society*, vol. 93, no. 4, 1984, pp. 345–98.
Bloch, M. (ed.), *Political Language and Oratory in Traditional Society*, Academic Press, London, 1975.
Brooke-White, V. (ed.), *Whaikoorero: Ceremonial Farewells to the Dead*, Continuing Education Unit, Radio New Zealand, Wellington, 1981.
Brougham, A. and A. Reed, *The Reed Book of Māori Proverbs*, Reed, Auckland, 1999 Publishing [first printed 1963].
Brown, A., *Mana Wahine: Women Who Show the Way*, Reed Publishing, Auckland, 1994.
Buck, P., *Ethnology of Mangareva*, Bulletin 157, Bernice P. Bishop Museum, Honolulu, 1938.
——, *The Coming of the Maori*, Whitcombe and Tombs, Wellington, 1966.
Caselberg, J. (ed.), *Maori is My Name: Historical Maori Writings in Translation*, J. McIndoe, Dunedin, 1975.
Cleave, P., *The Maori State*, Campus Press, Palmerston North, 1998.
Colenso, W., *Contributions Towards a Better Knowledge of the Māori Race: Part I. Legends, Myths, and Fables*, Kiwi Publishers, 2001 [first printed 1878].
Cowan, James, *The Maori Yesterday and To-Day*, Whitcombe & Tombs, Auckland, 1930.
Cox, L., *Kotahitanga*, Oxford University Press, Auckland, 1993.
Curnow, Jenifer Mary, 'Wiremu Maihi Te Rangikaheke: His Life and Work', MA thesis, Māori Studies, University of Auckland, 1983.
Del Mar, F., *A Year among the Maoris: A Study of Their Arts and Customs*, Benn, London, 1924.
Dewes, T. K., 'The Case for Oral Arts', in M. King (ed.), *Te Ao Hurihuri: Aspects of Maoritanga*, Hicks Smith, Wellington, 1977, pp. 46–61.
Douglas, B., *Across the Great Divide: Journeys in History and Anthropology*, Harwood Academic Publishers, Amsterdam, 1998.
Downes, T. W., 'Maori Ettiquette', *Journal of the Polynesian Society*, vol. 38, no. 150, 1929, pp. 148–67.

Duranti, A., 'Speechmaking and the Organization of Discourse in a Samoan Fono', *Journal of the Polynesian Society*, vol. 90, no. 3, 1981, pp. 357–99.
Durie, E. T., 'Ethics and Values in Māori Research', *Proceedings of Te Oru Rangahau Māori Research and Development Conference, 1998*, School of Māori Studies, Massey University, 7–9 July 1998, pp. 62–69.
Durie, M. H., 'Te Oru Rangahau – Concluding Remarks', *Proceedings of Te Oru Rangahau Māori Research and Development Conference, 1998*, School of Māori Studies, Massey University, 7–9 July 1998, pp. 408–15.
Edwards, M., *Mihipeka: Call of an Elder/Karanga a te Kuia*, Steele Roberts, Wellington, 1986.
Evans, J., *Māori Weapons in Pre-European New Zealand*, Reed Publishing, Auckland, 2002.
Firth, R., *Economics of the New Zealand Māori*, 2nd ed., Government Print, Wellington, 1959.
Green, Hohepa, 'Te Kawa o Ngāti Porou – He Pāeke', *Te Wharekura 46*, Learning Media Limited, Wellington, 1995, pp. 2–7.
Greenwood, W., 'The Upraised Hand or the Spiritual Significance of the Ringatu Faith', *Journal of the Polynesian Society*, vol. 51, no. 1, 1942, pp. 1–81.
Grey, George, *Nga Mahi a nga Tupuna*, 3rd ed., Reed, Wellington, 1928.
Grove, N., *Ngā Pēpeha a ngā Tūpuna*, 2nd ed., Department of Maori Studies, Victoria University of Wellington, 1984 [first printed 1981].
Gudgeon, C., 'Mana Tangata', *Journal of the Polynesian Society*, vol. xiv, no. 54, 1905, pp. 49–66.
——, 'Maori Religion', *Journal of the Polynesian Society*, vol. xiv, no. 55, 1905, pp. 107–30.
Haddon, A., 'The Hidden Teaching of the Maori', *Journal of the Polynesian Society*, vol. xxiii, no. 89, 1914, pp. 55–57.
Hanson, F. Allan and Louise, *Counterpoint in Maori Culture*, Routledge & Kegan Paul, London, 1983.
Harawira, W., *Te Kawa o te Marae: A Guide For All Marae Visitors*, Reed, Auckland, 1997.
Hazlehurst, K., *Political Expression and Ethnicity: Statecraft and Mobilisation in the Maori Word*, Praeger, Westport, Conn., 1993.
Henare, D., 'He Whakataki', in A. Brown (ed.), *Mana Wahine: Women Who Show the Way*, Reed Publishing, Auckland, 1994, pp. 16–23.
Heuer, B., *Maori Women*, A. H. & A. W. Reed, Wellington, 1972.
Higgins, R. and J. C. Moorfield, 'Ngā Tikanga o te Marae: Marae Practices', in T. M. Ka'ai, J. C. Moorfield, M. P. J. Reilly & S. Mosely (eds), *Ki te Whaiao: An Introduction to Māori Culture and Society*, Pearson Education, Auckland, 2004, pp. 73–84.
Hohepa, P. W., *A Maori Community in Northland*, A. H. & A. W. Reed, Wellington, 1964.
Introduction to Whaikōrero, Te Whare Wananga O Awanuiarangi [Coursebook for MAOR 217], 1995.
Joseph, D., *He Reo Pōwhiri/te Karanga, te Whaikōrero*, HANA, Wellington, 2004.
Ka'ai, T. M., 'Te Mana o te Reo me ngā Tikanga: Power and Politics of the Language', in T. M. Ka'ai, J. C. Moorfield, M. P. J. Reilly and S. Mosely (eds), *Ki te Whaiao: An Introduction to Māori Culture and Society*, Pearson Education, Auckland, 2004, pp. 201–13.
Ka'ai, T. M. and R. Higgins, 'Te Ao Māori: Māori World-view', in T. M. Ka'ai, J. C. Moorfield, M. P. J. Reilly and S. Mosely (eds), *Ki te Whaiao: An Introduction to Māori Culture and Society*, Pearson Education, Auckland, 2004, pp. 13–25.
Ka'ai, T. M. and M. Reilly, 'Rangatiratanga: Traditional and Contemporary Leadership', in T. M. Ka'ai, J. C. Moorfield, M. P. J. Reilly and S. Mosely (eds), *Ki te Whaiao: An Introduction to Māori Culture and Society*, Pearson Education, Auckland, 2004, pp. 91–102.
Ka'ai, T. M., J. C. Moorfield, M. P. J. Reilly and S. Mosely (eds) *Ki te Whaiao: An Introduction to Māori Culture and Society*, Pearson Education, Auckland, 2004.
Kāretu, S., 'Kawa in Crisis', in M. King (ed.), *Tihe Mauri Ora: Aspects of Maoritanga*, Wellington: Methuen Publications, 1978, pp. 67–79.
——, 'Ngā Waiata o te Ao Tawhito', He tuhinga kauhau [copy in author's possession], n.d.a.
——, 'Turanga waewae', Lecture notes [copy in author's possession], n.d.b.
——, 'Die Situation Der Māoriprache in Neuseeland', Lecture notes [copy in author's possession], n.d.c.
——, *Ngā Waiata me ngā Haka a te Kapa Haka o Te Whare Wānanga o Waikato*, Hamilton: University of Waikato, 1989.
——, 'Whaikōrero', Lecture notes [copy in author's possession], 1990.
——, *Haka: Te Tohu o te Whenua Rangatira*, Reed, Auckland, 1993.
——, 'E Aku Raukura' [a composition composed in 1995 and performed by Te Whare Wānanga o Waikato Kapa Haka Cultural Group in National Performing Arts Competition 1996], 1995.
Kawharu, H., 'Maori Sociology: A Commentary', *Journal of the Polynesian Society*, vol. 93, no. 3, 1984, pp. 231–46.
Kernot, B., *People of Four Winds*, Hicks, Smith & Sons, Wellington, 1972.
King, M. (ed.), *Te Ao Hurihuri: Aspects of Maoritanga*, Hicks, Smith & Sons, Wellington, 1977.
—— (ed.), *Tihe Mauri Ora: Aspects of Maoritanga*, Methuen, Wellington, 1978.

Kruger, T., 'The Qualities of Ihi, Wehi and Wana', Introduction to Whaikōrero, Te Whare Wananga O Awanuiarangi [coursebook for MAOR 217], 1995, pp. 92–99.
Leather, K. and R. Hall, *Tātai Arorangi, Māori Astronomy: Work of the Gods*, Viking Sevenseas, Paraparaumu, 2004.
Lord, Albert B., *The Singer of Tales*, Harvard University Press, Cambridge, 1960.
Mahuta, R. T., 'Whaikōrero', MA thesis, University of Auckland, 1974.
Mahuta, R. T., G. Schrempp and I. Nottingham, *A Whaikoorero Reader: Comparative Perspectives for the Study of Whaikoorero and Other Traditional Maori Speech Forms*, Occasional Paper no. 21, Centre for Maori Studies and Research, University of Waikato, Hamilton, 1984.
Maning, F., *Old New Zealand*, Whitcombe and Tombs, Christchurch, 1948 [first printed 1863].
Mataira, K., *Pukapuka Pānui* [coursebook for Te Kura Puaotanga. Kōwae Ako 6: karanga/whaikōrero], Te Ataarangi, Waikato Polytechnic, Kirikiriroa, 1995.
McGuire, E., *The Maoris of New Zealand*, The Macmillan Company, New York, 1968.
McLean, M., *Māori Literature: Poetry*, Department of Anthropology, Victoria University of Wellington, n.d.
——, 'Maori Chant (A Study in Ethnomusicology)', PhD thesis, University of Otago, 1965.
McLean, M. and M. Orbell, *Songs of a Kaumātua: Sung by Kino Hughes*, Auckland University Press, Auckland, 2002.
McRae, J., 'The Function and Style of *Ruunanga* in Maori Politics', *Journal of the Polynesian Society*, vol. 93, no. 3, 1984, pp. 283–93.
Mead, H. Moko and Neil Grove, *Nga Pepeha a nga Tupuna, Te Wahanga 4*, Department of Maori Studies, Victoria University of Wellington, 1996.
——, *Nga Pepeha a nga Tupuna: The Sayings of the Ancestors*, Victoria University Press, Wellington, 2001.
Mead, S., 'Imagery, Symbolism and Social Values in Maori Chants', *Journal of the Polynesian Society*, vol. 78, no. 3, 1969, pp. 378–404.
Mead, S. M., *Tikanga Māori: Living by Māori Values*, Huia, Wellington, 2003.
Melbourne, H. (ed.), *Maori Sovereignty: The Maori Perspective*, Hodder Moa Beckett, Auckland, 1995.
Melbourne, S., 'Te Rangatiratanga: Māori Chieftainship and Leadership', He tuhinga kauhau mō Encounter History, 02.227, Session Ten, Te Whare Wānanga o Waikato [copy in author's possession], n.d.
——, 'Ngā Kura Huna a Tūhoe Pōtiki', He Kohinga kōrero nō te kura wānanga o Tūhoe 1981, Rūātoki [copy in author's possession], 1987.
——, /First Encounters/ Lecture notes for Encounter History 02.227, Te Whare Wānanga o Waikato [copy in author's possession], 1992.
Metge, J., *In and Out of Touch: Whakamaa in Cross Cultural Context*, Victoria University Press, Wellington, 1986.
——, 'Returning the Gift – *Utu* in Intergroup Relations', *Journal of the Polynesian Society*, vol. 111, no. 4, 2002, pp. 311–38.
Milroy, J., 'Ko te Āhuatanga Ā-Iwi', Lecture notes for Ngā Tikanga o te Marae, Marae Ettiquette 66504 [copy in author's possession], 1991.
Mitcalfe, B., *Maori*, Coromandel Press, Coromandel, 1981.
Moon, P., *Tohunga Hohepa Kereopa*, David Ling, Auckland, 2003.
Moorfield, J. C., *Te Whanake 2. Te Pihinga*, Longman Paul, Auckland, 1995 [first printed 1989].
——, *Te Whanake 4. Te Kohure*, Te Whare Wānanga o Waikato, Kirikiriroa, 1996.
——, *Te Whanake 3. Te Māhuri Pukapuka Tātaki*, Pearson Education, Auckland, 2004.
Newman, A., *Who are the Maoris?*, Whitcombe and Tombs, Christchurch, 1912.
Ngata, A., *Nga Moteatea: He Maramara Rere No Nga Waka Maha*, Polynesian Society, Auckland, Part III, 1980.
——, *Nga Moteatea: He Maramara Rere No Nga Waka Maha*, Polynesian Society, Auckland, Part I, 1988 [first printed 1959].
Ngata, H. M., *English-Maori Dictionary*, Learning Media, Wellington, 1993.
Orbell, M., *Maori Poetry: An Introductory Anthology*, Heinemann Educational Books, Auckland, 1978.
——, *The Natural World of the Māori*, William Collins, Auckland, 1985.
——, *Hawaiki: A New Approach to Maori Tradition*, Canterbury University Press, Christchurch, 1991.
O'Regan, Tipene, 'TE KAWA O KAITAHU', Summary of meeting held at Ngāti Moki Marae, Taumutu, in 1971 [copy in author's possession], 1989.
Paora, Roka, 'Te Kawa o Te Whānau ā Apanui – Pāeke', *Te Wharekura 46*, Learning Media Limited, Wellington, 1995, pp. 10–15.
Pearce, G. L., *The Story of the Maori People*, Collins, Auckland, 1968.
Petersen, A., 'Signs of Higher Life', PhD thesis, University of Otago, Dunedin, 1998.
Piripi, Haami, 'Maori Need to Consider Women on Marae', e-mail correspondence, *The Dominion* [copy in author's possession], 8 December 2001.
Polack, J. S., *Manners and Customs of the New Zealanders; With Notes Corroborative of Their Habits, Usages, etc., and Remarks to Intending Emigrants, With Numerous Cuts Drawn on Wood*, James Madden & Co., Piccadilly, 1976.

Pomare, M. and J. Cowan, *Legends of the Maori* [volume one], Southern Reprints, Papakura, 1987.
Pool, I., *Te Iwi Maori*, Auckland University Press, Auckland, 1991.
Prytz-Johansen, J., *Studies in Maori Rites and Myths*, E. Munksgaard, Copenhagen, 1958.
Rangihau, J., 'Being Maori', in M. King (ed.), *Te Ao Hurihuri: Aspects of Maoritanga*, Hicks, Smith & Sons, Wellington, 1977, pp. 165–75.
——, 'Te Whakaako i te Reo Māori: He Whakaaro Noa', in T. Kāretu (ed.), *Te Hīnātore: Te Wāhanga Tuarua (Putanga Hou)*, coursebook for 66501 Te Reo: Maori Language, Oral and Written, Department of Māori, Te Whare Wānanga O Waikato, 1991, pp. 46–52.
Reed, A. W., *Myths and Legends of Maoriland* [3rd impression], A. H. & A. W. Reed, Wellington, 1950.
Reid, P., 'Dying to be Counted', *Proceedings of Te Oru Rangahau Māori Research and Development Conference, 1998*, School of Māori Studies, Massey University, 7–9 July 1998, pp. 267–71.
Reilly, M., 'He Kōrero Nehe Māori History: An Introduction', Lecture notes for Māori 207, Te Whare Wānanga o Otāgo, Te Tumu, n.d.
——, 'Whanaungatanga: Kinship', in T. M. Ka'ai, J. C. Moorfield, M. P. J. Reilly and S. Mosely (eds), *Ki te Whaiao: An Introduction to Māori Culture and Society*, Pearson Education, Auckland, 2004, pp. 61–72.
Rewi, P., 'Te Reo O Te Whaikōrero', conference proceedings World Indigenous Peoples Conference on Education in Alberta, Canada [copy in author's possession], 2003.
——, 'Ko te Waihanga me ngā Wehewehenga o te *Whaikōrero*: The Structural System of *Whaikōrero* and its Components', *Junctures*, vol. 2, 2004, pp. 16–32.
Ritchie, J. E., *The Making of a Māori: A Case Study of a Changing Community*, A. H. & A. W. Reed, Wellington, 1963.
Robb, Loren, *Kawa Marae: A Detailed Guide to Marae Visits*, GP Print/ Presbyterian Church of Aotearoa New Zealand, Wellington, 1992.
Royal, Te Ahukaramū Charles, *Te Haurapa: An Introduction to Researching Tribal Histories and Traditions*, Bridget Williams Books and Historical Branch, Department of Internal Affairs, Wellington, 1992.
——, *Kati au i Konei: Collection of Songs from Ngati Toarangatira and Ngati Raukawa*, Huia Publishers, Wellington, 1994.
——, *Native Traditions by Hūkiki te Ahu Karamū o Otaki Jany 1st 1856*, Te Wānanga-o-Raukawa, Otaki, 2003.
Ryan, P., *The Reed Dictionary of Modern Māori*, Reed, Auckland, 1995.
Salmond, A., 'Mana Makes the Man: A Look at Māori Oratory and Politics', in M. Bloch (ed.), *Political Language and Oratory in Traditional Society*, Academic Press, London, 1975, pp. 45–64.
——, *Eruera: The Teachings of a Maori Elder*, Oxford University Press, Auckland, 1980 [reprinted 1985].
——, *Hui: A Study of Maori Ceremonial Gatherings*, 2nd ed., Reed Publishing, Auckland, 1994 [first printed 1976].
School of Māori Studies, Massey University, *Proceedings of Te Oru Rangahau Māori Research and Development Conference*, School of Māori Studies, Massey University, 7–9 July 1998.
Schrempp, G. 'Introduction', in R. T. Mahuta, G. Schrempp and I. Nottingham, *A Whaikōrero Reader: Comparative Perspectives for the Study of Whaikoorero and Other Traditional Maori Speech Forms*, Occasional Paper no. 21, Centre for Maori Studies and Research, University of Waikato, Hamilton, 1984.
Schwimmer, E., *The World of the Māori*, A. H. & A. W. Reed, Wellington, 1974 [reprinted, Reed Education, 1977].
Shirres, M., 'Tapu', *Journal of the Polynesian Society*, vol. 91, no. 1, 1982, pp. 29–51.
——, *Te Tangata: The Human Person*, Accent Publications, Auckland, 1997.
Shortland, E., *Traditions and Superstitions of the New Zealanders: With Illustrations of their Manners and Customs*, 2nd ed., Longman, Brown, Green, Longmans & Roberts, London, 1856.
Siers, J., *The Maori people of New Zealand*, Sevenseas, Wellington, 1967.
Simmons, D., *Ngā tau rere: An Anthology of Ancient Māori Poetry*, Reed, Auckland, 2003.
Sinclair, D., 'Marae: Land: Maori View and European Response', in M. King (ed.), *Te Ao Hurihuri: Aspects of Maoritanga*, Hicks, Smith & Sons, Wellington, 1977, pp. 86–106.
Sinclair, J. (ed.), *Collins Cobuild English Language Dictionary*, Harper Collins, London, 1987.
Smith, J., 'Tapu Removal in Maori Religion' [memoir supplement], *Journal of the Polynesian Society*, vol. 83, no. 4, 1974, pp. 1–42.
Smith, P., 'Some Personal Habits or Mannerisms of the Polynesians', *The Transactions of the Australasian Association for the Advancement of Science*, Government Printer, Wellington, 1905.
——, *History and Traditions of the Maoris of the West Coast North Island of New Zealand Prior to 1840*, Thomas Avery, New Plymouth, 1910.
Stafford, D. M., *Te Arawa: A History of the Arawa People*, Reed, Auckland, 1991.
——, *Tangata Whenua: The World of the Māori*, Reed, Auckland, 1996.
Takino, Ngaronoa Mereana, 'Academics and the Politics of Reclamation', *Proceedings of Te Oru Rangahau Māori Research and Development Conference, 1998*, School of Māori Studies, Massey University, 7–9 July 1998, pp. 289–93.

Tauroa, H., *A Guide to Marae: Te Kawa o te Marae*, Trade Union Education Authority, Wellington, c. 1989.
Tauroa, Hiwi and Pat, *Te Marae: A Guide to Customs and Protocol*, Reed Publishing, Auckland, 1986.
Tautahi, Kapua, 'A Religious Narrative' [copy in author's possession], n.d.
Te Awekotuku, N., 'He Ngangahu', in A. Brown (ed.), *Mana Wahine: Women who Show the Way*, Reed Publishing, Auckland, 1994, pp. 24–31.
Te Hemara, H., 'Tikanga', in A. Brown (ed.), *Mana Wahine: Women who Show the Way*, Reed Publishing, Auckland, 1994, pp. 48–55.
Thomson, N., *A World Awakens: Te Puawai o te Ao: Traditions from Nga Tipuna*, Turakina Maori Girls' College, Marton, 2003.
Thornton, A., 'The Hidden Teaching of the Maori', *Journal of the Polynesian Society*, vol. 98, no. 2, 1989, pp. 147–66.
——, *Māori Oral Literature as Seen by a Classicist*, Reed, Wellington, 1999.
——, *The Birth of the Universe: Te Whānautanga o te Ao Tukupū*, Reed, Auckland, 2004.
Tregear, E. *The Maori-Polynesian Comparative Dictionary*, Lyon and Blair, Wellington, 1891.
——, *The Maori Race*, A. D. Willis, Wanganui, 1973 [first printed 1926].
Vayda, A. P., *Maori Warfare*, Maori Monographs No. 2, Polynesian Society, Wellington, 1960.
Walker, R., 'Marae: A Place to Stand', in M. King (ed.), *Te Ao Hurihuri: Aspects of Maoritanga*, Hicks, Smith & Sons, Wellington, 1977, pp. 21–30.
——, 'The Relevance of Maori Myth and Tradition', in Michael King (ed.), *Tihe Mauri Ora: Aspects of Maoritanga*, Methuen, Auckland, 1978.
——, *Ka Whawhai Tonu Matou: Struggle Without End*, Penguin Books, Auckland, 1990.
——, 'Opening the Fiscal Envelope', *Nga Pepa a Ranginui: The Walker Papers*, Penguin Books, Auckland, 1996, pp. 111–24.
Walsh, A. C., *More and More Maoris: An Illustrated Statistical Survey of the Maori Today*, Whitcombe and Tombs, Christchurch, 1971.
Ward, R., *Life Among the Maories of New Zealand*, G. Lamb, London, 1872.
Wharekura, Tamati, 'Te Kawa o Tainui – Tau Whakautuutu', *Te Wharekura 46*, Learning Media Limited, Wellington, 1995, pp. 8–9.
White, J., *The Ancient History of the Maori, His Mythology and Traditions*, vol. iv: Tainui, Government Printer, Wellington, 1888.
——, *The Ancient History of the Maori, His Mythology and Traditions*, vol. xiii: Ngā-Ti Whatua (Maori), University of Waikato Library, Hamilton, 2001a [published transcription of MS Copy Micro 447, MS papers 75 B21 Reel 3, Alexander Turnbull Library].
——, *The Ancient History of the Maori, His Mythology and Traditions*, vol. x: Ngā Puhi (English), University of Waikato Library, Hamilton, 2001b [published transcription of MS Copy Micro 447, MS papers 75 B20 & B24 Reels 2 & 5, Alexander Turnbull Library].
Williams, H., *A Dictionary of the Maori Language*, 7th ed., Government Printer, Wellington, 1975.
Williams, H. 1975. *A Dictionary of the Maori Language*. 7th ed (reprint). Wellington: Government Printer.
Wilson, O., *From Hongi Hika to Hone Heke: A Quarter Century of Upheaval*, John McIndoe, Dunedin, 1985.
Woodard, H., 'Karanga', MA thesis, University of Auckland, 1994.
Yoon, H., *Maori Mind, Maori Land: Essays on the Cultural Geography of the Maori People From an Outsider's Perspective*, P. Lang, Berne, 1986.

Audio and Audio-visual

Dewes, K. [casette-tape], *Tauparapara from Te Kawa o Te Marae*, Department of Anthropology, Victoria University of Wellington, Cassette-tape-SM-520, 1970.
MASPAC Video [video cassette], 'He pae kaumātua e whakautu pātai ana mō ngā tikanga Māori', Ko te wharekai o Kimiora, i Tūrangawaewae marae, Ngāruawāhia [copy given to the author by Hirini Melbourne], n.d.
Moorfield, J. [video cassette], 'Ngā Tapuwae', *Te Whanake 4: Te Kōhure*, Cassette 2, Te Whare Wānanga o Waikato, TVNZ Archive, n.d. a.
Moorfield, J. [video cassette], 'Te Reo', *Te Whanake 3: Te Māhuri*, Cassette 2, Te Whare Wānanga o Waikato, TVNZ Archive, n.d. b.
Ngā Pū Kōrero [cassette-tape], *Ngā Pū Kōrero o te Wā*, No. 8 TMC 398.209931 Puk, Te Reo Irirangi o Te Upoko O Te Ika, 1987.
Rangihau, John [cassette-tape], *Wānanga a Tūhoe* [cassette-tape in author's possession], 1978.
Te Kākano [video cassette], Cassette 2, TVNZ as part of a TV Open Learning course, n.d.

Online

2004 Study at Massey, online, accessed on 30 August 2004. Also accessible through Massey University, New Zealand: http://study.massey.ac.nz/paper.asp?paper_code=182.003

Awanuiarangi, online, accessed on 30 August 2004. Also accessible through Wānanga: http://www.wananga.ac.nz/

Biggs, Bruce, 'Williams, Herbert William 1860–1937', online, *Dictionary of New Zealand Biography*, updated 16 December 2003: http://www.dnzb.govt.nz/

Bishop Pompallier, online, accessed 11 January 2005. Also accessible through Dictionary of New Zealand Biography. http://www.catholic.org.nz/pompallier/legacy.html

Environment, Society and Design Division, online, accessed 30 August 2004. Also accessible through Lincoln University, Canterbury, New Zealand: http://www.lincoln.ac.nz/esdd/subjinfo/mast308.htm

Graduate Ceremony, online, accessed 4 March 2005. Also accessible through Māori and Indigenous Studies, University of Canterbury: http://www.maori.canterbury.ac.nz/about/gradceremony.shtml

History, online, accessed 21 January 2005. Also accessible through Te Taura Whiri i te Reo Maori: http://www.tetaurawhiri.govt.nz/maori/issues_m/hist/index.shtml

Karakia, online, accessed 16 November 2004. Also accessible through Names from Myths, Legends, Waka, etc.: http://www.embassy.org.nz/aotearoa/mmyths.htm

Koha, online, accessed 11 November 2004. Also accessible through maori.org.nz: http://www.maori.org.nz/faq/showquestion.asp?faq=7&fldAuto=82

Mackay, David, 'Colenso, William 1811–1899', online. *Dictionary of New Zealand Biography*, updated 16 December 2003. URL: http://www.dnzb.govt.nz/

Mana and the Human Person, online, accessed 19 January 2005. Also accessible through ā Māori Theology: http://homepages.ihug.co.nz/~dominic/mana.html

Māori Culture – Legends, online, accessed 27 September 2004. Also accessible through Uniquely New Zealand: http://www.uniquelynz.com/maori_legend.htm

Maori Women: Caught in the Contradictions of a Colonised Reality, online, accessed 28 October 2004. http://www.waikato.ac.nz/law/wlr/1994/article6-mikaere.html

MAOR 321 – Te Reo Karanga, Te Reo Whaikorero/The Language of Karanga and Whaikorero, online, accessed 30 August 2004. Also accessible through Victoria University of Wellington, New Zealand: http://www.vuw.ac.nz/home/catalogue/index.aspx?course=MAOR-321

Marae, online, accessed 31 March 2005. Also accessible through Maor.org.nz: http://www.maori.org.nz/tikanga/?d=page&pid=sp30&parent=26

Mātauranga Māori, online, accessed 30 August 2004. Also accessible through Te Wānanga o Raukawa: http://www.twor.ac.nz/programmes/matauMāori/dipms.html

Ngā Manu Kōrero, online, accessed on 27 August 2004. Also accessible through Te Kaupapa Mātauranga Mō te Iwi Māori: Māori Education Trust: http://www.maorieducation.org.nz/mk/pthj.html

Shirres, M., 'Noa', online, accessed 19 January 2005. Also accessible through Maori Theology. http://homepages.ihug.co.nz/~dominic/noa.html

Programme Description, online, accessed 30 August 2004. Also accessible through Te Wānanga o Aotearoa: University of New Zealand: http://www.twoa.ac.nz/frames/mainframe_search.htm

Raiatea, online, accessed 16 June 2009. http://en.wikipedia.org/wiki/Raiatea

Rangiatea, online, accessed 16 June 2009. http://rangiatea.natlib.govt.nz/RinAotearoaE.htm

Shirres, M., 'Mana and the Human Person: Pae Tukutuku', online, accessed 3 June 2010. http://crash.ihug.co.nz/~dominic/mana.html

Shirres, M., 'Mana Atua: Power from the Spiritual Powers', online, accessed 1 June 2010. http://homepages.ihug.co.nz/~dominic/mana.html

Shirres, M., 'Noa', online, accessed 19 January 2005. Also accessible through Maori Theology. http://homepages.ihug.co.nz/~dominic/noa.html

Tapu, online. accessed 19 January 2005. Also accessible through Māori Theology: http://homepages.ihug.co.nz/~dominic/tapu.html

Te Toi Hou, online, accessed 30 August 2004. Also accessible through Elam School of Fine Arts: http://www.elam.auckland.ac.nz/te_toi_hou.htm

Temara, Pou, 'Te Pairi Tuterangi ?–1954', *Dictionary of New Zealand Biography*, updated 22 June 2007. URL: http://www.dnzb.govt.nz/

The Mātaatua Declaration on Cultural and Intellectual Property Rights of Indigenous Peoples, online, accessed 5 April 2005. Available Maori Independence Site: http://aotearoa.wellington.net.nz/imp/mata.htm

The Return of the Remains of Bishop Pompallier, online, accessed 11 January 2005. Also accessible through Catholic Church New Zealand: http://www.catholic.org.nz/pompallier/legacy.html

The story of New Zealand wood carving, online, accessed on 27 September 2004. Also accessible through Tahu: http://www.nztahu.com/story2.htm
Wharepuni, online, accessed 2 September 2004. Also accessible through Wakareo ā-ipurangi: http://www.reotupu.co.nz/wakareo/

Oral Sources

Oral information was acquired through formal interviews, discussions, explanatory notes and lectures. The informants who have agreed to have their identities acknowledged follow. Names by which they are more commonly referred have been [bracketed] alongside their given names. Pseudonyms have been afforded to those who did not consent to having their identities revealed and have been bracketed with the explanation '[pseudo]'.

Dewes, Te Kapunga [Koro], Ngāti Porou, *Kaumātua* – Māori Tribal Elder. Interview, 4 November 1997.
Grace, John, Ngāti Porou, Pāpā. Explanatory note, 1982.
Herewini, Tony [Mehaka], Ngāi Tūhoe, *Kaumātua* – Māori Tribal Elder. Discussion, 17 February 1997.
Hohepa, Te Hiko-o-te-rangi [Hiko], Te Arawa, *Kaumātua* – Māori Tribal Elder. Interview, 19 August 1997.
Hohepa, Te Patu [Pat], Ngā Puhi, *Kaumātua* – Māori Tribal Elder. Interview, 24 March 1998.
Iraia, Pita [P.I.], Ngāi Tūhoe and Ngāti Whare, *Kaumātua* – Māori Tribal Elder. Interview, 7 April 1997.
Kaiwai, Mate, Ngāti Porou, *Kaumātua* – Māori Tribal Elder. Discussion, 28 November 2001.
Ka'ai, Tania, Ngāti Porou, Ngāi Tahu, Hawai'i, Samoan, Professor. 'Māori Renaissance and Assertions to Sovereignty', Lecture, University of Alberta, Canada, 2005.
Kāretu, Tīmoti, Ngāi Tūhoe and Ngāti Kahungunu, Professor. Interview, 2 November 1995.
Kereopa, Hohepa, Ngāi Tūhoe, *Kaumātua* – Māori Tribal Elder/expert. Interview, 13 August 1997.
Kingi, Mauriora, Te Arawa, *Kaumātua* – Māori Tribal Elder. Interview, 11 February 1998.
Kruger, Tāmati, Ngāi Tūhoe, Lecturer. Interview, 23 June 2003.
Kuia Te Wai [pseudo], Ngāti Kahungunu, *Kaumātua* – Māori Tribal Elder. Discussion, 24 November 2001.
Kuia Tiehi [pseudo], Ngāi Tūhoe, *Kaumātua* – Māori Tribal Elder. Discussion, 28 April 1996.
Kuia Te Rangi [pseudo], Ngāti Porou, *Kaumātua* – Māori Tribal Elder, 2001.
Mahuta, Robert [Te Kotahi], Waikato/Maniapoto, *Kaumātua* – Māori Tribal Elder, Executive leader. Discussion, 30 October 1997.
Malcolm, Joseph [Poroa], Te Arawa, *Kaumātua* – Māori Tribal Elder. Interview, 24 June 2003.
Melbourne, Sydney [Hirini], Ngāi Tūhoe and Ngāti Kahungunu, Professor. Interview, 18 September 1997.
Merito, Te Kei [Kei], Ngāti Awa, *Kaumātua* – Māori Tribal Elder. Discussion, 20 September 1997.
Milroy, James [Wharehuia], Ngāi Tūhoe, Professor/*Kaumātua* – Māori Tribal Elder. Interview, 7 November 1997.
Moorfield, John [Murumāra], Professor. Explanatory note, 2004.
Morehu, Derek [Te Ariki], Te Arawa, *Kaumātua* – Māori Tribal Elder. Interview, 9 February 1998.
Pouwhare, Taua, Ngāi Tūhoe, *Kaumātua* – Māori Tribal Elder. Discussion, 2 February 1996.
Pukepuke, Kimoro, Ngāi Tūhoe, *Kaumātua* – Māori Tribal Elder. Interview, 20 August 1997.
Rangi, Te Hue, Ngāi Tūhoe, Pūkenga. Interview, 23 June 2003.
Rangiaho, Sonny, Ngāi Tūhoe. Explanatory note, 1999.
Reedy, Tamati, Ngāti Porou, Professor. Interview, 4 November 1996.
Reilly, Michael, Ngāi Pākehā, Pūkenga Matua. Explanatory note, 6 January 2005.
Sharples, Peter, Ngāti Kahungunu, Māori Party co-leader, *Kaumātua* – Māori Tribal Elder. Discussion, 26 March 1998.
Stirling, Te Kepa, Te Whānau-a-Apanui, *Kaumātua* – Māori Tribal Elder. Explanatory note, 15 January 2005.
Tahuri, John [Rū], Ngāi Tūhoe, *Kaumātua* – Māori Tribal Elder. Explanatory note, 7 May 1996.
Tait, Te Kotahitanga [Bubba], Ngāi Tūhoe and Te Arawa, *Kaumātua* – Māori Tribal Elder. Interview, 14 October 1996.
Temara, Pou, Ngāi Tūhoe, Professor/*Kaumātua* – Māori Tribal Elder. Interview, 27 August 1997.
Tihema, Koro, Ngāi Tūhoe, *Kaumātua* – Māori Tribal Elder. Explanatory note, 3 February 2004.
Timutimu, Awanui [Mannie], Ngāi Tūhoe, University Lecturer. Interview, 10 November 1995.
Tupe, Hieke, Ngāi Tūhoe and Ngāti Raukawa, *Kaumātua* – Māori Tribal Elder. Interview, 16 October 1996.
Waiariki, Eric [Whitu], Ngāi Tūhoe, *Kaumātua* – Māori Tribal Elder. Interview, 18 June 1996.
Walker, Ranginui, Whakatōhea, Professor, *Kaumātua* – Māori Tribal Elder. Interview, 18 March 1998.
Winiata, Wīhapi [Hapi], Te Arawa, *Kaumātua* – Māori Tribal Elder. Discussion, 19 November 2002.

Index

ahi kā, 39
Akaroa mission station, 145
Anamata, 28, 173
ancestors, Māori, 48, 53, 181
Angas, George French, 87, 166
Archer, C., 68, 101
assimilation, 5, 41, 168
Auckland, 43, 44, 121; mission station, 145; *see also*, Elam School of Fine Arts; Hoani Waititi Marae; Te Tirahou Marae
Awanui, Epa, 61
Awatere, Arapeta, 33–34, 40, 136–7, 157, 180
Awhitu, 120–1

Barlow, C., 10, 11, 39–40, 129, 160
Bay of Plenty, 1, 20, 25, 83, 85, 121, 125, 131, 145
Beaglehole, E., 31
Bennett, Frederick Augustus, 86–87
Best, Elsdon, 2, 23–24, 51, 72, 97, 106, 115, 178
biculturalism, 179
Biggs, Bruce, 151
Binney, Judith, 105
Bloch, M., 46, 47
Brooke-White, V., 87
Broughton, Ruka, 81
Buck, Sir Peter, 3, 118, 121, 142, 159

chants, Māori, 33, 46, 53, 73, 87, 99, 104, 136, 137–9, 141, 152, 172
Christianity: introduction of, 68, 75, 144–5, 168, 169; references to in *whaikōrero*, 81–82, 144–5, 150, 155, 169; *see also*, hymns; mission stations; missionaries
Cleave, Peter, 63, 138
Colenso, William, 78, 178
colonisation, 11, 14, 22, 39, 68, 75, 144–5, 164, 168
competitions, speech; *see*, Korimako Contest; Pei Te Hurinui Jones competition; *whaikōrero*: competitions
Cowan, James, 141
Cox, L., 3, 25
cultural tokenism, 165–6
culture, erosion of, 21–23, 36, 179

deities, Māori, 7, 8, 11–12, 51, 64, 83, 85, 103, 120, 136, 137, 139, 140, 141, 144, 145, 169, 181
Delamere, Tuariki, 54
Dewes, Te Kapunga (Koro), 26, 34, 55, 66, 74, 141, 146, 147, 153–4, 169, 171, 181
Douglas, B., 64
Downes, T. W., 128
Durie, E. T., 2

East Coast, 34, 68, 85, 111, 171
education: distance, 28; Māori, 25, 28, 29, 154, 159–60, 164–5, 170, 173, 182; Pākehā, 86, 89, 145, 159–60, 164; *see also*, *wānanga*
Edwards, Mihipeka, 107, 134

Ehau, Kepa Hamuera Anaha, 86–87, 174
Elam School of Fine Arts, Auckland, 28
encounter rituals, 132–3
ethnographers/ethnography, 2–3; *see also*, Best, Elsdon; Buck, Sir Peter; White, John
eulogy, 34, 105, 135, 137, 145–6, 147, 148–50; *see also*, *tangi*; *whaikōrero*: and bereavement
Evans, J., 95

flax, knowledge of, 58

genealogy, Māori, 2, 3, 8, 20, 25, 27, 30, 32, 33, 49, 51, 56, 57, 58, 62, 64, 66, 73, 78, 83–85, 103, 104, 105, 128, 140, 144, 150, 158, 164, 171
geomentality, 8, 40, 43, 46, 53, 181
Gisborne, 1, 111
gods, Māori, *see*, deities, Māori
Governor General, 111
Grey, George, 79, 167, 178
Grove, N., 83
Gudgeon, C., 105, 169

haka, 24–25, 37, 53, 79, 87, 105, 108, 121, 135, 140, 150, 152–3, 154, 155, 167
Harawira, W., 118
Haumia-tiketike, 51
Hawaiki, 13
Herewini, Mehaka, 66, 96–97
Heuer, B., 32
Hine-ahu-one, 7, 12
Hine-nui-te-pō, 12
Hine-tītama, 12
history, Māori, 2, 22, 23, 24, 25–26, 29, 30, 32, 58, 83, 105, 150, 164, 181
Hoani Waititi Marae, Auckland, 169
Hohepa, Hiko, 12, 34, 60, 62, 91, 98, 114, 131–2, 134, 137, 139, 145, 160, 168, 173
Hohepa, Patu, 13, 43, 119, 124–5, 130, 151, 161
Hokianga mission station, 145
hongi, 49, 116, 121, 130
Horouta canoe, 85
hui, 1, 27, 29, 35, 68, 98, 100, 107, 133
hymns, 81, 154, 155, 169

identity: Māori, 7, 40, 82, 84, 170, 181; tribal, 39, 53–54, 88
Iharaira, 144
incantations, Māori, 35, 46, 53, 104, 110, 136, 137, 138, 139, 140, 171, 172, 183; *see also*, *tauparapara*
Io, 24
Io-matua-te-kore, 13
Iraia, Pita, 35, 44, 57, 61, 125, 145

Jones, Pei Te Hurinui, 83, 84, 137, 151

Kahungunu (iwi), 5, 6, 44, 67, 72, 74
kaikaranga, 146, 169

Kaipara mission station, 145
Kairau, 120
kākā kura, 127–8
kapa haka, 24, 98
karakia, 46, 53, 87, 136, 137–8, 139, 140
karanga, 25, 26, 70, 73–74, 75, 107, 128, 146, 149, 177, 181
Kāretu, Tīmoti, 13, 18, 57, 66, 77, 78, 79, 80, 95, 97, 100–1, 109, 128, 146, 151, 154–5, 157, 162, 166, 167, 178, 180, 181
kaumātua, 20, 30–31, 33, 34, 58, 147, 162
kaupapa, 70, 81, 150
kawa, 39, 65, 180–1
Kawhia, 84
Kereopa, Hohepa, 5, 18, 26, 31, 45, 66, 69–70, 79, 116, 129, 152–3, 168, 179
Kernot, B., 17, 58–59
King Country, 121
King Koroki, 34, 84–85, 137
King, Michael, 7, 42
Kingi, Mauriora, 13, 34, 43–44, 70, 122, 124, 128, 130
Kingi, Pihopa, 80
Kīngitanga, 84–85, 124, 144
knowledge, Māori, 2, 5, 13, 22, 23, 29–30, 58, 78, 80, 83, 181; and *whaikōrero*, 78; apprenticeship in, 28–31; preservation of, 2, 6–7, 164–5, 173; transmission of, 1–2, 6–7, 21–23, 24, 28–31, 36, 151, 164–5, 169, 174–5, 178–9; *see also*, genealogy, Māori; oral traditions, Māori
koha, 8, 54, 111, 131–4, 160, 168
Kohi, 176–7
Korimako Contest, 27
Kororareka (Russell) mission station, 145
koroua, 4, 10, 62
kotahitanga, 131
kotiate, 95, 96
Kotukutuku, Mihi, 67
Kruger, Tāmati, 11, 44, 47, 53, 64, 66, 76, 94, 98, 105, 157, 161, 166–7, 175
kuia, 4, 6, 34, 35, 67, 112, 181
Kuia Te Wai, 74
Kukutai, Ngapaka, 151
Kura Kaupapa Māori, 154
Kura Reo, 171
Kurahaupō, 120

land loss, 14, 18
landmarks, *see*, *whaikōrero*: references to landmarks in legends, Māori, 2, 23

magic, *see*, witchcraft and magic
Mahuika, Apirana, 80
Māhurehure Community Centre, 43
Mahuta, Robert, 15, 34, 55, 77, 78–79, 80, 85, 94, 99, 128, 129, 135–6, 137, 138, 139, 151, 152, 161
Maketu mission station, 145
Malcolm, Te Poroa, 13, 19, 26, 31, 34, 60, 156, 166, 168–9
mana, 5, 8, 39, 40, 56, 59, 61, 64, 68, 69, 72, 75, 77, 78, 79, 100, 103–13, 124, 138, 153, 161, 177
manaaki, 180
manaakitanga, 179
manawa wera, 139, 140
Mangakahia mission station, 145

Mangatoatoa, 176
Manihera, Te Uira, 21
Maning, F. 92–93
Manuera, Eruera, 173
manuhiri, 37, 39–40, 41, 45, 47, 48, 49–50, 53–54, 57, 64, 73, 107–8, 121–2, 130–1, 132–3, 136, 144, 146, 149, 181; *see also*, tangata whenua
Māori language, *see*, te reo Māori
Māori Language Commission, *see*, Te Taura Whiri i te Reo Māori
marae, 4, 8, 10, 14, 15, 16–17, 25, 30, 32, 38, 44–46, 47, 48, 49, 50, 52, 53–54, 57, 58–59, 62, 64, 65, 67, 68, 69, 70, 137, 144, 146–7, 153, 165, 166, 168, 169, 182; assigned roles on, 56, 68–69, 73; buildings on, 8, 23, 41, 44, 115, 116, 130, 132, 135, 144, 147–8; changes on 179–80; degradation of, 60, 169–70; functions of, 39–43; pan-Māori, 170; protocol on, 108–10, 117–18, 124–5, 127, 128, 132, 177; seating arrangements on, 8, 67, 68, 71, 72, 115–20, 157–8; urban, 43, 125, 170; *see also*, Hoani Waititi Marae, Auckland; Mātaatua Marae, Rotorua; Te Tirahou Marae, Auckland
marae-atea, 17, 41, 44, 52, 55, 68, 71, 76, 104, 118, 122, 169, 174
Marsden, Maori, 28–29
martial arts, Māori , 93
Mātaatua canoe, 85, 155
Mātaatua Marae, Rotorua, 118, 125
Mātaatua (*iwi*), 1, 71, 81, 83, 98, 106, 117, 118, 124–5, 126, 130–1, 133, 145, 146, 148
Mataira, Katerina, 14, 17, 19, 42–43, 46, 60, 68–69, 71–72, 74, 78
Matamata mission station, 145
Māui, 126
Māui-tikitiki-a-Taranga, 12, 64
Maungapōhatu, 48–49, 174
Maungatautatari (mountain), 84
mauri, 60, 130, 141–2
Mauriohooho, Waea, 80, 154
McClutchie, Whaia, 75
McGuire, E., 14, 25, 121, 167
McKillop, H. F., 115
McLean, M., 137, 152
Mead, S. M., 115, 155
meeting house, *see*, wharenui
Melbourne, Hirini, 11–12, 31, 39, 61, 70, 153
mere, 93, 95, 96, 98
Merito, Te Kei, 11, 35, 44, 45, 65, 134, 137, 141, 172
Metge, Joan, 61, 74
migration, Māori from Pacific, 13, 14, 83, 121, 132
mihi, 135, 144–8, 160
mihimihi, 45, 47, 49
Mikaere, Ani, 69
Milroy, Te Wharehuia, 7, 11, 15, 16, 17, 18–19, 26, 44, 45, 54, 77, 78, 80, 81, 89, 98, 127, 138, 159, 166, 170, 173
missionaries, 29, 145–178
Mitchell, Hamuera, 80
mnemonic ability, *see*, oral traditions, mnemonics of; Pacific Islands, retention of mnemonic ability in
Moorfield, John, 151, 154, 178
Morehu, Te Ariki, 12, 31, 45–46, 57, 66, 118, 134, 171, 175
mōteatea, 58, 135, 151, 154–5

Mount St John, *see*, Tiko-puke
Muriwai, 83
myths, Māori, 12, 22, 24, 32, 51, 83, 103, 145, 182; creation, 11–12, 52, 141

Ngā Puhi (*iwi*), 5, 74, 80, 82–83, 85–86, 114, 119, 120, 129, 130, 133, 155
Ngāhuruhuru, 166
Ngāi Tahu (*iwi*), 26, 29, 44
Ngata, Āpirana, 87, 112–13, 151
Ngāti Awa (*iwi*), 5, 67, 82, 134, 155, 173
Ngāti Haka (*iwi*), 13, 80
Ngāti Manawa (*iwi*), 13, 159
Ngāti Mutunga (*iwi*), 134
Ngāti Pikiao (*iwi*), 84, 156, 180
Ngāti Pōneke (*iwi*), 170
Ngāti Porou (*iwi*), 5, 6, 19, 26, 29, 60, 67, 68, 71–72, 74, 75, 80, 98, 129, 133, 134, 139, 141, 145, 146, 148, 149, 153, 154, 155, 156–7, 159, 169, 171
Ngāti Pūkeko (*iwi*), 65
Ngāti Rānana (*iwi*), 170
Ngāti Tarāwhai (*iwi*), 174
Ngāti Toa (*iwi*), 142–3
Ngāti Toarangatira (*iwi*), 147
Ngāti Wai (*iwi*), 85
Ngāti Whakaue (*iwi*), 26, 119, 174
Ngāti Whare (*iwi*), 5, 13, 57, 145
Ngāti Whātua (*iwi*), 6, 125
ngeri, 140, 150
noa, 21, 67, 73–74, 75, 117, 138, 153
Northland, 44, 111

Opotiki mission station, 145
Ōrākau, 139
oral traditions, Māori, 3–5, 22, 23–24, 87, 164, 182; centrality of in Māori culture, 3, 22; language of, 19, 164; mnemonics of, 3, 23, 24–27, 33, 89; transmission of, 3, 21–23; *see also*, chants; incantations; *karakia*; legends; poetry; *tauparapara*; *waiata*; *whaikōrero*
orators, 4, 6, 7; role of, 8, 18, 19–20, 46, 127–31, 133, 178; skills of, 8, 29, 56, 77–79, 90–91, 105, 109–10, 112–13, 154; speaking order of, 8, 19, 118, 120–5, 127–31; speaking rights of, 8, 56, 59–65; stance of, 8, 31, 126–7, 174–5; status of, 56–59, 104, 109–10, 128, 139, 161, 166
Orbell, Margaret, 22, 29, 100, 137
Otago, 146; mission station, 145
Ōtaki mission station, 145
Ōwae Marae, 120

pā, 42; *see also*, Tiko-puke (Mount St John) Pā
Pacific Islands, retention of mnemonic ability in, 24–25; role of women in, 69
pāeke, 19, 120, 122–3, 124, 125, 127, 130, 151, 170
paepae, 39, 58, 97, 114, 115, 116, 123, 128
Paia, 11
Paimārire, 144
Painoaiho, 153
pāpaka, 94, 126
Papa-tū-ā-nuku, 7, 11–12, 51–52, 120, 148
Parihaka, 120
Pariroa Marae, 120

pātere, 140, 172
patu, 97, 98, 99
Patuheuheu (*iwi*), 13
Pei Te Hurinui Jones competition, 27
pepeha, 58, 87–88, 140, 144
Pewhairangi, Ngoi, 30, 56–57
Piripi, Haami, 176
Piripi, Haupeke, 80, 82–83, 85–86, 155
poetry, Māori, 2, 22
pōhiri, 44, 49, 50, 107, 152, 171
pōhuatau, 138; *see also*, *karakia*
Poipiripiri, 170
Pompallier, Bishop Jean Baptiste François, 145, 178
Poutapu, Piri, 33, 85
Pouwhare, Taua, 61, 63, 66, 130
prayers, *see*, *karakia*
proverbs, *see*, *pepeha*; *whakataukī*
Prytz-Johansen, J., 52–53
Puhi-kai-ariki, 64, 83
Pukepuke, Kimoro, 12, 34–35, 66, 80, 106, 156

Queen Victoria, 68–69

Raglan, *see*, Whaingaroa
Rāhiri, 83
Raiatea, Society Islands, 13
rākau, 97
Rakiura (*iwi*), 6
rangatira, 57–58, 98
Rangi, Hue, 11, 57, 60, 63, 78, 98–99, 125, 130
Rangiaho, Te Kurapa, 174
Rangiaowhia mission station, 145
Rangiātea, 13
Rangihau, John (Hoani), 21–22, 60, 80, 107, 127
Rangi-nui, 7, 11–12, 51–52, 120
Rangitahi Marae, 156
Rangitāne (*iwi*), 6
Raukawa (*iwi*), 85, 159, 173
Reedy, Arnold, 68
Reedy, Materoa, 68
Reedy, Tamati, 20, 33, 59, 63, 70, 75, 83, 86, 118, 129, 139, 141, 161, 166, 175
Rei, Pateriki (Pat), 121, 139, 147
Reilly, M., 84, 129, 178
Reo Rua (Bilingual Units), 154
ringa wera, 39
Ringatū, 1 35, 144
Ritchie, J. E., 93
Robb, Loren, 42, 178
Rongo, 29, 51, 72–73, 98
Rongo-marae-roa, 51, 52–53, 72–73, 98
Rongo-mā-tāne, 51, 52–53, 72–73, 98
Rongowhakaata (*iwi*), 44, 119, 159
Rotoiti, 84
Rotorua, 84, 118, 168; *see also*, Mātaatua Marae
Royal, Te Ahukaramū Charles, 5, 22, 33, 112
Rua-i-te-pūkenga, 29
Ruamoko, 51
Rūātoki, *see*, Te Rewarewa Marae
Ryan, P., 16

Salmond, Anne, 16–17, 31, 33, 34, 35, 38, 41–42, 55, 61, 62, 79, 90, 91, 92, 93–94, 95, 100, 106–7, 108, 110, 111, 127–8, 131, 138, 140, 160–1, 169
Schrempp, G., 78, 80, 89
seating positions, *see, marae*, seating arrangements on; *whaikōrero*: seating arrangements for; women: and seating position on *marae*
settlement, European, 23
Sharples, Pita, 24–25
Shirres, M., 28–29, 73–74, 75
Shortland, E., 81, 85
Siers, J., 32
Sinclair, J., 46–47, 48
Smith, P., 14
Society Islands, *see*, Raiatea
song, *see*, *waiata*
songs, action, 154
Southland, 146
spirituality, Māori, 18, 40, 48, 53, 171, 181; *see also*, deities, Māori
status, sibling, 8, 64–65
Stirling, Eruera, 110–11

Tahu, 51, 53, 73
Tahuri, John (Rū), 34, 44, 62, 77, 80, 127, 146, 169, 179
taiaha, 95, 97, 98, 143
Taiepa, 93, 97–98
Tainui, 95
Tainui canoe, 121, 125
Tait, Te Kotahitanga, 15, 63, 69, 114, 140, 144, 157
Taituha, Pumi, 80
take, 135, 150, 153, 160–1
Takino, Ngaronoa Mereana, 38
Tākitimu canoe, 23, 85
Tamakaimoana, 63, 80
Tāmati, Whati, 33
Tāne, 11, 12, 13, 51, 52, 53, 137, 141
Tāneatua, 83
Tāne-i-te-wānanga, 29, 137, 174
Tāne-mahuta, 51, 52
Tangaroa, 51
tangata whenua, 37, 38–40, 41, 49–50, 53–54, 57, 59, 73, 108, 121–2, 130–1, 132–3, 136, 144, 181; *see also*, *manuhiri*
tangi, 34, 40, 43, 48, 66, 79, 81, 105, 106, 114, 115, 116, 119–20, 121, 124, 130–1, 134, 135, 137, 142, 146–7, 148–9, 150, 154, 169, 173; *see also*, eulogy; *whaikōrero*: and bereavement
taokete, 66
taonga, 92, 133
tapu, 21, 30, 67, 70, 74, 75, 105, 115, 117, 138, 140, 152–3
Taranaki, 122
Taranaki (*iwi*), 6, 26, 44, 80, 139, 145
Tarawera, 13
tauparapara, 19, 35, 49, 87, 100, 135, 136–41, 144, 145, 149, 160, 169, 172, 183; *see also*, incantations, Māori
Taupopoki, Mita, 93
Tauranga mission station, 145
Tauranga moana (*iwi*), 80, 159
Tauroa, Hiwi, 32, 39, 40–41, 56, 57, 63, 68, 69, 71, 107, 108, 112, 152, 160, 179

Tauroa, Pat, 32, 40–41, 56, 57, 68, 107, 112, 152, 160, 179
Tautahi, Kapua, 52
tauutuutu, 19, 67, 120, 121–5, 170
Tawhai, Wiremu, 151
Tāwhiri-mātea, 11, 51
Taylor, Richard, 29
Te Aitanga-a-Hauiti, 110–11
Te Arawa canoe, 121, 125, 159
Te Arawa (*iwi*), 5, 12, 13, 19, 26, 31, 34, 44, 60, 62, 63, 67, 68, 71, 73, 75, 80, 86, 93, 98, 108, 111, 115, 117, 119–20, 121, 124, 125, 128, 129, 131, 133, 134, 137, 140–1, 144, 145, 146, 147, 148, 149, 156, 157, 159, 166, 173, 174, 177
Te Awekotuku, Ngahuia, 75
Te Hauangiangi, 83
Te Hemara, H., 177–8
Te Hui Ahurei a Tūhoe, 27
Te Kawa A Māui, 27–28
Te Kooti Arikirangi Te Tūruki, 7, 13
Te Mātorohanga, Moihi, 57
Te Panekiretanga, 171
Te Papaiouru, 119
Te Puke, 62
te reo Māori, 13, 16–17, 41, 47; extinction/loss of, 36, 170–1; learning of, 34–35, 36, 164–6; proficiency in, 27–28, 30, 34–35, 58, 64, 77–78, 80–81; revitalisation of, 82, 89, 163–4, 171; suppression of, 36, 89, 163–4, 172
Te Rewarewa Marae, Rūātoki, 116, 125
Te Tairāwhiti (*iwi*), 6, 26, 67, 131, 140
Te Taitokerau, 108, 119, 124–5, 145, 151, 159, 169
Te Taura Whiri i te Reo Māori (Māori Language Commission), 176
Te Tirahou Marae, Auckland, 125
Te Tira Hou, 170
Te Waimana, 116, 126
Te Waipounamu, 6
Te Wānanga o Aotearoa, 28
Te Wānanga o Raukawa, 28, 173
Te Whakatōhea, 5, 35, 67, 79, 153
Te Whānau-a-Apanui (*iwi*), 29, 67, 71–72, 110–11, 151
Te Whanganui-a Tara (*iwi*), 6
Te Whare Wānanga o Awanuiārangi, 28, 173
Te Wherowhero, Potātau, 87
teina, 63, 64–65
Temara, Pou, 12, 26, 43, 44–45, 91, 96, 99, 102, 104, 123, 129, 137, 157, 175–6
tewhatewha, 95, 98
Tihema, Koro, 61–62
tikanga, 2, 40–41, 65, 182
Tiko-puke (Mount St John) Pā, 15, 115
Timutimu, Awanui, 53, 57
tohi, 28–29, 140
tohunga, 23, 46, 177
toki, 95, 98, 102
Tokomaru, 120
tokotoko, 95, 96–99
Toroa, 83
Treaty of Waitangi, 82, 86, 165
Tregear, E., 52
tribal differences, 7, 26, 28, 134, 141–2, 150, 159–60, 177
tuakana, 63, 64–65
Tūhoe (*iwi*), 5, 6, 21, 22–23, 25–26, 44, 45, 61, 63, 66, 67,

Tūhoe (cont'd) 68, 73, 75, 79–80, 98, 102, 117, 126, 128, 129, 131, 134, 137, 139, 144, 147, 149, 152, 153, 154, 156, 157, 166, 173, 175–6
Tūhoe-pōtiki, 64
Tūhourangi (*iwi*), 26
Tū-mata-uenga, 11, 12, 29, 45, 51, 52–53, 72, 98, 137, 166, 174
Tūnohopū, 119
Tupe, Hieke, 13, 30–31, 45, 78, 80, 106, 110, 171
Tūranga, 176–7
tūrangawaewae, 38, 39, 40, 104
Tūrei, John, 125
Tūrongo, 64
Tū-te-ihiihi, 137
Tutengaehe, Hohua, 70–71, 80, 124, 171
Tuterangi, Te Pairi, 79–80, 89, 102, 116, 126
Tuwhangai, Henare, 133, 176–7

University of Waikato, 24, 28, 49–50
urbanisation, of Māori, 36, 38, 164–5, 168, 169–70, 172
Urenui Marae, 120, 134

Victoria University of Wellington, 27–28

Waahi Marae, Huntly, 33
waerea, 141
waewae tapu, 49
wahaika, 95
Waiariki, Eric (Whitu), 34, 110
waiata, 2, 3, 25, 30, 70, 78, 81, 87, 92, 105, 112, 115, 126–7, 134, 135, 140, 150–61, 169, 181; *see also*, *mōteatea*; songs, action
Waikato, 44, 81, 121, 125, 145
Waikato (*iwi*), 75, 80, 84–85, 111, 119, 124–5, 133, 144, 145, 153, 159, 177
Waikato-Maniapoto (*iwi*), 5, 80, 129, 139, 176
Waikerepuru, Huirangi, 80
Waiohau Marae, 174
wairua, 40
Waitangi, 45, 68, 85
waka, as image, 127, 136, 137, 138
Walker, Ranginui, 15, 42, 43, 55, 70, 95, 104, 145–6
wānanga, 4, 6, 22–24, 25–26, 28, 33, 36, 137, 173
Wānanga o Aotearoa, 173
war and peace, intertribal, 14, 47, 53–54, 72
Ward, R., 14, 92, 167
Wellington, 43, 85; mission station, 145
whaikōrero: and bereavement, 15, 19, 34, 44, 48, 54, 66, 105, 140, 148–50; and conflict, 97, 108, 110–11; and disabled speakers, 174–5; and English language, 168–9, 173, 174; and humour, 48, 54, 82–83, 94, 105, 173; and Pākehā, 178–9; and sign language, 174; and trans-gender issues, 177; and use of archaic and figurative language in, 85–87; and use of gestures, 80, 89, 91–102; and use of hand props and weapons in, 95–99, 166–7; as ritual of encounter, 15–16, 37–50, 51, 54–55, 84, 93, 106–7, 122, 128, 131–4; as ritual of welcome, 56–57, 92, 115, 121, 140, 182; broadcasts and films of, 35, 94; competitions, 27, 95, 98; definitions of, 1617, 20; delivery of, 1, 6, 7–8, 31, 43–44, 47, 49, 73, 91–102, 174–5; formality of, 38, 45–50, 136; formulaic expressions in, 25, 31, 33, 36, 80–81, 89–91, 100, 162, 172; function of, 1, 14–16, 165; future of, 9, 162, 163–82; knowledge of, 2–3, 5, 25–27; language of, 16–17, 31, 34–35, 46, 47–48, 77, 80, 85–87, 100–1, 104, 111–13, 163–4, 166, 170–2; origins of, 7, 10–13, 144–5; physical attacks during, 44–45; protocol of, 122–5; references to landmarks in, 87–88; repetition in, 20, 149, 153, 172–3; seating arrangements for, 8, 115–20, 127, 157, 177; spiritual references in, 148; structure of, 8, 62, 81, 135, 157–60; theatrical qualities of, 1, 8, 91–102, 154, 171, 175; thematic development in, 18–19, 25, 78, 123, 144, 150; transmission and teaching of, 6–7, 23–28, 29–36, 59–65; variants of, 160–2
Whāingaroa (Raglan), 84
whakaaraara, 93, 135, 136, 140, 141–4, 145, 160
Whakaaturanga Māori (TV), 174
whakamutu, 135
Whakaotirangi, 131–2
whakapapa, 69, 83
whakapohane, 111
Whakatane mission station, 145
whakatau, 45, 49
whakataukī, 2, 3, 32, 33, 49, 53, 58, 71, 78, 79, 83, 87–88, 99, 105, 140, 144, 150, 164, 172, 174
whanaungatanga, 69
Whanganui (*iwi*), 6, 121
wharekai, 148
whare kau pō, 23
whare kura, 23
whare maire, 23
whare mate, 116, 117
whare pōrukuruku, 23
whare puni, 147
whare rūnunga, 147
whare takiura, 23
whare tipuna, 135, 147
Wharekauri, 6
wharenui, 16, 30, 34, 39, 41, 42, 45, 49, 73, 98, 115, 116, 118, 119–20, 133, 136, 146, 147–8, 160, 181
Whatihua, 64
Wharepuhunga (mountain), 84
Whiro, 11, 51
White, John, 2, 15, 23, 115, 120, 178
White, Sonny, 1
Williams, H., 16, 178
Wilson, O., 155
Winiata, Wīhapi (Hapi), 13, 56, 78, 91, 97, 101, 117, 130, 141
witchcraft and magic, 23, 29, 71, 96, 102, 126
women: and role on *marae*, 56, 68–69, 128, 139, 146, 147, 152–3, 156; and seating position on *marae*, 115, 177; and sexual abuse, 104; and *waiata*, 156–7; and *whaikōrero*, 8, 56, 66, 67–76, 111, 112, 152–3, 161, 175–8; *see also*, Pacific Islands, role of women in
Woodard, H., 149
World War II, 154, 164

Yoon, H., 46, 88